In memory of my father, who's appreciation for different cultures catalyzed my curiosity. His passion for music continues to serve as my muse.

Gringos Eating Tacos

A Progressive Case for Cultural Appropriation

Mason Scott

Copyright © January 8, 2025 by Mason Scott

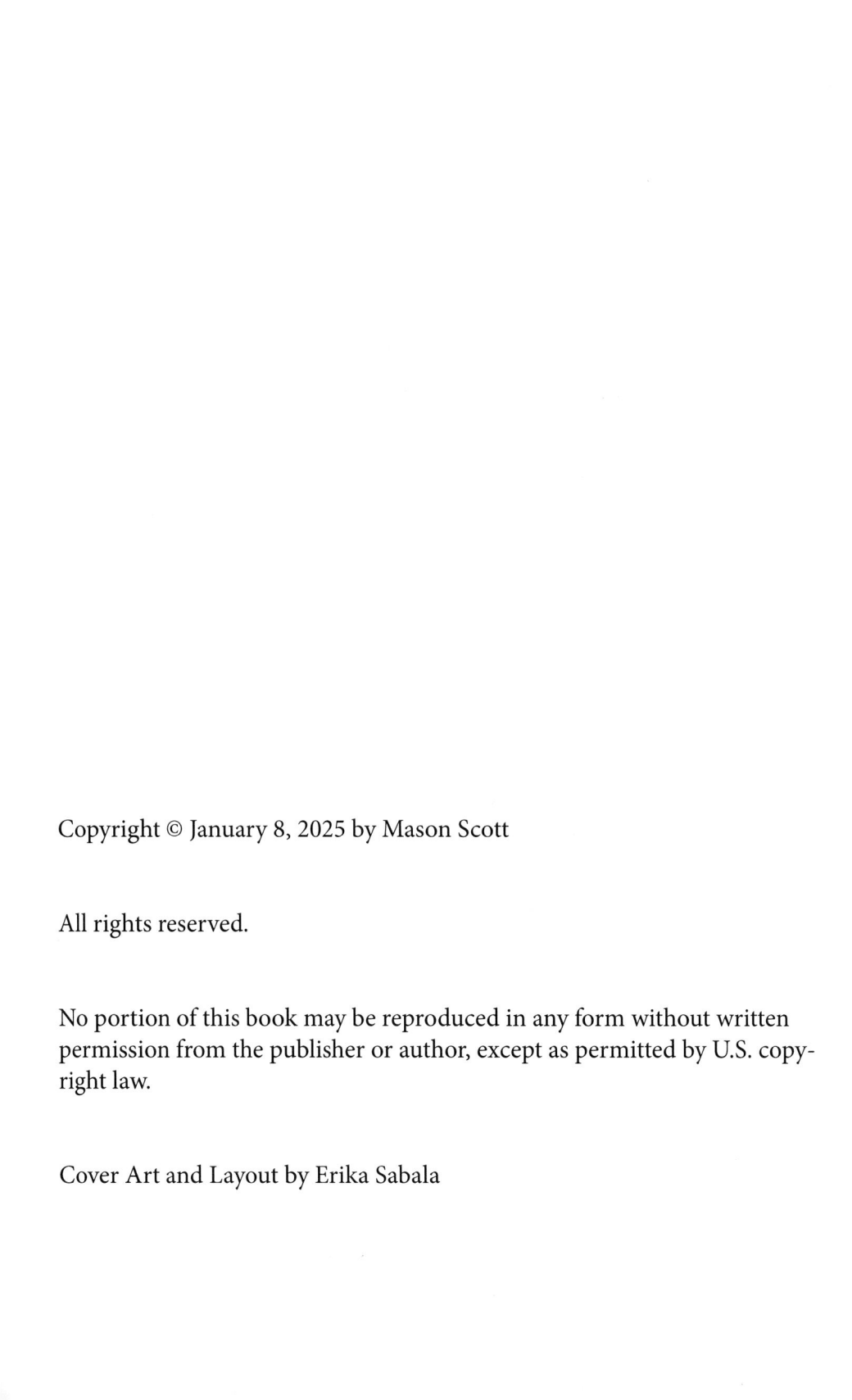

All rights reserved.

No portion of this book may be reproduced in any form without written permission from the publisher or author, except as permitted by U.S. copyright law.

Cover Art and Layout by Erika Sabala

"I am human. I think nothing human is alien to me."
— African writer, Publius Terentius of Carthage (a.k.a. "Terence")

Table Of Contents

Preface	1
Introduction	4
Part 1:	
Case-studies	14
The Relevance Of Intentions	21
Where Ethnic Fidelity Is Relevant; And Where It Isn't	28
Instances Of Commercialization	34
A Case Of Narcissism (Multi-Culturalism vs. Cultural Relativism)	44
Unintended Ramifications (The Misplaced Concern About Stereotypes)	55
Inconsistent Standards	62
Appropriation Or Annexation? (Cul-Ap vs. Cul-Ex)	68
Arbitrary Timelines	80
Literature	96
Elaborations	102
Concluding Remarks For Part 1	107
Part 2:	
A Continuation Of Our Critical Analysis	113
The Psychological Dysfunction Underlying Cul-Ap-Phobia	120
Affinities	132
More On Narcissism (Individual And Collective)	137
Who Are The Arbiters Of Memetic Transference?	152
Bespoke Temporal Framing (A Reprise)	163
Some Possible Problems	179
The Global Pantry	186
Learning Opportunities	193
Guidelines For Healthy Cul-Ap	202
Concluding Remarks For Part 2	208
Endnotes	214
Appendix: A Tale Of Two Debacles	251
Postscript	282

Preface

As I write here in Manila on a muggy afternoon, I have just passed a food vendor who's sign reads, "Oui Tacos: French tacos since 2019". (The image of a taco is accompanied by a cute, little beret.) What am I to make of such a quirky disjuncture? Is this eclectic branding a clash or a synthesis? It is possible that the proprietor of the kiosk is heedless of both Parisian and Mexican culture. I wonder: Shall I scoff at this odd culinary hybridization, or shall I simply be amused by such a slapdash combination of cultural elements? I chuckle and continue onward.

Having arrived at my destination, I am now seated next to a Christmas tree at an (Indian-owned) Indian restaurant, in which American Christmas carols are playing. Presumably, this exhibition of yule-tide cheer is meant to appeal to the predominantly Filipino customer-base. Again, the question arises: Is this apparent cultural incongruity to be seen as a discordance or as a confluence? It's a bit of both, I'd say. But for those who take umbrage with "cultural appropriation", all of this cultural intermixture is rather suspicious. Wherefore? That's not so straight-forward.

This book is based on an essay that was written a few years ago. It was compiled with subsequent material added in small installments over the course of the intervening time; and is now being published at the end of 2024, shortly after Donald Trump was elected POTUS for the second time in three election cycles. Such an eventuality was a glaring illustration of not only how horribly broken many people's moral compass is, but how nescient the general populace of the U.S. has become—when it comes to politics as well as basic economics. Such nescience is also the case when it comes to culture...even on the so-called "Left". As we will see, the demonization of "cultural appropriation" by alleged "Progressives" typically betrays an ignorance of the cultural element being cited. In addition, it shows a lack of understanding of how culture-in-general typically develops.

The 2024 presidential election result was a reminder how mis-informed much of the American electorate has become; and—yes—how exasperatingly dysfunctional the only viable alternative to MAGA (corporatist Democrats) remains. It is, after all, difficult to offer an appealing alternative to a proto-fascist movement when the only other viable political party sides with Wall Street Bankers…and the for-profit sickness-treatment industry…and the military-industrial complex…as well as with Judeo-fascists as they commit genocide in Palestine. The question arises: In trying to bring about civil society, are we devoting our time and attention to the right issues?

For the past couple decades, all that working class people have heard from the Regressive "Left" was: "You may not be able to keep up with the mortgage, but we're going to pillory you for your White privilege…and for something that we refer to as 'micro-aggressions'…and for something else we refer to as 'cultural appropriation'…and for mis-gendering people with ambiguous gender identity." It's hard to imagine how to better advertise the fact that one is completely out of touch with the concerns of the everyman. "Never mind about your low wages and all this crazy inflation; the stock market's doing great. So what's all the fuss? By the way, you should take those corn-rows out of your hair."

In *Robin's Zugzwang*, I made the case that those in charge of the Democratic Party focus on the wrong things. And as I will argue in this book, one of the things we often hear about that should NOT make the list of grievances is "cultural appropriation". Caviling about hipsters donning dreadlocks is not going to bring quality healthcare or gainful employment or affordable housing to those in marginalized communities. Hysterics about such matters is just going to annoy the shit out of a lot of people; and divert our attention away from far more pressing matters.

As I will argue, political correctness—effectively a program of weaponized etiquette—operates at the nexus of puritanism, authoritarianism, and censoriousness. Is this at all consummate with liberal democracy? The answer should go without saying; but let's say it anyway. No. So what gives? At the end of the day, the odd obsession with propriety has to do with luxury beliefs; and thus with luxury grievances. This is simply to say that political correctness comes from a place of privilege; as it is predicated on the supposition that one has the right to not be offended.

But is it true that we are each entitled to never experience discomfiture? Again, the answer is so obvious, it's not worth answering out loud.

All this aside, we can assess the practicality of instituting a strict regimen of political correctness. The question is worth posing: Is it effective in bringing about the results it (purportedly) aims to bring about? Upon surveying the mountains of evidence available to us, this ALSO has a resounding answer. There are very real problems (spec. of social injustice) with which we must contend; yet fussing over breaches of etiquette diverts vital time and energy away from where it is needed most. In any case, the working class does not want to be told that they are bad people for not hewing to the latest p.c. protocols; they want to hear practical solutions to so-called "kitchen table" (a.k.a. "bread and butter") issues. (For more on this, see the Appendix.)

My previous book sought to show how so many (otherwise reachable) people have been repelled by the so-called "Left"; which is largely comprised of ideologues masquerading as Progressives…who end up driving many Americans further to the political RIGHT. (If I were to be salty, the new subtitle to *Robin's Zugzwang* would be: I Told You So.) While those touting political correctness and identity politics seek to allay our concerns about inequities (spec. marginalization and exploitation) without addressing their root causes, ACTUAL civil rights activism seeks to actually rectify those inequities.

In the midst of all the disheartening setbacks, we Progressives must remain steadfast in our commitments to civil society. As we witness the self-immolation of the American Republic, we must not to let ourselves be overtaken by despondency. Instead, we must double our efforts—harnessing the untapped potential of a foundering movement. Step one is to recognize what is actually Progressive, and what isn't. To those who continue to hijack such efforts, we must put our foot down and say: Enough's enough.

The presidential election of 2024 was yet another reminder that those peddling a counterfeit Progressivism only succeed in shooting an otherwise noble cause in the foot. It is—in large part—thanks to them that the American far-right has been able to garner so much support amongst the working class since Obama left office—including amongst those who voted for Obama twice. (!) The lesson we must learn is that the only thing that can defeat *faux* populism is **real** populism. As we'll see, neither the weaponization of etiquette nor identity politics plays any role in the latter; it only cajoles people into embracing the former.

In the present book, I explore another area in which such rigamarole has turned off large swaths of the electorate, who's only alternative to the Regressive "Left"—so far as they can see—is the cult of Trump. This is not to say that we can place blame for MAGA entirely at the feet of Potemkin Progressives. But it is certainly a part of the problem.

Introduction

Since the turn of the millennium, a potpourri of buzz-terms have emerged in America's ever-changing political vernacular. Some of these trendy terms help us better understand the world in which we find ourselves; as they provide a conceptual framework within which we can more adeptly make sense of things. Other new terms, however, reveal a fundamental misunderstanding of the subject-matter to which they have been applied. The latter is the case with "cultural appropriation" (Cul-Ap). Typically used pejoratively, this has become fashionable amongst a particular strain of Potemkin Progressives—namely: identitarians. Extracted from the sudsy depths of academic lingo by practitioners of identity politics, the term is now a common fixture in the argot of the Regressive "Left".

Here, we will explore how and why the majority of scenarios characterized as Cul-Ap are not as objectionable as they may seem at first blush. There are, of course, cases of Cul-Ap that are problematic; but, as we'll see, they are not problematic due to the appropriation of exogenous cultural elements. There is invariably something else at play, the blame for which cannot be laid at the feet of those engaged in said "appropriation".

During our exploration, we will discover some interesting things. Is cumbia really a Colombian dance? What is the history of (what has come to be known as) the Star of David? Who started Christmas? How about Easter? Where does chess come from? How about corn-rows? The answer to such questions is more complicated than we might think. In many cases, it depends on where we opt to begin the timeline. Attempting to arrive at a definitive answer is often a quixotic venture. As cultures are always undergoing a metamorphosis, there is no discrete point in time at which we can proclaim definitively: This is when and where [insert cultural element] started. It is even difficult to designate a discrete time and place where a particular CULTURE began. We humans are suckers for a good story—especially "just so" stories, which are used to justify our favored conceptions of how things are. The most common form of this is an etiological myth, which typically takes the form of an ethno-centric origin tale (see Judaism, "eretz Israel").

As we shall see, using Cul-Ap as a cudgel rather than as an invitation serves to exacerbate the very problem its enthusiasts purport to solve. Instead of engendering amity between cultures, scorn for Cul-Ap only stirs up acrimony. How so? The vilification of those engaged in Cul-Ap requires us to (tacitly) prescribe a regimen of cultural segregation, thereby setting the stage for contrived indignation—often directed across confabulated borderlines, and targeted at an imagined OTHER. In other words: The anti-Cul-Ap crusade is diametrically opposed to the most vaunted ideals of cosmopolitanism. {1}

So how did "cultural appropriation" become a pejorative? As a neutral term, it simply points to the use of memes associated with cultures other than one's own. The implication, though, is that such an act is impolitic. The more zealous anti-Cul-Ap crusaders contend that there is something pernicious about adopting exogenous cultural elements. "Appropriation" is, after all, typically a bad thing, isn't it? {26}

I will argue that the act of "appropriating" an element of any given culture, while deemed ethically-questionable by anti-Cul-Ap crusaders, often has salutary repercussions. For embracing Cul-Ap involves an endorsement of what historian Iriye Akira referred to as "cultural internationalism", which—I hope to show—is integral to the cosmopolitan project. That the ham-fisted use of this term has wormed its way into the p.c. catechism is testament to how misguided otherwise well-meaning expositors have become.

First, a note on memes. {17} Memetics is a way of thinking about epidemiology, whereby pieces of information are seen as the analogues of genomes, and thus subject to natural selection. Put another way: As replicators of information (i.e. patterns of thought / behavior), memes are analogous to genes (i.e. biological replicators). A meme can be anything from a belief in a flying spaghetti monster to grandma's recipe for chicken pot pie. Memes might be symbols, names, catch-phrases, tunes, dance routines, hair styles, sartorial habits, culinary practices, superstitions, sacred rituals, or any of the countless other things that humans think and do. As they are replicators, successful memes tend to be the ones that are both sticky (memorable) and catchy (contagious). Memes propagate—and thus migrate—because that is what they are "designed" to do. Oftentimes, this involves migrating across different cultures, and so between ethnic groups. (Put simply: All memes originated somewhere; and that is not always the same place they end up.)

Some cultures are more robust—and thus resilient—than others. Memetic plasticity is proportional to the sanctity of the memetic lattice (a.k.a. memeplex). When pliable, a memeplex can be modified to accommodate changing exigencies—notably: the incorporation of new memes. Should a memeplex become petrified by a sanctified dogmatic system, though, it becomes brittle. (In memetics, consecration essentially entails calcification.)

In short: Some memetic lattices are ductile, and thus amenable to perturbation. But those that have been—in effect—sacralized tend to be quite brittle; so are not "designed" to adapt. In the latter case, the attendant ideology comes to depend on the memetic lattice remaining "as is"; so measures are often taken to prevent the memeplex from being tampered with by interlopers. Indeed, the entire dogmatic edifice is in danger of collapsing in the event an incompatible (read: foreign) element—one that does not "jive" with the incumbent memeplex—is introduced. {21}

And so it goes: When an ideology dominates a society, a matrix of cultural elements tends to become locked into place. Adherents believe that not only must the culture be protected from external influences, they will lay claim to the consecrated memes (proclaiming them to be exclusively THEIRS). Otherwise, said memes can't be seen as special; which means that the culture-in-question could just as well be otherwise. A consecrated memetic lattice (effectively comprised of sacralized social norms) cannot be seen in this way.

For the present purposes, we are concerned with memes insofar as they are widely-recognized elements of a designated culture. The preservation of certain memes becomes all the more imperative when they are believed to be unique to—and an integral part of—that culture. As socio-psychological "replicators", memes are analogous to their bio-chemical counterparts: genes. While the laws of biology (and ecology) dictate which mutations succeed; the ins and outs of social psychology (as well as geo-political exigencies) are the determining factors for meme-propagation. {17} In genetics, the phenotypes are anatomical / physiological features; in memetics, the phenotypes are ideals, creeds, narratives, and social norms.

While cultural elements can be understood as memes, this is not the only way to conceptualize—and analyze—them. So we might ask: Other than the logistics of memetics, what else is at play when it comes to an aversion to "Cul-Ap"?

Let's look at the ideological framework in which the (alleged) problem is couched. As a term of opprobrium, "cultural appropriation" tends to be invoked by those who subscribe to (an especially divisive form of) identity politics. For in order to be cast as an ethical transgression, Cul-Ap must be thought of in terms of people's membership in one or another demographic category. The problematic act is understood in terms of how said categorization relates to a (dubious) regime of cultural demarcation. This assumes such demarcation is possible (cultures with clear-cut edges; static boundaries that everyone can agree on, etc.)—which is, to put it mildly, a highly dubious assumption.

As I will argue, rather than fostering comity across ethnic lines, such an identitarian approach to human behavior serves to amplify latent ethnic animus: the opposite of the stated goal. This book will argue that the supposition that we should aspire to human solidarity without engaging in any inter-cultural memetic exchange is untenable. Not only is it paradoxical to come together by remaining partitioned, an anti-Cul-Ap protocol assumes distinct cultural boundaries where no such boundaries exist.

When people of different cultures interact with one another, one culture invariably blends into another culture; and this is usually a salutary development. If we devote our time and energy to spurning trans-cultural fertilization, we undermine any aspiration to a truly open, multi-cultural society.

Felicitous or not, "cultural appropriation" is ubiquitous; and often exists in places of which we are unaware. Cul-Ap is happening all around us, on a daily basis; and occurs without notice in largely anodyne ways. Little are anti-Cul-Ap crusaders aware: They are THEMSELVES engaging in Cul-Ap countless times each and every day with virtually everything they do and say. After all, each of us lives within a memetic microcosm that has no clearly-defined boundaries. Our locus of memes is perpetually shifting and fluctuating; as the constellation of cultural elements that play a role in our everyday lives changes over time.

While a pluralistic society is comparable to an ethnic salad, its supervening culture is effectively an ALLOY. Even as people may deign to maintain their distinct ethnic identities, the cultural milieu in which they live is a fluid amalgamation of ethnic components. This metamorphosis is based—in part—on external memes that happen to be impinging upon us at any given time. Understanding this, it is plain to see that the compartmentalization of cultures is not only inimical to pluralism, it is antithetical to the most fundamental principles of cosmopolitanism.

Granted, cultural segregation can be done along demographic lines—per a strict regime of identity politics. Yet an elementary fact seems to be lost on Cul-Ap-phobes: A melting-pot is not merely about the co-existence of disparate cultures; it is about the (discretional) MELDING of cultures. This is even the case when it comes to the most insular communities. For even as hyper-parochial enclaves are themselves not melting pots (insofar as they have impermeable boundaries), they are effectively petrified melting pots—having been, as it were, frozen in time by Reactionary forces that treat the CURRENT version as some (pre-ordained) destination.

Put another way: Insofar as a culture is seen as a static entity, we are indulging in an illusory impression of what it really is. Thus: Even when cultures are segregated, they can't help but be the products of Cul-Ap. A society that has been systematically partitioned into discretely-defined group identities cannot truly be said to be pluralistic. For it is such a society--a society that has not come to terms with the Cul-Ap, so is **closed**--that brought it to where it currently is. {29}

Cultural boundaries blur into each other because cultures inevitably intermix—and even MELD—whenever they interact. This process is more a matter of fusion than it is of superposition. Such intermixture can happen any number of ways for any number of reasons. One way: A culturally exogenous population that has recently arrived in a new land assimilates (wittingly or un-) elements of the indigenous culture. Another way: The native culture adopts elements of other cultures; though the latter is sometimes coerced into doing so due to the power asymmetry endemic to colonialism. The former (volitional adoption of cultural elements) is a matter of discretionary adoption; the latter (in the midst of forced assimilation) is a matter of imposition, so is better characterized as "Cul-Imp". These scenarios should be treated differently, because—morally—they ARE different.

Bottom line: ANY culture is—invariably—a hybridization of other cultures, which themselves are hybrids of other cultures, and so on, going back to time immemorial. Such hybridization is a good thing; as the alternative is insularity and stagnation.

In spite of this, anti-Cul-Ap crusaders insist that memetic transference across cultural lines is somehow deleterious to civil society. The only solution to this (purported) injustice, we are told, is a regimen of meme-sequestration…carried out along cultural lines. In other words, the prescription for respecting other cultures is cultural segregation: separate but equal. (This should sound eerily familiar.)

In my estimation, few of those engaged in the campaign against "cultural appropriation" are serious about making the world a better place; they are simply scavenging the world around them for an opportunity to cavil about imagined crimes…so as to APPEAR kinda-sorta Progressive. At the end of the day, they have no interest in substantive change; they are fine with changing the window dressing so long as the incumbent power structures remain fully intact.

In their eagerness to mete out memetic injunctions, the self-appointed arbiters of cultural exchange fail to realize that cultures cannot be "purified" any more than communities of people can be purified. We might recall that part of cultural purification is exclusivity…which is simply to say: Believers in a pristinely-maintained culture want to prevent things from leaking out as much as from leaking in. Consequently, they insist on some kind of memetic quarantine so as to preserve the (purported) integrity of their culture. But what, exactly, are we seeking to preserve with a regimen of memetic quarantines?

Calls for cultural segregation are a reminder that parochialism typically accompanies Reactionary thinking. This is where things get confusing. I contend that Cul-Ap-phobes are conservatives masquerading as "liberals". As it turns out, they are not advocates of pluralism; they are (cultural) Reactionaries who see any transference of memes across cultural lines as a ploy—by the adopters—to exploit those associated with the source-culture. Any incidence of domination / exploitation that DOES exist is thus attributed—at least in part—of whatever instance of Cul-Ap can be identified. As someone who is extremely concerned about social injustices (spec. marginalization and exploitation along demographic lines), I submit that this is a grave misdiagnosis.

When seeking to resolve issues of domination / marginalization / exploitation, cultural **integration** (what the sociologist, Max Weber dubbed "sinnzusammenhaung") is the answer. This invariably involves some sort of (intermittent) memetic co-optation; which is simply to say that the formation of a given culture is—ultimately—the result of incorporating elements from other cultures; and that this is not a bad thing. After all, such semiotic transmigration constitutes the warp and woof of ALL cultural life.

Cul-Ap, then, is not some insidious program of annexation; it is cultural integration taking its natural course. In other words: It is part of the natural course of cultural evolution (and, hopefully, cultural progress).

Therein lies the snafu: In order to depict Cul-Ap as some sort of dastardly deed, we must suppose that one can somehow annex the elements of another culture. The suspicion is that, by SEIZING this or that meme from its rightful owners, those (purported) owners are being short-changed. Consequently, the argument goes, Cul-Ap occurs to the detriment of the source-culture. It's as if, by adopting—or even just making use of—an exogenous cultural element, one were perpetrating some sort of memetic heist.

This supposition is, of course, entirely specious; as memes are non-rivalrous—which is to say: barring instances of intellectual property (copyrights, trademarks, and patents), the use thereof is non-exclusionary. Any attempt to treat cultural elements as deplete-able commodities proceeds from a fundamental misunderstanding of memetics. When one TAKES something, the source no longer has it. That is not the case when it comes to the propagation (and adoption) of cultural elements—what Franz Boas referred to as "cultural diffusion". When it comes to memes, diffusion does not entail dilution. Put another way: Meme-dispossession is not a sensical concept; as memetic transference is not a zero-sum game. In fact, when the cultural element being adopted is conducive to the commonweal, everybody wins.

In order to characterize Cul-Ap as a transgressive act, one is forced to contend that temporarily adopting—or blithely participating in—an element of another's culture is somehow trespassing on that culture's sovereignty over itself; and thereby either engaging in a kind of exploitation or committing a kind of desecration. Hence Cul-Ap—by its very nature—is deemed exploitative and/or derogatory toward those who most identify with said cultural element. (This indictment is made especially when the meme plays an integral role in the source-culture's heritage.) The unavoidable conclusion is that any act of unsanctioned participation must be forbidden...even if it is done in good faith.

There is something erroneous about this indictment.

My choice of the descriptor, "Cul-Ap-phobia" is deliberate. It is primarily intended to be descriptive; so is not merely used pejoratively. It is a diagnosis more than it is an aspersion. In fact, in opting for this neologism, I am giving those to whom it applies the benefit of the doubt; as it presumes that their contempt for cultural appropriation is sincere, stemming more from neurosis than from mendacity. While "phobia" typically refers to an irrational fear, it is often used instead to label a kind of unwarranted hostility. (Both fear and hostility stem from insecurity, so the two often go hand-in-hand.) That said, I suspect that an aversion to Cul-Ap is more a matter of (unfounded) antipathy than of (unfounded) fear. The problem is that antipathy often translates to an adversarial posture, which only serves to undermine cosmopolitan endeavors.

Anything that appeals to our baser tribal instincts should be handled with suspicion. The umbrage some take with Cul-Ap might be considered a form of "hamarto-phobia", as it largely involves a neuroticism about imaginary crimes. Rather than simply seeing the adoption of exogenous cultural elements as a sign of fecklessness, we are told they are a sign of malice. Just as the constables of p.c. feel obliged to police language (in order to curb alleged "harm"), anti-Cul-Ap crusaders feel obliged to police meme-transference (in order to curb alleged "harm"). This has dire repercussions. The prohibition of Cul-Ap entails what—taken to its logical conclusion—amounts to cultural segregation: "I shall keep my culture to myself; and you are expected to keep your culture to yourself." Endorsing such a mandate is especially ironic, as such onerous strictures are (ostensibly) meant to enforce a "respectful-ness" for all cultures. They do no such thing.

So there we have it: In the Cul-Ap-phobes' eagerness to condemn what they see as a morally problematic use of exogenous cultural elements, they neglect to see the implications of their own thinking. (Part of obtuse thinking is not recognizing such thinking **as obtuse**.) In a nutshell: Anti-Cul-Ap protocols backfire, creating effects that are counter to the ones (allegedly) intended.

To cure this phobia, it is necessary to address the myopia that underlies it.

The indictment of illicit Cul-Ap is shown to be frivolous the moment we attempt to universalize the maxims on which it is (purportedly) based. Taking the stricture to its logical conclusion, and applying it everywhere—especially where its proponents did not intend—exposes an inconsistency in its application. As we will see, by rebuking a gringo for snacking on tacos, one may as well castigate anyone who isn't a WASP for wearing a polo shirt. An anti-Cul-Ap crusade cannot help but be riddled with double-standards; as the standards it purports to uphold are, invariably, selectively applied. But as it happens, the standards can't NOT be applied in a selective manner…lest proponents of said strictures run headlong into a wall of their own absurdities. This book will provide many examples to demonstrate this.

Alas, we live in a world in which putative "liberals" denounce ethno-nationalism in their own back yard yet endorse it in a far-away land. Consistency is a rare commodity these days. Many have failed to grasp something as elementary as: If one is going to be truly anti-X, one must be against ALL FORMS of X—whether X is racism or fascism. And the push-back has to be about more than just optics.

In the final analysis, we come back to the (unavoidable) fact that Cul-Ap has always existed; and has usually been welcomed by all parties involved. While there are certainly some instances of exploitation and derogation (which shall be addressed forthwith), such cases are the exception, not the rule.

Only the most conservative (read: closed) societies on Earth have sought to curb adoption of memes from other cultures; or have claimed ownership of certain memes as though cultural proprietorship were somehow written in the stars. Time after time, history has shown that a robust, vibrant culture is one that readily incorporates new elements—even if from external sources—whenever such elements are found to be worthwhile. That is, after all, what a liberal (read: open) society entails.

As will be shown, societies the world over have been appropriating cultural elements from external sources since time immemorial. "The Persians are greatly inclined to adopt foreign customs" wrote the Greek historian, Herodotus about the Achaemenid Empire. In fact, Herodotus attributed the Persians' astounding success to precisely THIS modus operandi. As it so happened, the Hellenic penchant for Cul-Ap was inextricably linked to an embrace of multi-culturalism. In the Book of Ecclesiastes, written in Babylon in the 5th century B.C., there is a reason the authors noted that "there is nothing new under the sun." Whatever ONE people is using, it was invariably used by SOME OTHER people. True to form, that book was composed with many Persian and Aramaic loan-words; and—as we shall see—Abrahamic tradition is comprised largely of culturally-appropriated elements, cribbed from older traditions (spec. for those who codified Judaism: during the Exilic Period). {32} The passage from Ecclesiastes may as well have read, "We're just revamping what already exists. Others have used it; now we're going to use it."

Those who take umbrage with Cul-Ap fail to see that the admixture of cultures is socially beneficial; and that a crucial part of that mixture is meme-exchange. As a result of this blinkered thinking, they demand a memetic embargo at the imagined boundaries of each cultural enclave. But those boundaries are largely figments of their own imagination. It's not that any given cultural boundary is porous; it's that it is amorphous…nay, often vaporous. The location of any given boundary is not set in stone; it is in an ongoing state of flux. Why? Because it involves humans interacting in haphazard, unpredictable, often wonderful ways. Cultural cartography is more meteorology than astronomy. Predicting the position of celestial objects requires a bit of Newtonian physics (with a dash of general relativity). On the other hand, trying to prognosticate a given culture's metamorphosis would be like trying to forecast weather patterns a fortnight hence.

When we assess the rationalizations for anti-Cul-Ap sentiment, we find that the concern is the maintenance of cultural integrity. In calling for cultural segregation, they believe they are upholding a purist version of this or that culture against the dreaded scourge of meme-poachers. But what of cultural preservation? After all, the desire to preserve culture is an entirely noble one.

The assumption seems to be that cultural appropriation translates to cultural DISSIPATION. But does it? Can culture be diluted by being propagated? Are cultural elements exhaustible commodities? Can they be depleted—or sullied—by cultural diffusion? When memes proliferate, do they somehow lose their semiotic ballast? These are important questions; and this book aims to give some answers. As it happens, how we conduct such an inquiry boils down to how we think about culture. So it is worth articulating, up front, the conceptual framework within which I will be operating.

When harmonious, a culture might be thought of as a mellifluous memetic fugue. Yet even the most ordered cultures are a hodgepodge of elements culled from different places at different times for different reasons—usually by sheer happenstance. Cultures are rather messy things; and that is what makes them so fascinating. Any given culture—insofar as it can be discretely defined—is what Levi-Strauss called a "bricolage" of elements from antecedent sources; which is simply to say that any given culture is a salmagundi, the combination of which is an accident of history. Put another way: Any given culture is not some timeless blueprint inscribed into the fabric of the cosmos. For it could easily have been other than it now is; and it STILL CAN be something other than what it currently happens to be.

Cul-Ap-phobes seem unable to grasp this.

Another problem, as we'll see, is that the anti-Cul-Ap crusade is gratuitously tendentious. Being officious about (purported) meme-allocation rights is not a viable strategy for fostering comity across cultural lines. Rather than engendering respect for foreign cultures, the vilification of those who partake in Cul-Ap only succeeds in exacerbating a tribalistic mindset. Once participation in others' cultures is forbidden, we start going down a dangerous road—a road that leads to a raft of unintended consequences.

As it turns out, making Cul-Ap taboo is a way to keep THE OTHER (however demarcated) other-ized; which is simply to say that cultural segregation, like any form of segregation, reinforces alterity—and thus mitigates comity—between ethnic groups. Put plainly: The demonization of Cul-Ap flouts the principles of cosmopolitanism.

There are two elementary things that those who demonize Cul-Ap seem not to understand. First: No culture exists in a vacuum. Any given culture is a product of external influences; and has no discrete border. Second: No culture—as it has come to exist, however it has come to exist—emerges ex nihilo. Any given culture was likely ITSELF formed as a result of oodles of cultural appropriation.

Both of these things remind us that cultures are BASED UPON Cul-Ap. Moreover, cultures interact, and are perpetually in flux. Put another way: Cultures are a dynamic; not a stasis. Prohibitions against Cul-Ap are predicated on the illusion that there is some sacrosanct stasis that can be maintained indefinitely, whereby each ethnic group maintains sovereignty over a consecrated locus of memes…to which they lay claim due to a (largely fictional) "just so" story.

Reality tells a different story. Rather than a destination, culture is an on-going process; like a marriage or a friendship or—in a grander context—civil society. Yet the way anti-Cul-Ap crusaders cast the issue, one would think that any given culture has been magically conjured from stardust, then frozen in time "as is" for the rest of eternity. For them, this means that "preserving" a culture means protecting it from memetic leakage and/or memetic penetration. According to this thinking, a culture must be quarantined so as to preclude memetic transference TO or FROM other cultures. Never mind that it was the result of antecedent cultural diffusion that made any given culture what it is IN THE FIRST PLACE.

As will be discussed, anti-Cul-Ap crusaders treat appropriation either as a kind of annexation or a kind of imposition. They often react as though the source-culture were being picked dry by a horde of dastardly meme-scavengers. Thus Cul-Ap is taken to be deleterious to the culture of those who anoint themselves stewards of the memes-in-question. What we find, though, is that the ensuing imbroglio is nothing but an exercise in self-indulgent titivation—replete with maudlin theatrics about the ills of being "disrespectful" / "offensive" / "insensitive". The purpose of this book is to ascertain whether or not there is any credence to such grievances. Let's begin our exploration with a few case studies.

PART 1

Case-Studies

There are countless ways to illustrate the present thesis. Let's start with a simple inquiry. Shall we suppose that all Americans are denigrating pagan culture with festivities around the "Christmas tree"? The practice was originally part of a Germanic celebration of the winter solstice. For many of its earliest practitioners, it focused on the Norse god, Odin; and even made use of the colors red and green. The tree itself (the "tannenbaum") was based on the "koliada" from ancient Slavic (pre-Christian) winter festivals. Yet today we rarely hear those from Eastern Europe accusing the rest of the western world of "appropriating" a sacrosanct part of their culture. Why not?

Well, then, what about the occasion itself? The commemoration of the winter solstice (as an auspicious occasion) is as universal as just about anything—from the Hindu "Makara Sankranti" to the Persian "Yalda Night" to the Byzantine "Brumalia" to the Anglo-Saxon "Geola" ("Yule-tide") to the Incan "Inti Raymi[-rata]". (That last occasion is observed by the Quechua to the present day.) As it turns out, the winter solstice was a thing for virtually all peoples; so its commemoration cannot be tied to any specific culture. It's why Stone Henge was erected five thousand years ago.

Even the Georgians could accuse everyone else in Christendom of ripping off their yule-tide "chichilaki". But, then again, perhaps THEY were ripping off the Roman custom of "Saturnalia"—a winter solstice celebration that was common throughout the Empire. Saturnalia paid tribute to the god of time...and to his representative on Earth. (You read that correctly: The Romans used the occasion to commemorate a deity's incarnation.) During Saturnalia, homes were bedecked with wreaths of evergreen. This should sound oddly familiar. {28}

But why select the 25th of December? Lo and behold: The date that Romans—through Constantine, Rome's first ostensibly Christian emperor—celebrated the birthday of the godhead, Sol Invictus was December 25. That was also the day of the Mithraic winter solstice festival, in which the annual birthday of the sun was commemorated. Mithra-ism was still rampant throughout the Roman Empire during Late Antiquity—that is: when the Christianized version of this auspicious occasion was still being formulated by the Vatican's magisterium in the 4th century.

But that's not all. Christmas revelers today are all—unwittingly—riffing off the movement surrounding the canonized Greek bishop, Nikolaus of Myra (rendered "Sinter-klaas" in Frisian), on whom "Santa [Saint] Claus" is based. Why Nikolaus? Well, there was a cult surrounding him at the time…which, it turns out, had itself been modeled on a cult around the Pythagorean philosopher, Apollonius of Tyana (a man who lived in Cappadocia during the 1st century). In other words: Even the holiday's exalted mascot was purloined from antecedent pagan figures. {2}

So what's with the repudiation of Cul-Ap now?

The reason the charge of illicit Cul-Ap is spurious is that all cultures are based—to some not insignificant degree—on the co-optation of antecedent and/or exogenous cultural elements. Indeed, any given culture is—essentially—crystalized cultural hybridization. We speak of memetic "fusion" (think of music or cuisine) as if it is something exotic; when it is probably the LEAST exotic thing that humans do. There has never existed a culture that was NOT a pastiche of memetic precursors—with elements extracted from the various contemporaneous cultures with which it interacted. Put plainly: Every culture is derivative. (For a historical perspective on this point, see Michael Scott's **Ancient Worlds**.)

In Classical Antiquity, the Romans engaged in rampant Cul-Ap from the Greeks. During the early Middle Ages, the (Mohammedan) Arabs engaged in rampant Cul-Ap from the Nabataeans and Persians. And we might note that the Mongols were so incredibly successful because they engaged in Cul-Ap from the Uyghurs…and the Chinese…and the various Turkic peoples of the Eurasian Steppes…and the Persians…and pretty much EVERYONE ELSE they conquered. They may have done a lot of physical pillaging; but the adoption of exogenous cultural elements was one of the more admirable things they did. (While they were merciless when it came to slaughtering those who did not surrender, they never harmed anyone based on ethnic identity.)

Cul-Ap-phobes fail to realize that appropriation—whether calculated or unwitting—is the only way that any culture came to be in the first place. Over the course of human history, Cul-Ap has never been seen as problematic. Only recently has cross-cultural memetic transference taken on a contentious penumbra. This ersatz transgression is now a touchstone of those who are smitten with identity politics and/or preoccupied political correctness.

The aim of the present book is to show why proscribing Cul-Ap is wrong-headed. In a later chapter, I will explicate the crucial distinction between appropriation (which I take to be non-rivalrous / inclusionary) and expropriation (which I take to be rivalrous / exclusionary). {26} But first, let's consider some more relatable examples—just to see whether or not compunctions with Cul-Ap might possibly be stemming from misapprehension; or even, in some cases, a pointless moral panic. Note that this will require us to evaluate Cul-Ap as it actually is rather than how it is caricatured by Cul-Ap-phobes.

Let's begin by noting that the cooptation of cultural elements is generally celebrated in liberal democracies around the world. We see this in literature, in architecture, in music, in dance, in iconography, as well as in culinary and sartorial practices—from the most formal rituals to the most mundane social norms. We often fail to notice where Cul-Ap has actually yielded fruit because so much of it is encountered in everyday life.

Language offers us the best illustration. With idiosyncrasies in vernacular (like street-lingo and idiomatic expressions), any catchy turn-of-phrase that becomes fashionable can't help but be appropriated by those outside of the community that coined it. Indeed, that's how any snappy locutions propagate across cultures. ANYTHING that becomes sufficiently popular can migrate between ethnic groups that interact with one another.

By looking at some well-known instances of Cul-Ap, we can begin posing pertinent questions. As will soon become apparent, characterizing Cul-Ap as an illicit act leads to absurdities. Consider "Amazing Grace". This was sung by African slaves in the antebellum South as a way to keep hope alive during an epoch of unimaginable tribulation. So, today, can non-Black people sing this heartfelt song? According to the logic of Cul-Ap, the answer is a resounding "no". It's as if allowing White people to sing that particular hymn would somehow deprive African Americans of their legacy of empowerment through song.

Even further, the contention is that PREVENTING non-Black people from singing this song would somehow HELP them forge solidarity with Black people. Hence the Kafka-esque prescription: Universal inclusion via targeted exclusion.

But wait: It gets more complicated. For the song was composed in 1725 by a White (Anglican) clergyman...who was, it turns out, a former slaver. John Newton wrote the song as a way of expressing contrition (pursuant to his change of heart regarding the enslavement of Africans). So it is, in a sense, MORE appropriate for White people—remorseful of a past injustice—to sing this song.

We might continue along this line of inquiry. If Europeans play jazz, are they guilty of cribbing Afro-American culture...or are they simply paying tribute to great music? Should Buddhist musicians be allowed to perform Handel's "Messiah"? Can Taoists sing "Jingle Bells"? Can non-Germans play Pachelbel's Canon at their weddings? Can Caucasians sing the Blues? The legendary Egyptian pop-singer, Umm Kulthum (a.k.a. "Kawkab al-Sharq") incorporated an Occidental musical idiom. Was she guilty of Cul-Ap as well? And what about other Arabic pop-singers (like Samira Said and Elissar Zakaria Khoury)? What are we to make of these instances of adoption?

Let's pose the question this way: When Bing Crosby sang "Silent Night" (which would become a secular American classic), was he ripping off Austrian / Bavarian culture? After all, Franz Xaver Gruber composed the song ("Stille Nacht") for his church in Oberndorf bei Salzburg in 1818. Shall non-Bavarians be prohibited from singing this song? Should it be off-limits to non-Catholics? (If so, we should be thankful that Crosby was Catholic!)

According to the specious rational undergirding the charge of illicit Cul-Ap, sharing customs across cultural lines, however demarcated, without express permission to do so, is a morally dubious act, and so should be forbidden. For engaging in such an act, we are told, is indicative of (tacit) condescension; and even of derogation—especially if it is done in too flip a manner. But does anyone REALLY believe this? If so, it becomes a quandary that many of the most cherished Christmas songs were composed by Jewish men: Jay Livingston, Sammy Cahn, Irving Berlin, Jule Styne, etc. In such cases, who was appropriating who?

As I hope to show, the entire case for the vilification of those engaged in Cul-Ap unravels as we recognize that Cul-Ap is everywhere—even in places we might not suspect. If we were to apply the standards for Cul-Ap-prohibition consistently—and universally—we would end up implicating everyone's culture, everywhere, since the beginning of recorded history.

In order to bring to light the issue at hand, let's pose some other questions: Can Arabs perform Shakespearean plays...in Arabic...donning Bedouin attire? What about when Arabian dancers perform "Liwa", which was adopted from African folk dance? Do I need to be Irish to direct a production of River Dance? Can Irish who do not have a full appreciation of their Gaelic heritage do so? If the answer is YES to all these questions, and fidelity to the culture is not the ultimate standard, then are we to predicate eligibility on bloodlines? Birthright? Shall qualification be based on the adopter having spent some minimum amount of time acquainted with—nay, immersed in—the culture? Survey the criteria we shall use for allotting license to participate in another culture. The further we inquire, the more convoluted those criteria become.

If we are to aspire to a minimal level of rectitude, we are forced to use the same standards to answer analogous questions: Can anyone other than the Cantonese take Kung-fu lessons? Can non-Venetian film-makers use Vivaldi in their scores? Can non-Indian women wear saris? The more examples we consider, the more it becomes apparent that when Cul-Ap occurs—especially when done in good faith—the world is all the better for it.

It's worth reiterating that meme-adoption between cultures regularly occurs even when we don't realize it—not only with technical innovations and scientific insights (which are not necessarily cultural elements), but with folklore, superstitions, games, attire, culinary recipes, catch-phrases, and countless other things. This is salubrious in most instances; and it is salubrious for reasons that may not be immediately apparent to the parties involved.

Regardless of who one might be, I submit that succumbing to Cul-Ap-phobia is tantamount to (what might be sardonically described as) cultural masochism. For insofar as one identifies with a given culture, one is invariably forced to indict ONESELF for the illusory traducement. The fact is: Nobody is NOT currently enjoying a product of serial cultural appropriation. Cul-Ap is as endemic to culture as is breathing oxygen. It is safe to say, then, that grievances involving Cul-Ap demonstrate a fundamental mis-understanding of how cultures interact.

Let's continue asking questions. If I attend a luau and wear a lei around my neck, am I in some way desecrating Polynesian culture? In such a scenario, there are two different perspectives at play: For the Hawaiian, donning the flowered necklace is customary; yet to me, the accoutrement is simply nifty—even mildly exotic. Done flippantly, it's just for "shits and giggles". The perennial query is brought to the fore: At what point does "just for fun" become demeaning?

But wait. "Exotic," you say? What's THAT all about? Exoticism, we should bear in mind, is simply the result of differing vantages of familiarity, not the result of some invidious double standard. "Yet," proclaim some, "If you find it exotic, then you shouldn't be allowed to do it!" I contend that this is a rather harebrained declaration. Shall one also refrain from dating people one finds exotically attractive? Shall we deem exotic locals off-limits for holiday travel? Shall gourmands avoid any cuisine they happen to find exotic? Must we curb ALL curiosity in things that we find unfamiliar in an enchanting way?

We may as well criminalize fascination.

Well, then, how shall problematic instances of exotic-ization be addressed? What is typically identified as a problem is the FETISHIZATION OF exotic-ness. At issue, then, is not the (perfectly natural) fascination with the exotic that is problematic; it is the objectification of such things. But then again, fetishizing ANYTHING is indicative of dysfunction. For objectification is often accompanied by (oft-unwitting) dehumanization. But here's the irony: Cul-Ap-phobia is ITSELF based on fetishization; as it adjures us to treat cultural elements as sacrosanct totems—that is: as if they were the sole basis of dignity.

But that's not the worst of it. When it comes to "trying on for size" exogenous cultural elements, a censorious attitude ends up being just another form of parochialism. Indeed, a key facet of Cul-Ap-phobia is a nagging penchant for meme-sequestration; whereby one is obliged to hold in abeyance anything seen as foreign; or—heaven forbid—EXOTIC.

The notion that one should not be permitted to (intermittently) participate in—or temporarily adopt—some cultural element (esp. when one happens to find it exotic) is, in my estimation, ludicrous. Take, for instance, a non-Hindu attending a Navratri celebration, and opting to don a "bindi" (third eye) as part of his participation in the festivities. Fancying the practice, the person opts to do it again later on—of his own accord—in other contexts. In doing so, is he being patronizing toward Hindu culture? Not necessarily. (If it is done with a jeer, then we can conclude that mean-spiritedness is the motivation. But it is often NOT done with a jeer; and often out of an embrace of what one has come to see as a nice idea.) Supposing that doing this sort of thing is ALWAYS uncouth would be disingenuous; and, in some cases, to conflate homage with mockery, tribute with derogation.

Considering the spirit behind the gesture is key. Alas. As we shall see, so far as Cul-Ap-phobes are concerned, intentions are entirely beside the point; as the act is deemed PRIMA FACIE morally dubious. But the vilification of anyone, anywhere, at any time, in any way engaged in Cul-Ap misses what makes humans social creatures: curiosity of novel memes…especially those from other lands. Indeed, to hear those who kvetch about this alleged transgression, one would think the sky was falling every time a group of Asians formed a rock-n-roll band. (Based on this standard, K-pop would be a moral outrage.)

Ironies abound. For, as it happens, every one of the gormless enthusiasts who demonize Cul-Ap benefits from the fruits of Cul-Ap as much as anyone else; they just don't realize how much of what they do is the result of the very thing against which they inveigh. It can't be emphasized enough that all of us unwittingly engage in Cul-Ap on a daily basis, in even the most quotidian activities. We routinely participate in customs that were adopted from other cultures in days-gone-by, with nary the bat of an eyelash. Indeed, exogenous cultural elements suffuse our work-aday activities morning 'til night; and are now considered integral parts of OUR OWN culture.

Wherefore? In adopting one or another meme, people are simply being pragmatic. As Steven Lukes put it in his book, **Liberals And Cannibals**: "People often follow customs [prevailing social norms] blindly, even compulsively and without reasoning about what they do. But the fact that they don't reason does not mean that they don't have reasons." This goes for art, literature, music, dance, cuisine, clothing styles, religious dogmas, and virtually everything else that constitutes "culture". Trans-cultural fertilization is a natural consequence of amicable interactions between ethnic groups. Cul-Ap simply reflects the way that all cultures interact on any given day of the week. The alternative would be cultural stasis.

A culture in stasis is a culture in decline. After all, organic dynamism underlies the vitality of ANY system—be it biological or social.

In fact, meme-exchange is a spur for cultural FRUCTIFICATION; but the benefits are not always recognized until we have the benefit of hindsight. Whenever we are tempted to cast memetic transference as problematic, we should ask ourselves a few things. What happens if a Kurd puts a Persian rug in his home while a Persian puts a Kurdish rug in his home? Is that a fair trade? Can either hang a Native American tapestry in his foyer? If all of this is illicit, then what's really going on here? It would seem that even interior design must be subject to a regime of cultural sanctions. (And unless you're a Parisian of Italian descent, don't even think of putting Venetian blinds on French doors.)

Mehendi (a.k.a. "henna tattoos") is used ritually in Turkey, Pakistan, India, and Bangladesh amongst Muslimahs; yet it was originally a Vedic practice that predated Islam by many centuries. Does this make Dar al-Islam culpable in an elaborate memetic caper? Once we proscribe Cul-Ap in ONE context, where does it stop?

It might be noted that the two most popular sports in Japan are baseball and soccer. While soccer is international through and through, baseball is a hallmark of Americana. Shall Americans—even as they watch Dragonball Z and snack on some sushi—begrudge the Japanese for adopting this hallowed pass-time (and, it might be noted, infusing it with their own cultural flavor)? As it turns out, this is not a problem…any more than it is when, say, the Chinese drink root beer.

Some Russians practice their own version of ju-do (rebranded as "sambo") even as some Japanese fancy Asian-style matryoshka dolls (rebranded as "Russian nesting dolls", though with a Japanese aesthetic). As a result of this mutual "appropriation", no one is the worse for wear. In fact, such reciprocal meme-transference is oftentimes a means of trans-cultural solidarity (a refreshing change from the war of 1904-05). In the advent of this cultural interchange, Russians watch anime and read manga; and not a single Japanese person is up in arms about it.

More often than not, memetic cross-pollination enhances all cultures involved. The exceptions prove the rule. {36}

The point cannot be emphasized enough: The charge of Cul-Ap as some transgressive deed demonstrates a grave misunderstanding of how culture qua culture WORKS; and how it has ALWAYS worked. Making Cul-Ap taboo is—paradoxically—a gambit to celebrate our shared humanity via cultural segregation.

The Relevance Of Intentions

When the Japanese play baseball, are they in some way being "insensitive" to American sports-fans? Simply posing the question demonstrates the fatuity of this line of inquiry. Clearly, the adoption of exogenous cultural elements is not **inherently** disrespectful. Otherwise, we would be forced to insist that rap be off-limits to Eminem; that country music be off-limits to Lil Nas X; that curry be off-limits to anyone who isn't Indian; and that Brasilians can no longer practice jiu-jitsu.

So what, then, of ill will? Do intentions really matter to those for whom Cul-Ap is a moral outrage? Their bone to pick, it seems, is not really with Cul-Ap per se, but with the attendant sentiment. Perhaps it is morally dubious motives with which they are concerned. Maybe, at the end of the day, this is all about bad intentions.

Are good intentions always exculpatory when someone's actions have caused demonstrable harm? No. There are cases of negligence—and even recklessness—which involve a dereliction of responsibility. But generally, good will is the most important driver of pro-social activity; and should absolve those who are "guilty" of careless uses of exogenous cultural elements. By keeping things in perspective, we can recognize that there are much bigger fish to fry. In fighting for social justice, it is important not to get side-tracked by frivolous grievances, and thereby lose the plot.

Alas. So far as the more petulant anti-Cul-Ap crusaders are concerned, the matter of intentions is altogether moot. For them, good intentions don't matter; Cul-Ap is always bad. Full stop. Consequently, they are apt to feign indignation even if it is clear that no disrespect was intended. After all, their presupposition is: For people of one culture to adopt—or even to casually partake in—an element from another culture is IPSO FACTO derogatory. Even if no ill will is involved, the alleged culprit is somehow denigrating the source-culture; as the act itself—not what's behind it—is the problem.

For the vast majority of instances, nobody actually believes this; yet Cul-Ap-phobes pretend to think that it is true; full stop. So it goes with the puritanical mindset that is endemic to political correctness. The idea is to impute sinister motives to those engaged in (what are often) innocuous activities. This has become somewhat of a cottage industry in the precincts of the Regressive "Left". Participants are incentivized to take offense at virtually any breach of etiquette, no matter how trivial. As such, the vilification of those engaged in Cul-Ap attains regardless of intention.

Those who perceive themselves as having been mocked need only ascribe dubious intentions to whomever is seen as "crossing the line"…and presto! A crime has been committed. So the alleged transgression exists whether or not there is any attendant iniquity. Hence Cul-Ap should be seen as a personal affront…irrespective of the sentiment attending the act of the accused "appropriator". Good will is a moot point. So far as Cul-Ap-phobes are concerned, the use of an exogenous cultural element is iniquitous no matter how benign—or innocently intentioned—it might be.

If one FEELS patronized, then the accused is IPSO FACTO guilty of being patronizing / disrespectful. The idea is to prevent anyone from ever being disconcerted. But the scene of the crime ends up being solely in one's own mind.

The encouragement of such a tetchy cast of mind has consequences. The public square is soon flooded with dyspeptic interlocutors afflicted with a severe case of what the Danes refer to as "krænkelsesparat": a predisposition to quickly take offense at even the most innocuous of trespasses. (Such people seem to derive solace from acrimony.) Becoming apoplectic at trivialities is crucial to their campaign to vanquish Cul-Ap from the face of the Earth.

Being hyper-captious is not the same as being fastidious. More often than not, it just shuts down public discourse. An adversarial—nay, confrontational—approach to activism invariably backfires; so ends up doing far more harm than good. Aside from adopting a Reactionary mindset (puritanical, authoritarian, hyper-censorious), such an approach is tremendously off-putting to those who might otherwise be sympathetic to the cause.

When one assumes an accusatory posture in every interaction, one precludes fruitful conversation. In this scheme, a choreography is prescribed. Anyone who has the gall to step out of line is ostracized, and rendered a pariah. (Refuse to use my made-up pronouns? Well, then you're a fascist!) This is not a way to win over hearts and minds. Those who obdurately assert preposterous things (e.g. there is athletic parity between biological sexes) lose all credibility with the everyman. The thinking here is quite straight-forward: If their judgement is that off-base with something so elementary, then why should we take them seriously on anything else? Some people ARE bigots; but others are simply regular folk who would be receptive to the message…BUT FOR the proliferation of wacky claims…which become associated with otherwise estimable positions.

Are there assholes who engage in cultural appropriation in order to ridicule? Yes. In such cases, what is the problem: the Cul-Ap or the mockery? Alas, this question isn't even asked when intentions are deemed irrelevant. The fact of the matter is that, in the vast majority of cases where there IS a problem with Cul-Ap, it is not Cul-Ap per se that is the problem; it is the sentiment behind it. When invidiousness can be credibly attributed to derogatory usage of exogenous cultural elements, the actual crime is bigotry; and so can be explained AS SUCH. No need, then, to blame such things on Cul-Ap.

We can conclude that the issue here is not Cul-Ap itself; it is Cul-Ap that is done in bad faith. Consequently, the primary concern should be cultural obloquy, or—for that matter—ANYTHING that is not done in good faith. The fact is that not all participation in—or adoption of—an exogenous cultural element is demeaning. In fact, as we shall see, the vast majority of it is perfectly fine.

When Thais deck their urban shopping malls with copious amounts of tacky Christmas decorations, and play American Christmas carols throughout the concourse, is it a case of Buddhists being "insensitive" to Christians? (Make no mistake: The vast majority of Thai shoppers know almost nothing about Pauline theology; and even less about the Nativity legend.) Such use of kitsch is for entirely commercial purposes. {48} But, then again, the same could be said for Americans' use of Christmas themes. (After all, Christmas is hardly a RELIGIOUS occasion for the majority of Westerners.) Even the Japanese have gotten in on the action, celebrating "Kurisumasu" in laughably hokey ways.

As we saw earlier, Christmas is ITSELF the result of rampant Cul-Ap. Indeed, it is one of the most flagrant examples of Cul-Ap, based as it is on pagan precursors. It is no more OWNED by Christendom than it is owned by Thailand. The yule-tide holiday, celebrated on the winter solstice, has about as much to do with Jesus of Nazareth as the Easter Bunny has to do with Nicene soteriology. (A bunny-rabbit laying colored eggs in the springtime is, at best, a cartoonish metaphor for a resurrected savior-god.) Tellingly, it was in the Middle Ages that Epiphany-tide was appended to Christ-mas-tide, so as to incorporate the tale of the Nativity—confabulated in the Middle Ages—into the holiday. As mentioned, it is ALL traceable back to pagan commemorations of the winter solstice.

Ok. Fine. But how, then, are we to deal with those who are not being sufficiently deferential to the source-culture? This matter becomes especially salient when the element in question is considered sacred. The question answers itself: The issue at hand is ill will—something that can exist with or without Cul-Ap.

The concern about "insensitivity" seems straight-forward enough. Yet when someone is deliberately being derogatory, the point of concern is—again—the bad intentions. Being derogatory is a problem irrespective of HOW one is being derogatory. If it happens to be in the process of Cul-Ap, the problem is not the Cul-Ap. ANYTHING done out of ill-will is problematic—whether it is donning a sombrero or making sushi. After all, Cul-Ap can always be done in GOOD faith.

When those engaging in Cul-Ap are vilified, the implication is that they are being "disrespectful"—or, at best, insufficiently sensitive—merely in the act of trying a cultural element on for size. Cul-Ap is thus taken as a form of condescension BY ITS VERY NATURE. Yet framing the act-in-question as an illicit act does nothing to address concerns about discourtesy—that is: being "disrespectful" or "offensive" or "insensitive" (i.e. the very things that animate many Cul-Ap-related grievances). Here, the bone to pick is a chimera. The contention is as follows: By being cavalier—or even just insouciant—in the use of an exogenous cultural element, the culprit is demeaning the source culture. For he is not taking the cultural element—and by implication, the culture-in-general—seriously enough. Accordingly, the attitude ascribed to the culprit is: "I'm doing this simply because I find it amusing. Consequently, I am neglecting the fact that this meme is meaningful to certain people." According to the class-action grievance, anything short of a subscription to the culture WHOLESALE disqualifies a person from participating in any element of it.

If we were to proceed according to this maxim, questions arise that Cul-Ap-phobes are unprepared to answer. When world-renowned (Chinese) cellist, Yo Yo Ma plays one of Brahms' sonatas (German), bluegrass (American Southern), or a tango (Latino), is he paying tribute to different cultures or is he exploiting them? If the former, how can we know for sure? By what terms is he exempt from the proposed strictures on Cul-Ap? If the latter, how so? Might we suspect that his ostensive tribute really a veiled desecration? Is this acclaimed musician cribbing the material, or is he celebrating it

Such questions have obvious answers. Indeed, the mere posing of them reveals the inanity of vilifying Cul-Ap.

The gripe, we find, is often with participation that is conducted with an inadequate degree of solemnity (that is: when done cavalierly; and so–arguably–patronizingly). For when Yo Yo Ma plays a piece from a German composer, he is taking it very seriously; and inarguably doing the material justice. Here the idea seems to be that participation on the part of the casual "appropriator" is supercilious; and, in being supercilious, is dismissive of the cultural element's import to members of the (purported) source-culture. But this is clearly an untenable assumption. How are we to determine when someone is being too cavalier in their use of an exogenous cultural element? Yo Yo Ma is a clear-cut case; but what of the untalented Asian cellist who is simply dabbling in Mozart for his own idle amusement? Is he also exempt from charges of Cul-Ap? If so, what absolves him?

It would seem, then, that for those suspicious of Cul-Ap, it is CAPRICE that is the bone of contention. The accusation follows: "You are engaging in the act with an inadequate show of deference. Ergo you are being patronizing." Simply being care-free when participating in another's culture is seen as care-LESS. This seems to make sense...until we realize that we humans do this sort of thing all the time. In fact, it is almost unavoidable. WASPs impetuously get henna tattoos and counter-culture punk-rockers shave their heads in the Native American "Mohawk" style. Japanese music-stars simulate American-style punk...and goth...and boy-bands... and, yes, even cowboys. Are these exuberant adopters being insufficiently appreciative of the culture that first popularized the meme?

Shall we suppose that such acts somehow undermine human solidarity? When finding affinities is done flippantly, is the gesture morally suspect? Are we to suppose that the lackadaisical nature of the quotidian activities of daily life somehow disqualifies it from civility? Does care-free really equate with care-LESS?

Harboring contempt for Cul-Ap disregards the fact that day-to-day behavior is INHERENTLY mercurial. With respect to conduct in a setting where cultures routinely intermingle, people can't help but casually imitate memes they find amenable. It is inevitable that bystanders will emulate certain exogenous cultural elements—from locutions to attire—in extemporaneous ways. In most cases, such mimicry is a tacit form of flattery. Construing such behavior as IPSO FACTO patronizing—or even derogatory—is disingenuous. It may be clumsy. It may even be flippant. But it is rarely invidious.

If we take this uncharitable construal of cultural mimesis to its logical conclusion, we wind up in a maelstrom of absurdities. For we are forced to conclude that we all desecrate the memory of the Tang Chinese by celebrating with fireworks. And we demean the Mexican "vaquero" with our exaltation of the gun-toting, stetson-wearing Anglo-Saxon cowboy. We find ourselves enveloped in a whirlwind of Cul-Ap galore. Once we succumb to Cul-Ap-phobia, we wind up indicting every aspect of our daily lives. (!)

Of course, there are not always noble intentions afoot. So WHAT OF dubious motives? Here, we must contend with the question of where mere portrayal—cartoonish or not—ends and the alleged impropriety begins. We might ask: At what point does portrayal become exploitative? Alas, this is often very difficult to discern; for what may be merely a flubbed attempt at homage to one person is taken as effrontery to another.

But take heart. This disparity of sentiment needn't leave us in some insoluble quandary. We do not need protocols to tell us that Disney's film, "Song Of The South" was exploitative AND derogatory. We need only bring our moral intuitions to bear on the facts of the case. That said, there is a profound difference between "Song of the South" vis a vis African Americans and, say, "Ratatouille" vis a vis Parisians. Indeed, there is something amiss if someone does NOT find the former problematic; yet only the tetchiest Parisian would find the latter offensive. The explanation for this key difference, then, cannot be explained by couching things in terms of Cul-Ap.

So we might pose the question: At what point does conduct that is meant to be "all in good fun" become an act undertaken with an insufficient amount of "due respect"? According to whom? To what extent are we all obliged to cater to the sensibilities of every passer-by? The moment subjectivity is employed as the standard for ethical guidelines, we find ourselves unwitting bystanders in a deluge of extemporaneous prohibitions...subject to be updated at any moment...without notice...based on any random bystander's whim.

Admittedly, the "I'm just doing it for the fun of it" excuse only goes so far. How shall we verify that something is REALLY being done in good faith? Where does affinity end and perfidy begin? Sincerity is a notoriously difficult thing to gauge; so nobody can know for sure. Anyone who deigns to adjudicate such matters is forced to claim to have psychic abilities.

Let's pose the question another way: At what point does playfulness involving exogenous cultural elements become insufficiently heartfelt to be deemed acceptable? In assaying such scenarios, we soon find that no universal standard is possible. Short of mind-reading, no adjudication can be conducted on this matter. For even something done WITHOUT bad intentions can still be done a bit too flippantly—that is: in a ham-handed manner. After all, some mimesis is more pantomime than genuine immersion.

The mimesis of anything that happens to be a hallmark of another's identity can easily be construed as patronizing. But one person's impression cannot be the ultimate standard for evaluating another person's conduct. In any case, heedlessness is not tantamount to treachery. And being inconsiderate is not always the same as being immoral. To equate matters of propriety with matters of probity is a fundamental mis-step. There is a difference between ethics and etiquette.

Alas. Anti-Cul-Ap crusaders anoint themselves the arbiters of good form; and even fashion themselves as standard-bearers of good will. In their eagerness to appoint themselves the sentinels of cultural integrity, they fail to see that to vilify those engaged in even the most benign instances of Cul-Ap requires them to be complicit in the very activity against which they inveigh. For their prosecutorial zeal involves a sense of entitlement (exercised under the aegis of "respect") as well as a hefty dose of self-righteousness (which they construe as philanthropic fervor). The gimmick is well-known: Simply pass sanctimony off as a kind of humility.

It requires far more sense of entitlement to tell people that they are not allowed to participate in a bit of exogenous cultural activity than it does to—well—simply engage in it. The former requires one party to tell another party what they cannot do; the latter is simply an exercise of personal volition. One regards others' affairs; the other regards one's own affairs.

Yet the question remains: When people ARE being assholes, what are we to do? We are right to take exception to instances of Cul-Ap done with a scornful sneer, or in too flip a manner. In such cases, how are we to respond?

An anti-Cul-Ap crusade is not the answer. When contending with depravity, the proper focus is not the Cul-Ap that happens to accompany it. The focus, rather, should be on the depravity. Put another way: The diagnosis of an act done with ill will is not the act itself (which may sometimes occur in mundane contexts); it is the ill will.

To review: The demonization of Cul-Ap generally pertains to any act that is seen as demeaning—typically, because it is construed as condescending or derogatory. The prohibition aims to mitigate anything that is (purportedly) done "in poor taste". The problem is that proponents of this approach allege bad intentions to be around every corner. Once we adopt this frame of mind, suspicion of Cul-Ap almost seems to make sense. But in order for this to work, one must refrain from ever looking into ACTUAL intentions.

When, say, an Anglo-Saxon dons a Pocahontas costume, we must ask: What is BEHIND the act? Is it an attempt to mock or is it simply "all in good fun"? The charge of illicit Cul-Ap makes no such distinction. {10} Alas, for Cul-Ap-phobes, the act itself is seen as PRIMA FACIE pernicious. To recapitulate: Those who insist on treating the use of an exogenous cultural element as an opprobrious act are forced to pretend that all of it is derogatory BY ITS VERY NATURE. The Cul-Ap-phobe's credo amounts to the following precept: To casually partake in another's culture is to AUTOMATICALLY be patronizing—irrespective of what is behind the act.

What those who denounce Cul-Ap as inherently iniquitous fail to realize is that intentions matter. When something is done in a mean-spirited manner, the problem is not necessarily with the deed per se; it is with the mean-spirited-ness. If one is being a jerk while baking chocolate-chip cookies, that's not an indictment of chocolate-chip cookie-baking.

Where Ethnic Fidelity Is Relevant; And Where It Isn't

To what degree are we obliged to faithfully replicate exogenous cultural elements when we opt to "try it on for size". Nobody is a fan of cheap caricature… unless it is deliberately used for the sake of satire; and, even then, only when the satire is girded by good will. (Parody is a complex topic, which goes far beyond the scope of this book. Suffice to say, the question must always be: What is BEHIND the gesture?)

If a Westerner dresses up as a samurai "just for the fun of it", is he guilty of pilfering something from ancient Japanese culture? Is he demeaning the ancient "sho-gun" culture with this whimsical act? By countenancing a simulacrum of the medieval warrior in a somewhat cavalier manner, might he be patronizing the "bushido" creed? Is such an act too casual for the consideration such an outfit warrants? After all, short of donning an authentic "hatomune do", he risks caricaturing something that used to be taken very seriously. These are all fair questions. Yet denigration would seem to be an overly harsh indictment. (Generally-speaking, a lack of consideration is not tantamount to being unethical.) Yet the way Cul-Ap-phobes characterize incidents, one would think a grave moral transgression has occurred…whereby members of the source-culture have incurred harm.

Such complaints, assuming they are sincere (which is not always the case), stem more from neurosis than from moral principle. It could even be said that it is the ACCUSATION ITSELF that is doing the real damage. For it engenders trepidation in those who are curious about other cultures…yet are reticent to do anything that might be construed as untoward. In the midst of such accusations, we are expected to forget how commonplace cultural exchange has been since the beginning of time.

Upon even cursory scrutiny, we find that those who insist that everyone be "politically incorrect" are often being rather petty. Take, for instance, grievances about the portrayal of people of color in the HBO series, "Game of Thrones"—a mythical land based on medieval European tropes. (The show was itself adapted from the novel series, "A Song Of Ice And Fire", which did not pretend to be doing anything other than trafficking in stereotypes often found in modern fantasy.) Those griping about this popular HBO series neglected to note that the beautiful, noble Dornish warrior sisters—like the "unsullied"; and like the Dothraki of Essos—did, indeed, have darker skin.

But were these churlish identitarians REALLY concerned about a fictional world denigrating entire races? It seems not. After all, similar complainants pretend not to understand why elves and mermaids (mythical creatures) are White or East Asian, but are almost never depicted as Black. {4} Presumably, these are the same people who claim to be "offended" that there were no dark-skinned elves in "The Lord of the Rings". Shall we also be confounded by the fact that so few Punjabis are cast as Vikings? {30}

Whether or not the figure in question is fictional is beside the point. The Greek gods were, in fact, NOT East Asian; so it would be peculiar to portray, say, Aphrodite as Japanese in a production that deigns to depict Greek myth. Even so, there is no problem with Asians dressing up as Aphrodite "just for the fun of it". How shall we account for this discrepant assessment?

We can all agree that one does any given culture a disservice by caricaturing it—that is: portraying in a way that cheapens it by making light of its most hallowed traditions. There are two possible scenarios. Cos-play can be used either for portrayal (where fidelity to the folklore IS important) or for recreational caricature (where there is no pretense of fidelity to the folklore invoked). In any given instance, which is the most salient? Here is where we encounter the shaky basis for Cul-Ap-phobia. It's considered fine when Asians dress up as cowboys; yet woe to any girl who isn't Native American if she decides to dress up as Pocahontas. {10} When ascertaining the legitimacy of meme transference across ethnic lines, by which criteria are we to base our judgement? The best answer is exigent power asymmetries; so this will be explored at length in the present book. For now, it suffices to say that, when done flippantly, many cases of mimesis are little more than hackneyed simulations—done out of mockery. This is a problem; and it is worth addressing. For the moment, though, let's set aside the fact that there will always be the occasional asshole who engages in cheap imitation to make fun of those who are not like him.

It is fair to say that, when it comes to the PORTRAYAL OF certain things, it is important to maintain a modicum of ethnic fidelity. For instance, a Black vampire makes about as much sense as a Nordic Ninja or a Siamese Santa Claus. This should NOT prevent Scandinavians from dressing up as ninjas or people in Thailand from wearing Santa Claus costumes "just for the fun of it". But it SHOULD prevent those deigning to proffer a serious portrayal of medieval Japanese culture or of "Western" Christmas traditions from engaging in cultural mis-representation.

When playing dress-up ("cos-play" in the current lingo) that involves personages from other cultures, there is no pretense to ethnic fidelity. People are, as it were, just playing around. This is why it is fine for a non-Native American to dress up as Pocahontas for a festive occasion (where there is no pretense of ethnic fidelity)…even as it is wrong to cast a non-Chinese actress as Mulan in a film (where there IS a responsibility to maintain ethnic fidelity). The former is a matter of festivity; the latter is a matter of dishonesty. {10}

So, yes, Disney can make a live-action version of Mulan for an audience dominated by WASPs; but only if they make an honest effort to do the tale's legacy justice (and give credit where credit is due). This means not betraying the spirit of the story; and not pretending that Mulan was anything but Chinese. Casting anyone but a genuinely Chinese actress to play the role would, indeed, be daft. (Recently, Jada Pinkett Smith made herself a laughing-stalk by depicting Ptolemaic Pharaoh, Cleopatra II, a Macedonian monarch in Egypt, as Black.)

This elementary principle can be illustrated by making further queries. Shall we pretend that Alexander the Great was Swahili or that Jesus of Nazareth was Slavic? To do so would not only be factually inaccurate; it would be silly. However, this should not prevent Africans from donning Macedonian warrior costumes or the Irish from dressing up as the Messiah…when it's "all in good fun".

In the event that there is any pretense of ethnic fidelity, an accurate characterization is warranted. This is not rocket science. If one is going to do a biopic on Martin Luther King Jr., casting Jackie Chan in the lead role is probably not the most prudent choice. Why not? Because the famous American civil rights activist wasn't Chinese. Simply noticing this is not a slight against everyone from Hong Kong. {15}

In considering this matter, we have two different scenarios:

Upholding fidelity to ethnic exigencies when purporting to portray what are cultural realities.

Casually participating in exogenous cultural elements–be it sartorial, musical, culinary, literary, or anything else.

The imperative of (A) is not mutually exclusive with the prerogative to engage in (B). The former involves responsibilities; the latter involves liberties.

In sum: Ethnic fidelity is important; yet it does not preclude the prerogative to engage in play-acting ("cos-play" for idle amusement). There is nothing inherently profane about playful experimentation—even if done puckishly, with a wink and a nudge. Very few of those who are playing dress-up are seeking to MOCK the thing they are ostensibly EMBRACING. In the event "cos-play" is done in a waggish manner, we mustn't ascribe ill-intent to what is—more often than not—nothing more than irreverent playfulness. (The thing with chiding is that it can be done out of insensitivity or out of cruelty. There is a difference worth noting. Being inconsiderate is difference from being mean; and the degree of malice ACTUALLY involved cannot be ascertained merely from surveying the personal impressions of bystanders.) In assessing cases of botched emulation, we should bear in mind that being heedless—or even callous—is not the same being malicious. There is a long way from being inconsiderate to being insidious.

Yet when it comes to instances of play-acting that involve ethnic caricatures, compunctions remain. How are we to proceed? It is, of course, no surprise that subjective takes don't always align. What is "all in good fun" for one party may be mischief to another. Therefore any given party's sensibilities cannot be the ultimate standard by which any given behavior is proscribed. How any given person might happen to feel about it is another matter entirely. We cannot establish moral standards based on this or that party's sentiment. In a global society, the only basis to which we have recourse is to (categorically) universal moral principles (i.e. that which TRANSCENDS cultural differences).

The inconsistent standards of the anti-Cul-Ap crusade become evident the moment we start applying them universally. So far as Halloween costumes go, culture-segregationists seem not to consider donning lederhosen a mockery of Bavarians…or wearing a kilt a mockery of the Scots…or dressing up as "Swiss Miss" a mockery of the Schweizer…to say nothing of pirates, ninjas, and gypsies. But why not? Because, like all other indictments leveled by those obsessed with political correctness, the charge of illicit Cul-Ap is based on selective application. When White women wear hoop earrings, we are notified that it is a slight against African culture; yet if they embroider "Hello Kitty" on their purses, well, then the Japanese have nothing to complain about. {3}

The protocols of political correctness only work by being inconsistently invoked. The modus operandi is invariably: "It's fine if THIS group does it; but opprobrious if THAT group does it." When it comes to the vilification of those engaged in Cul-Ap, it is INEVITABLE that standards will be applied ad hoc. And it is not merely that double standards are permitted; they are—effectively—MANDATED. Even a cursory survey brings such inconsistency into stark relief. Rarely do Scandinavians become incensed when Indians or Africans dress up as Vikings. Rarely do the Irish get their hackles up when Arabs or Asians dress up as leprechauns. And the Japanese have no scruples whatsoever with Western women dressing up as geishas. Such widespread equanimity goes precisely to the crux of the matter: The rules apply only to some, not others.

Trying to put oneself in another's shoes is important; as it is the basis for empathy. Cosmopolitanism is based on an expansion of one's sphere of empathy beyond the confines of one's own ethnic group. The ultimate goal, global empathy, is what happens when trans-ethnic empathy is taken to its logical conclusion. Be that as it may, it is important that we not confuse putting oneself in another's shoes with suddenly knowing what it's like to BE that person. We rightfully take exception to those who design to experience the plight of an oppressed / marginalized group by engaging in a superficial emulation of some element of that group's culture…and who then pat themselves on the back for being stalwarts of empathy. It makes sense to be wary of those who assume to know for certain what it is like to be someone other than themselves. (By donning a sombrero, a gringo does not suddenly know what it's like to be Mexican.) The problem with such posturing is that it trivializes the tribulation of others by role-playing. It's as if temporarily adopting the outward accoutrements of a people was tantamount to feeling their pain. Such empty gestures are, indeed, problematic; as they are more pantomime than a genuine effort to empathize. Performative morality is not morality; it is theater.

The best that might be said of such posturing is that it is very tacky. In some cases, such participation is a puerile attempt at exoticism—which invariably ends up as exoticism-as-theatrics (read: FAUX exoticism). The act is typically a gambit to assert a novel identity within one's own community via superficial (spec. cosmetic) means. In doing this, one invariably plays into stereotypes. Even so, superficiality is not a transgression, it is a character flaw. The issue at hand is obtuse thinking, not Cul-Ap.

The problem with trafficking in tropes—and adopting crude caricatures—is that it is tremendously disingenuous; and, rather than paying tribute to an ethnicity, only ends up perpetuating oft-demeaning stereotypes. The "catch" is that, in leveling the charge of Cul-Ap, one is often forced to COUNTENANCE said stereotypes. {52}

Even so, the protocols of political correctness are not a requirement for being honest. In fact, political correctness is—in many cases—predicated on DIS-honesty; as it reduces morality to a regime of propriety. As a consequence of such thinking, being "good" ends up being more about putting on airs than it is about rectitude. It comes as no surprise, then, that most p.c.-mongers are primarily concerned with keeping up appearances; not with solving underlying problems.

Civil rights activism is about far more than optics.

So the question remains: Shall we EVER consider it objectionable to flippantly "try on for size" a meme from a culture other than one's own? Yes; if it is done IN ORDER TO mock. In cases where the motivation is to demean, we are right to take exception. What is opprobrious about such instances, though, is the mean-spirited-ness; not the Cul-Ap per se.

It is possible to temporarily "try on for size" a cultural element without being mean-spirited; but are there still problems of which we should be cognizant? To shed light on possible dilemmas, we can make further inquiries. Can Asians dress up as cowboys? Can Latinos dress up as Flappers? Can ANYONE dress up as slutty nuns? If not, then the question remains: Who shall be the official adjudicator when it comes to such matters? More to the point: A subset of a group cannot claim to be offended on behalf of the entire group. So do some people's offense matter more than the fact that most others are NOT offended? How, exactly, does the calculus of offense-taking work?

For those of us who genuinely care about culture, the primary concern is desecration—or some sort of vulgarization—of a hallowed piece of heritage. Such an act can take the form of feckless misrepresentation or intentional debasement. This pertains to portrayals (where there is a pretense of ethnic fidelity), not to dressing up just for fun (where there is no such pretense). Deliberately misrepresenting folklore is not so much pernicious as it is DAFT. There is nothing wrong with "cos-play" involving, say, Bantu Vikings...or Dutch geishas...or Celtic sheiks; but we should not pretend that such cultural chimeras have any legitimacy beyond tongue-in-cheek play-acting.

This is simply a matter of common sense: If one is directing a play about Zulu warriors, don't cast a Korean actor. A Nubian Queen? Don't cast a Russian actress.

A documentary on Ashkinazim? Don't cast Bengalis. Whether or not the character is fictional or not is entirely beside the point. (Pretending that Tevye—a milkman from a shtetl in Volhynia—may have been Bengali does nothing to empower the Desi community.) {4} Granted, some mythical beings are race-neutral—as with werewolves, witches, and the myriad versions of fairies (sprites, pixies, sylphs, nymphs, etc.) And certain roles transcend ethnicity—as with, say, Catwoman in the DC universe or Elphaba in Wicked. {40} Be that as it may, we now encounter a daft conception of demographic "representation", whereby movie producers pretend that social justice can be effected in the real world by casting fictional characters in a strategic way. {15}

It seems not to occur to those afflicted with Cul-Ap-phobia that the sharing of culture might be impelled by good will (or even just good cheer). King Arthur was Anglo-Saxon; it would be silly to suppose otherwise. But why can't, say, Indonesian revelers dress up as the medieval knights of Europe…if, that is, it's all in good fun? (Most Crusaders were actually Frankish.) The hysterics over Halloween costumes attests to the neurosis undergirding Cul-Ap-phobia. I submit that such confectionary indignation is more a matter of self-ingratiation than it is about the sincere expression of moral opprobrium.

Those who are most irked by Cul-Ap exhibit a state of moral panic that is entirely disproportionate to the alleged transgression—as if Korean girls wearing sexy genie costumes on Halloween might be a worse problem for the world than, say, systemic socio-economic injustices. The "djinn" are from the Middle East, but no Persian or Arab has ever incurred harm from people dressing up as genies…any more than Jews would be harmed by people dressing up as "shedim" or Buddhists would be harmed by people dressing up as "asuras". The only difference is that many Muslims STILL BELIEVE in "djinn". That shouldn't be anyone else's problem.

Instances Of Commercialization

What of the dysfunctions that are endemic to commercialization? At what point is the commercialization of culture done in bad faith? Such queries lead to another question: At what point are we to qualify appropriation as a commercial venture? This is an important issue; as, whenever the profit-motive is involved, dubious motives are invariably a factor.

We are right to be wary of the appropriation of a cultural element becoming the COMMODIFICATION of a cultural element. But are we to suppose that every instance of Cul-Ap involves an attempted commodification of someone's cultural heritage? No. As with the peculiar instance of the French tacos mentioned in the Preface, the profit motive may be a red flag; but they are not proof positive that something iniquitous is afoot. While dubious motives abound whenever there is commercial enterprise, it does not follow that every act of cross-cultural invocation is done in bad faith. Cultural diffusion is not resource extraction.

In assessing the probity of any given act, the focus should be on the ultimate of all common denominators: our shared humanity.

Making queries about concretes may help discern which principles are most salient. When those in "the West" take yoga classes, are they hijacking a key element of Hinduism…or are they simply adopting a practice they find advantageous? In a sense, American-style yoga IS a mere caricature of Indian culture: hokey, superficial, and—yes—commercialized. Yet it does not follow that there is something iniquitous afoot when someone opts to throw on some Lululemon tights and participate in a Vinyasa seminar.

Here's the thing: ALL culture is cheapened by being commercialized—regardless of who might be doing it. One need only experience a tourist-trap in any country to note that most countries often commercialize—and so cheapen— THEIR OWN cultures when it is economically advantageous. (!) Nobody makes super-tacky kitsch more than people trying to cash in on stereotypes **of their own culture** by peddling tchotchkes to naive tourists seeking memorabilia.

It is no secret that Cul-Ap is sometimes more a matter of the cheapening of culture-in-general (as with commercialization) than it is the judicious use of cultural elements by thoughtful parties. What some fail to understand is that culture—of whatever ethnicity—is not a marketing gimmick; it's part of people's lives. Thought-provoking commentaries on the "culture industry" (spec. the commodification of culture) can be found in the writings of Theodor Adorno and Max Horkheimer under the aegis of the Frankfurt School of critical theory. {48}

The film industry sheds light on the issues arising from trans-cultural commercialization. We might begin by asking: Should the French be offended by the fact that the best cinematic production of "Les Liaisons Dangereuses" was made by Chinese director, Jin-ho Hur ("Wi-heom-han Gyan-gye")? The Chinese rendition (2012) re-conceived Pierre Choderlos de Laclos' 18th-century tale, setting it instead in Shanghai's high society during the 1930's; and, I might add, is arguably the greatest rendition ever done. Hollywood had also adapted it to New York City during the 1990's ("Cruel Intentions"). Yet Parisians were not irked by these instances of appropriation. Pourquoi pas?

Should the British be up in arms over the fact that the Americans ripped off "Romeo And Juliet" with the Broadway musical, "West Side Story"? The American classic (by Arthur Laurents) re-conceived Shakespeare's tale to have taken place in 1950's New York City (with Tony & Maria) instead of in medieval Verona, Italy. (The Montagues and the Capulets were replaced by the Jets and the Sharks—that is: gringos and Latinos.) The next year, the famed Japanese author, Yamada Futaro (a.k.a. "Yamada Seiya") wrote "Koga Ninpocho" (a.k.a. "The Kouga Ninja Scrolls"), in which the ill-fated lovers (re-named Gennosuke and Oboro) were members of warring clans in feudal Japan c. 1600.

Meanwhile, the Broadway musical, "Hello Dolly" was lifted from a musical by the Viennese playwright, Johann Nestroy (via Thornton Wilder). No Austrian was irked by this instance of theatrical appropriation. There was then an American version of the classic French novel "Phantom of the Opera" by Gaston Leroux. This did not elicit any acrimony from Parisians. In Russia, Nikolai Leskov appropriated Shakespeare for his production, "Lady Macbeth Of The Mtensk District". There was no outrage. Why not? Upon surveying the resplendent tapestry of the world's artistic achievements, we can only conclude that the admixture of cultures is often—and usually should be—encouraged.

Admittedly, Cul-Ap is not always an estimable affair. A prime case of cultural vandalism was the cynical re-purposing of Beethoven's 9th symphony (a.k.a. "Ode To Joy"), named after the poem, "An die Freude" by the German Freethinker, Friedrich Schiller; who was writing about universal human brotherhood. Alas, the piece of music is now often used by the Roman Catholic Church. In 1907, the American minister, Henry van Dyke changed Schiller's lyrics, expunging the feminine idiom (pertaining to the daughter of Elysium) from the verse; and re-branded the song, "Hymn Of Joy". Beethoven would almost certainly not have approved. Should we consider this memetic adaptation an instance of cultural desecration or simply a harmless instance of meme-adoption? This is not an easy question to answer. {56}

There is a difference between appropriating art and perverting it. We can encourage the former while discouraging the latter. It is not the case that every time non-Lutherans perform, say, one of Bach's devotional pieces, they are misappropriating German culture. For it is honoring the "spirit" of the artistic work that counts. Artistic tribute is not the same as artistic defacement. This is why it is perfectly fine for atheists to sing Gospel music...so long as they do so with a full artistic appreciation for the material. Subscription to Pauline Christology is not a prerequisite for performing music composed with a Christian theme. For one does not need to espouse the dogmatism of the material's authors to appreciate its artistic value.

In music, there are many examples of Cul-Ap *as tribute*. When British poet laureate, Robert Bridges (an Anglican) composed lyrics for one of Bach's cantatas (rendering the familiar hymn, "Jesu, Joy Of Man's Desiring"), the world was treated to a felicitous case of Cul-Ap. The key is that Bridges' gesture did not betray the spirit of the piece. Also note the use of Beethoven's masterpiece, "Egmont" by the Hungarian filmmaker, Janos Vadasz for the score in his film, "Overture".

There are hits and misses. Richard Strauss may have approved of Stanley Kubrick using "Also Sprach Zarathustra" (spec. Sunrise) as the theme song for the film "2001: A Space Odyssey". However, Nietzsche probably would NOT have approved of the musical theme to his magnum opus (which, sadly, he never had the chance to hear) being used for nationalistic or religious purposes, as it—unfortunately—often is. (When Christians play "Sunrise" from "Also Sprach Zarathustra", it is especially grating…if not oddly hilarious.) Meanwhile, one wonders whether Strauss would have endorsed the use of "Sunrise" by the punk band, Blink-182 as the overture for their live concerts…or as fanfare for the USC Gamecocks as they enter the football stadium.

Even as Tchaikovsky may have been fine with Disney using his material in the score for "Fantasia", Shakespeare may have balked at the plot of "Hamlet" being recruited for animated, singing animals in the Serengeti—as Disney opted to do in "The Lion King" (with the special, added touch of turning tragedy into triumph).

Speaking of "The Lion King"; it might also be noted that Disney's animated feature amounted to a Westernized version of the Japanese movie, "Kimba" from 1950 (replete with the film's hallmark set-pieces), though Disney did not admit as much at the time. It could be argued that this makes the American film more a matter of plagiarism than it was of cultural appropriation. The irony here is that the creator of "Kimba", Osamu Tezuka, had made Japanese versions of Bambi and Pinocchio in 1951. The difference is that Tezuka did so with permissions; and without any pretense of novelty. (In other words: He admitted that he was engaging in Cul-Ap—reminding us that, at the end of the day, it is honesty that counts.)

We are often oblivious to Cul-Ap when it DOES occur; and tend to be perfectly fine with it whenever it suits us. In a twist of irony, the music for the national anthem of the United States is lifted from a BRITISH song ("To Anacreon in Heaven"), even as it uses lyrics composed during the War of 1812 AGAINST the British (by a captive on one of the British ships, Francis Scott Key, as he witnessed the attack on Fort McHenry in Baltimore).

On the fourth of July, Americans often play Tchaikovsky's 1812 overture, which was composed to celebrate a RUSSIAN victory (against Napoleon). Another patriotic song, "My Country, 'Tis Of Thee" is simply a rehashing of Britain's stridently monarchical "God Save The King"—thus extolling the very thing that the American republic was founded AGAINST.

Incidentally, the United States wasn't the only nation to adapt the melody of "God Save The King" to fit their own patriotic motif. The Swiss made it "Rufst du, Mein Vaterland"; the Russians made it "Molitva Russkikh"; the Prussians made it "Heil dir im Siegerkranz"; and the Norwegians made it "Kongesangen". In these instances of Cul-Ap, one could make the case that such appropriation was problematic, as the revamped versions betrayed the spirit of the original. (Hence the phrase "B is a rip-off of A" is used whenever people have compunctions about certain adaptations.) But this illustrates, yet again, that it is not the appropriation ITSELF that is the issue; it is the MODE OF appropriation.

In America, the appropriation of cultural elements is riddled with ironies. Anti-Cul-Ap crusaders might ask themselves if we are to become disgruntled about Americans' use of other nations' music. The point, it seems, is that it is important to recognize the legacy of the cultural element being invoked. When we alter the wording of a classic piece of writing to suit their own (puritanical) sensibilities, it is sometimes profane. It does not follow from this, however, that those from outside the source-culture should be disallowed from making JUDICIOUS use of the material. Memetic emulation is not inherently impertinent.

Problematic occurrences of Cul-Ap serve as reminders that REAL problems arise not from Cul-Ap per se, but from a lack of appreciation for—and/or a failure to give proper attribution to—the cultural element at hand. Our tendency to indulge in collective narcissism makes us blind to such things. (Conceit is, after all, a hallmark of a tribalistic mindset.) Denying the origins of a cultural element (because we are, after all, tempted to make everything ALL ABOUT US) is a problem that has nothing to do with cultural diffusions. The problem is conceit.

Normally, however, the commercialization of cultural elements is taken in stride. Hollywood has been festooned with Cul-Ap since its earliest days. In American cinema, some of the all-time classic Westerns were "Spaghetti Westerns", so named because they were produced and/or directed by Italians. The acclaim of such films was not undermined by the fact that Europeans were "appropriating" the characters of the fabled "wild west" (i.e. folklore about the American frontier that tends to involve overwrought caricatures). Meanwhile…LITERAL spaghetti is a staple of American cuisine which was "appropriated" from the Italians. This was not some premeditated cultural exchange. Shall we wonder whether or not cowboys for pasta is a fair trade? (To be fair, Americans STARRED IN the Spaghetti Westerns…as Italian food earned an exalted reputation worldwide.)

When it comes to "Westerns", there was trans-cultural fertilization afoot in several other ways. The American classic "The Magnificent Seven" was an adaptation of Akira Kurosawa's "Seven Samurai". (Maclean's "The Guns Of Navarone" was also an adaptation of the Japanese classic. Yes, the Japanese are to thank for one of America's most beloved cowboy movies AND most beloved war movies.) Nihon-jin had no problem with this. Kurosawa's films also served as the basis for the classic Western, "Fistful of Dollars" (a re-imagining of his "Yojin-bo")…and even as inspiration for "Star Wars" (a re-imagining of his "The Hidden Fortress"). Is such cultural interchange a slight against either ethnic group?

But nobody is above Cul-Ap. When Kurosawa made his critically-acclaimed movie, "Ran", nobody begrudged him for having regurgitated Shakespeare's "King Lear"…which was itself adapted from Raphael Holinshed's hagiography of the Briton King known as "Leir". Meanwhile, Kurosawa's "Ikiru" was a revamping of Tolstoy's "The Death of Ivan Ilyich". (Thank you, Russians.) And when he made "Throne Of Blood", nobody begrudged him for having riffed off of "Macbeth". (Human nature as it is, the anti-hero in this amazing story could have been a Danish king or a Japanese Emperor.) Thank heavens for thematic cross-pollination!

Cultural elements, it turns out, are not commodities to be traded and bartered; they are PUBLIC GOODS…from which we might all benefit. Meme-harvesting, it turns out, is the engine of cultural flourishing.

Granted, memetic transference across cultural lines is not always reciprocal. Humans operate in a globalized commercial environment, and find themselves incorporating various things from various places at various times for various reasons. So unilateral memetic transference does not necessarily indicate that some sort of domination is afoot. Much of cultural exchange is INVARIABLY one-directional, as it occurs extemporaneously.

In proscribing ALL Cul-Ap, we would be forced to concede that Disney was guilty of illicit Cul-Ap by making "Aladdin". But a problem arises: Appropriated from WHOM? In fact, "Aladdin" was not even authentically Arab! The tale was a medieval European invention involving a fantastical caricature of Arabian culture… which was itself based on PERSIAN literature (namely: the medieval Pahlavi work, "Hazar Afsanah"). So who's the victim in such a case?

It's not just Aladdin and his magic lamp. Also best known from One Thousand And One Nights (a.k.a. Arabian Nights) are the tales of Sinbad The Sailor as well as Ali Baba And The Forty Thieves. None of these stories were in the Arab original. A (Syriac) Maronite Christian, Antun Yusuf Hanna Diyab of Aleppo (Ottoman Syria) penned ALL THREE in the early 18th century…which were then added (in French, by the translator, Antoine Galland) to the medieval Arab anthology…presumably in an attempt to appeal to European sensibilities. Was this a bad thing?

We can pose further queries about the commercialization of culture simply by surveying animated feature films. Was Disney guilty of Cul-Ap when it made…

"Pinocchio" *(Italian)*
"Pocahontas" *(Algonquian)*
"The Emperor's New Groove" *(meso-American)*
"The Princess And The Frog" *(African American)*
"The Hunchback Of Notre Dame" *(Romani)*
"Beauty And The Beast" *(French)* {22}

"Hercules" *(Greek)*
"Mulan" *(Chinese)*
"Tangled" *(German / Dutch)*
"The Little Mermaid" *(Danish)* {4}
"Brave" *(Scottish)*
"Frozen" *(Scandinavian)*
"Moana" *(Polynesian)*
"Coco" *(Mexican)*

...or "Saludos Amigos" starring Donald Duck *(Latin American)*?

How about when Dreamworks made "Prince of Egypt" *(Hebrew)*? How about when 20th Century Fox made "Anastasia" *(Russian)*? How about when Sony made "Hotel Transylvania" *(Romanian)*? How about when American film-makers made "Kubo and the Two Strings" *(Japanese)*? How about when Irish film-makers made "The Breadwinner" *(Afghan)*? What's going on here?

Granted, the use of cultural leitmotifs in such films was more a matter of unsanctioned culture-INVOCATION than it was a matter of appropriation. The fact remains, though, that most were rather puerile caricatures of the cultures they deigned to represent. Shall we suppose that the above companies were pillaging the world's cultures to make animated films? {5}

While these were all commercial productions done primarily for their entertainment value (and, perhaps, with an oblique concern for other cultures), it is no secret that they were created for financial gain. One might say such products were done "all in good fun", as the saying goes; yet the question persists: Were these movies exploitative? Did any of them demean or trivialize the source-culture? Puerile—and inaccurate—as they may have been, we might consider that they served other purposes (e.g. spurring curiosity about alternate cultures amongst a youthful audience). In the grand scheme of things, all these animated films were relatively anodyne.

By contrast, Disney served as the distributor (and English language over-dubber) for Japanese films like "Ponyo", "Princess Mononoke", and "Spirited Away". In such cases, the most significant thing that was being appropriated was Hollywood's muscle...BY the Japanese. So who was exploiting whom?

In 2004, renowned Japanese director Hayao Miyazaki made the blockbuster hit, "Howl's Moving Castle"...which was "appropriated" (with consent) from British author, Diana Wynne Jones. Shall this be given a pass simply because Jones was compensated handsomely? (Consent is more straight-forward when something is treated as intellectual property.) In 2010, the acclaimed Japanese director, Maro made "Arrietty The Borrower"...which was "appropriated" (with consent) from the late British author, Mary Norton. And in 2013, a Japanese version of Clint Eastwood's "Unforgiven" was made—entitled "Yurusarezaru Mono". Eastwood was happy to extend the rights.

Meanwhile producers of the Japanese blockbuster, "Kimi no Na-wa" [Your

Name] insisted that a Hollywood studio render the film in a (live-action) Western idiom. And the French did their own version of the Japanese film, "Himitsu"—entitled "Si J'étais Toi". Were the Japanese being taken advantage of by heedless Francophiles? Hardly.

Might Cul-Ap be an act that is reduce-able to a financial transaction? Let's hope not. We like to think that there is more to cultural diffusion than the profit motive. Irrespective of motives, though, it is important that—with each trans-ethnic adaptation—there is a respect for the source material. The question must always be asked: Are we cheapening an ethnic group's heritage by commodifying its cultural elements? Is the process in any way exploitative?

Realistically, it's worth acknowledging that commerce is often a mixture of the profit-motive and—we hope—a sincere interest in generating cultural awareness. We have already mentioned the Chinese adaptation of "Dangerous Liaisons", which was originally French...before it was Anglicized. The French seemed fine with this. And Tinsel Town has recently adapted the acclaimed French film "Intouchables" (as "The Upside") without eliciting any accusations of illicit Cul-Ap from the French. These are not isolated incidents. The same went for adaptations of:

> The French "La Cage aux Folles" (as "The Birdcage")
> The German "Wings Of Desire" (as "City Of Angels")
> The Italian "Profumo di donna" (as "The Scent Of A Woman")
> The Spanish "Abre los Ojos" (as "Vanilla Sky")
> The Swedish "Let The Right One In" (as "Let Me In")
> The Norwegian "Kraftidioten" (as "Cold Pursuit")
> The Indian "Parinda" (as "Broken Horses")
> The Cantonese "Internal Affairs" (as "The Departed")
> The Japanese "Ju-on" (as "The Grudge")
> The Korean "Oldu-boi" (as "Oldboy" in the U.S.; as "Zinda" in India)

Hollywood studios were appropriating something in each of these cases. That it was sometimes done purely for financial gain is where the potential problems lie. So to treat the profit-motive (commercial interests) as a means of exculpation from the charge of illicit Cul-Ap seems odd. In any case, all these instances of appropriation were relatively innocuous...which reminds us that Cul-Ap is more ubiquitous than we realize. Indeed, Hollywood is not the only participant in cinematic Cul-Ap. Bollywood did an Indian rendering of Thomas Hardy's "Tess Of The d'Urbervilles" ("Trishna") without any recriminations from the Brits. In fact, there have been dozens of Indian renderings of American films—from "Primal Fear" ("Deewangee") to "When Harry Met Sally" ("Hum Tum"). There was an adaptation of "48 Hours" ("Andar Baahar"); there was one of "My Best Friend's Wedding" ("Mere Yaar Ki Shaadi Hai"); there was one of "Mrs. Doubtfire" ("Chachi 420"); there was one of "There's Something About Mary" ("Deewane Huye Paagal"); there was one of "Disclosure" ("Aitraaz"); there was one of "Reservoir Dogs" ("Kaante"); and there was even one of "I Know What You Did Last Summer" ("Kucch To Hai").

(There were TWO done of "Unfaithful": "Murder" and "Hawas".) Jim Carrey fans needn't despair; Bollywood's got that covered too. They did a version of "Liar Liar" ("Kyo Kii") and "Bruce Almighty" ("God Tussi Great Ho"). Nobody was bothered by any of this.

Such adaptations show how certain themes translate remarkably well between cultures. Trans-cultural resonance reminds us of our shared human nature. (In the forthcoming chapter on literature, we'll see how certain things transcend ethnicity. And in Part 2, we'll look at the tale of Robin Hood across different cultures.) To the objection that film adaptations don't count as (illicit) "cultural appropriation", the only response is: Given the logic undergirding Cul-Ap-phobia, how could they possibly NOT be?

Granted, films are intellectual property; so rights to them can be bought and sold. Commercial interests are clearly involved. But are we to suppose that ***iconic*** films (all of those listed above were critically-acclaimed in their original form) are not an integral part of the source-culture?

This brings us back to the issue of fidelity (to the source-culture). In Japan, anime has often riffed off of Arthurian Legend—from The Seven Deadly Sins and Lance N' Masques to Million Arthur and Claymore's Knights. One anime series is even called "King Arthur And The Knights Of The Round Table"…though it is suffused with Japanese sensibilities. Such material does not attempt fidelity to the European legend that inspired it; yet each of the above films was—nevertheless—considered a fun and creative revamping of the source-material.

So where does this leave us?

"Cultural appropriation, you say? Well, by all means!" is the most reasonable retort to charges of illicit Cul-Ap. And so, it turns out, there was nothing iniquitous about Disney making an animated version of "Cinderella"…even without permission from the world's Italians (who first offered the world the tale of the "Cinder" maiden). Were Americans aware that the vaunted movie studio was using material from German authors ("Aschenputtel" by the Brothers Grimm c.1812)? And that the Brothers Grimm had taken it from a French author (Charles Perrault's "Cendrillon" from his 1697 "Contes du Temps Passé")? And that Perrault had taken it from a Neapolitan author (Giambattista Basile's "Cenerentola", a tale included in his 1634 anthology, the "Pentamerone")? Yet no Italian was offended. In any case, Basile was likely inspired by a recounting of the tales of "Cupid and Psyche" by the Roman writer, Apuleius of Numidia. And Apuleius was likely doing a rendering of an even older GREEK legend (that of the slave-girl, Rhodopis, who won the love of the Egyptian king in the 7th century B.C.) Jumpin' juniper, it's Cul-Ap all the way back to the Iron Age!

Nor were many fans of this cherished fairytale aware that many other cultures had ALREADY "appropriated" the character of the "Cinder" maiden—notably:

Norwegian ("Katie Woodencloak")
Irish ("Ashey Pel")
Jewish Polish ("Raisel")

Georgian ("Conkiajgharuna")
Serbian ("Pepelyouga")
Filipino ("Maria and the Golden Slipper")

Even the Russians incorporated the character into legends of "Baba Yaga". YET, according to Cul-Ap-phobes, the Greeks should have sequestered the leitmotif during its initial run in Classical Antiquity—staking their claim on the folktale so that none of these other pesky cultures could have gotten their grubby hands on it (and refashioned it to suit their own respective cultures). Heaven forbid. {19}

When Woody Allen used Rhapsody in Blue for the score of his film, "Manhattan", he was paying tribute to a fellow Jewish New Yorker, Jacob Gershowitz (a.k.a. "George Gershwin"); but Woody Allen needn't have been EITHER a New Yorker OR Jewish to have done this. According to the contorted logic of Cul-Ap-phobia, though, had the producer / director of this classic film been a WASP, something sinister may have been afoot.

All this is beside the point anyway, as Gershwin HIMSELF engaged in Cul-Ap. As it turns out, he employed musical idioms from R&B, which had been pioneered by African Americans.

It's worth repeating: We are often unaware of when Cul-Ap happens; as trans-cultural fertilization usually occurs organically—which is to say: unwittingly. So when we identify instances that are allegedly problematic, we have invariably engaged in cherry-picking. In other words, an anti-Cul-Ap crusade can't help but be highly selective. The same hypocrisy undergirds much of the putative "anti-racism" hoopla that passes for civic-mindedness in Regressive "Left" circles. {51}

Games are another illustration of how Cul-Ap is typically benign…and generally welcomed by everyone. The Russians play chess even though the game originated in Magadha (India) during the Gupta epoch. In the early 6th century, it was known as "c[h]atu-[r]anga" ("four arms" in Sanskrit); and was possibly Babylonian (Assyrian) prior to that. Chaturanga would eventually lead to various other games: "xiang-qi" (Chinese), "jang-gi" (Korean), "sho-gi" (Japanese), "sittuyin" (Burmese), and "mak-ruk" (Siamese). In Late Antiquity, it was adapted by the Sassanians, and eventually popularized in Persia as "chatrang" (later rendered "shatranj" in Arabic). The term "rook" derives from the Middle Persian "rukh", meaning chariot. The "bishop" was originally an elephant ("fil"); the "knight" was originally a horse ("asp"); and the king was originally a "shah". Shall Persians NOW be offended that the Occident switched their elephants to clerics? One might say that taking a sacred animal and turning it into an ecclesiastical figure was a form of cultural vandalism.

As it turns out, nobody cares. Why not? Because cultural adaptation is what happens with virtually EVERYTHING. As we all know, the game was eventually brought to Europe—via Andalusia—by the Muslims. (How the meme migrated from the Moors to the Russians is anyone's guess.) The number of Indians and Persians rankled about this? Zero.

Rummy is another case in point. The Israeli game, "rummik[y]ub" was inspired by the well-known card game, "gin rummy"...which was, in turn, based on the French game "conquian"...which was itself an adaptation of the (Qing) Chinese game, "mahjong". The number of Chinese dismayed by this? Zero.

That's not the end of it. We find that this lineage of cultural appropriation continued elsewhere. For the Indian game, "paplu" is a spin-off of "gin rummy" as well. Like any other meme, whom the meme has been appropriated FROM is based on where we draw the line in history. No Parisians are incensed at Indians by this...just as nobody in China is incensed at anybody in France. As it turns out, playing cards IN GENERAL derived from the medieval Chinese game, "tien gow" [ninth heaven], which dated back to the 12th century. It eventually came to Europe via the Mamluks. So whether you happen to be playing "go fish" or "canasta", you are engaging in Cul-Ap...though now with Occident-style kings, queens, jokers, and knaves (later rendered "jacks"). The jester is now a "joker". And we play everything from poker to bridge using materials imported by Turkic Muslims in the early modern period.

That Cul-Ap was allowed to occur in all these places should be seen—according to the logic of Cul-Ap-phobes—as some sort of travesty. But it wasn't. Why not? Well, because virtually anything to be found in ANY culture is likely the result of this sequence of historical accidents, often occurring between cultures. Should someone in the future opt to "appropriate" the Indian game "paplu", then so be it. It's the kind of thing that's been happening for millennia.

A Case Of Narcissism (Multi-Culturalism vs. Cultural Relativism)

What might be the psychology behind Cul-Ap-phobia?

Much of the grievance expressed regarding this hobgoblin seems to be based not on the unilateral memetic transference PER SE, but on the fact that certain instances of said transference happen to bug some people sometimes. Offense-taking, then, is the issue; not Cul-Ap. My theory is that the majority of anti-Cul-Ap hysteria is insincere; and results from the puritanical sensibilities—and, often, peevishness—endemic to political correctness. This bit of didactic gimmickry works as follows: "I'm offended, therefore you did / said something wrong. (The collective version of this is no better: "The gesture offends certain people, therefore it must be considered odious by everyone on the planet.")

All this stems from a scenario where self-absorption becomes an epidemic. The mentality here can be summed up as: "It bothers me, so nobody should be allowed to do / say it" is not a moral statement; it is an expression of conceit. "My taking offense means that the position I have taken has credence" is emblematic of narcissism. Note that this does not necessarily involve vanity; as narcissism is more a way of viewing one's relationship to the world than it is about self-admiration. Instead of chortling, "Look how great I am" (the hallmark of vanity); the narcissist obdurately insists, "It's all about ME; and how I happen to feel." We see, then, how self-absorption is proportional to a lack of intellectual curiosity: "I have no interest in understanding the world; I merely want the world to hear my sentiments." (The etymology of "narcissism" notwithstanding, the use of the term in psychology has little to do with being vain—which, in Greek lore, was Narcissus' problem.)

In terms of ethics, only insofar as an activity is disruptive to others in empirically verifiable ways—thereby imposing a LOGISTICAL burden—does it become a matter of ethics. Discomfiture is not a barometer for moral status. Alas, for the anti-Cul-Ap crusader, everyone is expected to cater to a given party's subjective state. But to suppose that one party's sentiment is translatable to a universal ethical mandate is untenable—as it cannot help but lead to an anarchy of incompatible moral standards, each claiming precedence. In a world of moral relativism, tenets are treated as consumer products, hawked and sold in a marketplace of competing doctrines. Meanwhile, the speech codes proffered by p.c.-mongers make it verboten—sometimes, even illegal—to employ anything other than the approved phraseology. So far a they are concerned, if one uses the wrong wording, it is a calumny.

Those struggling to make ends meet are not worried about speech codes. (Someone on the verge of going bankrupt from exorbitant medical bills is not apt to spend their time complaining about the name of Cleveland's baseball team.) They—and most others—are understandably annoyed by those who suggest that everyone should be concerned with such things (see the Appendix). The weaponization of etiquette only serves to divert attention away from more important problems.

Alas, this is what happens when morality is transplanted by formality. In the proposed scheme, certain expression is considered odious simply because it (purportedly) "offends" someone. Consequently, inter-cultural mimesis is deemed a sort of trespass…leading to "injury". Responsibility for one's own psychical well-being is transferred to bystanders, who are expected to comport themselves in a way that accommodates all of one's hang-ups.

And so it goes: With the wave of a magic wand, those who are determined to find an excuse—ANY excuse—to be "offended" can turn even the most milquetoast expression into a devastating infraction. It comes as little surprise, then, that the censorious attitude of the anti-Cul-Ap crusader is predicated on a friable disposition.

The problem with this line of thinking is that—in reality—offense is taken, not given. WE decide what offends us. As the ancient Stoics noted, certain things befall us; and it is up to us how we respond. When one has a frangible constitution, one becomes one's own worst enemy. In the event one experiences unease, one is more inclined to blame others. One is then tempted to mete out indictments accordingly. Accordingly, one expects the rest of the world to cater to one's neuroses.

The mantra of political correctness is: Blame your own psychical quirks on everyone else. "If I'm unsettled by something, it must be someone else's fault. It can't possibly have anything to do with my own insecurities. For that would require me to engage in introspection." It does not occur to such a person to ask himself: Shall everyone else on Earth be at the mercy of my peccadillos?

Mental discipline is anathema to the aficionado of political correctness. {21}

Are we to acquiesce to such perfidy? More to the point: Is censorship to be exacted according to some designated party's sensibilities? Establishing municipal ordinances on meme-transference requires there to be gate-keepers of cultural diffusion…which requires that the rest of us cede sovereignty over our own lives to those who claim to know better.

A logistical problem arises, as one party's subjective state is used to impose restrictions / obligations on everyone else. Any bystander is invited to allege injury due to a bout of discomfiture—as if unease was an indication that some sort of semiotic battery had occurred. According to this modus operandi, one can whimsically designate anything a sacred cow...and thereby render certain acts off-limits to everyone else. This attests to the hubris underlying Cul-Ap-phobia.

Such subjectivism-gone-haywire privileges whimsy—nay, caprice—over critical deliberation. What's the end-game? Is the ultimate goal to bring an end to every (perceived) slight? If so, then how shall we proceed? Should tacky-ness be forbidden? Unseemliness? Stupidity? Even if the aim is to make public spaces more agreeable to everyone's taste, we must ask: Is it possible to eradicate poor taste by forbidding it?

It is de rigueur amongst aficionados of political correctness to pass self-serving endeavors off as a public service. Here, propriety is (mis)construed as probity. The ornery constables of cultural demarcation seek out an excuse to be offended; then feel empowered by having taken offense. Taken offense at what? Well, at anything they find unsettling. They then indulge in fits of pearl-clutching...before embarking on their next ax-grinding expedition.

The most churlish practitioners of this craft are, it seems, determined to be offended. By what? Well, by something. ANYTHING. The most vociferous p.c. vigilantes could look at a potted plant and see a devious scheme of exploitation. Once one has adopted this attitude, a cloudy day can be seen as a sign of a devious plot to sully another culture. And even on the sunniest day, they see ominous stormclouds of oppression forebodingly gathering on the memetic horizon, threatening the fabric of civil society.

As it happens, there are some perks to participating in this charade. Anti-Cul-Ap crusaders do what they do because it has a certain utility. An excuse to grouse about imaginary crimes is an occasion to brag about standing up for some illusory ideal—an ideal that, in their own minds, ONLY THEY are qualified to fully comprehend. It is also a way to accrue social capital. Feigning outrage over such frivolous matters is a way to earn approval from those participating in the same charade.

As a result of all this, Cul-Ap-phobia is often more about scoring points in some kind of virtue-signaling tournament than it is about promoting civility. Such posturing is the hallmark of political correctness. Like persnickety schoolmarms with an ax to grind, the arbiters of meme-transference take it upon themselves to police the agora, seeking to cleanse it of (perceived) improprieties. With self-righteous indignation, they carry out this mission by leveling a litany of denouncements in a frenzy of finger-wagging—as if scolding had magical didactic properties. Like an incantation, all ill will can be tsk-tsk-tsk-ed away.

For the vituperative anti-Cul-Ap crusader, taking offense is seen as taking a moral stand. This is, of course, fallacious. Rather than their grievance being a mark of intrepidity, it is nothing more than a craven emotive ejaculation. Such contrived indignation not only misses its mark, it ends up having the opposite of the intended effect: sowing division instead of solidarity. This irony seems to be lost on those who've been swept up in anti-Cul-Ap hysteria. {**18**}

No matter. The demonization of Cul-Ap is a chance for the haughty proprietors of cultural demarcation to engage in boorish rants about how some people are not staying in their own lane (a lane to which they have been assigned by accident of birth). Pearl-clutching is passed off as a sign of injury; hand-waving is passed off as sound argumentation.

Can we rid the world of those who are impolitic by tsk-tsk-tsk-ing them into oblivion? According to p.c.-mongers: yes. So they proceed accordingly. In a flourish of virtue-signaling splendor, anti-Cul-Ap crusaders imagine themselves to be de-contaminating the public discourse. Little do they realize: virtue-signaling is about the signaling, not about the virtue.

Semiotic prudery is every bit as retrograde as sexual prudery. Alas, one is obliged to undertake this campaign of discursive de-contamination as if, by deploying a raft of sanctimonious declarations, one could somehow make the world a better place. As it turns out, though, what is seen as **contamination** is often just the messy—often clumsy—intercourse endemic to free expression. Lost in all this is a simple truth: Free speech is not important because everyone will enjoy it; it is important in spite of the fact that NOT everyone will enjoy it.

Anti-Cul-Ap crusaders' mawkish exhibition of moral panic is just an opportunity to engage in moral preening. They recognize that, in the current climate, virtue-signaling affords one a chance to tout some fatuous notion of social justice. But all of it is little more than theatrics—meant to flatter more than to empower.

Political correctness, we should bear in mind, is entirely performative in nature; as it is primarily a matter of putting on airs rather than adhering to underlying moral principles. What makes political correctness and identity politics so insidious is that they often masquerade as a quasi-Progressive enterprise. This is why anti-Cul-Ap crusaders have been able to convince themselves—and persuade others—that, in excoriating those engaged in Cul-Ap, they are somehow promoting social justice.

With performative morality, one does not require recourse to moral principles; one need only stick to the script. Who writes the script? Well, the self-appointed adjudicators of cultural exchange, of course. How does this work?

Once we espouse performative morality, our behavior—insofar as it is seen as acceptable—primarily becomes a matter of keeping up appearances. We are obliged to follow whatever choreography has been prescribed by the self-appointed impresarios of propriety. (Another word for this is "decorum".) The result of this charade is an odd combination of peevish-ness and glib-ness. (Acrimony and sanctimony often go hand-in-hand.) Not only does a commitment to p.c. protocols incentivize people to be tetchy, it urges people to go on the offensive. Hence anti-Cul-Ap crusaders operate in an incentive structure that has been designed to promote—and reward—priggishness.

When it comes to virtue-signaling, the intent is to arrogate social capital to oneself—from like-minded compatriots—by shunning those who refuse to accede to the latest mandates. By "getting with the program", the prime directive is to shame others. For what? Well, for (what amounts to) blasphemy…as defined by the arbiters of acceptable meme-transference.

People participate in this charade not to be better people, but simply to earn approval–that is: to feel validated.

By participating in this pageant of virtue-signaling, one can't help but enter into any interaction with a chip on one's shoulder. Taboos can be conjured out of thin air. After each "call-out", one can then congratulate oneself for enforcing those taboos…even if in an ad hoc manner. For the aficionado of p.c., propriety is king. But here's the problem: Obsessing over propriety does nothing to promote the commonweal; it only obliges everyone to perform in the prescribed manner.

To thrive in such environs, everyone is obliged to hew to token formalities, which often entails disregarding moral principle. Those who refuse to play along are summarily scorned—even ostracized. (Shame is the primary weapon of the p.c.-monger.) It bears worth repeating: Performative morality is not morality; it is theater. {49}

Participants in this cloying charade are adjured to abide by the latest version of cultural demarcation; yet nobody is actually moved to ground their deeds in moral principles. Participants are moved to signal that they are on board with the latest strictures; yet are NOT encouraged to cultivate any appreciation for other cultures. The grievances of the self-appointed guardians of unsullied culture have little to do with respecting culture; yet they are thoroughly convinced that their mission is ALL ABOUT respect for culture. Instead of edifying themselves, we are asked to feign contempt for anyone who breaches whatever the etiquette-du-jour happens to be.

All the while, Cul-Ap-phobes are blissfully unaware of the self-contradictions in their condemnations. (Ideological zeal serves as an anesthetic for cognitive dissonance.) How can we be so sure that anti-Cul-Ap hysteria is much ado about nothing? The experiment has been run countless times, so it is not difficult to simply observe. When a non-Chinese female dons a "cheong-sam" (a.k.a. "chi-pao"), what actually happens? Even as some grouse about the horrors of Cul-Ap, the vast majority of Chinese (the alleged victims) see the gesture for what it is: a sign of cultural appreciation—even TRIBUTE. Such vicarious offense-taking reveals not only the neurotic disposition of those who are enamored with politically correctness; it exposes the fatuity of using "cultural appropriation" as an indictment.

But wait. As it turns out, the Han Chinese THEMSELVES appropriated the "cheong-sam". Centuries ago, they adopted it from the Manchu peoples of the northeast, who were ethnic Jurchen. And even then, the sartorial style originated during the Liao dynasty…which was Khitan (a nomadic Mongolic people related to the Xian- bei). Shall modern-day Chinese be apologizing to the Manchurians? Ironically, subsequent designs of the dress were influenced in large part by the fashions of the OCCIDENT…which, ironically enough, is one of the reasons it was banned in Maoist China. That's right. The Chinese DELIBERATELY sought to Westernize the design!

The moral of the story? The "cheong-sam" is a beautiful dress for all women; and we should only celebrate the fact that more women around the world are incorporating it into their fashion repertoire.

But no matter. Those determined to be offended on others' behalf will forge on, undeterred by common sense. Grievances about Cul-Ap are revealed to be bogus when those doing the hemming and hawing claim to be offended ON BEHALF OF the (imagined) victims of the (imagined) crime...even when the real-world counterparts are not at all offended. It requires a high degree of conceit to indulge in vicarious offense-taking—the sort of conceit that only a Cul-Ap-phobe might have.

Another explanation for the penchant to hold Cul-Ap in contempt—and to summarily vilify anyone who engages in it—is the confusion between multi-culturalism (the precondition for an open, pluralistic society) and cultural relativism (an utterly inane paradigm). From whence does this confusion come?

Amongst those of the Regressive "Left", there seems to exist a fear of comparing cultural elements across cultures. Such comparisons are seen as a kind of sacrilege for relativists—who demand that EVERYTHING be shown deference (because, hey, who's to say what's better and what's worse?) Hence indiscriminate "respect" for all cultural elements everywhere, no matter how dysfunctional, is mandated. Never mind that promiscuously allotted respect renders the exhibition of respect an empty gesture. (Only when judiciously granted does respect mean anything.) Estimable cases of discrimination—characterized by prudence and careful discernment—are invariably based on standards that are universal.

Relativism lies at the root of this misapprehension. But what do I mean by CULTURAL relativism? Let's begin with what it is NOT. The relativity of different perspectives, which obviously exist and clearly offer advantages (New vantage points from which to see the world we all share). Even as we all inhabit the same Reality, nobody would argue that each of us is enculturated, so inclined to see things through the lens of our own culture—according to certain habits of thought, couching things from within a certain conceptual framework.

So far as the cultural relativist is concerned, though, there are no universal standards by which to compare an element in one culture with its counterpart in another. To make comparisons of analogous elements between cultures is to risk assessing the relative MERITS OF those cultural elements; and so must be seen as a form of chauvinism. The supposition—entirely groundless—is that people derive their humanity EXPLICITLY FROM the designated element; and so are INHERENTLY tied to it as if by some cosmic force. Everyone on the planet is therefore obligated to show "respect" for the element...so as to avoid hurting the people who identify themselves with it. (Make fun of purple tortillas, and one is impugning all Mexicans.)

In the most outrageous instances of anti-Cul-Ap hysteria, comparative critiques of analogous cultural elements is portrayed as an oblique form of "bigotry" (against all those who are affiliated with the element deemed inferior). It's as if one could be bigoted against a *custom*. But one can't be bigoted against memes; one can only be bigoted against people. And isn't it PEOPLE we should care about most?

So for the cultural relativist, making judgements about the relative merits of this or that custom is seen as a kind of hubris. But the problem isn't judgement; it is POOR judgement—which includes premature (hasty) judgement; also known as prejudice. Not only is there nothing wrong with assessing the merits of any given social norm; it is the responsible thing to do. This sometimes leads to unsavory conclusions (that a cherished tradition may not, in fact, be conducive to the commonweal). Yet those engaged in such heretical critiques are at risk of being assailed for simply pointing out cultural trends (viz. statistical realities that stem directly from prevailing social norms). For such critiques involve that precarious thing known as JUDGEMENT. Alas, "judgement"—especially when it involves brute candor—is off-limits in p.c. precincts.

We find ourselves dealing with a charge that only makes sense if one denies the existence of universal standards. The cultural relativist must realize, though, that treating everything as sacrosanct does not help ANYBODY. Pretending that everything has comparable moral valence—and so must be treated with parity—is untenable. Some cultural elements ARE objectively better / worse than others; and the standard by which we determine this cannot itself be derived from how much stock any given party happens to place on them.

The contention that there can be no universal standards is not only inimical to cosmopolitanism; it is at odds with Reality. What relativists fail to see is that it is not judgement PER SE that is problematic; it is judgement that is UNSOUND that is problematic.

Stating that something is part of someone's culture does not exempt it from judgement. Civic responsibility demands that we assay which memes most comport with the kind of society to which we all—as fellow humans—aspire. This attains irrespective of whether the meme is from our own or another's culture. The idea, then, is not to compare cultures wholesale (as if any given culture was destined to be as it eventually came to be). Rather, it is to compare analogous memes—on a case-by-case basis—on their own merits (rather than according to the culture with which they happen to be affiliated, which is—after all—merely an accident of history).

We cannot pick the culture we were born into; but we CAN choose what we do with that culture. There has never existed a culture that was pre-ordained. More to the point, no one is tied by some ethereal cosmic decree to this or that culture. So, in assessing the merits of any given cultural element, we must bear in mind that there is nothing inevitable—or ineluctable—about this or that culture.

What we want to avoid is cultural chauvinism. We should—all of us—be wary of the notion that certain memes are better by dint of the fact that they happen to come from a certain culture (our own); or simply because they are affiliated with a certain ethnicity (our own). Alas, the trappings of ethno-centricity can be found within every ethnic group. Each culture deals with its own dysfunction in its own way…to varying degrees of success. Suffice to say: There are pitfalls everywhere. Those affiliated with a designated culture can't help but contend with the temptation to romanticize that culture; and thereby commit themselves to the quixotic venture of maintaining both a sense of purity and of exclusivity (only WE are entitled to such and such).

There are dire repercussions to such thinking. For cultural purity is often conflated with ethnic purity; and THAT often blurs into racial purity…which, in turn, redounds to demands for cultural purity—especially in insular communities. (Haredi communities are an obvious example of this.) The prohibition of Cul-Ap entails championing a chronic parochialism…all in the name of "staying in our own respective lanes". {23}

Wonder how bad this can get? Think of all the scenarios in which we have heard some ethnic group declare: "Nobody else should be allowed to do this." Has such a decree ever been issued for noble reasons? Has it ever led to good things? It's worth bearing in mind: Whenever there is a preoccupation with the exalted status of the in-group's rightful claims, the penchant for ethno-centricity is always lurking beneath the surface.

We want cultures to be HEALTHY, not just THERE. One does a culture no favors by pretending every aspect of it is beyond reproach. No culture is flawless; as every culture is a reflection of some combination of human creativity and human depravity. The same West African can wear a beautiful kente cloth while endorsing female genital mutilation. The same Pashtun can make a delicious pulao while forcing his wife to wear a burka. And an American WASP can play Paganini's Cantabile beautifully on the violin…yet be a member of an exclusive country club that admits only White Protestant men. The full range of human feats and human foibles are on display in virtually any culture that has ever existed. It should not be considered "rude" to point this out. Not all memes are equally conducive to civil society.

There are incontrovertible answers to certain moral questions, and it is dishonest to pretend otherwise. Indulging in a tribalistic mindset is the most expedient way to shirk the responsibility to think for oneself. Though we will never quite achieve perfect impartiality, we should always strive to get as close as we can. Humans' relationship to objectivity is asymptotic. (That we can **never actually get there** doesn't mean we shouldn't aspire to do so.) Put another way: Impartiality is an ideal; so is aspirational. Even though it will never perfect, it is something we should shoot for.

How shall we handle constructive criticism? For those identitarians who are extra smitten with political correctness, the answer is: not very well. The trick, it seems, is to tie one's very humanity to the cultural elements with which one most identifies. So any critique of said elements is taken as a personal affront—even an act of de-humanization. In the event that others fail to honor the exaltation of one's own ethnic group, one can bask in a warm bath of one's own crocodile tears…and thereby elicit sympathy for one's veiled hubris. (All-too-often, cupidity is tolerated so long as it can be disguised as humility.)

Frank criticisms of beliefs / practices is not the same as despising those who embrace those beliefs / practices. One cannot be bigoted against DOGMAS, only against PEOPLE. (One can want the best for all Jews / Christians / Muslims while taking exception to Judaism / Christianity / Islam.) We short-change the people affiliated with a culture—ANY culture—by supposing they are incapable of overcoming their own cultural deficiencies; and embracing things that might not be endogenous to their traditional way of life.

Cultural relativism needn't play any role in multi-culturalism. While the former is a sign of fatuity, the latter is an embrace of ethnic diversity. This embrace involves a sincere interest in learning about other cultures. By contrast, cultural relativism does not require one to know ANYTHING about—nor genuinely care about—ANY cultures. Cultural relativism—like all relativism—is characterized only by a dereliction of intellectual integrity. While discrimination between people is a bad thing (when predicated on anything other than merit), discrimination between memes is an integral part of a free (open) society.

Happily, multi-culturalism does not require us to indulge in cultural relativism. Quite the opposite, it requires us to find a universal common ground—to operate on principles that transcend any and all cultural division.

Cultural relativism stems from a failure of intellectual curiosity–not to mention a complete abdication of rectitude. (The same might be said of epistemic relativism and its demented cousin, moral relativism.) It is also a mark of mental laziness. After all, cognitive exertion is required to critically evaluate any given culture—especially one's own; and then make judgements about any given cultural element according to universal standards. (A modicum of perspicacity also helps.) Note that doing so is NEVER about judging a culture wholesale; as each element must be assessed individually, on its own merits. Being multifaceted, ANY culture is—invariably—a mixture of better and worse facets. (A culture is not rendered null simply by modifying one of its constituent elements...or by introducing a NEW element.)

Here, as anywhere, relativism is a cop-out. After all, mental discipline can be extremely difficult; especially when it requires one to contend with deeply entrenched biases, and overcome conflicts of interest. For we ALL—every last one of us—have vested interests that sabotage even the most sincere attempts at objectivity.

But the key here is intellectual curiosity (that is: giving a shit about other cultures). As we find upon even cursory scrutiny, those who level charges of illicit Cul-Ap have no sincere desire to effect inter-cultural comity. (They don't even have a genuine interest in learning about other cultures.) Mutual understanding is not their goal. Their primary objective is to cavil; and thereby earn brownie points from like-minded compatriots for "fighting the good fight" against those dastardly cultural appropriators. But the fact of the matter remains: Engaging in an anti-Cul-Ap crusade has nothing to do with giving a shit about other cultures.

It is crucial to recognize the ideological distinction between multi-culturalism and cultural relativism if one is to understand Cul-Ap-phobia. Multi-culturalism is the hallmark of cosmopolitanism. Cultural relativism is inimical to cosmopolitanism. This is a difference worth recognizing. These two oft-discussed-yet-little-understood ideals, then, are unrelated both logistically and morally. Alas, it is a common mistake on the part of both overt Reactionaries and those on the regressive "Left" (that is: covert Reactionaries) to conflate multi-culturalism and cultural relativism—an irony that is lost on both contingents.

One does not support a culture by refusing to EVER be critical of it. When assaying any given culture, we invariably find that both human wisdom and human folly are endemic to CULTURE PER SE. One only demeans an ethnic group by supposing its members are uniquely incapable of grasping what are categorically universal principles. The denial of universals is sheer folly—the hallmark of that untenable epistemological blunder: relativism. As it turns out, we are all human, and so all possess the same capacities to recognize universals. For, as human beings, we—every last one of us—have access to immutable principles—which, by definition, transcend any and all cultures.

Immutable principles are not social constructs. By contrast, the elements of any given culture are ONLY social constructs. Much as some might like to believe their own customs are somehow hardwired into the cosmic order, they are deluded. One should always bring a critical eye to that which one most cares about. (High standards show respect.) "I think highly of you, so I expect more from you" is the spirit behind the adage: "Dissent is the highest form of patriotism." This is why we are hardest on those we most esteem. We may not all share a family or nationality, but we all share our humanity. And that fact must inform all interaction. We do a grave disservice to an culture by supposing its participants cannot handle an honest evaluation of its pro's and con's.

Thoughtfully critiquing X is indicative of genuinely caring about X. It shows we give a shit. Identifying the salubrious aspects **as well as the dysfunctions** of a given culture is something that ANYONE is capable of doing; as humanist standards are transcendentally prior to social constructs...which are, after all, just historical accidents. We are all human, so we are all—pace those with mental handicaps and/or psychopathy—equipped with the requisite cognitive faculties AND moral intuitions to engage in such a critique. Accident of birth does not confer upon anyone a unique Providential appanage. For each one of us, all memes present themselves for audit. It is up to us to employ sound reasoning; and to bring to bear the (universal) moral principles to which we all have access (that is: if we care to look). Astute discernment requires perspicacity.

In the event that we find an ethical lapse in what we have confronted, those who have a sense of civic duty have an obligation to openly denounce it. And when we really like what we see, we are apt to adopt it. This process is typically known as "being human". We will explore the role of affinities in Part 2; but for now it suffices to say that certain things resonate with certain people for a panoply of possible reasons; and, in the midst of it all, there are certain things that categorically transcend ethnicity and/or culture.

Multi-cultural is an integral part of cosmopolitanism. With this in mind, whenever we consider people of other cultures, we should come to the encounter with our shared humanity at the fore. In other words: While appreciating our differences, it is important to be mindful of what we all have in common.

Cul-Ap-phobia only seems to make sense insofar as cultural relativism is seen as a prerequisite for (or corollary of) multi-culturalism. That is: It is–like most neuroses–based on illusion. The fact of the matter is that pluralism does not require relativism. In fact, pluralism is enabled by the recognition of universal moral principles (that is: a shared vision of what constitutes a civil society). After all, common purpose is the lifeblood of pluralism.

In understanding what each means, it becomes clear that multi-culturalism neither requires nor entails cultural relativism. In fact, multi-culturalism only works when we all proceed from a common ground. Without universal principles, pluralism degenerates into an epistemological—and moral—free-for-all: a cacophony of artificially-constructed "realities" whereby one is behooved to declare, "That's just how we do things around here, so take your maxims elsewhere."

What does this have to do with dubious motives like the profit motive? We are right to be wary of commercialism run amok; as the commodification of culture—and the concomitant hyper-consumerism—auger cultural deterioration. (Want an example of modernity without a soul? Commerce bereft of culture? Prosperity without morality? Look no further than Dubai: a petroleum-funded, Arabian monarchy that has created a Truman Show for the privileged…even as it enslaves countless subalterns…behind the scenes. Out of view, out of mind.)

In the final analysis, there exists no culture that needs to be either embraced or eschewed wholesale. As humans, we are all entitled to assess whatever our fellow humans do. So long as this is done on a case-by-case basis, we do not risk being unfair. The point is to come to trans-cultural encounters from what is ultimately a HUMAN perspective. This entails that—in the midst of our appreciation for the resplendent variety of mankind's social norms—we are all in a position to judge. Universal standards demand nothing less.

Unintended Ramifications (The Misplaced Concern About Stereotypes)

The concern about being condescending toward a certain culture is understandable. This is especially true insofar as one is playing fast and free with stereotypes. However, by crying "cultural appropriation", one often ends up committing the very crime that one deigns to prevent. For one assumes a homogeneity amongst the people over which a designated culture supervenes—a homogeneity that does not really exist. Not every member of a given culture is equally wed to this or that cultural element; nor does every member identify with a particular cultural element in the same way (or even AT ALL). Moreover, a culture is not demographically homologous. This is only made more complicated given the fact that even those WITHIN any given culture cannot necessarily agree on what its signature traits might be. A culture is rarely a unified block, as it contains a diverse assortment of constituents, each of whom emphasizes some of its aspects over others. (Not all Americans identify with baseball and apple pie.) The problem, then, is with stereotypes; not with a cavalier adoption of—or participation in—exogenous cultural elements.

Question: How are we supposed to determine who the gatekeepers of each culture are supposed to be? This is an insoluble quandary.

Every frivolous charge of Cul-Ap is invariably predicated on a regime of "identity politics", whereby all questions are asked and answered according to one or another dimension of everyone's demographic profile. Beyond the problem of seeing humans in such monochromatic ways, it is never a good idea to divide the world into insiders and outsiders—allotting entitlements and restrictions according to the demographic category in which someone happens to (ostensibly) belong.

In addition, the iron-clad demarcation of distinct cultural elements invariably runs into problems of definition. Who owns which contemporary cultural element? Since when? Is R&B the exclusive province of Black folk? Is classical music the sole province of White folk? Can only Koreans create "maedeup"? (The beautiful use of knotted string was prominent during the Silla era.) Should only Algonquin people be allowed to hang dream-catchers in their bedrooms? (The "bwaajige ngwaagan" originated amongst the Anishinaabe and Ojibwe of the Great Lakes region; yet I got mine from a craftsman in Bahia, Brasil.) Shall Afghan rugs henceforth be exclusively for the Pashtuns and Uzbeks? How about Persian rugs for only Persians, Kurdish rugs for only Kurds, and Turkish rugs for only Turks?

All of these absurd queries assume that there exists a network of bright, flashing neon lines between cultures…each of which is a definitive collection of sacralized customs, belonging exclusively to itself…for all eternity. This is nonsense. Cultures are AMORPHOUS. They do not have rigid boundaries; they have hazy penumbras. They don't ABUT one another, they BLEED INTO one another. They merge and diverge. The lines we pretend demarcate one culture from another are actually fluid and always blurry…which means that there really are no lines.

Moreover, cultures are not monoliths. The virtue of any given culture is that it is NOT any one thing; it is a melange of myriad elements—memes that have been incorporated into its repertoire at different times from different places. This belies the notion that cultures are confined spaces with clear-cut edges. As Steven Lukes put it: "Cultures are never coherent, never closed to the outside, never merely local, and never uncontested from within and from without" (ibid.) In any case, countenancing signature features of a culture is not stereotyping; it is simply acknowledging statistical reality (vis a vis prevailing social norms). What does THAT entail? Paying tribute to a key element of a culture, or even one of its hallmark features.

If one wants to call this a stereotype, then so be it.

In many cases, the indictment of Cul-Ap focuses on any expression that SEEMS to countenance stereotypes. This is an eristic complaint. For the use of stereotypes is unproblematic so long as one is forthcoming about the fact that stereotyping is, indeed, what one is doing. As with parody, the point is to be open about the fact that the tropes that one is employing are, indeed, tropes; and are being used with a "wink and a nudge", not with a scornful sneer. (There is a difference between laughing WITH someone and laughing AT someone.) The "catch", then, is that this needs to be done out of good will.

Cheeky humor is not verboten in civil society; and we must be permitted to be impertinent when it is all in good fun. Stereotyping can be done for didactic purposes, not to demean. Even the most biting of satire seeks to rouse, not to quash. Hence the countenancing of negative stereotypes makes sense within the delimited domain of satire—where snark is the point. The only proviso is that, in order to be respectable, this must be done in a (clearly) playful manner. While tongue-in-cheek, the employment of stereotypes mustn't ever be mean-spirited.

We should bear in mind that negative stereotypes are oftentimes perpetuated by some of the very people who are the subjects of those stereotypes. That is to say: In some cases, many of the culprits are members of the group being (negatively) stereotyped; as they are unabashedly EMBODYING the stereotype rather than rebuking it. They are the ones who should MOST know better. I would submit that it is they for whom fellow members of the relevant group should reserve contempt. Especially notable is the diminution of standards for a designated identity-group—often done in a fumbling attempt to "help" them. (Rather than help you clear the bar, you poor things; we'll just lower the bar for you.) Such treatment—the equivalent of a pat on the head—leads to (what amounts to) inverted bigotry. {58} Far from empowering, being condescending only plays into rationalizations for further discrimination.

Stereotype or no stereotype, one's ethnic identity has no bearing on what one can and cannot do in a free (open) society. At the end of the day, every human is morally obligated to assess every other human AS a fellow human being—based on standards that are universal.

Ironically, in an attempt to deter stereotypes, anti-Cul-Ap crusaders end up re-enforcing them. For, in order to get an indictment of Cul-Ap to hold water, the complainant is forced to countenance the very stereotypes he decries. Accordingly, anyone who engages in behavior / speech that happens to correlate with certain stereotypes is accused of perpetuating those stereotypes...with sinister motives explicitly ascribed to those they indict. The thinking is as follows: "It is something that someone who is bigoted might do / say; so you doing / saying it makes you bigoted-by-association." Such an indictment often has the effect of buttressing the very stereotypes it ostensibly seeks to stymie. {52}

Most of what is derided as Cul-Ap is simply an instance of nescient people propounding puerile caricatures of (certain parts of) a culture. Such caricatures are invariably based on stereotypes, typically propounded in a sophomoric fashion. Doing so is callow; it is patronizing; and it is usually based on ignorance. In such cases, the aim is to be derogatory. There is much to be said about what is wrong with such instances, but NONE of it has anything to do with "appropriation". Suggesting Cul-Ap is to blame for such problematic conduct only makes things worse. It confuses **the manifestation of** the mean-spirited-ness with **the basis for** the mean-spirited-ness. The ill will itself cannot be attributed to the means by which it is conveyed.

Vilifying those engaged in Cul-Ap because they are being jerks is not an indictment of Cul-Ap. To ascribe the ill will to the Cul-Ap ITSELF is to miss the point. The frivolous charge exacerbates the very dysfunction it deigns to ameliorate, as it tethers cherished cultural elements to specific groups (which, as we've seen, are often racially defined by the complainants). The repercussion of this is cultural segregation and–even worse–a reinforcement of STEREOTYPES: hardly a recipe for pluralism.

To expect cultures to exist in memetic silos is rather unrealistic; not to mention a recipe for eternal parochialism. When it comes to certain cultural elements, shall usage rights be accorded per the decrees of the designated stewards of the culture-in-question? But then again, who shall be appointed for ascertaining what is and what isn't a permissible instance of meme adoption?

In some cases, there seems to be inadvertent racism undergirding indictments of Cul-Ap as unacceptable—another manifestation of the inconsistent standards already discussed. Let's look at some examples where racialist thinking seems to be operative.

According to the commissars of Cul-Ap, even attire must be allotted according to some ethereal license—rendering even wardrobes proprietary. Sartorial restrictions seem to entail the most obvious reductio ad absurdum. If a European man dons a turban, from whom is he appropriating: Berbers of the Maghreb, Bedouins of Arabia, Pashtuns of the Hindu Kush, Sikhs of the Punjab, Hindus of India, or ALL of them? Isn't it strange that we talk about "Arabs" when the Hashemites, Alawites, and Saudis so often despise one another? Which one has the most credible grievance, then, when non-Arabs appropriate something that is considered "Arab"?

One might be tempted to respond: All of them. But this is not the issue. The point is: What would THEY think? And, as it turns out, THEY will often tend to disagree amongst themselves. For each constituency fashions itself as the truest and greatest representative of "Arab" culture. They are all equally right; and so are all equally wrong. Hence the reductio ad absurdum of the logic employed by Cul-Ap-phobes.

If a Palestinian man decided to wear tartan fabric whilst a Scottish man decided to wear a keffiyah, is this MUTUAL theft? Can either of them claim to have been somehow "ripped off"? Exploited? In the meantime, can either of them wear a Mexican poncho? According to Cul-Ap logic, even Latino culture must be divvied into disparate enclaves; as anyone other than meso-Americans mustn't don a huipil. If we are to take charges of illicit Cul-Ap seriously, we must suppose that these parties are smuggling memetic contraband. A regime of meme sequestration, then, would be the only answer. This is an ersatz solution to an ersatz problem. The present book aims to make the case that cultural segregation helps nobody—least of all marginalized communities; and that strictures against Cul-Ap do nothing to maintain the cultural integrity so ardently sought by those who—understandably—are concerned with heritage.

The way Cul-Ap-phobes would have it, the cultures of the world would be rendered a network of memetic cordons, separated by impermeable membranes. But wait. Is the charge of illicit Cul-Ap really about CULTURE? Let's pose a few other queries to see. Can any woman who isn't Japanese wear a kimono? As it turns out, yes: any ASIAN women can without receiving much guff. Can any woman who is not Ashanti wear kente cloth? As it turns out, yes: any BLACK woman can without receiving much guff. Can any woman who isn't Navajo wear a manta? As it turns out, yes: any NATIVE AMERICAN woman can without receiving any guff.

Suddenly, the true logic of anti-Cul-Ap fervor is revealed. Cul-Ap-phobia, it seems, is NOT about culture after all; it is about phenotypic features. For, given the geo-political history, Chinese culture is often AT ODDS with Japanese culture. Africans, you say? The Nubians, Oromo, Swahili, and Zulu are quite far from the Ashanti. Native Americans, you say? The Algonquins, Iroquois, Shoshone, Pawnee, and Sioux had little to do with the Navajo. In many cases, these phenotypically proximal groups spent much of their history fighting and killing each other. So what's going on here? Rather than being based on genuine concerns about protecting the integrity of anyone's culture, Cul-Ap-phobia seems to be based more on vaguely racialist criteria and categories specious generalizations…all of it concocted ad hoc to suit the purposes of the anti-Cul-Ap crusade du jour.

What of nationality, then? Even that poses problems. The Ashanti are Ghanan. However even fellow Ghanans (e.g. Mande, Akan, Fula, Yoruba, Igbo, Hausa, etc.) are culturally distinct. Be that as it may, virtually no one who complains about Cul-Ap would give people a free pass simply because they have a shared **nationality**. The free pass is only given, it seems, if there is shared **ethnicity**. But that often becomes a mandate for RACIAL parity…or even, in some cases, some sort of racial similarity. We should find this standard very disturbing. For the conditions are now no longer about culture, but about RACE.

How, then, are we to proceed with exigent racial affiliations—that is: common associations of certain cultural elements with a particular race?

Tying culture to a specified demographic is not just untenable due to the indeterminate nature of CULTURES, it is untenable due to the indeterminate nature of DEMOGRAPHIC GROUPS. For who's to say where any given group begins or ends? In a world where one demographic blends into another, one is obliged to *pretend* demographics can be discretely defined…even though such a thing is intractable.

In reality, the boundaries of a given group—however defined—are vague and fluctuating. One therefore encounters the same issues as when one tries to define phenotypic populations in terms of RACE. That is: One is forced to concoct social constructs ad hoc, based on superficial criteria—criteria that have no discrete boundaries. If red people are allowed to tap-dance but not blue people, then what about purple people? So the notion of collective ownership of a meme—especially along ethnic lines—is LOGISTICALLY untenable. In every case, the designation of WHO, exactly, the (purportedly) rightful owners is quite difficult—if not downright impossible—to pin down. Cultural stewardship is ephemeral, and forever elusive. This indubitable fact is not acknowledged by those who opt for cultural essential-ization—that is: insisting that cultural elements are INHERENT TO a certain population.

When one impugns those engaged in Cul-Ap by making appeals to "cultural ownership", one is in danger of not merely cultural essentialization, but of ETERNALIZED cultural essentialization—that is: insisting that those cultural elements must remain proprietary, and tethered to a designated ethnic group forevermore. This only seems to make sense if we forget that the constituent parts of any given culture are what they are by sheer accident of history; and that even OUR OWN culture is "ours" by accident of birth.

In the end, we're all human. Considering the sequence of historical accidents that led to certain cultural elements being associated with a certain ethnic group, we might conclude that we are all equally entitled to—at our own discretion—try the memes of the world on for size.

Pointing out that a particular custom (be it a social norm or a tenet) is dysfunctional / immoral is not an act of bigotry. This is true even if that custom happens to be a hallmark trait of a particular ethnicity. Elements of a culture / creed can be—nay, MUST be—assessed in a way that has nothing to do with harboring contempt for any ethnic group with which that culture / creed may be affiliated. Recognizing when one cultural element is more conducive to the commonweal than another is not a conceit; it is the mark of a discerning mind.

Criticizing iniquitous practices / dogmas which happen to be rooted in this or that culture does not constitute a slight against humanity. For one cannot be racist against a meme. Why? Because social norms are not humans. Indeed, what makes us human is not the particular memes we happen to adopt; it's that we have a choice. The indictment of a particular custom (for being either morally-dubious or counter to the commonweal) is not a devious scheme to denigrate an entire community, however that community may be defined. Being against gulags doesn't make one anti-Russian.

Alas, p.c. aficionados would have us believe that simply noticing social norms within a society (i.e. the signature features of a culture) is somehow a matter of "stereotyping". This is erroneous. Statistical realities are not generalizations; nor are they caricatures. We might be reminded what makes stereotyping objectionable. A stereotype requires one to engage in gross generalization, which behooves one to lend credence to a disingenuous portrayal of anyone who might be included in that generalization. And THAT leads one to pre-judge (read: mis-judge) individuals according to a fraudulent charge of collective culpability; which can then be used as an excuse for collective punishment.

Stereotypes are the lifeblood of prejudice; and are often leveraged to make gross generalizations, which may then be used to rationalize rash actions directed toward entire groups.

But that is not what we're doing when we apply a critical eye to MEMES. Prevailing trends—insofar as they are recognized AS TRENDS—are not iron-clad laws of the universe; so there is no need to treat them as such. Whenever an ethnic group happens to espouse this or that custom, it is an accident of history; not an indelible feature of that group. It is not written in the stars that subscription to certain memes—whether rituals or doctrines—be the basis for any given community's humanity.

It is worth acknowledging trends qua trends; and investigating how / why they came to be. During the course of this investigation, moral evaluations are warranted. Such evaluations are possible because they are conducted according to objective standards–that is: standards that TRANSCEND culture. After all, moral principles are universal.

So what of gringos dancing the tango? It's not deemed Cul-Ap if LATINOS do the tango; yet the Tango is explicitly Argentinian. So if Brasilians do the Tango, it is still technically Cul-Ap. Shall the Tango be off-limits to all non-Argentinian Latinos? Likewise, the Samba would be off-limits to all non-Brasilian Latinos? This is, of course, preposterous. Each Latin American country has notably different cultures. (And, in this case, they don't even speak the same language!) Yet, according to the logic of Cul-Ap phobia, all Latinos must be considered a monolithic demographic bloc; so it's fine for ALL Latinos to dance the Tango and the Samba; but maybe not gringos. Again, we find the issue is more about some vaguely-defined notion of RACE, not about culture per se. The reductio ad absurdum here should be obvious, as many Argentinians and southern Brasilians are White (mostly Germanic). After trying to reconcile the internal contradictions of the indictment, the logic eventually implodes in upon itself.

Things get even more convoluted the more we inquire. Can Japanese Brasilians dance the Tango? Are they "properly" Latino? Is it because of their Brasilian nationality that Japanese who also happen to be Paulistas get a free pass? (But wait. Wasn't the Tango originally Argentinian? Or was it Uruguayan? When it comes to who decides to practice this fine art, does it really matter?) We once more find ourselves engaged in a highly selective application of the purported restrictions.

Can non-Japanese artists create their own version of anime (geared to a non-Japanese fanbase)? The use of Japanese-style animation in Kansas is no more meme-theft than is bukkake in Arabia or origami in Iceland. How about manga for Latinos? (Shall that be permitted only insofar as Japanese are "allowed" to dance the tango? Is that a fair trade?) Should sub-Saharan Africans be allowed to belly-dance? Can non-Austrians do the Viennese waltz? Can non-Andalusians learn Flamenco?

Are we to suppose that because a meme started in ONE place, nobody in any other place should be permitted to adopt it? Or are we to suppose that ethnicity dictates which memes are off-limits to whom? If Kiwi rugby players perform the Maori "haka" prior to a sporting match, are they desecrating Maori-tanga; or are they simply celebrating their country's heritage? How about if Samoans do it? Such queries can only lead to one conclusion: Anti-Cul-Ap hysteria invariably backfires, undermining the very cause its proponents claim to be helping.

Inconsistent Standards

In ***Robin's Zuzwang***, I discussed at length the problem of inconsistent standards—that is: the selective application not only of ethical standards, but of acquiescence / opprobrium. The prime case of this is the tendency for many Americans on the so-called "Left" to speak out against ethno-nationalism at home while supporting it abroad (spec. with regard to Israel). **{51}** As Immanuel Kant pointed out, moral principles mean nothing unless one is willing to apply them even when doing so is inconvenient; as a deontic moral system has no basis in utility. Principles only matter when they are NOT self-serving.

If one claims to be against fascism, one must be against ALL FORMS of fascism. (The same goes for such things as bigotry, oppression, and exploitation.) If one is in favor of something only when it happens to suit one's fancy, then one is flirting with hypocrisy. Those who apply standards only when / where it is convenient to do so are being dishonest about their justifications. They fail to see that principles don't matter because they are USEFUL to oneself; they matter because they help us to be good people. There is nothing instrumental or self-serving about rectitude.

By engaging in an anti-Cul-Ap crusade, one can't help but be ad hoc in one's application of the indictment—cherry-picking grievances as it suits one's purposes. This is made apparent by the fact that complaints of Cul-Ap have only recently become fashionable; and have been lent credence only insofar as we stopped acknowledging the distinction between condescension and acclamation.

In 1999, Natalie Portman donned maiko-style (Japanese) make-up and a Mongolian-style head-dress for her role as Padmé Amidala of Naboo. This occurred without any scandal; as doing so was not seen as problematic at the time. Despite the fact that it is now one of the most decimated cultures in history, no Mongols complained. The Japanese press actually celebrated the use of their culture in an American sci-fi extravaganza.

In the next Star Wars film, Portman donned a Russian "kokoshnik". No Russians were incensed. As it turns out, such stylization did not constitute a debacle of unsanctioned mimesis; the motley alien wardrobe was—like most science fiction—an eccentric sartorial pastiche. YET…only a decade later, George Lucas would surely have been excoriated by legions of Cul-Ap-phobes for such eclectic stylization.

The problem with those who cavil about "cultural appropriation" is that they are forced to be highly-selective in their indictments. Yo-Yo Ma is no more begrudged for his choice of non-Chinese cello material than someone of non-Latino ancestry is begrudged for taking up salsa dancing. Yet woe to a non-Chinese woman who dons a cheongsam! How can this double standard be justified? To understand this, let's look at some other (inexplicable) exceptions to (purported) Cul-Ap strictures.

Americans don't pay tribute to Caribbean islanders every time they have barbecue chicken. {7} Why not? It's the same reason women around the world don't feel the need to commemorate Catherine de Medici every time they wear high heels. {8}

The Japanese tend to CELEBRATE other countries' use of anime—each invariably adapted to its own culture. Anime (and manga) have morphed into a resplendent array of offerings around the world. It would be rather odd to accuse Westerners of something uncouth when partaking in this gem of Japanese culture… even if the participants are not as sophisticated as one might prefer them to be. (Anime is, after all, as much about entertainment as it is about artistic prowess.) Shall Japan establish memetic embargoes so as to ensure nobody bootlegs its cultural bounty? This would be rather hypocritical, as much of Japanese pop-culture is comprised of bootlegged Western culture—from baseball to "B-style". {9}

In cases where there is an asymmetry along one metric or another (geo-politically, economically, or the magnitude of a given nation's pop culture), is it bad when Cul-Ap turns out to be a unilateral affair? If so, then samba in Tokyo is fine, but there shall be no Manga in Brasil. And what of Brasilian waxing? Gosh-golly, now gringos do it too! Is this particular style of anatomical landscaping unethical when anyone but Brasilians do it? Might such waxing be open exclusively to Latinos? How about to those who are HALF-Latino? What about Latinos who do not identify all-that-much with Latin American culture?

What's going on here?

The simple answer: Cultural diffusion. Cul-Ap can have—and, indeed, often does have—pro-social effects. Just ask those who now practice capoeira (established by African slaves in Bahia), which is now simply considered Brasilian. (What does "Brasilian" even mean? Legal citizenship? A specific ethnicity? A certain degree of dedication to upholding cultural heritage in a former Portuguese colony?) Ballet was originally an Italian dance form from the Renaissance. It was promptly rendered into its quintessential form by the Russians…after, that is, it had already been appropriated by the French. Matcha tea is rightly associated with Japan—especially its tradition of "chanoyu". The signature green color is achieved by a preparation known as "temae", developed in the 16th century, at the beginning of the Edo period. But wait. THAT was actually appropriated from the Chinese, who'd been using it throughout the Ming period. Was the Japanese adoption of this Chinese beverage a bad thing? No more than was the Russians' adoption of ballet…or Americans' adoption of capoeira.

Regarding meme-allocation protocols: Who's to say what constitutes a distinct element of a particular culture? Which culture shall stake its claim on which meme? Based on what? Inevitably, it becomes a convoluted matter as to what, exactly, is being "appropriated"…and from whom? We are expected to keep track of who supposedly "owns" which element, which requires us to establish the terms by which the members of a culture are to be demarcated. This becomes an intractable task once we go back far enough in history. For any given culture, almost every element was appropriated from somewhere, at some point.

Clothing fashion illustrates this. In the modern era, the propagation of sartorial practices is demonstrated by the necktie…itself based on a European ascot... which was based on the French cravat...which was appropriated from the Croats.
{16}

It seems non-Europeans are given an exemption from the charge of Cul-Ap in many instances—ostensibly due to centuries of European colonialism; which engendered a Euro-centric approach to "civil society". Fair enough. Having been subjected to systemic subjugation, victims of imperialism might be granted license to certain things that are off-limits to Europeans. Be that as it may, the problem with colonialism is the COLONIALISM. When enculturation is the handmaiden of imperialism, the culprits are those who see fit to become foreign governors of the source-culture; NOT those who happen to be associated with the colonizers' culture when they opt to adopt cultural elements from those who have been colonized. There is nothing inherently imperialistic about memetic transference…in EITHER direction. Cultural inter-penetration does not—in and of itself—involve either domination or exploitation or marginalization.

How, then, shall we treat the (Ottoman) Turkic "kaftan", a robe which yielded variations in Persia (the "xalat" / "chapaan") and even Hasidic Jewish culture (the "bekishe")? The article of clothing also made its way east through Kurdish, Tatar, Russian, and Mughal cultures. It even transformed into FEMALE attire in the Maghreb (as the Berber "kafta"). So who is guilty of Cul-Ap in THOSE instances? Everyone? No one? Where are the lines to be drawn? Based on what criteria? When Arabs, Persians, and Indians wear polo shirts, it is not memetic embezzlement from unsuspecting, preppy American WASPs. Why not?

Cultural diffusion on a global scale is sometimes referred to as "cultural globalization". The globalization of certain cultural elements strengthens social relations across cultures; as it sets the stage for an inter-connectedness amongst the world's populations. That sounds fine. However, for those concerned about systems of domination / exploitation, the worry is less about cultural globalization than it is about (what has mistakenly been called) "cultural imperialism". But to recapitulate: Cosmopolitanism is not imperialism; it is its antithesis. In the event that one party encounters another party's culture and–of its own volition–simply "tries it on for size", nothing odious is afoot. It is when this is done so as to denigrate that dubious motives may be afoot. Yet even then, it is not the adoption PER SE that is the problem, it is the hubris underlying the gesture.

We might also note that headscarves are not the sole province of Muslimahs; as they have been a sartorial practice for THOUSANDS of years (primarily for women)—from the Armenians and Russians to the French and Dutch. Recently, such garb is often taken to be emblematic of Muslim-ness. So, we might ask, what constitutes a MUSLIM headscarf? That is: What, exactly, is it that distinguishes a hijab or abaya from, say, a dupatta or an apostolnik? Would a sanction on headscarves for non-Muslimahs include BONNETS? What about plain ol' kerchiefs, which were popular amongst female WASPs in America throughout much of the 20th century? **Individual memes**, it turns out, are as amorphous as **entire cultures**. What constitutes one type of head-scarf from another? There is no way to answer such a question. So how are we to establish the boundary conditions for proper meme usage?

In virtually all cases of Cul-Ap, the spirit behind incorporating "foreign" memes into one's cultural repertoire is a cosmopolitan one. In the best cases, it stems from the recognition that the way WE currently do things might not be THE BEST way. We needn't shy away from the realization that it is sometimes prudent to adopt elements from other cultures. So the hang-up seems to be based on something more nebulous than the transference of memes PER SE.

The universality of the right of expression is best captured by art. One might say that much of the point of making art—and, by the same token, the basis for APPRECIATING art—is putting oneself in another's shoes; especially those from other walks of life. Such a global perspective is what makes artistic expression such an effective vehicle for human solidarity. It is also what makes art arguably the greatest pedagogical medium for inter-cultural understanding.

Cul-Ap is one of the key components in the art one encounters in ANY country. Such co-optation is not a matter of ransacking others' cultures; it's a matter of celebrating the best of what the world has to offer. When Matisse and Picasso incorporated African themes into some of their paintings, are we to suppose that they were trafficking in (African) memetic contraband? Of course not. They were simply doing what artists do. Their works were a pastiche: more a matter of adapting than of cribbing. Picasso conveyed this point with his cheeky comment: "Good artists copy; great artists steal." (T.S. Eliot echoed the sentiment. William Shakespeare's entire career was based on it.) This is not to say that all art is merely "derivative"; it simply reminds us that even the greatest artistic achievement is never done in a cultural vacuum. Indeed, it is often the INTERACTION BETWEEN cultures that enables the best artistic inspiration.

In the art world, to "appropriate X" simply means to "make use of X"—as when Andy Warhol "appropriated" the Campbell's soup can. If we indict this kind of appropriation, then Henri Matisse and Pablo Picasso are in deep trouble.

We might recall that artistic expression—from paintings to literature—is largely about seeing the world from the perspective of someone from a different walk of life. Art is rarely limited to inspiration from one's own culture. As such, it often furnishes us with a pan-cultural—one might even say META-cultural—vantage point for seeing the world. Art affords one the chance to empathize with those who are different from oneself. Indeed, that is one of its greatest virtues.

To reiterate: Art reminds us of the importance of putting oneself in someone else's shoes…even if one is not afforded the opportunity to walk a mile in them. Even when the participation is fleeting, there is no harm in temporarily "wearing the hat" of another—even if it's just being done "for the fun of it". So long as it is done in good faith, Cul-Ap is the lifeblood of pluralism.

Alas, the upshot of demonizing Cul-Ap is that we mustn't ever try to put ourselves in another's shoes; at least, not in this way. This is inimical to the cosmopolitan ideal. Taking measures to put oneself in another's shoes is a laudable act; and should be applauded, not derided.

The obdurate demand, "Know your place!" should be a red flag. Such a regressive attitude misses a crucial fact: Global human solidarity is about TRANSCENDING cultural divisions, not reinforcing them.

Again, the matter of power asymmetries comes to the fore. Those who argue that only enfranchised demographic groups can be guilty of Cul-Ap (as, indeed, only the more-privileged are in a position to dominate the less-privileged) miss what makes oppression oppressive. The contention is that when someone from a marginalized group (esp. when a minority demographic) does it, it doesn't count as "cultural appropriation". But does this make any sense?

We should note that this same double standard is employed in the argument that certain demographic groups (spec. those that are marginalized) are exempt from being bigoted—as if racial minorities are incapable of being racist and women are incapable of being sexist. This changes the definition of racism from something that is race-neutral (prejudice based on race qua race) to something more tailored to one's own interests (anything a certain racial group does that I don't like)…which, ironically, is itself racist. Such an ad hoc application of this criterion prescribes a regimen of worthiness along RACIAL lines. This is the crux of racism.

The selective application of indictments should clue us into the hypocrisy involved here. We don't begrudge non-French girls who—on a lark—put their hair in French braids. Why not? If, say, a Desi girl opts to put her hair in a French braid just for fun, it is technically an act of Cul-Ap; yet not in the way that anti-Cul-Ap crusaders find objectionable. Their rationalization for this exemption? Such practices are not especially cherished in—nor integral to—French heritage. And, in any case, aren't the French more privileged than the Desi community overall? The answer is not always straight-forward.

To reiterate: One of the mistakes made by the anti-Cul-Ap crusader is to treat cultural elements as exhaustible commodities. Should someone contend that he likes this part of another's culture, and that he might like to incorporate it into his life, the Cul-Ap-phobe's response is: "Keep your grubby hands off THEIR memes!" But one cannot copyright an element of culture. Elements of culture are not a kind of property; so they are not subject to the kinds of strictures germane to intellectual property rights.

Most would agree that the most IN-appropriate thing to treat as a mere commodity is art. Once we recognize that artistic expression ultimately transcends demographic categories (gender, sexuality, ethnicity, etc.), we soon find that many other things do as well—be it social justice or common courtesy.

It is often forgotten that even the best art is based in part on a non-trivial degree of mimesis (that is: creative imitation of what came before). As the adage goes: Imitation is a form of flattery. This has been illustrated throughout history. To this day, art—be it music, dance, literature, or painting—remains the touchstone for all inter-cultural appreciation.

The genealogy of musical genres demonstrates the fact that all culture is invariably derivative. Even the greatest compositions remind us that this is not something to lament. Pop music borrowed from rock-and-roll, which borrowed from jazz. But jazz was itself a cultural appropriation from Afro-American culture... which was itself inspired by indigenous African idioms. At which juncture in this memetic lineage shall we say someone is "guilty" of Cul-Ap? We are asked to suppose that there is a clearly-demarcated boundary that exists in the aether between "Black" music and "White" music (both highly dubious categorizations in themselves). Moreover, we are asked to suppose that such a threshold is memetically impermeable. Presumably, this entails a mandate for ETHNIC separateness which shall endure 'til the end of time.

It turns out that some who complain about Cul-Ap are themselves racist. For according to the most zealous anti-Cul-Ap crusaders, nobody other than Black musicians should be allowed to perform jazz, rhythm and blues, reggae, funk, scat, ska, doo-wop, hip-hop, mo-town, or southern gospel. This would be a ridiculous stricture, to put it mildly. Taking this to its logical conclusions, we run into some hairy problems. For every Hispanic on Earth would even be on shaky ground when enjoying salsa, merengue, samba, mambo, and tango. After all, such genres are also derivative of African idioms.

According to the same logic, nobody who is not White should be allowed to perform classical music. Imagine proposing such a prohibition; and imposing it on all the world's musicians of color.

Considering rock'n'roll's antecedent in Afro-American musical idioms, the scope of influence is breathtakingly extensive. Barring Cul-Ap would preclude most of the world's contemporary music. After all, boy-bands adopted elements of hip-hop...which, in turn, led to K-pop. Are Koreans to be prosecuted for taking culture from African Americans? If the proposed standards were to be applied universally, we would wind up instituting all sorts of nutty restrictions across the planet.

Thankfully, we needn't consider such wide-ranging memetic embargoes. For all artists are influenced by other artists. And oftentimes, such influence includes artists from different cultures. Cul-Ap animates even the most novel artistic expression. So we should not be surprised to find that most art is NOTHING BUT Cul-Ap. It has been that way for thousands of years.

Appropriation Or Annexation? (Cul-Ap vs Cul-Ex)

First, a word on the terms "appropriation" and "expropriation". In common parlance today, the two terms are used interchangeably. In effect, they are treated as synonyms; so they are BOTH taken to mean: making use of—or even exercise control over—something without permission. For the purposes of the present book, it is crucial to make a distinction between the two terms.

I take "appropriation" to mean: making use of something for a (new) specific purpose (for which it was not originally designated). This is generally innocuous. Hence "cultural appropriation" is to be held in contradistinction with the illicit act to which it has lately often been applied (an act for which the term "expropriation" can be duly reserved). This terminological mis-step has led to the semiotic conflation on which Cul-Ap-phobia is based. {26}

When it comes to elements of culture (i.e. memes), Cul-Ap-phobes insist that appropriation be construed as EX-propriation—as though a memeplex could be looted. This misapprehension only attains if memes are treated as commodities. According to such blinkered thinking, Cul-Ap is seen as a kind of resource-extraction...even as the resource is un-deplete-able. So, in order to get their indictments to hold water, anti-Cul-Ap crusaders are forced to (effectively) commodify cultural elements; thereby reifying the very terms of exploitation they impugn. (!)

The anti-Cul-Ap crusade is predicated on the conflation of appropriation with expropriation. Wherefore? As it turns out, the demonization of Cul-Ap only makes sense insofar as it is construed as one of two things: Either a kind of **exploitation of** the source-culture or a kind of **annexation of** the memes in question. Here, we'll look at the latter, which (purportedly) amounts to exercising control over cultural elements—specifically in a way that denigrates those who are affiliated with them. The problem with this indictment is that Cul-Ap is virtually never a matter of exercising control.

To illustrate this point, let's consider, again, the world's greatest cellist. Does

Yo Yo Ma in any way try to exercise control over German music when he plays Brahms? Does he deprive Germans of their heritage each time he performs? We could ask the same of American culture when he plays bluegrass; or—for that matter—of Latin American culture when he plays a tango. He enjoys doing both. We should ask him why.

There is, of course, a legitimate concern about instances of EX-propriation—cultural or otherwise; as expropriation of X DOES involve an exercise of control over X. It is, after all, a kind of annexation—that is: taking control over something that is rightfully the province of others; and typically doing so to their detriment. The inevitable result of such domination is marginalization and/or exploitation. But Cul-Ap is NOT a kind of annexation.

Generally speaking, what does it mean to "appropriate" something? In the event that X is non-rivalrous, "appropriating" X can not be a matter of exercising control over X; nor can the use of X be in any way mutually-exclusive with another's use of X). Think of using someone else's recipe for a delicious meal. In spite of all this, Cul-Ap-phobes speak of such an act as if it were tantamount to EX-propriation—that is: as if it would entail depriving its rightful stewards of their exclusive province. Are we to suppose that an annexation of Caribbean culture is taking place any time White hipsters put their hair in dread-locks? {11} How about when (White) American Southerners eat "jerk" chicken while listening to reggae music? Are we to inventory cultural elements–some of which are tacitly marked "proprietary"—according to the decree of some arbiter of cultural exchange?

The non-rivalrous (that is: non-exclusionary) nature of memes means that–pace intellectual property–they can only be invoked, not seized; celebrated, not confiscated. This is why incorporating–into one's personal fashion repertoire–a clothing style normally associated with another culture does not constitute some kind of sartorial larceny. Elements of a culture are–after all–non-rivalrous BY NATURE.

Thomas Jefferson put it well when he said: "He who receives an idea from me, receives instruction himself without lessening mine; as he who lights his taper at mine, receives light without darkening me." In the event that a gringo dons a sombrero while throwing a taco party, the world's Mexicans have lost nothing; well, at least no more than when gringos eat popcorn or Caesar salad (which were—incidentally—also invented by Mexicans). {20}

The conflation of appropriation with expropriation asks us to construe (benign) instances of Cul-Ap as (malign) instances of Cul-Ex. The former is what the present book endorses, as there are no "losers" in the memetic transference. By contrast, the latter describes something that is done to the detriment of the source-culture. {26}

Outside of commercial activity (in which the profit-motive is explicit), it is difficult to discern how, exactly, one culture could profit off of exogenous cultural elements "at the expense of" the source culture. After all, cultural elements are non-rivalrous. (Memetic transference is rarely a zero-sum game; and so is typically not exclusionary.) The point of contention, then, is either commercialization or derogation. In the former case, one party is profiting off of the cultural heritage of another party. In the latter case, the source-culture is diminished in some way. In neither case is Cul-Ap the salient factor.

It is no secret that memetic transference is often not a reciprocal affair. Pursuant to the Desi immigration into Germany, Bavarians may welcome having the new options of, say, Kabuli palaw and Afghan carpets to enjoy at their leisure; yet we are not inclined to suppose that the culture of the Hindu Kush may be soon enhanced by Schubert in the air and Schopenhauer on the bookshelves. While Deutschland welcomes the perahan tunban, it might be unreasonable to expect female Pashtun villagers to don a dirndl whenever the mood strikes them. {6} And while curry-wurst is now a popular snack at German pubs, there will probably not be lots of sauerbraten in Indian kitchens anytime soon.

So what of the supposition that Cul-Ap constitutes some kind of inequity? In the event that a significant power asymmetry is involved, this is feasible. The question becomes: If the semiotic transmigration is unilateral, under what circumstances is it to be considered exploitative?

It sometimes makes sense to think of this in terms of SOME SORT OF asymmetry. After all, communities which are unaffiliated with incumbent power structures are more susceptible to being assimilated…or even marginalized; and are thus more prone to being exploited by those with more socio-economic leverage. It is, indeed, those belonging to underprivileged / marginalized communities who incur the brunt of social injustices. While power asymmetries often end up being relevant factors when different groups of people interact, such matters are beside the point when it comes to trans-cultural fertilization. (After all, who is more marginalized: a Deutsch fraulein donning a dirndl in Waziristan or a Pashtun donning an abaya in the Rhineland?)

Let's evaluate that (admittedly hyperbolic) hypothetical. In both countries, the dominant demographic would be adopting a meme from the minority demographic. The explanation for this uni-laterality, then, must be accounted for in another way. As it turns out, far from being explained by Cul-Ap, the key difference IN PRACTICE boils down to a fundamental ***socio-political*** disparity: a cosmopolitan society vs. a provincial society. This is why we find halal kebab carts in Paris yet no ham 'n cheese crepe stands in Kabul. To wit: There IS an asymmetry; but the asymmetry lay in the societies' respective open-ness.

The lesson here is obvious; but let's spell it out. It is CLOSED (viz. illiberal) societies that disdain Cul-Ap; as they seek to maintain ethnic purity. Hyper-traditionalism is—after all—predicated on systematically-enforced parochialism. There is a term for refusing any influence / input from the outside world: nativism. THAT, it would seem, is the real problem.

So what of possible explanations for unilateral memetic flow when the liberal-illiberal distinction is NOT salient? While the French did not adopt Vietnamese cuisine during their time in Indo-China, the colonized adopted some things from their colonizers. Baguettes (known as "banh mi") and croissants became a big hit in Vietnam as a result of France's odious colonial enterprise. Even the hallmark of

Vietnamese cuisine, Pho, was an adaptation of the French "pot au-feu" (with noodles and lots of broth added to the mix). It is no coincidence that the instances of (allegedly illicit) Cul-Ap tend to only occur in one direction: toward the culture of those who enjoy higher socio-economic status. But this is the antithesis of some sort of cultural IMPOSITION. Discretionary adoption mustn't be confused with coerced assimilation—whereby a minority group is pressured into adopting the ways of the dominant group in order to pass muster. It is, then, cultural imposition with which we should be concerned.

Cul-Imp can, of course, occur in a piece-meal way; however it is often systematic. Insofar as this is the case, it is, indeed, a problem. After all, Cul-Imp is the hallmark of imperialism. Throughout history, such memetic hegemony has often been concomitant with colonialism. A prime example is the Spanish and Portuguese forcing Roman Catholicism onto the indigenous populations of (what is now) Latin America (as well as the Philippines). In instances of colonialism, there is SOME memetic transference that is innocuous—as when the British introduced tea to India during its colonialist enterprise on the subcontinent. Be that as it may, Cul-Imp is typically a sign of domination; as it is unilateral AS A MATTER OF COURSE. In other words: It proceeds from the more powerful to the less powerful. In such cases, the former expects the latter to not only integrate, but to assimilate.

Though coerced assimilation occurs in some circumstances, it is not operative in any of the examples of salutary Cul-Ap enumerated in the present book. In the cases presented here, those within the "appropriating" culture were not obliged to assimilate into the source-culture. When Yo Yo Ma plays Bach, he is not trying to be more German. When gringos eat burritos, they are not trying to be more Mexican. And when Muslimahs shed their hijabs, they are not (necessarily) trying to be more "Western". {6}

So back to actual instances of cultural *appropriation*. When volitional, meme-adoption is not the result of some calculated program of co-optation—as when an indigenous population has been assimilated by an impinging (dominant) power. The fact that most former British colonies—from Uganda to Bengal to Hong Kong—now drive on the left side of the road (and are now smitten with the pseudo-sport, cricket) is a vestige of their colonial past. Obviously, having adopted some of the cultural elements of their occupiers, the unwilling subjects of European geo-political dominion cannot be considered guilty of an infelicity. After all, they were the victims. The problem in such circumstances was not memetic transference; the problem was COLONIALISM. In other words, it was the systematic domination—replete with exploitation—with which we should have qualms; not with the fact that there are now cricket clubs. And it certainly has nothing to do with the fact that Brits now enjoy eating dim-sum. Leveling charges of illicit Cul-Ap does nothing to diagnose the underlying problem.

This is why Antonio Gramsci spoke about cultural hegemony (i.e. cultural imposition) rather than about "cultural appropriation". To cavil about Cul-Ap is to invert his diagnosis of social injustice. Indeed, the obloquy directed toward Cul-Ap-philes is something he would have found bewildering; as one does not exploit someone by simply participating in what they are doing.

Colonialism is objectionable because it involves a domination / subjugation dynamic—replete with a system of marginalization / exploitation of the colonized. Of course, Cul-Ap is sometimes a ***byproduct of*** colonialism. But in what ways does this place a (further) burden on the subaltern population? When the Dutch eat Bami Goreng, we are reminded that some Indonesian cuisine made its way into the Dutch cuisine; and it is no secret that that occurred as a result of the Dutch colonizing Indonesia. But in such cases, what was wrong with the colonialism was the COLONIALISM, not the transference of culinary practices. All the harm wrought upon the Indonesians had nothing to do with the fact that a few people in Holland adopted some of their tasty dishes. (As it happens, the Indonesians ended up adopting some tasty Dutch dishes, like hagelslag and poffertjes; so the memetic transference was bi-lateral.)

Even in the midst of colonization, memetic cross-pollination ends up being one of the few salubrious consequences (along with the introduction of new technologies—especially medical knowledge—into the developing world). During the British colonization of the subcontinent, Indians adopted "chai" (tea) from their colonizers, the British...who themselves adopted it from the Chinese. (Ancient Indians did not drink tea.) Meanwhile, the Brits started eating Vindaloo...which, it turns out, the Indians had actually adopted from the Portuguese ("vinha d'alhos"). That was in addition to the introduction of de-spiced versions of korma and tikka masala into the British culinary repertoire. Of all the horrible things the British did to the Indians (and there were a lot), such memetic transference does not make the list.

We mustn't be distracted by the fact that Cul-Ap (which is generally benign) is often concomitant with colonialism (which is invariably malign). Denouncing colonialism does not require one to demonize Cul-Ap.

Compunctions with Cul-Ap do not translate to an indictment of colonialism. Anti-Cul-Ap crusaders take umbrage with the migration of memes between ethnic groups, not the subjugation of one ethnic group by another. When memetic transference occurs between ethnic groups, should we always suspect that some sort of iniquity is afoot? No. Granted, some unilateral Cul-Ap may be by design. In other words, sometimes Cul-Ap results from a deliberate integration of exogenous memes (from the subaltern population) into the dominant group's cultural repertoire. When it is done by design, the transference is invariably unilateral. However, such uni-laterality does not—in and of itself—entail exploitation. Oftentimes, it is a mark of AFFINITY, and serves as a gesture of solidarity. Sharing memes is, after all, a way for people from different walks of life to relate to one another.

In any social interaction, there are, of course, legitimate concerns about the repercussions of power asymmetries; as there is the possibility that those in a more powerful position will abuse their privileged status (i.e. to lord it over everyone else). But insofar as this (very real) problem is cast in terms of Cul-Ap, we needlessly create conceptual vexations that undermine our ability to solve it.

It makes sense that those who worry about Cul-Ap are often focused on power asymmetries: cases in which those from a dominant group adopt cultural elements from those who are being dominated. Some of this may have to do with a sense of entitlement on the part of those with more socio-economic leverage: "Not only do we stake our claim on YOU (humans), we stake our claim on your WAYS (memes)." In other words: "We assert a right not only over the subaltern population; we assert a right over their signature cultural elements." In effect, the imperialists say: "We shall use them AND their customs."

This is a problem. But one does not rectify socio-economic inequities or help marginalized / exploited communities by circumscribing meme-usage. Any alteration in social norm—on ANYONE'S part—is a symptom—not an underlying cause—of interactions between ethnic groups.

Let's leave aside the obvious fact that one cannot pilfer memes. (After all, one can only exploit PEOPLE, not customs.) It is a mistake to see cultural elements as exhaustible commodities; or as exclusionary resources. YET…anti-Cul-Ap crusaders are forced to treat cultural elements like commodities. Ironically, it is the commodification of culture that they claim they want to PREVENT.

Let A be the culture of those who happen to dominate a society (socio-economically) and B be the culture of those who happen to be subjugated / marginalized. Even as A might incorporate elements from B into its memetic repertoire, the problem lies with the mechanism of subjugation / marginalization, not with the transference of memes. Consequently, to focus on Cul-Ap per se is to completely ignore the source of the problem.

In other words: Those afflicted with Cul-Ap-phobia find themselves obliged to countenance the very thing they purport to be against: the commodification of cultural elements.

Cul-Ap-phobes prattle on about non-existent dispossession—as if a grave injustice were being done whenever memetic transference occurs. But the alleged injustice is illusory. The demonization of Cul-Ap rarely—if ever—solves the problems it purports to solve. It only diverts our attention from the crux of the matter. Of all the potentially effective ways to ameliorate power asymmetries across demographic lines, an anti-Cul-Ap crusade is not one of them.

In sum: Even as structural inequalities may sometimes be concomitant with Cul-Ap, they do not exist BECAUSE OF Cul-Ap.

Cul-Ap-phobes focus their ire on the allocation of meme-usage. It's like trying to rectify an unhealthy diet by restricting the manner in which one sets the table. (Shall we suppose that one can make the food one eats more nutritious by only using one's own dinnerware?) Herein lay the irony: One of the ways in which a subaltern population is marginalized is through the marginalization of their CULTURE. While a PEOPLE can remain marginalized, a CULTURE cannot be said to be marginalized if its elements are being adopted by those in a more privileged position—thereby being INCORPORATED INTO the dominant culture. One cannot at the same time elevate something and suppress it.

Admittedly, problems arise when those cultural elements are adopted while the people remain marginalized. However, such an eventuality cannot be attributed to Cul-Ap PER SE. The solution to the marginalization of people is not the sequestration of their culture (into a space that has been cordoned off from the rest of the world). Some are inclined to say: "WE can partake in this cultural element, but YOU cannot; because you aren't one of us." But cultural segregation is never a good idea. For it paves the way for—and subsequently reinforces—other modes of segregation. Indeed, it is a slippery slope from cultural segregation to ETHNIC segregation.

In sum: Memetic embargoes (based on purported meme-ownership) do nothing to reduce power asymmetries. If anything, they create yet another obstacle to effecting social justice.

We mustn't lose sight of the fact that trans-cultural fertilization is a key feature—dare I say, PERK—of multi-culturalism. Indeed, it is the hallmark of a pluralistic society. Would those who deride Cul-Ap urge us to embrace other cultures yet simultaneously insist that we keep our distance? In other words: "Let's commune together, yet hold each other in abeyance!" Such "respect it but stay away" approach can only be described as a kind of cultural schizophrenia.

In virtually every case, we find that the embrace of Cul-Ap is a sign of (delimited) cultural affinities, not of animosity. This is why cultural exchange tends to dissolve alterity, and even engender comity. The prohibition of Cul-Ap, then, is an (inadvertent) invitation to subsist in a tribalistic mindset. In this respect, anti-Cul-Ap crusaders encourage the very thing they deign to mitigate.

The question remains: Why the skittishness when it comes to embracing exogenous cultural elements? Cul-Ap-phobia stems—in large part—from a Reactionary mindset, whereby people are exhorted to be suspicious of novelty—especially when it involves anything deemed foreign. "It's not ours, so we should keep our distance!" It all comes back to an in-group / out-group mentality; whereby everyone is exhorted to stay on their own side of the fence. (The Cul-Ap-phobe's imperative to "protect your turf" is simply about memetics rather than geography. Think of blood-and-customs instead of blood-and-soil as the central conceit.)

Power asymmetries are relevant when it comes to populations interacting—especially when there is a significant geo-political imbalance; and especially when systematic domination / marginalization / exploitation is afoot. But such a problem cannot be diagnosed in terms of Cul-Ap; nor can it be resolved by mitigating Cul-Ap. Of course, domination / marginalization / exploitation is always bad—irrespective of who is doing it, who it is being done to, and the manner in which it occurs. But here's the thing: Being socio-economic in nature, such social injustices can—and often do—occur WITHIN a culture. (Intra-ethnic oppression is a thing.) So clearly, Cul-Ap cannot be the clinching factor.

Those who treat Cul-Ap as if it were an ethical transgression are implicitly calling for meme-ownership along cultural lines. They are—effectively—prescribing a regime whereby each meme is consigned to (what they surmise to be) the source-culture (which is, in many cases, not the ORIGINAL source-culture). Meanwhile, they are calling for the prohibition of un-sanctioned meme usage, which amounts to an embargo on cross-cultural memetic transference. According to this thinking, the only solution to problematic meme-usage is some sort of meme-requisition program along (imagined) cultural lines—lines that, it turns out, don't exist.

One must wonder: Is it even possible to requisition memes? No. But this does not prevent Cal-Ap-phobes from calling for the repatriation of cultural elements. Nor does it deter them from promoting an ad hoc program of cultural segregation so as to maintain the sanctity of (oft chimerical) cultural demarcations.

Whenever taking a stand, we must ask what principles we are ultimately championing. Proscribing Cul-Ap is antithetical to cosmopolitan ideals. For to limit ourselves to using only endogenous cultural elements is to succumb to our baser tribal instincts; and espouse provincialism in lieu of cosmopolitanism. If we are willing to eschew such ideals, then what shall be the guiding principle for our decisions? Are we prepared to put forth a program of ethnic puritanism?

If not, then we should take pause before rushing to judgement about inappropriate meme-usage. Barring the oft-abused legalistic construct, "intellectual property" (alt. "proprietary information"), genuine knowledge cannot be "owned" by ANYONE. Generally speaking, knowledge belongs to all mankind; and so cannot be stolen. How, then, can one steal something simply by way of expression? Any given mode of expression is a HUMAN act; ergo no one party can claim sovereignty over it. (Imagine claiming: We own the exclusive rights to handshakes; so they're off-limits to everyone else.) Where do we draw the line? Does it make sense to claim ownership of, say, high heels? Henna tattoos? Peace signs? Pony-tails? {8}

In his book on "rethinking identity", Kwame Anthony Appiah, made the point well. After noting that the Ghanaians of west Africa had developed the distinct art of "bodom" (glass beads) after having adopted the craft from the Venetians, he asked: "What sorts of progress would have been advanced by insisting that the Venetians owned the idea of glass beads, and policing their claim?" The mistake, he noted, was treating elements of culture as (intellectual) property. "Unfortunately, the vigorous lobbying of huge corporations has made the idea of intellectual property go imperial. [The idea] seems to have conquered the world. To accept the notion of cultural appropriation is to buy into the regime they favor—where corporate entities, acting as cultural guardians, 'own' a treasury of IP, [thereby] extracting a toll when they allow others to make use of it." He concluded that those who make indictments based on Cul-Ap "in terms of ownership have accepted a commercial system that is alien to the traditions they aim to protect. They have allowed one modern regime of property to appropriate THEM."

The self-appointed officiants of cultural diffusion seek to impose a strict regimen of meme-allocation; yet they can never provide a consistent logic to how the lines shall be drawn. In this dialectical shakedown, each officiant fashions himself a sibyl—arrogating to himself the magical power to divine what does and does not qualify as Cul-Ap. The rest of us are expected to await judgement; and cease on demand…whenever we are called out for illicit meme-usage.

Even more absurd: Cul-Ap-phobes believe that the only way to do this is to refrain from ever showing curiosity about any culture other than one's own. This stricture includes—it seems—acknowledging that a foreign culture may seem, well, FOREIGN. (This is especially the case if one happens to be WHITE—whereby being curious about other cultures is, we are notified, tantamount to a non-physical kind of COLONIALISM.) Sound too loony to be true? Note the bullying of knitting enthusiast, Karen Templer on Ravelry.com in early 2019. (You read that correctly: KNITTING.) Templer was excoriated for the sin of wanting to incorporate Indian aesthetics into her repertoire; and—to make things worse—for noting OUT LOUD that Indian culture was foreign to her (which, of course, it was). Meanwhile, when Oprah Winfrey chastised Indians for using their hands when they eat (a wonderful idea), she was called out neither for her arrogance nor for her ignorance.

This is where "identity politics" becomes so perfidious as to be Kafka-esque. For Cul-Ap-phobes, to SIMPLY NOTICE differences between one's own culture and another, and to subsequently express a genuine interest in acquainting oneself with the other culture, is seen as INIQUITOUS. This gripe extends even to the realm of FABRICS. No kidding. Some denizens of the aforementioned knitting forum felt the need to decry the menacing prospect of interwoven cultures (pun intended) when it came to the stylization of innovative textile prints.

In essence, Templer was castigated for being COSMOPOLITAN. Her crime was being fascinated by another culture. All the more terrifying: She was looking forward to actually visiting India—a land as alien to her as another planet; thereby learning more about how THEIR craft may have related to HER craft.

No doubt the world would be a more beautiful place if MORE people were so inclined. Alas, the most fanatical identitarians could walk by a lamp-post and see a hidden scourge of White Supremacy; so Templer was accused of…White Supremacy. (Noting that you find something that is foreign to you to be FOREIGN? How dare you?) This brings to mind the putative "anti-racists" who—it often turns out—are themselves virulently racist. {51}

Karen Templer's on-line assailants were clearly pernicious actors; and they demonstrated that they had nothing but contempt for cosmopolitan ideals. In their eyes, to strive to be worldly was to engage in imperialism. But what in heaven's name was the real problem supposed to be? (Before attempting to answer this question, note that Templer was invited to India by an Indian family, and was planning on staying with them—in their home—to better familiarize herself with their time-honored sartorial practices.)

Here's what we can gather from this bizarre incident. So far as bad-faith interlocutors are concerned, to find something "exotic" is to engage in some devious scheme of alterity. If Templer—as a White woman—had the gall to celebrate the Indian aesthetic when it came to fabrics, and incorporate any element thereof into her own practice of this handicraft, she must be guilty of "cultural appropriation"! (Cue audience gasps.)

Here's the contention: If you fail to countenance the strict parochialism that the self-appointed arbiters of cultural exchange have mandated, something downright invidious must be afoot. You will therefore be summarily harangued for the bigotry that Cul-Ap-phobes refuse to see in themselves. There is no other way to characterize Templer's phalanx of persecutors than as hyper-puritanical cultural segregationists—each of them demonstrating that it is possible to simultaneously engage in pearl-clutching and finger-wagging.

What can we learn from this episode? Anti-Cul-Ap crusaders often engage in Reaction Formation—projecting their own bigotry onto those who are, in fact, the OPPOSITE OF bigoted. (If only more Americans were as interested in Indian culture as Templer was!)

What is most ironic—and reprobate—about such bullying is that p.c.-mongers do absolutely nothing to mitigate the iniquities that they claim to be so deeply concerned about. How many of Templer's persecutors actually knew ANYTHING about the depredations of British colonialism in India, and WHY it was so awful? Well, you see, there's no time to actually learn anything about the world when one is busy patting oneself on the back for faux activism.

We are once again reminded that virtue-signaling requires no ACTUAL virtue. And, once again, we are shown that the purported victims can't decide whether they are supposed to be on their high horse or on a cross. Sanctimony loves a good persecution complex…even if the alleged persecution involves woven materials that combine motifs from two different cultures. (The horror!)

But was there some sort of EX-propriation going on? Unlike Cul-Ap, Cul-Ex is exclusionary. {26} When one TAKES something, the source no longer has it. When one claims rights over usage, others are deprived of the right to make use of it. That is not the case when it comes to the adoption of cultural elements–whether temporarily or permanently.

So what does THAT look like? An example would be Disney's attempt to copyright the Swahili saying, "hakuna matata" ["no problem"] due to the fact that the phrase had become somewhat of a hallmark of the cinematic blockbuster, "The Lion King" (an animated film released in 1994, itself a rip-off of the Japanese "Kimba"). All reasonable people would agree that trying to monetize a cultural element is highly objectionable. Worse, the attempt by a large media conglomerate to take legal ownership of a LOCUTION (to fuel its already-gargantuan corporate profits) is downright obscene. The culprit here, though, was greed; not Cul-Ap. What Disney was attempting to do was annex a phrase, thereby claiming exclusive rights to it (effectively taking ownership of a Swahili saying…in order to use it as a marketing gimmick).

In a twist of irony, the phrase had ALREADY BEEN appropriated: in the making of the film itself.

Gladly, Cul-Ap is rarely about using a meme for strictly commercial purposes. Any given cultural element X is non-rivalrous; which is simply to say: Appropriating X is not an act of seizure, as it does not entail depriving anyone else of X; nor of their ability to avail themselves of X of their own accord. (The same would be the case with, say, the "appropriation" of an IDEAL.) EX-propriation of X, on the other hand, involves seizure of—or the exercise of control over—X. The latter act DOES entail depriving someone else of X (that is: of their right to make use of it).

In light of these fundamental differences, it is a mistake to conflate the appropriation of X with the EX-propriation of X. The former is not exclusionary (as X is non-rivalrous). The latter IS exclusionary (when X is treated as property, as when Disney attempted to copyright a Swahili phrase).

This crucial distinction can be captured explicitly: When those enjoying more power say to those who are less powerful, "Hey, that's a nifty thing you do; we'd like to give it a try," it is consummate with the cosmopolitan spirit. Doing so is the OPPOSITE of declaring: "Hey, you are no longer allowed to do that; you now need to do things OUR way." The former is born of open-mindedness; the latter is born of hubris. Cul-Ap is germane to the former; Cul-Ap-phobia is germane to the latter. In any case, one can no more pilfer a meme than one can embezzle an ethos...or abscond with a zeitgeist.

The way Cul-Ap-phobes talk about cultural elements, Cul-Ap entails a deprivation of another's ability to partake in his own culture. Yet cultural elements being non-rivalrous, this makes no sense. One party's participation in culture in no way compromises another party's prerogative to do the same. In reality, Cul-Ap is not resource-extraction; it is simply part of cultural diffusion—which, it might be noted, is the inevitable consequence of cultural efflorescence. Cultures are actually STRENGTHENED by cultural diffusion; not diluted by it.

When anti-Cul-Ap crusaders accuse anyone engaged in inter-cultural exchange of "taking" something to which they are not entitled, they are treating cultures as (deplete-able) commodities instead of something within the public domain. Indeed, cultural elements are, in a sense, a public goods—like the air we breathe. (Friendly neighborhood reminder: Sometimes we happen to share the air with those who are not in our own group.) In this sense, culture belongs to humanity itself; which is to say it is a GLOBAL public good. As such, there is an open invitation for every person—qua member of mankind—to participate in the gloriously diverse panorama of cultures of which the global community is comprised.

The Cul-Ap-phobe's dubious enterprise seems viable only insofar as cultural elements are treated as something other than public goods. It's not for nothing that, in broaching the topic of participation in cultural life, the Universal Declaration of Human Rights stated: "Everyone has the right to the protection of the moral and material interests resulting from any scientific, literary, or artistic production of which he is the author" (Article 27). This pertains to *intellectual property*; and the concern was primarily about seizing the fruits of others' creativity—namely, the artistic achievement of identifiable people. But the thing with cultural elements is that no singular party—let alone any particular person—is the author. Elements of culture, then, are NOT like intellectual property. Moreover, the concern in Article 27 was a Marxian one: those with more power EXPROPRIATING the creative output of artists, who typically have much less leverage than, say, a gigantic corporation.

Applying this to culture, though, makes no sense; as the authorship is categorically indeterminate. Usage rights for designated cultural elements would make about as much sense as placing a patent on, say, a religious sacrament; or a copyright on a magical incantation. Hence cultural tort makes no sense.

Pace the legal construct of I.P. (or of private property more generally), memes—be they stylistic choices or formal rituals—cannot be treated as though they were articles of which one or another party can claim ownership. Generally speaking, ideas belong to all mankind. An attempt to proscribe unsanctioned meme-usage—or to prohibit memetic cooptation across cultural lines—is thus based on a category error.

We might explore the flawed logic here even further. Take the suspicion that some sort of meme-poaching operation is afoot whenever those of one culture adopt elements from another culture (spec. when they do so without express "permission"). This gripe is based on zero-sum thinking (the supposition that one party's gain is another party's loss). But to repeat: cultural elements are non-rivalrous (that is: communal); and so cannot be thought of in the same way we think of private property.

In pursuing this dubious indictment, we are forced to define Cul-Ap as the seizing of "cultural expression" (alt. "cultural knowledge") without permission. Yet here, the indictment falls apart. For it is unclear what "seizing" and "permission" here could possibly mean. (Can one pilfer a meme?) Permission from WHOM? From an appropriations panel? From an officially designated representative of the entire culture? From some supreme arbitration authority? Indeed, it is not specified how, exactly, one is supposed to secure "permission" from a "culture".

What would it mean to be the anointed spokesperson of an entire culture?

Once we posit that a particular cultural element "belongs" to THIS set of people, but not to THAT set, insoluble problems arise. Who would be the ultimate adjudicator in such matters? Based on what criteria? What would the qualifications for such a position be? Can ANY one person (that is: any ONE person) speak on behalf of everyone in the world who is affiliated with a given culture? Such an arrangement would prove itself to be intractable within the hour. So what, then? Are we to undertake a worldwide referendum every time someone wants don attire or try a hairstyle or perform music or prepare cuisine that is generally associated with an ethnicity other than their own? Shall allotted entitlement (i.e. exclusive access to memes) be determined by plebiscite? The questions go on and on. Anti-Cul-Ap crusaders cannot answer any of them. Why not? Because they are un-answerable.

When memes propagate, so long as they are adopted organically, moral problems generally do not arise. It is when memes are imposed from above that charges of cultural imposition hold credence. Even then, insofar as it is a descriptor, Cul-Ap pertains to the opposite of this. That is to say: appropriation does not involve imposition; it involves adoption. In the normal course of global cultural diffusion, imposition is typically not what's going on; it is simply a matter of SHARING.

To summarize: The self-styled proprietors of the source-culture are concerned with the taking of memes AS IF it were the taking of property. This only makes sense insofar as one treats memes AS property (spec. as intellectual property), collectively held by all those affiliated with the designated culture. But such a conceptualization cannot attain.

Arbitrary Timelines

As already discussed, the demonization of Cul-Ap involves a conceit regarding the origins of the cultural element at issue. As we saw, hairstyles are a familiar illustration of this. When thinking of things in terms of cultural EX-propriation, questions arise: By donning corn-rows, are we to suppose that White hipsters are not embezzling a meme? Or are we to simply note that they are trying a meme on for size?

Even if adopting this particular coif is done heedless of the prevailing ethnic associations with hair-style, we need not assume that something odious is afoot. After all, corn-rows do not "belong" to either African or Caribbean culture; as the hairstyle's origins lay elsewhere. They could be found throughout the Greco-Roman world during Classical and Late Antiquity. Yet such history has no bearing on the legitimacy of anyone doing such things with their hair today.

Alas, everyone with a parochial mindset—irrespective of their culture—likes to believe that world history began with the inauguration of their own culture. In this sense, there is a conceit underlying Cul-Ap-phobia: "It is integral to OUR culture; therefore we shall assume it originated with US."

The fact of the matter, though, is that EVERYONE is deriving cultural elements from bygone eras; and often from other lands. When a caucasian opts to don corn-rows, she is no more being exploitative than when a Black woman straightens her hair and dyes it blond. This equivalence is in no way affected by power asymmetries. Pace the issues related to overt tribal signifiers, political oppression never had anything to do with who wore which hair-style.

Socio-economic inequalities are a serious problem, but establishing an embargo on MEMES will do nothing to rectify them. If anything, such an embargo only serves to REINFORCE disparities along tribal lines.

The charge that someone has smuggled memetic contraband across cultural lines requires one to engage in a quixotic attempt to identify the ULTIMATE source-culture of the designated meme. Such an identification is invariably based primarily on present exigencies, not on historical realities. As it turns out, exactly which culture is anointed as the TRUE OWNER depends on how far back in history one opts to terminate one's inquiry. Such a temporal threshold is—invariably—arbitrary, if not self-serving.

As I will try to show, in order to assert that a designated meme "belongs" to a certain culture, one is forced to ignore all of the history that preceded the purported source-culture's adoption of it. Such conceit is illustrated by iconography and holidays (especially when they are sacred). Yet it is even illustrated by catch-phrases and clothing fads. Where did it begin? And who started the trend? Oftentimes, a discrete origin simply does not exist.

To reiterate the point: Any given culture is not a fait accompli; it is a work in progress—the result of having incorporated memes from extant cultures during its own development. That process is STILL HAPPENING.

Cultural elements generally have a history that predates the culture that now claims the element as its own. Beer is originally from Egypt. Mocha is originally from Qatar. Coffee is originally from Ethiopia. Yet we never associate the consumption of such things with their source-cultures. Why not? We choose to start the history of beer, mocha, and coffee at some point LATER ON. This is only natural. Each culture is inclined to take credit for a meme that it fancies to be a signature trait of itself. So we are apt to associate wine primarily with French and Italian culture...even though it was originally PERSIAN. (Thanks, Shiraz.) If we were to enforce the strictures suggested by Cul-Ap-phobes, tea would be off-limits in England; as it was appropriated from the Chinese.

Contrary to the popular adage, apple pie is originally British, not "American". (Apples originally came from Kazakhstan, by the way. And pie goes back to ancient Greece.) "Just as American as apple pie," it turns out, means NOT (originally) American after all.

As mentioned, the iconic (white) cowboy of the "wild west" in American folklore is a derivative of the Mexican "vaquero". Peanut butter was first used by the Incas and Aztecs. And don't get Italians started on the origins of REAL pizza. Why aren't the Nahua people incensed by Skippy? Well, probably for the same reason Neapolitans aren't incensed by Pizza Hut. One people's cultural heritage is not threatened by another's adoption of this or that cultural element; as their pride need not be anchored to any particular meme. Alas. If we were to take the logic of Cul-Ap-phobia to its logical conclusion, only Yemenis could eat mocha and only Ethiopians could drink coffee. (Both were traded by the Aksumites.)

We all incorporate elements from various cultures into our own repertoire... then, eventually, fancy it to be our own. Paying tribute to antecedent adopters undermines cultural pride; so we tend to elide any heritage that countermands our own. This goes for technology as much as it does for cuisine. Gunpowder, the concept of vaccination, paper, and moveable type are originally from China; yet rarely do those in the Occident commemorate these vital Oriental contributions.

Though certain memes might currently be integral parts of a given culture (by sheer accident of history), those memes cannot be said to eternally "belong" to any given culture. To illustrate this point, we might harken back to the pantheon of Roman gods: Jupiter, Venus, Neptune, Minerva, Hercules, Vesta, Mars, Mercury, Pluto, Juno, Diana, Nike, Bacchus, Vulcan, Ceres, Harmony, and Saturn. Who are these deities? Lo and behold, they are the Italic version of Hellenic gods: Zeus, Aphrodite, Poseidon, Athena, Heracles, Hestia, Ares, Hermes, Hades, Hera, Artemis, Victoria, Dionysus, Hephaestus, Demeter, Concordia, and Kronos (respectively). Heavens to Mergatroyd; the Romans poached the entirety of Mount Olympus!

As it turns out, this is usually how deities are established. Even the Hebrew "Yahweh" seems to have been appropriated from the antecedent godhead of the "Shasu": an Edomite / Amorite clan that hailed from the southern Levant (ancestors of the Jebusites). Shall we begrudge the world's Jews for filching the Abrahamic deity from Canaanite forebears? Perhaps not, as there are no Shasu left to file charges. But that's neither here nor there; for virtually ALL deities are derivative.

Whichever ethnicity one might be, most of the elements of one's own culture are the (tentative) culmination of a very long sequence of Cul-Ap. This makes contempt for Cul-Ap a kind of semiotic masochism. Want to find someone guilty of Cul-Ap? Look no further than a mirror. Regardless of who you might be, you are likely (unwittingly) engaged in myriad instances of Cul-Ap every day.

We are more prone to a bout of Cul-Ap neurasthenia when we fail to come to terms with the fact that a cultural inheritance is, indeed, a concatenation of various inheritances. Most of those inheritances are probably not even recognized as such. So the question arises: Are we to deny everyone else the right to do with OUR cultural elements what we have already done ourselves with others before us? Virtually anything we now fancy to be "ours" was, at some point, someone else's.

As we have seen, the point can be illustrated by something as trivial as what people opt to do with their hair—be corn-rows or dread-locks. We might even explore this matter further. Let's look at French braids and Bantu knots. French braids were not originally French, they were Numidian; which is to say PUNIC (an ethnicity that included a mixture of Carthaginians and Berbers). And they were used by the Chinese before that; and by the Mycenaeans even before THAT. Bantu knots were Zulu knots before they were used by the Bantu diaspora. And they were Nubian before that. And Egyptian even before THAT. It is plain to see, then, that nobody owns that hair-style either.

This is how we can account for the fact that few are in a tizzy about the "Dutch braid", an adaptation of the "French braid"...which was an adaptation of the Berber braid...which, as mentioned, was an adaptation of an ancient Numidian stylization—possibly used by Punic peoples in Classical Antiquity. It is no wonder, then, that the French don't even call French braids "French braids"; they refer to braided hair as "tresse", "plait", or "natte"; and sometimes even "African braids" (due to affiliation with the Berbers of Algeria). For similar reasons, they don't call french toast "french toast" because it actually isn't French.

But, then again, EVEN THAT is not accurate; for, as mentioned, this Maghrebi braiding style was ALSO used by the ancient Greeks. In any case, the Ancient Egyptians were braiding their hair long before anyone else—though not necessarily in the precise style now known as "French" or "Dutch". Tellingly, women braiding their hair was evidently an issue in Palestine during the 1st century, as Paul's first letter to Timothy admonishes against it. (!)

So are we to then suppose that the girls of Holland are guilty of Cul-Ap? From where? How far back shall we go? Should the Greeks be in an uproar about hair-styles in the Netherlands? How about the Chinese? Where, exactly, are the lines to be drawn? I dare say: With all the serious problems in the world today, who is and isn't donning this or that hair-style should be the least of our concerns.

Yet anti-Cul-Ap crusaders are determined to problematize any instance of un-approved meme transference. In their eyes, Cul-Ap amounts to a kind of memetic larceny. By suggesting that someone is somehow "stealing" something from another culture, one sets oneself up to explain how the designated source-culture conjured the idea out of thin air. Unless one is referring to the Sumerians (or perhaps the Indus Valley and Yellow River Valley civilizations), whatever one is fixated on likely came from somewhere else...which, according to Cul-Ap, makes all mankind a swarming throng of memetic thieves.

The ubiquity of meme-appropriation is also illustrated by the ramification of iconography around the world. But, even more so, iconography gives us a window into the fact that the GENESIS of any given cultural element is nary impossible to pinpoint with any precision.

Let's look at another set of examples--this time in the realm of iconography. The cooptation of symbolss has occurred throughout human history. Here, there are a few well-known examples of memetic transference.

Christianity fancies itself to be a movement rooted in unstinting forbearance. In an odd twist of irony, though, after being adopted by the Roman imperium, its iconography underwent a queer inversion. The transmogrified (Nicene) religion took as its emblem a Roman torture device. The use of a "cross" to represent Christianity likely stemmed from the use of the staurogram in the Greek manuscripts for the Pauline Letters and the canonical Gospels (beginning in the late 2nd century). It bears worth mentioning that preceding the use of a crucifix to symbolize the Faith, the movement had already espoused a series of appropriated symbols.

The initial following of Jesus of Nazareth (known as "the Way") was based on universal compassion; and used a FISH as its insignia. In Koine Greek, the symbol came to be called the I-Chi-Th-Y-S, an acronym for "Iesous Kristos Theou [h]Yios Soter" [Jesus, anointed son of god, savior] (a.k.a. the "icthys"). In place of a fish, the movement eventually adopted the pagan "Vesica-Pisces"; as most of the earliest followers of Jesus of Nazareth were fishermen. It makes sense, then, that Jesus would have characterized his ministry as fishing for followers—as attested in the first chapter of the original Gospel: Mark.

The fish seems to have been appropriated from antecedent iconography, much of which had to do with the Roman worship of Venus...who was, in turn, based on the Greek goddess, Aphrodite. The leitmotif was also likely influenced by the pagan goddess, Atargatis (often associated with fish)...whose origins were in the Middle East. It is yet another irony that—after all this—Christianity would become an obdurately patriarchal institution.

Pursuant to Emperor Constantine's purported conversion in the 320's, the Chi-Rho (the first two letters of the Greek term, "Kristos") was used as an emblem of the newly-minted Roman religion. It was also in the 4th century that the Tau-Rho caught on as a symbol—itself based on its function as a nomen sacrum in biblical manuscripts.

Only when Nicene "Christianity" (based largely on the tenets diametrically opposed to the original movement) became the prevailing version of the creed—during the reign of Emperor Theodoseus—did the cult adopt the crucifix as its insignia. And it is quite likely that THAT was inspired by the Egyptian Ankh. {12}

In sum: Christian iconography was a veritable orgy of appropriation.

Examples of appropriated iconography are endless. The staff of Hermes was a dagger enwrapped by a helix of one or two snakes, sometimes topped by a pair of wings. The symbol seems to have originated in Mesopotamia during the 4th millennium B.C. It eventually served as the icon of the Sumerian demi-god, Nin-gish-zida: messenger of the Earth-mother. It was then "appropriated" by the ancient Egyptians—as attested on the Djed pillar at the Dendera temple. During Classical Antiquity, it was used by the ancient Greeks as the "kerukeion": an icon for the deity associated with healing, Asklepios. (Here, it incorporated the serpent known as "Python".) It was thus often known as the "Rod of Aesclepius" in Greco-Roman lore.

As it turns out, THAT icon was the same as the herald used by Hera's messenger, Iris in Greek mythology. Even so, it continued to be associated with the aforementioned god of medicine, Asklepios. This may have been the basis for its subsequent symbolism: its use for warding off ailments. (Hermes was sometimes seen as a god of protection.)

The staff eventually made an appearance in Judaic lore as well—in the form of a protective brass pole for the Israelites (meant to ward off the lethal bites from serpents). In the Book of Exodus, Moses presented the Israelites with a depiction of a snake coiled around a wooden staff. He did this in order to protect them from, well, snakes; as serpents generally symbolized evil in Abrahamic lore. In the Book of Numbers (beginning of Chapter 21), Moses was given the staff by Yahweh in order to protect the Israelites from the poisonous snakes that Yahweh had himself sent to accost them as they wandered the desert. (Numbers is a rather deranged book.)

Thereafter, the talisman represented a magical prophylaxis against poison—both actual and spiritual. It is telling that a Judaic prophet opted for pagan iconography when seeking an antidote to (literal and theological) venom. But as it turns out, such appropriation was not uncommon in Abrahamic lore; as MUCH of what was eventually considered Hebraic had been appropriated from Hellenic sources. {31}

The staff then came to be dubbed the "caduceus" by the Romans; and would subsequently be associated with Mercury—especially in medieval astrology. Meanwhile, the icon was used in India as the "mudra" under Mauryan king "Ashoka the Great". It is now used to symbolize medicine.

So…shall we inform most of the medical associations around the world that they are guilty of appropriating culture from the Sumerians? Well, it's not a problem, you see; as the Sumerians don't exist anymore. So who cares, right? Neither do the ancient Egyptians. But wait. What about the Greeks and Indians? Do they have a case to make? If so, the American Cancer Society better rethink its logo.

The ways in which we NOW characterize things (that is: how we happen to think of things CULTURALLY) is a function of many historical accidents; and is far from how they were always characterized. Prevailing semiotic schemes are a reflection of the time and place. Iconography, then, results from a concatenation of salient semiotic factors—factors that are perpetually in flux, and determined by a variety of social forces. Because semiotics plays a significant role in collective (read: tribal) identities, we often lose sight of the fact that CURRENT symbolism was not written in the stars at the beginning of time.

The relationship between a collective identity and semiotic exigencies is rather complex; as each is—ultimately—a historical accident; so could have just as easily been otherwise. {29} The "catch" is that everyone likes to think that their iconography is unique to them. We all want to take ownership of our own signature semiotic repertoire. So we see novelty even when things are derivative. We are moved to do so…lest we be forced to concede that what we hallow is merely an accident of history; and may have been different had circumstances been different.

Once something has been sanctified, such a concession becomes untenable.

So when assaying how a given group identifies with a certain set of memes at any given time, it is necessary to take into account the social psychology underlying nascent memetic resonance. (More on cultural affinities in Part 2.) But what of collective identity? Just as there can be individual narcissism, there can be collective narcissism; as conceit can also operate at the group level. Ergo tribal chauvinism. This is the basis for ethno-centricity—effectively self-centered-ness mapped to the in-group. While there are problems with basing personal identity explicitly on one's own demographic profile (nationality, race, gender, sexuality, etc.); doing so with a tribalistic mindset leads to severe problems.

We all subsist within a locus of memes from different places. As individuals, we customize our memetic repertoire as an expression of personal identity, which may or may not be a function of collective identity. The result is a motley assortment of cultural elements—some of which are, invariably, from cultures other than our own. Is this a bad thing? Of course not. Manifesting the elements of different cultures in one's own behavior is the hallmark of multi-culturalism. Indeed, it is also how any given culture formed in the first place. The question, then, is: Is one being conceited when doing so?

Amidst all this, we are faced with a choice. We can quibble over who "owns" which cultural gem; or we can all feast at a communal table. The genealogy of cultural elements WITHIN any given culture is testament to the on-going co-optation in which we are still partaking—a process that shall hopefully continue indefinitely. Pretending that it all started with OUR culture is delusive.

Once again, iconography offers a good illustration. Consider the phoenix. As it happened, the "feng-huang" in medieval Chinese art inspired its use in medieval Persian art (as the "simurgh"). This posed no problem for anyone involved—a fact that becomes especially apparent once we consider versions of the icon predated BOTH cultures. We in the Occident now know this leitmotif from its Roman incarnation: a bird rising from the smoldering ashes. From whence did the Romans get the idea? The Greeks. Okay, then where did THEY get the idea? From their predecessors, the Mycenaeans (the "gryphon"). And where did THEY get it? From the ancient Egyptians (the "Bennu")—a fact attested by Herodotus. Those in the Vedic world rendered it the "garuda". Later, during the Middle Ages, Christians adopted the leitmotif as a symbol for Christ's resurrection; and thus for metempsychosis. Meanwhile, the pagan Slavs rendered it the "zhar-ptitsa" / "zhar-ptak" [firebird]. And on and on.

Ok, then what about the double-headed eagle? This nifty symbol has been used for regimes in Austro-Hungary and Russia; and, before that, by the Franks (as an insignia for the Holy Roman Empire). Yet it originated in the Bronze Age with the Hittites of Anatolia. It was alternately rendered the "ganda-berunda" by the Hindus; and was later used by the Byzantines as the "Palaiologos"…then by the Seljuk Turks in the pre-Ottoman era. Should it now be deemed off-limits to anyone but eastern Europeans, Indians, and Turks? Shall we now suppose that those who use the insignia are guilty of ripping off the Hittites? The Prussians adopted it as the "reichsadler" in the 19th century. In doing so, was there something iniquitous afoot in Bavaria? Albanians and Serbians liked it so much, they made it their national symbol. Cultural appropriation in the Balkans!

The so-called "Star of David" ("megan David" in Hebrew) offers another case-study in appropriated symbols. It originated in ancient Canaanite iconography. Thereafter, the hexagram served as a sacred symbol in Phoenician, Assyrian, Roman, Armenian, and Ethiopian iconography. Each version used what was a catchy and straight-forward design: two triangles (one inverted) superimposed upon one another.

The Semitic origins of the hexagram will likely forever remain unclear. Why did some of the early Semitic peoples adopt it? One possibility is that it was the pagan symbol for "Kewan" / "Kaiwan", the Canaanite star-god rebuked in the Book of Amos (5:26). This moniker was—mistakenly—rendered "Re[m]phan" / "Raiphan" in Koine Greek (when the Septuagint was composed in the 2nd century B.C.) "Kewan" was probably a Semitic adaptation of the Assyrian "Kayawanu" (as in the reference found in Acts 7:43).

The familiar star was eventually adopted by Kabbalists for use on "segulot" (talismanic protective amulets) during the Middle Ages. Kabbalists originally referred to it as the Seal of Solomon—which appeared in two versions (as either a pentagram or a hexagram).

It is oft-forgotten that the original emblem of Judaism was the "Aryeh Yehuda" [lion of Judah]. Long before it was the lion of Judah, though, it was the lion of Ishtar—as depicted in murals on the gates of Babylon, which feature winged lions with serpentine forms. (The "mush-hushu" was a sacred animal of the Babylonian godhead, Marduk.) So, in effect, the early Hebrews simply re-purposed the symbol from the Neo-Assyrians.

In a twist of irony, lions were prominently depicted in the throne room of none other than Nebuchadnezzar II—the ruler that exiled the Hebrews to Babylon in the early 6th century B.C. Sure enough, the adoption of the "aryeh" in Abrahamic iconography occurred during the Exilic Period. It turns out that the Judaic adoption of this particular symbol was contemporaneous with the Greeks' usage of "Leo Nemeaeus" (lion of Nemea) from the popular tales of Heracles—wherein it symbolized victory over death. The inspiration for the Hellenic leitmotif was likely ALSO Assyrian iconography. It turns out that memes have been going viral since the Iron Age.

But wait. EVEN THAT is not the beginning of the story. Nebuchadnezzar II was HIMSELF guilty of Cul-Ap. This catchy iconography actually dated back to the 4th millennium B.C., when lions guarded the gate of the city of Nineveh. Meanwhile, the "temple of lions" (dedicated to Dagan) at Mari dated from the 22nd century B.C. (!)

So the ancient world was rife with cultural appropriation. The question arises: Shall we begrudge the Mycenaeans AND the Hebrews for "appropriating culture" from the Assyrians? Or was it permissible in such cases simply due to the fact that the source-culture eventually became extinct?

Ok, then. So exactly what Judaic icon WAS used during the Iron Age? Hebrew rulers opted for an assortment of winged insignias—as were used on the [L-]M-L-K seals of Judean king Hezek-i-yah ben Ahaz in the late 8th / early 7th century B.C. Much later, pursuant to the Hellenization of Beth Israel during the Seleucid era (that is: post-Exilic, pre-Hasmonean), we find the major icon used by Jewish leaders was…*an owl*. Wherefore? Well, this was inspired by Athena's owl (which would later be known by Romans as the owl of Minerva). Goodness gracious.

The only symbol that has ever been unique to Judaism is the candelabrum (known as the "menorah"), which came into use during the Hasmonean era. It commemorated the Maccabees' fortitude after having successfully staved off the Seleucids. (As the story goes, the candles in the temple miraculously burned for over a week, using a surprisingly small amount of oil.) Just as we'd expect, the iconographic shift from the (winged) lion and the owl to the candelabrum occurred in the 2nd century B.C. {32}

While it had been in use for centuries by other creeds, the hexagram (later fashioned as the "Star of David") did not emerge as an insignia *for Judaism* until the Late Middle Ages. It arose from within the smorgasbord of esoteric Kabbalist semiotics; and was eventually presented as the (purported) "Seal of Solomon". The earliest JUDAIC use of the hexagram appeared on the cover of a Masoretic text now known as the Leningrad codex from c. 1009. Thereafter, the star soon came to be used in various "segulot" and grimoires—mostly by aficionados of the Kabbalah. But for the time being, that was initially a niche use.

The hexagram was first used as an emblem for Beth Israel IN GENERAL by the Jews of Prague; but that wasn't until the 14th century. It was then popularized in the 16th century by the Jewish mystic, Isaac Luria when he presented his version of the "Etz [c]Hayim" (diagram of the "Tree of Life"). Thereafter, the familiar star caught on, and came to be used in mainstream Judaica.

Thus Judaic iconography went from the Lion of Judah (during the Exilic period) to an owl (during Classical Antiquity) to the candelabrum of the Maccabees (during the Hasmonean era) to the hexagram of medieval Jewish mystics (during the Renaissance). Once a movement is wed to certain iconography, it likes to fancy it as sui generis. After all, to be presented as authentic, it cannot be admitted that it is derivative in any way. So connoisseurs of Judaica today are inclined to pretend that the "Star of David" literally dates back to, well, King David himself, over three millennia ago. (This seems to go hand in hand with the risible supposition that Judaism ITSELF goes back to the Bronze Age.)

There is, of course, a reason to eschew the original iconography: While the lion had clear pagan origins; the menorah was, indeed, unique to early Judaism. And so it went: During Late Antiquity, and into the Middle Ages, the predominant symbol of the Mosaic Faith was the **menorah**—as attested by the Babylonian Talmud (which never mentions a star). It makes sense, then, that when Roman Emperor Domitian erected the triumphal "Arch of Titus" to commemorate the Roman victory over the Jews in 70 A.D., the latter were associated not with a star, but with the familiar candelabrum.

The menorah was still the go-to symbol in the 5th and 6th centuries A.D.—as demonstrated by the Jewish Catacombs of Rome and Venosa.

Assuming King David even existed, were he to have seen this star, he surely would not have associated it with either himself, with his people, or with the Abrahamic deity. In fact, he would have had no idea what it meant. Consequently, it stands to reason that this was NOT what Solomon would have used for his royal seal. A lion symbolized his creed, not the Canaanite hexagram.

As mentioned, only around the 11th or 12th century A.D. did those involved in the Mosaic tradition start incorporating the fabled hexagram into their iconography—a convention that was mostly limited to the Kabbalist tradition. The star was thereafter used as an insignia for Masoretic texts (as attested by the aforementioned Leningrad codex). Beth Israel then adopted the hexagram: ANOTHER formerly pagan symbol—one that was, admittedly, much more snazzy…yet NOT unique to Judaism. Doing so meant eliding the fact that this new symbol had any history before that.

Through the Renaissance, the hexagram was alternately known by Jews as the "Shield of David" or "Seal of Solomon". Yet it was hardly exclusive to Judaism. During the Crusades, the same star was used by the (vehemently anti-Semitic) Knights Templar! Cul-Ap, it turns out, is not without its ironies.

In 17th-century Prague, the hexagram was just another cool-looking insignia. But today, ANYONE who sees the symbol immediately identifies it as the "Star of David": an emblem of Beth Israel (as well as the symbol used on the flag for the modern nation, "Israel"). {32}

It was not until the 19th century that Jewish communities within the Pale of

Settlement (i.e. the Ashkenazim of Eastern Europe) adopted the hexagram as an insignia for Judaic identity. By the end of the 19th century, in the advent of modern Zionism, the iconography had been thoroughly instantiated. Consequently, the star ("Judenstern") was used by the Third Reich as a Judaic symbol, which is why the regime eventually forced Jewish people to don it—in yellow—on their sleeves. (Yellow had been the color used in the medieval Islamic world as a sartorial designation of Jewish people…though, tellingly, NOT as a star, but as the "Judenhut", which were typically yellow badges featuring the shape of a pair of Mosaic law tablets.)

Considering how iconography usually works, we should not be surprised to find that this particular star is not unique to Judaism; as Albanians and—ironically—Palestinians have been using it as an emblem for centuries. In fact, prior to the 20th century, it was just as much an Islamic symbol as it was a Jewish one. The hexagram was on the Moroccan flag until 1915, when it was altered to a pentagram. So it had been used by Muslims in the Balkans, in the Levant, and on the Barbary coast long before the theocratic ethno-State of "Israel" was established.

But wait. There's more. The symbol was also used in the Far East as well. It was used in Bactrian, Indian, Tibetan, AND Japanese iconography. Practitioners of Shinto have been using the hexagram—as the "Kagome" crest—since the 5th century B.C. And it was often used on Hindu mandalas EVEN BEFORE THAT. In fact, the "Shatkona" antedates ALL THE OTHER versions of the hexagram. The two triangles—one pointing up, the other down—represent "Om" and "Hreem" in Vedic lore; or, alternately, Shakti (representing Vedic "prakriti") and Shiv[a] (representing Vedic "purusha") in later Hindu lore. **So, gee-wiz. Who's symbol is it?**

As it turns out, Jews of the modern age are the LAST people on Earth to have adopted this familiar symbol…which is now most associated with the modern ethno-State of "Israel". Shall we cry "cultural appropriation" against the world's Jewish people each time we see them using this "star of David"? According to the logic of Cul-Ap: YES. But we don't. Why not? Because doing so would be ridiculous. Like anyone else, Jews have a right to adopt things from other cultures. The symbol was not ORIGINALLY theirs; yet they now use it as their own nevertheless. And that's perfectly fine.

To summarize: The iconography that is familiar to us NOW is often the result of a long line of Cul-Ap. It is important to recognize that what we now call the "Star of David" originally had a very different semiotic existence—be it the Shatkona yantra in Hinduism; or the Kagome crest in the Shinto tradition; or any of the other occurrences of the symbol over the millennia. And when we see the hexagram's use in Judaism, we should note that that was a later development; and that the Anahata mandala existed long, long before.

It is worth noting that many instances of the hexagram around the world emerged independently, not from Cul-Ap; but the point remains: It is the height of conceit for anyone who adopted the meme later in the timeline to claim exclusive ownership. {25}

Another Abrahamic example drives the point home. Dar al-Islam implicitly (and unwittingly) pays heed to its pagan roots by retaining the crescent moon as its icon-of-choice. This was a hold-over from pre-Islamic Arabia, when it symbolized the moon-god—alternately S[ay]in or Hubal. Naturally, Mohammedan lore was designed to elide this fact. For it is de rigueur for virtually ALL iconography to obfuscate its own genealogy. Indeed, failing to do so risks revealing the fact that—whatever it might be—the meme BEING WHAT IT IS is an accident of history.

As it happened, the crescent moon and star combination was also used in Persian (Sassanian) iconography. Meanwhile, the Sabaeans—then Aksumites—used a crescent moon and sun combination throughout Classical Antiquity; and even referred to their godhead as "al-Rahim" (the merciful). It is no surprise, then, that this symbol was eventually adopted as a key element in Islamic iconography.

Many memes have genealogies that don't necessarily accord with the stories we like to tell ourselves. This is especially the case when it comes to memes that we fancy to be OUR OWN. Consequently, each iteration in the genealogy of a symbol deems itself to be sui generis (i.e. NOT derivative). When it comes to sacred symbols, this is done to claim authenticity, and thereby to assert legitimacy. To concede that a hallowed cultural element is derivative would be to concede that it was merely a social construct.

So it goes with Christianity vis a vis the crucifix; so it goes with Judaism vis a vis the Star of David; and so it goes with Islam vis a vis the crescent moon. Symbols like the staff of Hermes, the phoenix, and the double-headed eagle further illustrate the point.

Though awkward to broach, one prime example remains worth mentioning.

When it comes to symbols, the tendency for things to not be as they now seem is most blatantly demonstrated by the Hindu / Jain—and then Buddhist—swastik[a]. This is a tragic tale of mal-appropriated iconography. The sacred symbol was sullied by its appropriation by the Nazi party after it had already been in use for thousands of years. But how in heaven's name did THAT happen? Eureka: by a series of memetic appropriation. The symbol-in-question was actually used in Greek iconography since the 10th century B.C. as the "tetra-gamma dion" [four-gamma shape]. And it was used on Scythian coins going back to Classical Antiquity. In Vedic Sanskrit, "swasthi" means good fortune, blessed-ness, prosperity, and/or well-being (roughly comparable to "eudaimonia" in Greek). Meanwhile, "laksh[a]" means progression toward a goal; which seems to have served as the etymological basis for the lexeme's suffix, "-ka". Ergo "swastik[a]". {13}

The symbol's history in Europe is calumnious. At the turn of the 20th century, Germanic occultists like Guido von List and Adolf Josef Lanz von Liebenfels made use of the Teutonic "haken-kreuz" [hooked cross]; the latter for his virulently anti-Semitic, hyper-nationalistic "Order of New Templars". The Thule Society also made use of the symbol for its own nefarious purposes. The basis of this iconography was—ostensibly—ancient Nordic mythology. (The symbol, signifying some kind of preternatural power, seems to have been associated with Thor's hammer.) In the advent of the first World War, the German Freikorps got the idea to use the symbol from Teutonic shrines that made use of it (as some medieval Germanic churches tended to do). The proto-fascists were also probably aware of the Templars' use of it as an emblem of the Teutonic legacy. They most likely did NOT have Hinduism, Jainism, or Buddhism in mind. In other words, the hakenkreuz has nothing to do with the swastik[a].

Considering the symbol's association with militant "Völkisch" Supremacy, it was only natural that the brown-shirts opted to adopt the symbol soon thereafter. Nazi leadership had connections to the Thule Society. So far as they were concerned, the symbol was the "hakenkreuz"; not the "swastik[a]".

It might be noted that some Native American tribes ALSO made use of this particular symbol (e.g. the Navajo; with the whirling log); though they likely did not appropriate it from anyone else. The symbol was even used as the insignia for the U.S. Army's 45th Infantry Division until 1939—as a homage to Native Americans. (!) Once the symbol became inextricably associated with the Third Reich, the U.S. military felt obliged to refrain from using it anymore.

Tragically, throughout the Occident, the symbol's association with Nazism has stuck; and along with it the odious stigmatization. Regardless, the swastika STILL IS what it has been for THOUSANDS of years. The world's Hindus, Jains, and Buddhists needn't let the fact that an Austrian psychopath appropriated this particular iconography in the 1920's deter them from continuing to make use of it.

Most would agree that the Nazis' hijacking of the symbol (as the "hakenkreuz") was probably the most vulgar case of Cul-Ap in modern history. Nevertheless, if we were to enumerate a hundred of the most execrable things the Third Reich did, mimicking a Hindu / Jain symbol would probably not make the list. In other words, even when it comes to the most egregious case of Cul-Ap, it is STILL not an issue that needs to be addressed in terms of "cultural appropriation".

What the Nazis did with this particular symbol is more accurately characterized as a semiotic swindle. It is due to a failure to understand how meme-adoption works that many still primarily associate this hallowed symbol with Nazism…and erroneously refer to it as a "swastika". (It is perverse to refer to the Nazi version of the symbol by its Vedic name, as doing so is extremely misleading.) It makes sense to take measures to curb such zany memetic hijinks. But this does not require one to demonize Cul-Ap per se. Even the most opprobrious cases of Cul-Ap do not warrant the kind of anti-Cul-Ap hysteria found in the precincts of the Regressive "Left".

To summarize: While the swastik[a] is a hallowed icon from ancient Eastern traditions, the hakenkreuz is an odious insignia—lifted from Teutonic iconography—used by a megalomaniacal fascist for his deranged movement. Semiotically, the two are not the same…even as there is a tragically superficial resemblance. So to refer to the latter as the former is a misnomer. It is high time for the Hindus, Jains, and Buddhists of the world to reclaim the swastik[a] for the beautiful symbol that it is; and for everyone on the planet to recognize that the Nazi symbol was, in fact, NOT a swastik[a].

The bottom line is that the black hakenkreuz superimposed on a white circle (spec. within a red field) should be shunned for what it was…and NOT conflated with something that it is not. Integrity demands that the distinction be made between Nordic / Germanic symbol and the Vedic symbol, as the latter has been in use for several millennia by a people that have no connection to Nazism. {33}

Alas, stigmas are stubborn things; and tend to persist far beyond their expiration date. As with embellishments to folklore (be it the urban legends or ancient myths), stigmatization has a ratcheting effect: Once a stigma is sufficiently ingrained in the collective consciousness, it is difficult to revert back to the original semiotic instantiation. This is why it's still okay to name a girl "Swastika" in India, but such a choice would be uncouth in the West.

This ratcheting effect can be found throughout onomastic conventions. An athletic company has permanently stigmatized the female name "Nike"; and an automobile company has permanently stigmatized the female name "Portia" (based on the homophonic Bohemian family-name, "Porsche"). Mass-inculcation is rarely reversible, especially when the stigmatization is poignant. But if we are to hew to the strained logic of Cul-Ap-phobia, should we not demand that "Nike" (Greek) and "Portia" (Roman) be returned to their rightful homeland?

What of the Apple command symbol? Appropriated from the Swedes. The dollar sign? Appropriated from the Portuguese. The glyph for female? That was originally the alchemical symbol for antimony. And on and on. Cul-Ap is all over the place. It ALWAYS HAS BEEN.

The swastika is perhaps the most poignant—if tragic—instance of memetic hijacking. The (Judaic) Star of David, the (Christian) cross, and (Islamic) crescent moon are the most un-acknowledged instances. Even so, this is how iconography usually works. The Maori of New Zealand understand this—which is probably why they don't complain that one of their tribal marks is now used as the symbol for "biohazard". (!)

In sum: A cultural element is not always what we fancy it to be. Rushing to judgement about who can and cannot use it, then, invariably proceeds from a host of spurious assumptions. It's like the Scot who insists that tartan (a.k.a. plaid) is exclusively Gaelic, failing to realize the patterned fabric was used on continental Europe—and even in ancient China—long before it made it to Alba. (It did not appear in Scotland until the 16th century…hundreds of years after William Wallace fought for independence.) The Celtic peoples, recall, originated on the continent.

As it turns out, Cul-Ap-phobes are only concerned about Cul-Ap when it suits them; glossing over all the other instances that populate their own world. There are countless examples of such selectivity. How often do we hear complaints about Halloween being a tacky re-branding of Hallow-mas (a.k.a. "All Hallows Tide"; "All Hallows Eve")? Never. Yet, as it so happens, the origins of this occasion lay in the Gaelic "Samhain", commemorating the end of the harvest season. Medieval Christians appropriated the pagan idea, and refashioned it as "All Saints / Martyrs Day". The carved pumpkin (now known as the "jack o'lantern") was appropriated from traditions found in the Cornish version of the occasion, Kalan Gwav (a.k.a. "Allan-tide")…which was a variation on the Brythonic / Welsh "Calan Gaeaf". Yet Cul-Ap-phobes are not up in arms that a Gaelic holiday has been turned into a mawkish commercial enterprise by the rest of the world. Why not?

"But it's okay, as the Irish were not an oppressed minority" is an objection that could only be uttered by those unfamiliar with the earliest era of the American colonies. The Irish were routinely discriminated against in America; yet they do not have an aneurism every time non-Irish revelers don a shamrock on Saint Patrick's Day.

Just as with Halloween, St. Patrick's Day has been "appropriated" from hallowed Gaelic folk-traditions by the rest of the Occident. Is the entire Western world denigrating the Irish by celebrating these holidays in such a care-free manner? According to the contorted logic of Cul-Ap-phobia, Americans must somehow be desecrating an entire people's heritage by engaging in daffy activities on such festive occasions. (Is this bigotry via conviviality?) No sane person—least of all the Irish—is tempted to make such a contention.

As is often the case, there is appropriation going as far back as our timeline can take us. When it comes to memes, what is now seen as endogenous was at one point exogenous. (In other words, indigeneity is sometimes over-ascribed.) Cul-Ap-phobes fail to recognize this. So what they aim to do is terminate the very process that brought the culture-in-question to where it now is. It's like trying to protect butterflies by prohibiting the formation of cocoons. To spurn those who CONTINUE the very process that brought one's own culture to where it is today, then, is the height of hypocrisy. For it is to undermine that which one is aiming to protect.

Judaic traditions illustrate the point as well. Would we be right to assail the world's Jewish people for appropriating the Persian festivals of "Jashn-i Mehr" (a.k.a. "Mehr-i Gan") and/or "Fravashi" (a.k.a. "Fravard-i Gan") in their observance of Purim? The Judaic occasion (initially dubbed "Masekhet Megillah") was ostensibly based on the commemoration of the apocryphal Persian queen, Esther; but its origins lay elsewhere in Persia's history.

And shall we take umbrage with Beth Israel for having based "Yom Teruah" (a.k.a. "Rosh Ha-Shanah"; meaning head of the year) on the Assyrian festival of "Akitu[m]" (a.k.a. "Resh Shattim", also meaning head of the year)? The Day of Ashura was rendered the Tenth [Day] of [the month of] Tishri (alt. "Yom Ashura"), which came to be known as "Yom Kippur" in Judaic tradition. ("Ashura" means "tenth" in Aramaic.) Incidentally, the Day of Ashura was also the inspiration of the Muslim "Laylat al-Qadr" [Night of Power], as well as for the Shiite mourning of Hussein ibn Ali at Karbala during the month of Muharram. (Arabic also adapted the onomastic from Aramaic, via Nabataean Syriac.) Sure enough, the earliest Mohammedans fasted during the Day of Ashura: an Arabian tradition that predated Islam. {14}

There's more. Shall we begrudge Jews for riffing off of the Egyptian harvest festival dedicated to Min when establishing the holiday of "Chag ha-Asif" (a.k.a. "Sukkot")? The occasion was ostensibly based on the Mishnah (as well as passages from the Books of Nehemiah and Zechariah); yet it was really just another case of appropriated lore. Even one of the most sacred Judaic practices, circumcision, was adopted from the Egyptians (which Canaanites started practicing during the Amarna period).

"But that was a really long time ago," comes the objection. Granted. But how, then, shall we proceed? Does memetic provenance have a sunset clause? Is it the case that if the appropriation occurred a while ago, then we are permitted to let it slide? To qualify for exemption, where shall the cut-off be? A millennium ago? A century ago? Last year? Exactly how far back do we need to go before Cul-Ap is deemed to have been copacetic? The problem is: Whatever threshold one might propose, it will invariably be arbitrary.

The ad hoc rational for the indictment reveals the inconsistency of Cul-Ap demonization. Once more, we see that indictments of illicit "cultural appropriation" are, by their nature, highly selective; and thus based on an inconsistent application of the touted principle. We encounter the same selectivity when it comes to much of the "anti-racism" rhetoric spouting from Potemkin Progressives. {51}

Shall we chide Jews for cribbing their holidays from pagan antecedents? The answer is, of course, no. It makes perfect sense that such adaptations occurred within Judaism. After all, Judaic lore was codified in Babylon during the Exilic Period. Consequently, it is no surprise that those forming the new creed opted to simply adapt the existing traditions of the dominant cultural milieu to their own Faith.

What of Islam? The myriad traditions involved in the "Hajj" (Muslim pilgrimage) were ALL appropriated from antecedent pagan rituals—replete with ablutions, animal sacrifice, and the circumambulation of the Meccan cube ("kaaba"). Throwing stones at an edifice which represents evil forces (for the expiation of sins)? Appropriated. Drinking from the Zamzam well (for spiritual purification)? Appropriated. Kissing a black stone (to garner blessings)? Appropriated. Running between the Safa and Marwah hills? Yep, that was appropriated too. If we were to treat Cul-Ap as a transgression against the source culture, we'd be forced to contend that pre-Islamic Bedouins (spec. the Nabataeans) were the "victims" of rampant Cul-Ap.

Even the tradition of fasting for a lunar month (Ramadan) was appropriated from the extant tradition of the Nabataeans, in commemoration of the moon-god, Dashura. In fact, one would be hard-pressed to find an element of Islamic practice that was NOT lifted from antecedent (pagan) practices. {14}

Another example of a religion co-opting elements from antecedent tradition is Theravada Buddhism's adoption of Hindu lore—replete with Ganesh, Hanuman, and the legend of Rama. {19} As it turns out, virtually every Faith—especially those of the Abrahamic tradition—arrived at its present form as a result of Cul-Ap galore. Any given religion is the culmination of a meandering process of ad hoc co-optation—a process that few votaries care to acknowledge. For in consecrating a memeplex, one is inclined to fancy it to be sui generis. (It doesn't make sense to sanctify something that one admits is derivative.) Bottom line: A creed is invariably a bespoke agglomeration of pre-existent memes.

In leveling an accusation of "appropriation" from the purported source-culture, the question must be posed: Where do we draw the line? How far back in time are we willing to go before we settle on an official ORIGIN? We agree that practitioners of Zoroastrianism—a monotheism that predates Judaism—cannot indict Beth Israel for cribbing their (Persian) sacraments. So shall we suppose that Cul-Ap has a statute of limitations? Is it to be sanctioned retroactively? Or was it okay all along? If Cul-Ap was wrong last weekend, how was it not wrong a few millennia ago?

The lesson here is simple: Leveling charges of illicit Cul-Ap requires absolutely no knowledge of the ACTUAL HISTORY of the cultural heritage in question. The faux sophistication of the anti-Cul-Ap crusader is revealed by the fact that one does not really need to know anything about any of the world's cultures in order to level the indictment.

In proscribing Cul-Ap, we are not only obliged to specify the PUTATIVE source-culture (to designate the alleged victim), we are—by the same logic—obliged to specify the ULTIMATE source-culture of the meme-in-question. Doing so would, of course, be a quixotic task; but, more importantly, it is an unnecessary one. For in appropriating an exogenous cultural element, we are merely continuing a process that got that element—insofar as it can be discretely defined—to the current (purported) source-culture in the first place.

Again, the question arises: What is the optimal time-frame for claiming exclusive rights to a given cultural element? Such an inquiry is utterly inane; as there can be no solid basis for ANY answer. As Kwame Anthony Appiah once noted: the "putative owners" of cultural elements may well have been the "previous appropriators" of those elements. He could have gone so far to say: Their ancestors USUALLY WERE earlier appropriators. After all, that's how culture works.

When the license for meme-usage has an expiration date, who determines who gets the license, and for how long? In demanding everyone stop making use of the designated source-culture's memes (because Cul-Ap is inherently bad, you see), we are decrying a process that brought things to **where they are now**. As it turns out, the designated source-culture (whichever one it happens to be, depending where we draw the line in history) was ITSELF guilty of Cul-Ap.

To reiterate: Grousing about Cul-Ap is usually a sign that someone does not know much about the history of the culture being cited. In the campaign to paint Cul-Ap as something untoward, we are admonished to disregard the fact that every culture is a unique conglomeration of material, which was almost entirely culled from other cultures. That's not a bad thing. In fact, in each case, we find that Cul-Ap is a GOOD thing so long as we tap into our capacity to give a shit about one another—ESPECIALLY those from different cultures. Embracing exogenous cultural elements better equips us to summon our nascent humanity, expand our sphere of empathy, and thereby bolster human solidarity.

At the risk of flogging a steed that is already deceased, it is worth pursuing this line of inquiry in other contexts. Let's look at literature.

Literature

In assaying the incidence of Cul-Ap in the literary sphere, we might start by noting that the father of American drama (the Nobel laureate and Irish playwright, Eugene O'Neill) adopted his style from Russian "realism" (esp. the works of Anton Chekov). Was this a problem? If not, then why not? We might then ask: Was American "imagist" poet, Ezra Pound's gravest sin is that, in composing his verse, he employed an idiom appropriated from the Chinese (and possibly even the Japanese)? Considering that he also happened to harbor fascist sympathies, how shall we prioritize our moral qualms?

With respect to literature, Cul-Ap goes back thousands of years. A prime example of literary cross-pollination is the Hindu "Ramayana", a Sanskrit epic from Classical Antiquity. Key elements in the work owe a debt to the Mycenaean epics of Homer. Several of the motifs are the same–as with the abduction of a lady, as well as the subsequent conflict based on forbidden love: Sita by Ravana, Helen by Paris. Unsurprisingly, influences flowed in the other direction as well. As it turns out, the Hellenic "Aeneid" exhibits influences from the Vedic "Mahabharata". {19} Shall Indians be mad at the Greeks?

Throughout the Middle Ages, the Silk Road—stretching across Eurasia from the Middle East to the Far East—was not just a means of interchanging goods, it was a means of interchanging ideas (including theological tenets, artistic idioms, and fashion). Without rampant Cul-Ap, the Kushan Empire would not have existed. (Gandhara art was the result of Buddhist motifs being infused by Greek motifs. The Bactrian language was the result of Greek letters being used to write an Aryan vernacular.) An illustration of this **cultural alloy** is the panoply of Buddhist terms that ended up in the Persian vernacular; and the panoply of Syriac / Sogdian terms that ended up in Manichaean liturgy. The propagation of Pahlavi literature across Eurasia attests to the fact that there was an exchange of memes as well as of merchandise…in both directions. This was a reminder that cultures are not clearly-demarcated domains that can be memetically quarantined. {19}

Even the father of English literature, Geoffrey Chaucer, appropriated many of his motifs from French and Italian sources for his "Canterbury Tales"; yet neither the French nor the Italians were bothered by this. And when Japanese author, Minae Mizumura penned a Japanese rendition of Emily Brontë's "Wuthering Heights", the British didn't seem to mind. Why not?

Regarding contemporary literature, it might also be asked: Can black female authors write novels in which major characters are white men? How about vice versa? If an author cannot compose a heartfelt narrative involving characters that are anything other than the demographic to which the author himself belongs, then all fiction would be reduced to verging autobiography. Shakespeare was neither a wayward Moorish military officer nor a disillusioned Danish prince. Nevertheless, the English playwright was able to create the principal characters of "Othello" and "Hamlet". The great bard was certainly not a lovesick Venetian teenager. Yet we now have "Romeo and Juliet".

I have mentioned "West Side Story" (1957), an Americanized adaptation of Shakespeare's "Romeo and Juliet" (1595). But that wasn't all there was to it. As it turns out, the Elizabethan playwright HIMSELF adapted a tale that had already been widely published...both as an Italian novella by Matteo Bandello AND as a French novella by Pierre Boaistuau (about Reomeo Titensus and Juliet Bibleotet). And even that was not the beginning. For the Italian and French renditions that inspired Shakespeare had themselves been adaptations of William Painter's "Palace of Pleasure" (1567)...which had, in turn, been taken from Arthur Brooke's "The Tragicall Historye of Romeus and Juliet" (1562). And THAT had been taken from Luigi da Porto's tale of Romeus and Giulietta (1524)...which had been taken from Masuccio Salernitano's tale of Mariotto and Giannozza, entitled "A Newly Found Story Of Two Noble Lovers" (1476). And Salernitano had taken HIS tale from John Metham's "Amoryus and Cleopes" (1449)...which had been an adaptation of a Florentine tale in Giovanni Boccaccio's "Decameron" (from the 14th century). And EVEN THAT was lifted from antecedent Roman lore—notably found in Ovid's tale of Pyramus and Thisbe, published in 8 A.D.

Gadzooks! It was Cul-Ap from Broadway all the way back to ancient Rome. (!) In virtually every case of Cul-Ap, the very people who are purportedly the victims were guilty of the indiscretion themselves. How far into the past shall we venture before we just resign ourselves to the fact that memes propagate across cultural lines?

Don't think the tragedy of Romeo And Juliet counts as "appropriation" due to the fact that everyone was—as it were—IN ON the chain of adaptation? Think again. Each party in this sequence of appropriation sought to make the tale an integral part of their own culture. In each case, the fact that it had already been a part of someone else's culture posed no problem; and was often even elided. With each iteration, the adaptors sought to make it their own. They all asserted ownership by imbuing that which had come from another culture with a distinct (indigenous) cultural flavor. We can, then, better understand George Bernard Shaw's cheeky quip that "Shakespeare was a wonderful teller of stories so long as someone else had told them first."

So the question arises: Is Shakespeare's vaunted legacy in any way diminished by him having co-opted other cultures' material? Au contraire. If anything, his work was ENHANCED by him having done so. For the ability to transcend one's own lot in life—and to imagine what it's like to be someone else—is what enables great art. In fact, if the proprietors of Stratford-up-Avon were beholden to proscriptions against Cul-Ap, almost NONE of the great bard's timeless oeuvre would have been permitted on their stage.

Imagine Danes begrudging Shakespeare for Hamlet; or Italians begrudging him for the way he depicted the Montague-Capulet feud. Shall Andalusian Muslims be incensed over the use of a Moorish protagonist in Othello? As it turns out, we rarely hear complaints about such works; as the more sober aficionados of political correctness know better than to grouse about something so patently absurd. It seems they would rather focus on the indiscretion of gringos hitting piñatas at kids' birthday parties.

This is a reminder that the charge of illicit Cul-Ap can't help but be highly selective; thereby reflecting the biases of those leveling the charge. Double standards are routine in the demesne of political correct-ness. Tragically, doyens of identity politics fail to see that great literature—like all great art—elucidates our shared humanity; and thus transcends culture. Such identitarians may want to reflect upon the fact that Shakespeare has given us some of the great Svengalis in literature—from a conniving Scottish virago (Lady Macbeth) to a conniving Venetian soldier (Iago). We find this character in Germany (as with Mephistopheles) and in France (as with the Marquise Isabelle de Merteuil). In the final analysis, the lamentable tendency of tragic heroes—manipulated by the subterfuge of scheming villains—reflects something about humanity. It is a vulnerability that exists irrespective of demographic profile.

Humanity transcends ethnicity.

Shakespeare reminds us that certain themes are timeless; and that the most profound insights are immune to the artificial boundaries we have so unscrupulously constructed to demarcate one culture from another. Artistic expression cannot be reduced to its creator's ethnic identity. Shakespeare's plays illustrate that certain themes are HUMAN themes; so are not constrained to this or that cultural milieu.

Alas. Not everyone sees it this way. In early 2019, the most obdurate of anti-Cul-Ap zealots opted to pillory Chinese author, Amélie Wen Zhao for penning a novel in which one of the themes was indentured servitude. According to the complainants, as someone who was not Black, Zhao **had no right** to write about anything having to do with one group enslaving another group…as if African-Americans were the only people in the world who had ever experienced slavery. {**24**} This is nothing short of insanity. It is also a textbook example of racial bias (otherwise known as "racism"). Moreover, such a blinkered "take" requires one to know virtually nothing about world history.

Authors are on notice: If you want to pen a story involving minority characters, you risk being accused of exploitation if you do not personally belong to that minority. Were we to begrudge artists who attempt to put themselves in the shoes of "the other" (a.k.a. virtually ALL ARTISTS), so adopting idioms from outside their own culture, we would be forced to censure much of the world's greatest artistic achievements—musical, sartorial, architectural, culinary, AND literary. In doing so, we would also betray the most fundamental principles of humanism.

Looking around the world, we find that memetic transference is ubiquitous in literature. Take, for instance, the notion of the quintessential seducer: From Don Giovanni (Italian) to Don Juan (Spanish) to Cyrano de Bergerac (French)…each of them flawed in their own way. In Europe, this was nothing new. The famous "Chansons de Roland" from medieval France (starting in the late 11th century) were eventually adapted by Italian writers four centuries later (as the tales of "Orlando"; first by Matteo Maria Boiardo, then by Ludovico Ariosto). Hollywood then offered its own rendition with Anglo-Saxons in the lead roles: the film Roxanne. The tale went from medieval Franks to small-town America.

If we were forced to censor the literary repertoire in the manner suggested by anti-Cul-Ap crusaders, we must ask: Who would benefit? Shall only Asians write about Asians, Africans about Africans, Scandinavians about Scandinavians, and Latinos about Latinos? Or shall we ALL—as fellow humans—be permitted to recognize that we share in the same humanity? As we have seen, for the answer, we need only look to Shakespeare. His entire repertoire was a bacchanal of Cul-Ap. Was this in any way detrimental…to ANYONE? Harold Bloom put it well: "The idea that you benefit the insulted and injured by reading someone of their own origins rather than reading Shakespeare is one of the oddest illusions ever promoted." Of course, insofar as one wants to be educated about a specific literary tradition, it makes sense to focus exclusively on the ethnicity of the authors and their impact on their own culture; but it does not follow that, in order to be edified, we must all use the ethnic background of an author as the primary criterion for determining merit.

Sometimes an author seems to be writing from within one ethnic identity, yet turns out to belong to another. When "Danny Santiago" penned a critically-acclaimed novel about Chicano barrios ("Famous All Over Town"), he was revealed to be an upper-class WASP named Daniel Lewis James. This revelation did not detract from either the insightfulness or the literary value of the work. He no more needed to be Hispanic to tell the gripping story than Shakespeare needed to be a Bohemian to craft "The Winter's Tale". (Did we mention that the Elizabethan bard was neither a Danish monarch, nor a Moorish general, nor a Venetian gamine?) Indeed, James was actually knowledgeable about—and genuinely CARED about—the Chicano communities about which he wrote; as he had worked with them intimately in the past.

This should remind us that it is the SPIRIT BEHIND the work that is truly important. Fidelity and good intentions matter more than the demographic profile of the author. When Kathryn Stockett penned "The Help", the fact that a White woman had written a compelling novel about the travails of Black maids in the American South during the Jim Crow era did not compromise the story's credibility. She no more needed to be an African American to craft a poignant narrative about White privilege in Mississippi than, say, Khaled Hosseini needed to be a woman to write his novel about Muslimahs dealing with Afghan patriarchy in ***A Thousand Splendid Suns***.

Felicitously, J.R.R. Tolkien engaged in OODLES of cultural appropriation (primarily from ancient Norse culture) when he composed "The Hobbit" and "The Lord of the Rings". Eight decades later, renowned British author Neil Gaiman engaged in his own creative appropriation with his "Norse Mythology". Should Scandinavians be incensed by this? Well, no more than Danes should be incensed by the fact that Shakespeare ripped off their 12th-century saga, "Vita Amlethi" (itself an adaptation of a tale in the "Gesta Danorum") when he wrote "Hamlet". As it turns out, they don't begrudge ANYONE for appropriating Norse folklore…any more than they would begrudge somebody for adopting quotidian Nordic customs.

The 1990 animated Japanese series, "Nadia Of The Mysterious Seas" (a.k.a. "Nadia: The Secret Of Blue Water") was lifted from Jules Verne's classic, "Twenty Thousand Leagues Under The Sea"—composed 120 years earlier. A decade later, Disney decided to do a take-off on the Japanese rendition–entitled: "Atlantis: The Lost Empire". So who's ripping off whom? Well, nobody. The ideas in the story transcend culture. For instance, the notion of a lost city of "Atlantis" originated in ancient Greece (ref. Plato's "Timaeus" and "Critias"); and was then taken up by the Jewish thinker, Philo of Alexandria in the early 1st century A.D…then by the English author, Thomas More in 1516…followed by Francis Bacon in 1626. And on and on. Virtually all classic literature is appropriation.

And what of, say, the quest for the Holy Grail? Yep. That too was lifted from antecedent lore: the ancient Persian legend of the Grail of Jamshid (believed to be a magical cup of immortality). Versions of the quest would later be done by Goeznovius of Cornwall (the "Legenda Sancti" under the pseudonym, "William"; in the 6th century)…then by Nennius ("Historia Brittonum" in the early 9th century)…then by Geoffrey Monmouth ("De Gestis Britonum" c. 1136)…then by Chrétien de Troyes ("Perceval: The Story Of The Grail" in the 1180's)…then by Wolfram von Eschenbach ("Parzival" in the 1210's). So the tale went from Persian to Cornish to Welsh to English to French to German. The appropriation is endless…and even crosses religious contexts: from Zoroastrian to Christian to secular. (Another prime case-study of this phenomenon is the tale of Robin Hood, as we'll see later, in Part 2.)

Even Arthurian legend, the touchstone of medieval (Christian) Anglo-Saxon lore, was likely adapted from an antecedent (pagan) source: "Beowulf". In fact, the two tales likely harken back to the same place and time (England, c. 500), and possibly even the same cast of characters. (The primary figure seems to have been based on either the Briton king, Riothamus or the fabled king Eomer.) Once we consider the narrative parallels, we can surmise that the tale of Arthur was a Christianized re-vamping of the Old English epic. Consider the nemesis in each case: Grendel's mother (a creepy sorceress named Aglaecwif / Aglaeca) was from a mysterious place in the middle of a lake. Meanwhile, Mordred's mother (a creepy sorceress named Morgan[na]) was from a mysterious place in the middle of a lake (the Isle of Apples, in Avalon). Few in Christendom would concede the derivative nature—let alone the pagan origins—of their cherished story. This is a reminder that Cul-Ap has been the norm even when it comes to our most hallowed folklore. So from whence do compunctions with Cul-Ap come?

It turns out that those trafficking in ersatz Progressivism are not cosmopolitan at heart. They are not impelled by a yearning for human solidarity; and they certainly don't seem to care much about actual history. (But, hey, at least they have a Trans-inclusive rainbow flag on their social media profile…and preferred pronouns specified in their bio.) Potemkin Progressives are more concerned with virtue signaling than with actual virtue. All the while, they put their own ideological purity over integrity. This is because their ersatz Progressivism (which operates at the nexus of political correctness and identity politics) is more a veneer than a sincere effort to promote social justice; part of it is simply corporatism.

There was a particular incident that captures the lunacy of the anti-Cul-Ap crusade. In 2017, the popular Canadian writer, Hal Niedzviecki was pilloried for stating that "anyone, anywhere, should be encouraged to imagine other peoples, other cultures, other identities." In other words: We should all aspire to be cosmopolitan; and—in the spirit of curiosity and empathy—strive to put ourselves in the shoes of others who might be different from us. Art—be it literature or music or anything else—is a great way to do this. Yet, for this estimable position, Niedzviecki was castigated…**and ultimately evicted from Canada's Writer's Union**. Why? For the intolerable act of endorsing "cultural appropriation". No kidding.

This is the sort of errant—I dare say, wacky—thinking germane to Cul-Ap-phobia.

To understand literary tradition, and to simply appreciate literature, is to embrace the vital role that Cul-Ap plays in the life of the mind. From Hermann Hesse's rendition of "Siddhartha" (Indian) to James Joyce's rendition of "Ulysses" (Greek) to Ursula K. Le Guin's rendition of the "Tao Te Ching" (Chinese), there are endless examples of laudable "appropriation" in literature. We find that in virtually every case, belletristic appropriation is something to be celebrated, not repudiated.

This isn't just about literature. ALL art is a reminder that embracing the cosmopolitan spirit means trying to put oneself in the shoes of those who are different from oneself—that is: to make the foreign more familiar. This is the mechanism which enables global empathy. This is the only way to override our basest tribal instincts. For the "citizen of the world" (as Thomas Paine called himself) strives to see the humanity in THE OTHER. This comes from a meta-tribal perspective—what Karl Marx referred to as "species-being" and Paul Tillich referred to as "trans-moral conscience". This requires one to see all things, first and foremost, as a fellow human being (rather than as a member of this or that identity-group).

To truly understand the merits of this approach, one must travel extensively—experiencing other cultures first-hand. In lieu of traveling, one can take a journey in one's own mind by reading a book written about someone in a distant land. And once one cultivates sufficient knowledge of that distant land, one may even write about it.

Elaborations

One of the main themes of this book is that a tribalistic mindset acts like an acid on human solidarity. In virtually every way, ethno-centric thinking behooves us to abandon focus on our shared humanity, and focus instead on some ethereal notion of cultural purity. While the former attitude is predicated on a cosmopolitan outlook, the latter is predicated on collective narcissism (spec. ethno-centrism). Each is diametrically opposed to the other; so we cannot possibly uphold both.

Another important theme is that conceit—whether on the individual or group level—renders us incapable to seeing the bigger picture; as we are more inclined to become self-absorbed. By not grasping universals, we tend to adapt an adversarial / confrontational posture toward *the other*; and subsequently insist that anything that *the other* says / does that we find unsettling is some sort of affront. Here, unease is construed as HARM. Any episode of mild irritation is thus wielded as a rhetorical cudgel…which can then be used to bludgeon anyone with whom one opts to have an ax to grind.

For aficionados of political correctness, the key is use even a fleeting bout of discomfiture as justification to be gratuitously tendentious whenever doing so might serve one's interests. This is the stock in trade of the p.c.-monger. Such people can see a toothbrush of the wrong color and take offense. These (largely-manufactured) internal calamities are seen as signs that some sort of injustice is afoot; which means that those on whom the bout of discomfiture can be blamed are guilty of some sort of transgression.

To get this scheme to work, everything must be taken personally. Accordingly, "offense" is seen as something GIVEN rather than TAKEN. The positing of these miniature cataclysms is known as "catastrophizing"; as being "bothered" by something is treated as a personal catastrophe…in dire need of remediation. This leads to the demand that we all take measures to ensure everyone feels at east—thereby ensuring that the most squeamish person in the room might avoid the harrowing experience of feeling a bit unsettled. (In the argot of the p.c.-monger, to feel **unsettled** by X is to be **injured** by X.) Participants put themselves on a hair-trigger response, eager to claim effrontry whenever it suits them.

This stage-managed tetchy-ness gives rise to a raft of problems. For whenever "offense" is leveraged in this manner, it is typically invoked in place of sound argumentation. In short order, global empathy is precluded; the prospects of comity between interest groups are severely hampered; and meaningful public discourse becomes a pipe-dream.

Back to the matter at hand: It makes no sense to become apoplectic every time one encounters Cul-Ap. Appropriation only becomes problematic when it is exploitative, fails to give credit where credit is due, reinforces negative stereotypes, or plays into prejudices. But such things do not occur in most instances of Cul-Ap. How can we be so sure? As it so happens, the vast majority of Cul-Ap passes without notice. Just because we don't acknowledge it doesn't mean it's not there. Many of us sing Auld Lang Syne (a Scottish song) during each New Year's celebration; yet we never feel indebted to the Albannaich. Why not? It wouldn't make much sense. The Scots aren't being exploited when inebriated revelers in distant lands lift their champaign flutes at midnight, so there's no reason to fret.

In the advent of identity politics on the (so-called) "Left", accusations of illicit Cul-Ap have become one of the rhetorical cudgels used by identitarians and p.c-mongers. Aside from distracting from far more important matters, this ill-advised approach to social justice provides right-wing commentators with bounteous ammunition for attacking the "Left"; as it enables the former to portray the latter as petty, obstreperous, and completely out of touch (see the Appendix). In caviling about this or that impropriety, Potemkin Progressives are doing little more than putting on airs. Such posturing is a reminder that virtue signaling rarely involves any ACTUAL virtue.

Those who are determined to be "offended" at every opportunity will always find an excuse to cavil. In discovering how frivolous many of these grievances are, it becomes plain to see that touting p.c. protocols is more a hustle than it is a sincere effort to foster civility. True activism is about far more than just keeping up appearances.

When we obsess over token formalities, the first casualty is common sense. As we survey the world's vast, undulating cultural landscape, with all of its knolls and glens, we can admire a panoramic memetic vista. We might then, at our own discretion, opt to explore each hillock, each vale, discovering nifty tidbits that compliment our own repertoire of cultural elements.

There are countless ways to illustrate the fact that—generally—Cul-Ap is a salutary development. Let's consider martial arts. Already mentioned was the Russian adaptation of Japanese "ju-do", rebranded "sambo". Further into the past, Ju-do had been inspired by "Kito-Ryu"—a product of the "Ten-jin Shin-yo-Ryu" school of "ju-jutsu", which was used in Japan by the Samurai during the the Sengoku period (starting in the 16th century). After the Second World War, a Jewish Hungarian martial artist named Emrich Lichtenfeld created ANOTHER spin-off of ju-do, inspiring the craft of ai-ki-do (as it was derived from a style of ju-jutsu established by the "Daito-Ryu" school of "ai-ki"). This led to an Israeli martial art known as "Krav

Maga". (In Korea, Hap-ki-do was also adapted from "Daito-Ryu".) The Japanese were not up in arms over these adaptations of their craft by other ethnic groups.

Also after the Second World War, Japanese martial artist, So Doshin (working off the practice of "Muneomi Sawa-yama") adapted the Chinese craft of "quan-fa", which had been established by the monks of Shaolin centuries earlier, rendering it "Ken-po" (meaning "first method"). ("Quan-fa" was a kind of wu-shu, which was dubbed "kung-fu" in Cantonese.) When Doshin did this, the Chinese didn't seem to mind. Neither did those who cherished the Shaolin legacy.

"Karate" has an even longer history. It began in the 15th century in the Ryu-kyu archipelago of the South Pacific…which has since been claimed by both the Japanese and Chinese. Subsequently, the Japanese and Chinese each adapted this martial art, each in their own way. After the First World War, its Okinawan incarnation came to be dubbed "Motobu-Ryu". Then, after the Second World War, Korean practitioners melded "karate" with their indigenous "Taek-kyeon" to yield "Taek-won-do". The appropriation of this craft soon made its way to the United States…without anyone in the Far East taking umbrage.

In my estimation, one of the best arguments in favor of cultural appropriation (and thus against the supposition that it is something to be held in contempt) is "jiu-jitsu": originally a Daito-Ryu method of combat known at the time as "yawara" (which later influenced the development of the aforementioned "ju-jutsu"). This famous martial art migrated to Brasil in the mid-20th century; and was famously appropriated by the Gracie brothers—who extensively refined its techniques. (It remained in Japan as the aforementioned "ju-jutsu"—most notably with the practitioner, Takeda Sokaku--where, as we have seen, it incorporated the principle of "ai-ki". Now it is BRASILIAN jiu-jitsu that is the most revered form of the craft (with regard to grappling and submissions).

Are we to say, then, that the Brasilians were guilty of appropriating Japanese culture? In a sense, yes. And thank heavens for it. It was appropriated and ENHANCED. Its Latin American incarnation is far more useful than its Samurai precursor; so it is now the most revered approach to grappling.

That wasn't the end of it. A hybrid of (Japanese) ju-do, (Siamese) Muay Thai, and (Brasilian) ju-jitsiu was then created—dubbed "sanda". Who did THAT? The Chinese. This is hardly a development to be repudiated. On the contrary, such hybridization is to be celebrated; as all culture is NOTHING BUT hybridization. (And, in any case, this lethal trifecta is the most effective for mixed martial arts.)

Think of it this way: If even one person outside the (purported) group-of-origin is allowed to make use of a meme, then everyone must be allowed to use it. Otherwise, we are obliged to start designating sanctioned groups; which would entail specifying additional terms of circumscribed entitlement. Memes would need to be sequestered according to ethnicity. Such a tendentious enterprise would require us to posit demarcations that are invariably ad hoc…thereby compounding the very problem we purport to be solving.

In the case of jiu-jitsu, shall we accord exemption from the charge of Cul-Ap exclusively to Brasilians (or, more narrowly: only to the descendants of Helio and

Carlos Gracie)? No. Of course not. YET…today, compunctions often emerge when Cul-Ap occurs. Again, we encounter regimes of selective censure (which is to say: self-serving and inconsistently-applied censure).

How selective? In early 1990, Madonna adopted the house dance style known as vogue-ing, which had evolved out of the Harlem ballroom scene of the 1960s amongst African Americans and Latinos—especially those in the queer community (notably with the drag-queen pioneer, Paris DuPree). This was universally embraced as high tribute…even though Madonna was White…and straight. Alas, times have changed. Today, were a straight, White, cis-gender musical artist to do something like this, he/she would almost certainly be castigated. Wherefore? The aversion to Cul-Ap (especially in cases where there is racial disparity) seems to have gone into overdrive. This is especially so in the wake of a newfound hyper-sensitivity to the (all-too-common) blithe dismissal of the interests of marginalized communities. While this concern is entirely valid, the ways in which it has recently manifested itself do not always serve the purported cause.

Part of appreciating excellence is recognizing when people from one culture embrace something from another culture and take it to new heights—as was the case with the Gracie brothers' modification of jiu-jitsu and Madonna's popularization of vogue-ing. Another example is one of the most talented electric guitarists on the planet: a young Muslimah from Indonesia who's online handle is "MelSick-ScreamoAnnie". This Javanese hijabi has mastered heavy metal in ways that astound even the most avid American guitar aficionados.

What's going on here?

We now find ourselves in a global-culture—a world where ethnic boundaries are being magnificently blurred. It is a time when the best chess player to ever live is Norwegian, one of the best golfers in history is half-Thai half-Black, the best slugger in baseball is Japanese, the greatest female Taekwon-do artist is Punjabi, the greatest billiards player in history is Filipino, and the best freestyle rapper is a White guy from Portland, Oregon. As was the case with the Gracie brothers… Mel, Magnus Carlson, Tiger Woods, Shohei Ohtani, Rayna Jade Vallandingham, Efren Reyes, and Harry Mack have all excelled in crafts that did not originate within their own cultural milieu. This is something to celebrate.

The charge of illicit Cul-Ap precludes us from being at liberty to appreciate—and subsequently judiciously select—the best elements from other cultures; and incorporate them into our own. To prohibit Cul-Ap is to deprive people of a prerogative that animates all cultures--that fuels the efflorescence of culture in its most estimable forms. After all, nobody can "steal" a custom. Barring intellectual property, memes belong to the world.

Those of us who genuinely care about other cultures revel in the (judicious) appropriation of exogenous cultural elements. Indeed, such a gesture is a hallmark of cosmopolitanism.

The lesson here is simple: If cosmopolitan ideals are to prevail, the appropriation of exogenous cultural elements is to be celebrated in most cases. What is to be discouraged is not memetic transference PER SE, but conduct that is in any way mean-spirited or exploitative. In other words, we should focus on the iniquity, not on the Cul-Ap. (To repeat the point made at the beginning of the book: When a person is being a jerk while baking chocolate-chip cookies, that's not an indictment of chocolate-chip cookie-baking.) In keeping with the spirit of cosmopolitanism, one comes away with a markedly heterodox attitude: If only MORE "cultural appropriation" were undertaken, then more people around the world might try, say, the Vedic principle of "ahimsa" on for size; and maybe even emulate the pedestrian courtesies of the Japanese. Most cultures have something to offer the world; and the world would be remiss to neglect such offers. As far as Americans are concerned, perhaps they might take a queue from the Europeans—and the Chinese—and consider a society in which daily life is oriented around mass transit. To familiarize oneself with the world's resplendent variety of cultures is to recognize that trans-cultural fertilization is integral to civilizational advance.

Always has been. Always will be.

Concluding Remarks For Part 1

We are all embedded in the ambient culture in which we live our lives. Consequently, we are apt to view all memes through a certain prism, whereby we experience comfort when encountering familiar memes (which are often associated with compatriots) and suspicion—even trepidation—when encountering foreign memes (which are often associated with outsiders). We have developed this default setting for obvious reasons; yet it does not serve us well when operating in a modern, global society—that is: in a society where tribalism has become, if not obsolete, rather antiquated.

As I have tried to show, in evaluating the nature of cultural appropriation, it is important to maintain a global perspective. The world offers a treasure trove of great ideas—many of which are beyond our immediate purview. Memetic cross-pollination is not only a way to engender cosmopolitanism, it is a way of bringing to the fore our shared humanity.

At any given juncture, when we attempt to ascertain which customs merit our consideration, it helps to broaden our scope beyond the confines of our own cultural milieu. After all, cosmopolitan ideals are diametrically opposed to a parochial mindset. So, in considering our default setting, the question arises: If we urge cosmopolitanism in one breath, why would we mandate parochialism in the next?

Our survey has demonstrated that the appropriation of exogenous cultural elements is ubiquitous; and often felicitous. Cul-Ap is not synonymous with the desecration of the (purported) source-culture; nor is it tantamount to the dis-empowerment—nay, denigration—of members of that culture. Even when done cavalierly, there is typically no condescension intended; and—far more often than not—no harm done. After all, the propagation of memes across cultures—whether deliberate or unwitting—is simply a matter of memetic diffusion; which, as we have seen, is how any given culture came to be in the first place.

Alas, for those afflicted with Cul-Ap-phobia, this is all a moot point. For according to their tortured logic, Cul-Ap is prima facie invidious, and therefore must be decried. Anti-Cul-Ap crusaders call for (what amounts to) a memetic quarantine...as if the (imagined) boundaries between this and that culture were iron-clad and forever indissoluble. Pretending that the world is comprised of immutable ethnic demarcations does not foster pluralism; it mandates cultural segregation... which, we are notified, must be enforced in perpetuity (for reasons that even anti-Cul-Ap crusaders themselves don't even seem to understand).

As I have attempted to show, any culture that has ever existed is a concatenation of cultural elements that antedate it...in addition to a merging of contemporaneous cultures that have impinged upon it. Indeed, the proliferation of such acts is how any given culture came to be what it now is. Recall the global migration of the hexagram: Such memetic propagation reminds us that memes are transferable across both epochs and cultures.

Every meme started somewhere with someone for some reason; and was then adopted by others elsewhere for other reasons. This has never been considered a problem. In fact, barring those obsessed with some delusive notion of cultural purity, it has always been seen as fairly routine.

If we define Cul-Ap as the adoption of elements of one culture by another, then we soon find that Cul-Ap is something we should celebrate; and even encourage. For it is one of the best ways to generate awareness about "the other". Meme-exchange is the substrate of inter-cultural pro-sociality. When there is trans-cultural fertilization, everyone usually wins.

Embracing Cul-Ap is a matter of availing ourselves of what the human race has produced at various times, in various places, under various circumstances. Americans especially should remind themselves that American culture is almost entirely derivative; and still has a lot to learn from other cultures (and, in certain cases, beneficial memes to adopt). This is not a bad thing; it's how society evolves.

Those in pluralistic societies don't see the incorporation of exogenous cultural elements as some kind of contamination; they see it as a potential enhancement. Consider the maxim: "The way we currently do things must forever remain the same; and don't anyone else ever try ANY of it." Such an attitude is diametrically opposed to cosmopolitanism. It also vilifies those who cross cultural barriers to seek communion with their fellow man. To cast such a gesture as TAKING ADVANTAGE OF one's fellow man is rather disingenuous. Exploration is not exploitation.

The bottom line is this: The co-option of exogenous cultural elements is the basis for every culture that has ever existed; and is one of the reasons that cultures flourish. The prohibition of Cul-Ap, then, ends up being just an ill-conceived social ordinance that one violates simply by living life to its fullest. To constrain meme-usage to memes that can be readily tied to one's own heritage (or one's own ethnicity) is to ignore history. Even worse, it flies in the face of the cosmopolitan spirit. Meme-sequestration is a recipe for hyper-parochialism. Such an attitude is sure to lead to the Balkanization of mankind into a network of insular cultural redoubts, where cordons are erected to ensure that one ethnicity never try walking in the shoes of another. This is not a world we want to live in.

And what about social justice? Good question. The onus is on anti-Cul-Ap crusaders to point to a single case in which the mitigation of Cul-Ap moved the cause for civil rights forward in some way. (Hint: This will be a difficult task considering no such case exists; or, I dare say, possibly could exist.) The demonization of Cul-Ap does nobody any good. If our aim is to forge global human solidarity, a regime of strictures against cultural diffusion is not the way to go about it. This even goes for cases in which those with more power adopt the customs of those with less power. (It turns out that those with less power often have better ideas than the power elite.)

And so it goes: Cul-Ap-phobia engenders insularity along ethnic lines. This invariably translates to tribal chauvinism. For by supposing Cul-Ap to be iniquitous, one mandates strictures that exacerbate fissures between cultures rather than engendering human solidarity. We mustn't mistake the Cul-Ap-phobe's pluralism-via-parochialism as a clarion call for cosmopolitanism.

Based on the preponderance of evidence, we find that what is often called "cultural appropriation" is a good thing. Anyone confident in the integrity of their own culture is inclined to say: "Please, by all means, appropriate elements from my culture 'til your heart's content! We may all be all the better for it."

Culture is a dynamic in which to participate, not a commodity to be rationed. It is a process, not a piece of property. To partake in a cultural element is not to loot the source-culture...any more than using a recipe entails looting its originator's kitchen. Sometimes it is commercialized and branded (Hello Kitty); sometimes it is mal-appropriated (the Nazi's vulgar imitation of the swastika); and sometimes it is reified and passed off as one's own (the Christmas tree). Each of these scenarios warrants a different response; and each kind of problem calls for a different solution.

As I hope to have shown, culture is more like a swirling kaleidoscope than a stained-glass window. It is a dynamic; not something that has been set in stone. So purporting to assert what any given culture "REALLY IS" is like beholding the twinkling spectrum of refracting light in a kaleidoscope and trying to discern the "true color" of the pattern. It is no one thing; and it is certainly not static. Put another way: Culture is ongoing synthesis; which means culture is metamorphosis.

What cultural purists fail to understand is that every culture that has ever existed is a hybridization of previous cultures. What we refer to as this or that culture is just a snap-shot in time of an on-going process, where we often pretend—for heuristic purposes—that we are beholding some calcified arrangement with discrete boundaries, which emerged "as is" from the aether. Those of us who are smitten with a given culture imagine it to be a consecrated monolith that might be maintained 'til the end of time. This fanciful thinking is anodyne...until we start begrudging others for not playing along. So we often find ourselves in an imbroglio wherein everyone is inclined to protect their own memetic turf. This is inimical to the cosmopolitan vision. Cultures are not meant to be hoarded; they are meant to be shared.

While Cul-Ap-phobes are busy inventorying memes in an attempt to enforce cultural patrimony, those of us who embrace cosmopolitanism are happily engaging in a resplendent festival of trans-cultural fertilization. It is only natural for cosmopolitans to encourage Cul-Ap...at least insofar as we see something of ourselves in other cultures, and seek to embrace it. This means recognizing the shared humanity that underlies even some of the most foreign cultural elements.

Civilization, it might be said, has been NOTHING BUT one culture appropriating elements of other cultures—ad hoc—in an effort to enhance itself. Decrying Cul-Ap as a social ill would be like decrying foreign ingredients as a culinary sin. When we learn more about other peoples, we learn more about ourselves. For THEY are—after all—other instances of humanity (which is simply to say that they are other versions of US). Hence human solidarity is best realized via inter-cultural exchange. This is ESPECIALLY so when it is the more-privileged adopting—or participating in—the culture of the less-privileged. For the sphere of empathy is broadened by a sharing of ideas. Without cultural diffusion, the Balkanization of mankind would persist indefinitely. It is only with cultural sharing that ethnically-based tribalism can be attenuated; and we can start to see each other more as kindred spirits than as different peoples.

The problem is that we are all—to one degree or another—unwittingly ethno-centric to some degree; as we make sense of the unfamiliar by analogy to the familiar. Alas, we cannot help that the accident of our own environs shapes the lens through which we see the world in which we find ourselves. Much of that lens is formed via an enculturation process we do not fully recognize; as it infuses our daily lives. We no more notice it than the oxygen we inhale. But if we engage in some critical reflection, we realize how myopic we often are when prizing the native over the foreign as a matter of course. The best parts of human civilization, it turns out, are not ALL to be found within one's own cultural heritage. Mankind is like a library where, as John Donne put it, "all books lie open to one another." It might be added that nobody OWNS any one of the books.

Even as Cul-Ap-phobes are perfectly fine with PEOPLE FROM different cultures intermixing, the intermixture of the CULTURES THEMSELVES is something that they urge us to rebuke. What they fail to realize is that cultural intermixture is salubrious for the same reasons that miscegenation is salubrious. Maintaining purity in either context is a fool's errand. When it comes to the global meme-sphere, we are all immigrants; and every one of us is entitled to a green card.

At the end of the day, seeing things from the vantage-point of HUMANITY rather than from ETHNICITY is important; but it is easier said than done. Recognizing that mankind is ultimately a commonwealth of kindred spirits sounds all fine and dandy; but acting accordingly is extremely difficult; as it requires us to overcome our baser tribal instincts. We might begin by embracing cultural diffusion...even when it makes us uneasy. For once we look around us, we come to realize that sometimes cultural appropriation is indicative of cultural INFUSION, which is an eventuality to which everyone should be open.

What's the alternative? In addition to the Balkanization of mankind, the demonization of Cul-Ap contributes to the dumbing-down of our own culture; and of EVERY OTHER culture, for that matter; as it discourages people from putting themselves in others' shoes. Cultural segregation is inimical to humanism, as it flouts our shared humanity in favor of a more provincial attitude, whereby we are obliged to remain within our memetic comfort zones and eschew cultural exchange.

How, then, shall we proceed? As a point of departure, we should recall the perspective articulated in the 2nd century B.C. by the Carthaginian playwright, "Publius" Terentius Afer (the African slave better known as "Terence"): "Homo sum, humani nihil a me alienum puto."

Amen.

PART 2:

A Continuation Of Our Critical Analysis

In Part 1, we saw that cultural appropriation (Cul-Ap) and cultural expropriation (Cul-Ex) are not to be confused with one another; as appropriation / adoption and expropriation / exploitation are very different things. We also saw that there are several problems with memetic sequestration. Proclaiming the appropriation of memes from other cultures off-limits not only undermines the cosmopolitan enterprise, it consigns each culture to a condition of permanent stasis and insularity (conditions which render cosmopolitanism untenable). Forbidding Cul-Ap is a mark of parochialism, not of respect.

While Cul-Ap does not always have positive repercussions, more often than not, it does. Going about the mundane activities of our daily lives, we often don't notice the merits of trans-cultural fertilization; or even that it has occurred. Yet if we look deeper, we find that there are more salutary cases than we might realize. When Paul Simon did a collaborative project with Zulu musicians in 1985, a strange thing happened—at least by today's standards. No one accused him of wrongfully "appropriating" African culture. As it happened, "mbaqanga" permeates Simon's landmark album, "Graceland". His trans-cultural effort was lauded by fellow musicians around the globe. Very few people begrudged him for incorporating Zulu music and dance into his repertoire; and—during performances—even donning traditional Zulu garb.

Times have changed. 36 years later, when Gwen Stefani did a collaborative project with Jamaican musicians, Sean Paul and Shenseea, there was an outcry amongst a cadre of pettifoggers. Never mind that Jamaican musicians were actively involved in the project—which was celebrating Jamaican culture. {44} Right on cue, anti-Cul-Ap crusaders feigned indignation. What's going on here?

In considering this juxtaposition of (surprisingly disparate) receptions over such a brief period of time, one wonders what might have happened to alter attitudes toward (what is now often referred to as) "cultural appropriation". Looking back at pop music in the late 20th century, we might ask: Did it matter that Teena Marie was not a Black woman? Her avid fans—overwhelmingly African Americans—were flattered by the adoption of soul in her repertoire. Most took it as tribute to their culture; so she was (almost) never begrudged for some sort of infelicitous "appropriation". In the same vein, we might wonder: Did Country Music fans—who are overwhelmingly White—take exception to the fact that Charley Frank Pride was Black? Barring a segment of those who may have racial biases: No. Why not? He took their favorite musical idiom to wonderful new heights; so his demographic profile was not a salient factor.

Let's review. Before even trying to explicate what "cultural appropriation" is, we might begin by defining what **culture** is. In terms of memetics, culture might be though of as a collection of social norms (customs and beliefs). {17} In other words: It is a regimen of ideals and rituals, as well as the narratives employed to explain them. However, simply listing a series of STYLES (iconography, cuisine, attire, literature, architecture, music, dance, sport, etc.) seems inadequate. More than a set of practices and ideas, culture is a pattern of meaning—a pattern that is made manifest in everyday life. Culture is how we interpret and give meaning to the world in which we find ourselves. It informs what we value. It is how we express ourselves—and how we make sense of things; and—here's the key—do so in a **communal manner**. This includes a shared heritage and a shared vision. A Grand Narrative is a sense-making device, which furnishes us with an etiology (where the in-group came from) and an eschatology (where the in-group is headed), in order to help us orient ourselves in an otherwise bewildering universe. Done communally, participation in such a scheme provides us with a sense of belonging. Tribal narratives create a collective identity, which answers questions like "Who are we?" and "Why are we here?" and "What's the point of it all?" {62}

Naturally, when people at different times and places do this under different circumstances, they end up relating to each other in different ways. Consequently, we can't help but wind up with different cultures. (This outcome is not only inevitable, it is—I would contend—usually quite salubrious.) Since we are all human, we can often relate to how people who are different from us go about doing all this; as we are invariably doing some version of it ourselves. We realize that, while cultures are all rather different, they are all doing **the same kind of thing**. At the end of the day, we're all just interpreting and giving meaning to the world in which we find ourselves; and the WAY we end up doing this is largely a product of some sequence of historical accidents.

In sum: Culture is a mechanism for meaning-making and for social cohesion. It's how human activity can be orchestrated; and how humans make sense of that activity. Being part of the a group—however defined—means participating in a well-defined set of traditions that distinguish the in-group from all out-groups. This involves—implicitly if not explicitly—positing what amounts to memetic ownership: "X defines who WE are; so we lay exclusive claim to X." Accordingly, cultural diffusion is seen by some as a kind of memetic leakage—threatening to dissolve those crucial demarcations; thereby compromising the structural integrity of their consecrated memetic edifice.

In other words: Cul-Ap is believed to jeopardize the parameters of group identity.

Herein lies the rub: We are all engaged in *the same kind of thing*. So the question must be posed: Are these demarcations to be upheld for the rest of eternity? I submit the answer is: NO. Cross-cultural interaction not only helps us learn more about each other, it helps us learn more about ourselves. And, most importantly, it shows us—irrespective of our culture—what it is to simply be human.

Cosmopolitans embrace cultural diffusion because it affords us the opportunity to put ourselves in another's shoes.

So how do we get from this to the reproach: "Gringos making tacos?! How dare you?!" Well, for any marginalized community, defense mechanisms have been built up in order to protect—that is: to preserve—their culture AS SUCH. This is done by maintaining an ever-elusive memetic integrity. Such an endeavor involves establishing clear-cut lines as to where a culture begins and ends. This is, after all, about staking one's claim on what defines one's community as a distinct thing…to be revered and maintained forevermore…AS IS. Little do we realize how quixotic this endeavor really is. As we cannot revere or preserve an amorphous abstraction, we are inclined to posit discrete boundaries…even where those boundaries may not actually exist; then insist that such boundaries should be impermeable. The problem is that such stringent demarcation, and the demand for memetic proprietorship, engenders parochialism.

Insularity is never a good thing, as it makes it far more difficult to relate to anyone outside of the designated in-group. Tribalistic mindsets are soon inculcated, thereby attenuating human solidarity. Lo and behold: This is when "cultural appropriation" becomes a point of contention.

There is an alternative. By adopting a cultural element of another, we are opting to partake in their way of life. We are putting ourselves in their shoes. This is salubrious so long as it is done out of good will; it is deleterious when it is done to demean. So the issue becomes: Is the cultural participation we're witnessing being done in good or bad faith?

An aversion to Cul-Ap seems to be a relatively recent phenomenon; so it's worth asking: From whence does all this disputation come? In **Robin's Zugzwang**, I called out the Regressive "Left" (which, to be clear, is not the REAL "Left") for their errant approach to social (spec. racial) justice. My indictment was directed toward those who masquerade as "Progressive", yet who betray the most fundamental tenets of (genuine) Progressivism—most notably: the ideals of cosmopolitanism.

I am happy to report that the hallmark features of a "Potemkin Progressive" are easy to spot. Such actors are both narcissistic and dogmatic. Many are tribalistic, in which case the narcissism and dogmatism operate at the group level. It is, after all, a combination of collective narcissism and groupthink that undergirds identity politics—the former born of conceit; the latter born of obsequiousness.

Potemkin Progressives are often neurotic; and often adopt (succumb to?) a censorious, puritanical, authoritarian mindset. As a result, this counterfeit version of Progressivism exists at the odious nexus of political correctness and identity politics. The result has been calamitous for "Leftist" politics: the emergence of a brigade of insufferably captious interlocutors…whose primary accomplishment is handing the right wing an endless supply of ammunition to ridicule ACTUAL Progressives. If one were to ever try to sabotage Progressivism from within, instituting a strict regime of p.c. protocols—and a mandate for identitarian (read: tribalistic) thinking—would be the optimal way to do it.

To recap: Political correctness is a patently right-wing phenomenon, characterized as it is by a mindset that is both authoritarian and puritanical. It is, in effect, illiberalism pretending to be liberal. (One might consider p.c. a kind of inverted liberalism with latitudinarian window-dressing.) Given the evidence, we are forced to conclude that those who countenance political correctness are not genuine Progressives; they are imposters.

And so it has gone: The weaponization of etiquette has defined what has come to be an ersatz Progressivism—what with its perfunctory nods to civil rights with a superficially-Progressive veneer. The idea is to put formality over rectitude; so participants in this charade end up policing demotic language instead of focusing on moral principles. By focusing on the personal rather than the institutional, those who weaponize etiquette tend to squander their time and energy grousing over frivolities. They then demand that **everyone else** squander their time and energy as well.

In the midst of all this, genuine Progressives strive to keep our head above water as we await the next deluge of empty gestures from those in power…who are more than happy to play along with the rigamarole dolled out by the impresarios of this ersatz Progressivism; as said rigamarole does nothing to actually challenge incumbent power structures (see the Appendix).

Unfortunately, the program proffered by the Regressive "Left" often passes muster with credulous audiences, who are taken in by its rhetorical flourishes… which seem to vaguely resemble Progressive ideals. It's as if the movement were designed for those anxious about showcasing their "woke" bona fides, thereby proving to the world—and to themselves—that they are "with it". In reality, they are anything but. For, as it turns out, political correctness is entirely performative in nature. Its appeal lay in the hankering to be recognized as one of the good guys; which is to say: it stems from narcissism.

At the end of the day, a regime of political correctness amounts to little more than a pageant of virtue-signaling: a self-ingratiating display that has a tenuous relation to rectitude. (Probity, we should bear in mind, has nothing to do with earning approval from peers.) So instead of civil rights activism, we wind up with a schmaltzy exhibition of token gestures.

Alas, in a nation that has no formidable Progressive party, performative morality often wins the day. Consequently, the stage is set for corporatism-with-a-smile. So long as people are content to participate in said virtue-signaling pageant, the powers that be are willing to play along. However, those who aren't satisfied with merely putting on airs—who dare to stand up to corporate power—are made pariahs. (There's only one thing corporatist Democrats despise more than MAGA: Progressives.) And so it goes: Democratic leaders would much rather stonewall a genuine populist like Bernie Sanders than take a bold stand against [insert corporate interest here]. Indeed, the Democratic party has done far more to quash Progressivism than the G.O.P. could ever dream. (Just ask Nina Turner, Cori Bush, Jamaal Bowman, Jessica Cisneros, or any other p.o.c. who had the gall to promote Progressive policies.)

As I discuss in the Appendix, the diabolically brilliant trick of the MAGA movement (effectively, a Tea Party redux) was to tie the Democrats to the insufferable strain of "Leftist" thought that puts identity politics and political correctness over common-sense solutions. Right-wing pundits were thereby able to frighten the rank and file away from anything that might be associated with the rubric, Progressive—including genuinely populist legislation.

Long story short: The proliferation of ersatz Progressivism has done significant damage to the public discourse in myriad ways; but for the purposes of the present book, we'll focus on the flap about "cultural appropriation". Why the umbrage with memetic transference across (perceived) cultural lines? And from whence does the aversion to Cul-Ap come? To answer this question, let's continue our investigation.

As mentioned, ignorance—and even a smug embrace of that ignorance—is at the root of Cul-Ap-phobia. Whenever hearing Cul-Ap-phobes rail against the "appropriation" of this or that cultural element, one can be quite certain that they do not have a keen grasp of the cultural element that they are talking about; or the history of the culture to which they are referring. One can also be quite certain that they have no genuine interest in learning the history of the culture-in-question, let alone in fostering pluralism. As I hope to show here in Part 2, the rationalization for their grievance is specious; and their attitude is antithetical to cosmopolitan ideals.

In between their paeans to multi-culturalism, Potemkin Progressives are apt to decry any instance of cultural diffusion that is incommensurate with their own sensibilities. The thinking is as follows: "We associate this cultural element with our own ethnic group; therefore nobody else should be allowed to use it." Such conceit only advertises an ignorance of what culture PER SE is; as well as a glib disregard for how any given culture forms (their own or anyone else's).

Meanwhile, those of us who DO understand how culture works should not put up with such nonsense...let alone accede to unreasonable demands to never participate in exogenous cultures. For unless one is a nudist, one is almost certainly engaging in Cul-Ap every time one puts on an article of clothing. Lest one refrain from exhibiting ANY art, and playing ANY music, and eating ANY food, and dancing in ANY way, it is inevitable that Cul-Ap is involved in one's everyday life. We can say the same thing about the culinary arts or architectural / interior design or religious rituals or holiday celebrations or literature or film or countless other things that have become part of this or that culture...anywhere...at any time. Indeed, a concatenation of cultural appropriation is what any given culture IS.

As I have pointed out, we are often heedless of how much any given culture came to be what it now is. Nobody is exempt from being aloof in this way; but we should bear in mind that heedlessness is not the same as insidiousness. Countless people don designer Yankees baseball caps throughout Europe, Africa, the Middle

East, India, and Southeast Asia; and often have no idea what the logo stands for.... or even that it has something to do with that peculiar American sport, baseball. So when a German or Russian or Gujarati or Filipino dons the distinctive cap, he/she is appropriating American iconography in a rather naive way. (The Japanese are a different story, as they are avid baseball fans, so are far more familiar with Major League teams.) What are we to make of phenomena such as this? The vast majority of it is utterly innocuous. Aside from the obvious issues with the profit motive, one of the worst things about globalized commercialization is the rampant commodification of culture. Much of this has to do with exploiting foreign consumers who are simply trying to be hip (read: "Western").

When it comes to the devaluing of culture, commercialization is always a concern. The problem is that some take an aversion to meme-propagation (spec. across cultural lines) too far. Commercialization is not endemic to all cultural diffusion. In an agora roiling with Cul-Ap-phobia, avoiding charges of illicit Cul-Ap requires us to engage in de facto cultural segregation—something that is antithetical to cosmopolitan ideals. While such a measure may curtail instances of Cul-Ap, it is diametrically opposed to ACTUAL multi-culturalism. For in order to prevent that which it deigns to prevent, we are all forced to erect barriers between memetic enclaves.

Commissioners of this dubious municipal ordinance are not seeking to prevent people of different cultures from intermingling; they are simply positing a kind of (strictly circumscribed) collective meme-ownership. What they prescribe is not so much DEMOGRAPHIC Apartheid as it is a kind of SEMIOTIC Apartheid.

What are the consequences of this misguided approach to cultural preservation? Rather than involving the (intentional) segregation of PEOPLE, it involves the (de facto) segregation of behavioral norms. The question arises: How much better is the latter than the former?

Another question: What, exactly does this (de facto) cultural segregation entail in practice? We soon find that it is, effectively, a regulation of deportment based on memetic inheritance. The ordinance amounts to: Indigenous memes only! It's as if by adopting—or temporarily partaking in—a cultural hallmark from outside one's own culture, one is somehow engaging in some sort of meme-embezzlement.

And then the most pressing question: Are those engaging in Cul-Ap somehow "taking advantage of" denizens of the (purported) source-culture? The present book has attempted to show that, in the overwhelming majority of cases, the answer is: no.

So what of instances of Cul-Ap that ARE—arguably—exploitative? Even then, the problem is the exploitation, not the Cul-Ap itself. The fact is that virtually anything can be done with sneering condescension. The key, then, is: What is BEHIND the act? (Indeed, virtually anything can be done in bad faith. If I do X in bad faith, the solution is not to forbid X; the solution is to entreat people to do X in good faith.) To reiterate: When creative exploration of other cultures transmogrifies into creative exploitation, the problem is the EXPLOITATION.

Should Germans feel exploited every time Yo-Yo Ma performs one of Bach's cello suites? Why not? Because there is no exploitation going on; only Cul-Ap.

Cul-Ap-phobes call for a scenario in which each culture stakes its claim on a locus of sanctified memes. These are—by dint of this tacit claim—designated as memes that anyone else is prohibited from adopting, or even participating in. They might be reminded that a hermetically-sealed culture is a culture held in stasis. It seems that those who vilify anyone engaged in Cul-Ap would be content if all the world's cultures were to languish in a state of enforced parochialism. We should bear in mind that the entire point of pluralism is to eschew notions of purity—whether ethnic or cultural.

In reality, forbidding memetic transference between the world's cultures would bring most cultural flourishing to a halt. The fact is that, when it comes to cultural globalization, trans-cultural diffusion is ubiquitous. After all, that's what happens when global human solidarity prevails.

Is the license to partake in a designated cultural element—insofar as the element can be discretely defined—transferable? On who's terms? What would the conditions be for transferring such a license? In positing this ersatz transgression, one is forced to posit collective ownership of a meme (alt. monopoly power over a meme); which is nonsensical.

The constables of meme-sequestration aim to protect the declared inventory of memes like skittish security guards posted at a warehouse that has been put under quarantine. They obdurately insist that each culture—insofar as it can be explicitly demarcated—be cordoned off. Such memetic cordons are necessary, we are notified, lest those of the dominant culture persist in their domination with impunity.

This is a bad idea. Not only does it fetter the lifeblood of culture (to wit: memetic cross-pollination); it exacerbates cleavages—nay, FISSURES—along cultural lines, thereby engendering tribalistic mindsets. This can't help but lead to the fragmentation of a polis based on ENTIRELY ARTIFICIAL (read: un-necessary) boundaries. Put plainly: Segregation of cultures leads to segregation of PEOPLE.

It is an irony that those of us who embrace pluralism are most prone to breach this (fanciful) municipal ordinance. After all, the modus operandi of cosmopolitanism **entails engaging in Cul-Ap as a matter of course**. In fact, it is impossible to be a genuine cosmopolitan without enthusiastically engaging in rampant Cul-Ap at almost every turn.

No pluralistic society has ever been sullied because too many people were at liberty to evaluate—and, if the evaluation turned out to be salutary, to adopt—the fruits of one others' cultures. If only we engaged in MORE cultural appropriation, provincial Americans might start appreciating things like Buddhism and soccer. We might even discuss the issue over a nice, cold yogurt drink—be it "kefir" (the Russian version), "ayran" (the Turkish version), or "lasi" (the Indian version).

The Psychological Dysfunction Underlying Cul-Ap-phobia

Let's begin with a profile on the Cul-Ap-phile. In addition to recognizing universal principles (which transcend any and all tribal divisions), the cosmopolitan opens himself up to the full range of human cultures. This includes a sincere appreciation for all the fruits of human activity…in whatever cultural milieu those fruits might be found. In adopting this orientation toward the world, the cosmopolitan does not prejudge anything according to its tribal affiliation; for he recognizes that, just as humanity itself transcends ethnicity, creative achievement transcends culture; and the MERITS OF those achievements can be assessed on a basis that exists outside any given cultural context. Such an orientation means being receptive to—nay, fascinated by—the new, the different, even the odd and peculiar. For the Cul-Ap-phile, novelty indicates opportunity. He wants to turn the seemingly foreign into the more familiar; as everything that is human is—at root—familiar to him.

However, not everyone adopts this orientation toward the world. For those who have developed a dependency on routine, the prospect of such open-ness is terrifying. Consequently, they cling to the familiar; and—here's the catch—expect everyone else to do the same. (!) Whenever the outsider "tries on for size" a cultural element with which such a person identifies, he views it as a transgression on the part of THE OTHER. It's as if the foreigner had broken an unspoken covenant between all the world's ethnic groups: *stick to your own culture*. (What else is parochialism than finding security exclusively within the memetic horizon of one's own culture? It is also wanting the accoutrements of one's culture only to oneself.)

This cast of mind has dire implications. Those who are beyond the designated cordons are not seen as fellow humans; they are THOSE OTHER PEOPLE. For anyone who views the world in this way, human solidarity (what Marx called "species-being") is anathema. There can be no "citizen of the world", only us and them. In such a world, everyone knows their place.

This in-group / out-group thinking undergirds Cul-Ap-phobia. For only in this way does it make sense to assert "cultural ownership"; and begrudge others for straying from their pre-ordained path.

Naturally, riffing off of something that others take seriously will sometimes be taken as a kind of blithe devaluation. In such cases, the designated culprit's cavalier gesture—BECAUSE it is done cavalierly—is seen as an affront; or perhaps as a sign of indolence. For reasons that should be obvious to most bystanders, perfunctory emulation (the mercurial "just for the fun of it" mimicry that is an entirely self-involved exercise) can be seen as patronizing by those who have sanctified the meme (so see it as exclusively THEIRS). Their perspective is essentially: "We define ourselves by X; whereas you are simply trying X on for size." Hence the participant in Cul-Ap is perceived as condescending. ("It's a triviality for you; but it is very important to US.")

So it is incumbent upon us to hear the grievance: "You're participating in—or temporarily adopting—X just for the heck of it; but X matters a great deal to us!" Shall such disparity in valuation preclude all Cul-Ap? No; for two reasons. First: One party's ability to enjoy the full sanctity of X is not undermined by another party's cavalier treatment of X. (The religious fundamentalist is not stymied in his doctrinal fealty by the casual observer of the same Faith.) Second: In a ham-fisted effort to STYMIE stereotypes, one is forced to base one's grievance on them.

The moral of the story: All members of a society do not define themselves according to the same cultural elements.

It is no secret that some people are insecure about their ethnic identity. Such insecurity manifests in various ways. In a ponderous attempt to address a gnawing sense of besiegement—and thus ameliorate a deep-seated insecurity—they come to see our multi-cultural society not as a learning opportunity, but as an inter-culture turf war where there are winners and losers. In response to this imagined plight, they adopt a "circle the wagons" approach to (what they see as) cultural preservation. Subsequently, the chance for different ethnicities to learn about one another is lost in a vortex of antipathy.

The self-appointed sentinels of ethnic demarcation proclaim with morbid relish the inevitability of ethnic stasis, whereby ethnicity is taken as a tribal signifier rather than a constellation of cherished cultural elements. For those who urge cultural segregation, pluralism requires a **cordoning off** rather than **merging of** ethnic groups—replacing calls for intermixture with calls for ethnic purity. As a consequence of this ill-advised precedent, we are each adjured to mark our territory, and forevermore hold each other at arm's length. A "siege mentality" often ensues.

This has dire repercussions—one of the more perfidious of which is "reverse victimization". Here, the bullies masquerade as victims so as to rationalize their bullying. The trick is, in the midst of one's offensive, to earn sympathy by acting verklempt. This is largely a matter of **projection**; as the idea is to impute to others sins that are actually one's own; and to insist that the REAL injury is incurred by the assailant. Instead of introspection (looking within), participants opt for vilification (lashing out). Anti-Cul-Ap crusaders engage in their own form of tribalism. They then pretend that all their kvetching is simply a call to "respect" those who've been marginalized. Contrary to this claim, their posture is based on tribal chauvinism… though of a different kind from the one against which they so vociferously inveigh.

Reverse victimization is the most weaselly of all underhanded rhetorical tactics. Intellectually, it is of the same caliber as "I know you are, but what am I?" Yet it is remarkably commonplace; so—in some cases—we wind up with bigots accusing civil rights activists of being the REAL bigots; and—in the most extreme cases—those who are supporting terrorism accusing those standing up for human rights of being the REAL terrorists (see Revisionist Zionism; genocide in Palestine). {35} This explains why gas-lighters often accuse those who they are gas-lighting of doing the gaslighting. (They claim to be the victims rather than the perpetrators of the gas-lighting: a textbook case of reverse victimization.) Projection is part and parcel of a siege mentality; as this is how neurosis typically works. {57}

In sociological terms, a "circle the wagons" approach to social interaction makes sense when one feels besieged by THE OTHER. The siege mentality operates on the individual and/or group level, and invariably involves some sort of persecution complex. When singular, the persecution complex is epitomized by paranoid dictators like Kim Jong-il / -un of North Korea. When collective, the persecution complex is epitomized by Revisionist Zionists…who insist they be allowed to get away with anything, no matter how heinous, if it is done in the name of self-preservation. (Hence the right-wing Zionist version of ethno-centric lebensraum. Note that ethno-nationalism is ethno-centricity in its most extreme—and malign—form.)

In addition to a persecution complex (on the individual or group level), narcissists have an unwillingness to apply the same principles to themselves that they apply to others. This is entirely predictably, as when it comes to narcissism, empathy is limited to oneself (or one's own tribe), so could never possible extend to anyone else. For the narcissist, other people have no inherent value. (For those in engaged in collective narcissism, those outside the tribe have no inherent value.) Those who have embraced narcissim at the group level are apt to eschew human solidarity in favor of tribal fealty. Ergo tribalism. Humanism is inimical to narcissism; and vice versa.

And so it goes with Cul-Ap-phobia: Ethnic groups are urged to hold each other in abeyance. As a consequence of this adversarial posture, we are faced with those who are eager to claim "offense" at any instance of cultural **participation**. What are we to make of this ultra-tetchy disposition? It's difficult to make sense of it; but here I will try.

In the noxious wake of the ascendency of political correctness on the putative "Left", some have made a career out of feigning offense. It turns out that gripes about "cultural appropriation" are just another consequence of the same mentality that undergirds every other form of political correctness. (Some degree of neuroticism seems to always be operative. A zealous anti-Cul-Ap crusader could see a peanut-butter and jelly sandwich and cry, "cultural appropriation!")

As with narcissism, reverse victimization can occur at either the individual or group level. When **collective** narcissism is operative, we find that reverse victimization infuses international relations—as is the case with Revisionist Zionists who level bogus charges of anti-Semitism in order to rationalize the suppression of any speech wherein Judeo-fascism is denounced. In this Kafka-esque twist, protesting the slaughter of tens of thousands of innocent civilians is cast as a form of bigotry. (Those committing "defensive" genocide along ethnic lines can then accuse their critics of being the racists. Sadly, such projection often proves effective.)

Whether singular or collective, reverse victimization—and the siege mentality that undergirds it—has all the key features of narcissism. *So the harassers pretend that they are the ones being harassed.* Such a maneuver works in both inter-personal relations and in geo-politics. (For another example of the latter, we might note China's posture vis a vis Japan, Taiwan, and Philippines.) In virtually every case, the bully simply pleads self-defense.

Neuroticism cannot be the entire story. Insecurity manifests itself in other forms—forms we find underlie an aversion to "cultural appropriation". That brings us to (collective) narcissism.

To make sense of Cul-Ap-phobia, it is necessary to assay the psychological underpinnings of both political correctness and identity politics. Doing so requires an understanding of narcissism on both the individual and group level. We might begin with the two basic traits of all narcissists:

They have difficulty with mentalization. This has two ramifications. First, such people are incapable of reflecting CRITICALLY on their own internal mental states. Second, they are incapable of putting themselves in another's shoes. (The only perspective is THEIR perspective.) *This accounts for their lack of empathy; as well as their predilection for acrimony.*

They tend to suffer from some sort of neurosis. This has two ramifications. First, such people see anything that doesn't sit well with them as a personal slight—or even as an attack. Second, they have a delusive estimation of their own righteousness. *This accounts for their friability; and thus their frenetic offense-taking.*

A combination of narcissism and ignorance undergirds all Cul-Ap-phobia, which—like political correctness more generally—is characterized by a sense of entitlement. ("I have a belief about X, and it needs to be validated by everyone I come into contact with. Moreover, I have this hang-up, and THAT TOO needs to be accommodated by everyone I come into contact with.") But narcissism is about far more than being self-centered; it is about being tetchy. In other words: Not only are narcissists delusive; they interpret anything that fails to comport with their expectations as an incursion…even as an ASSAULT. It makes sense, then, that the narcissist's specialty is guilt-tripping. A narcissist is always looking for ammunition to use against anyone who does not play by his/her rules…which, make no mistake, are HIS rules.

Undergirding an obsession with political correctness—so a crucial element of Cul-Ap-phobia—is **vulnerable** narcissism. Rather than (overtly) grandiose, the vulnerable narcissist is irritable, resentful, and passive-aggressive. As all narcissists lift themselves up by putting others down, vulnerable narcissists are apt to engage in reverse victimization. Hence they are self-righteous *while also having a perse-*

cution complex.

Those who go out of their way to be offended often have no (actual) significant problems in their lives…even as they are hell-bent on playing the victim card at every opportunity. For them, the airing of petty grievances is a sport. This has negative repercussions for the rest of us: as, in their fervor to garner sympathy for their phony plight, they divert attention away from those who have legitimate grievances.

Vulnerable narcissists pretend that they are perpetual under siege by a scourge of heinous improprieties—which they demand must cease, lest the world be knocked off its axis. As with any other narcissist, shame is their primary social currency, so they become maestros of the guilt-trip in order to get their way. {34} The insecure self-esteem of the narcissist is predicated on an insatiable craving for perpetual validation from all those around him/her. Any deficiency in validation is seen as a travesty. Says the narcissist to everyone around him/her: "You are obligated to be how I want you to be. If you default on this obligation, I will accuse you of some sort of egregious violation; and apoplexy will likely ensue."

Empathy is a precondition for the cultivation of moral virtue. {53} As self-absorption is endemic to narcissism, the narcissist becomes incapable of probity. So far as the narcissist is concerned, the only value anyone might have is their utility—which is simply to say: others have worth only insofar as they serve the narcissist's purposes. (This is a breach of Kant's Categorical Imperative, whereby every person is to be seen / treated as an end in him/herself; and not as a means only.) The usefulness of others generally comes in the form of validation, but—in the more extreme cases—may come in the form of servility and/or veneration. As such, narcissists have ulterior motives with virtually anything they do and say. (To wit: All that they do / say is designed to bolster their own stature.) For every seemingly gracious word / deed, there is always an angle. Such duplicity stems from a staggering sense of entitlement. Accordingly, narcissists come out of many interactions thinking that they are owed something.

A sense of entitlement involves no genuine self-esteem. Rather, it stems from a need to erect one's self-esteem on the backs of others. "Those in my orbit exist to placate me. If I prefer it, it should be considered GOOD by everyone; if I don't like it, it should be considered BAD by everyone." This leads to: "You shouldn't be allowed to do / say X because X makes me feel uncomfortable." The narcissism here is palpable. For the narcissist takes everything personally, and expects everyone else in the world to cater to his/her sensibilities.

It is in light of these diagnostic criteria that Cul-Ap-phobia becomes an explicable phenomenon. Here, we should bear in mind that Cul-Ap-phobe is a certain breed of p.c.-monger. After all, both exhibit all the hallmarks of narcissism. Moreover, both exhibit tell-tale features of neurosis. Put them together, one we wind up with a singular directive: "You are obligated to enable my neuroses, lest I claim injury." Any given person's subjective state can thus be used as justification for imposing obligations / restrictions on everyone else.

The present book makes the case that, in the spirit of cosmopolitanism, not only is "cultural appropriation" not a bad thing; we should push back against the demands of Cul-Ap-phobes. Indeed, we should push back against anything that is grounded in identity politics or political correctness.

What is the point of standing up to identitarians and p.c.-mongers? Narcissists tend to wither when they are deprived of their supply. They only thrive insofar as everyone around them is an enabler.

It is not merely that identity politics is not required for a Progressive cause to succeed; it's that identity politics works at cross-purposes to a Progressive cause. Case in point: Amidst all its misogyny and devotion to the Catholic Church, Mexico elected a Jewish woman as president. Why? Because she championed the working class—pushing for investment in basic public infrastructure and vital social services. Those who are not bigoted (that is: malignantly tribalistic) tend to pay more attention to ideas than to demographic profiles.

What proponents of identity politics cannot seem to understand is that, though it is perhaps a quick fix for some, such an approach to social justice does nobody any good in the long run. For one focuses primarily on the personal, thereby neglecting the structural. Even as they pay lip-service to pluralism, identitarians end up opting for ethno-centricity instead of human solidarity.

While they fashion themselves as resplendently Progressives, identitarians are, in fact, RE-gressive; as they care nothing for cosmopolitan ideals. Rather than eschew a tribalistic mindset altogether, they simply re-define the terms of tribalism. Passing judgement on people because of their demographic profile is something genuine Progressives would never abide.

Well, then, what about political correctness? I submit that there is no (legitimate) problem that political correctness purports to solve that cannot be solved without it. Using propriety as a cudgel is a way of vilifying those whom one would prefer remain muted. As is the case with other recriminations in the p.c. ambit, the cynical accusation of ransacking another's culture is a matter of guilting people into silence; so that one need not engage them in serious discussion.

The weaponization of etiquette does nothing to foster civil society; it only motivates people to put on airs. For p.c.-mongers, politics is more about presentation than substance; and ethics is rendered performance art. Social injustices persist… even as everyone is obliged to keep up appearances. The p.c.-monger steps onto his giant soapbox and thinks that doing so gives him the moral high ground. He confuses the prominence of his position for a loftiness of principles. To reiterate: political correctness is entirely performative; so has virtually nothing to do with rectitude.

So long as p.c.-mongers and identitarians are allowed to hold sway in our public discourse, they will be given free reign to dictate the terms of social interaction. It is worth bearing in mind that most of these actors are bullies masquerading as victims. (It is also worth bearing in mind that political correct-ness is a tool of puritanical authoritarian minds; identity politics is an outgrowth of a tribalistic mindset.) When this dictatorial approach to social interaction takes the form of Cul-Ap-phobia, the result is invariably a mandate for cultural segregation. In other words: Those who inveigh against Cul-Ap are effectively cultural segregationists. (I could have just as easily subtitled the present book, "The Case Against Cultural Segregation".)

A call for meme sequestration flies in the fact of cosmopolitan ideals. And, as I tried to show in Part 1, taking such a mandate seriously leads to a slew of odd predicaments. Consider culinary practices. Anyone who eats quinoa is subject to accusations of "cultural appropriation" from those claiming Incan ancestry. (Peanut butter? Yep, that's from the Incas too; so that would ALSO be off-limits to virtually everyone on the planet.) And seeing as how hamburgers were invented by Russians during the Renaissance (then brought to England and North America by Germans, who opted to name them after a northern port-city), shall we harangue anyone who isn't either Russian or Anglo-Saxon for serving this popular fare?

Such a stricture may put a damper on many a backyard cook-out.

Some who clearly do not understand what culture IS—or how culture WORKS—have offered half-baked definitions of that dastardly thing, "cultural appropriation". Such definitions typically have something to do with TAKING something called "traditional knowledge" (a nonsensical term if there ever was one) or "cultural expression" without permission. Permission from WHOM, exactly, cannot possibly be specified. Such unauthorized-use-of-meme, we are notified, may include the illegitimate use of an exogenous culture's music, dance, dress, cuisine, folklore, and even LANGUAGE ITSELF.

Wait. Language?

What on Earth could this possibly mean? We should bear in mind that language is part of culture. So we engage in Cul-Ap whenever we make use of a term or phrase from any language that is not the lingua franca of our homeland. (Call it lexical cooptation, something that every vernacular has done since the beginning of speech.) English, for example, is an amalgamation of Norman (i.e. French) and Germanic vernaculars—with an infusion of Vulgar Latin, Koine Greek, and Old English. Lexical cooptation has occurred with virtually every language that has ever existed. So unless one speaks Classical Chinese, Sanskrit, Old Turkic, Avestan, Aramaic / Syriac, Coptic, Koine Greek, Vulgar Latin, Old Norse, or Old Gaelic, one is engaging in Cul-Ap every time one opens one's mouth.

Some Cul-Ap-phobes warn against taking someone else's "cultural knowledge". But how can one "take" knowledge? And what in heaven's name is "CULTURAL knowledge"? Does it mean knowledge ABOUT a particular culture? It cannot possibly mean such a thing, as knowledge of other cultures is a GOOD thing. In any case, as with any other knowledge, when one acquires it, one has not TAKEN it. (Supposing knowledge can be "taken" requires one to traffic in epistemological nonsense.) Knowledge is not a commodity to be bought and sold. More to the point: It is not a commodity; which is to say that it is non-exclusionary / non-rivalrous. (Knowledge is like love: It grows the more that it is given.) What, then, could this queer locution possibly mean?

In hearing about "cultural knowledge", are we to suppose it is possible for a designated "culture" to OWN certain knowledge? If knowledge can be said to BE-

LONG TO a culture, then we are ascribing agency to an abstraction. Are we to suppose that social constructs can have agency? The answer to such questions becomes clear once we realize that one can only oppress / persecute / injure PEOPLE, not memes.

Progress is effected—in part—by allowing new (i.e. foreign) memes to penetrate one's own memetic microcosm. Proponents of an open society ask that people be willing to adopt an exogenous cultural element whenever doing so might—in some way—enhance their own culture. {6} We might note that in an open society, such an eventuality is seen as unproblematic; even serendipitous. After all, cosmopolitanism is predicated on the recognition that one's own culture does not have a monopoly on all the good ideas; and that we are all better off when we embrace each other's attainments.

Yet, then again, we homo sapiens are all tribal animals; so comity across ethnic divides is often easier said than done. In our efforts to transcend our differences, we are always drawn back to our baser instincts by the Siren call of tribalism. By demonizing Cul-Ap, we are given permission to embrace our in-group / out-group biases…and do so in the name of "respecting" those who are not like us. Yet prohibiting those in a more privileged position from making use of memes that originated from within the culture of a marginalized community does nothing to attenuate the marginalization.

Again, it is worth noting the lack of consistency involved when Cul-Ap-phobes become disgruntled over instances of "cultural appropriation". Such disgruntlement may even occur during the Yuletide season. Consider music. Imagine if Austrians became incensed every time non-Germanic Americans sang **Silent Night**; or if Silesians got a bee in their bonnet whenever Americans without East European ancestry sang **O Christmas Tree**. The Irish may as well throw a fit each time a WASP sings **Christmas In Killarney**. (While we're at it, we should ensure that no gringos sing along to **Feliz Navidad** ever again. Heaven forfend WASPs became more acquainted with Latino culture.) Does any of this make the least bit of sense?

Cul-Ap-phobes fail to understand how culture works—both what it is and how any given instance of it comes to be in the first place. {29} Mimesis is as much a part of culture as is novel creation; perhaps more-so. Cultures interact, so memetic transference between cultures is inevitable. Sometimes this involves synthesis with indigenous cultural elements; sometimes, it leads to outright adoption. This is as only as good or bad as the meme in question.

As we've seen, those afflicted with Cul-Ap-phobia interpret cultural participation as a kind of cultural exploitation…or even ***expropriation***. Yes, exploitation exists, and is morally problematic. This is especially the case when it involves political or socio-economic domination (that is: the marginalization of a cultural minority). However, every instance of cultural mimesis between ethnic groups is not exploitative. {26} Nor do alleged cases of "cultural appropriation" necessarily involve marginalizing those who are affiliated with the source culture. In fact, oftentimes, cultural mimesis is a matter of cultural ENRICHMENT—something that stems from human solidarity. (Friendly neighborhood reminder: Human solidarity is a good thing.) In the 1960's, few Japanese had compunctions when Americans started performing "Ue o Muite Aruko" (renamed "Sukiyaki"); and few Brasilians had compunctions when Americans started performing "Garota de Ipanema" (otherwise known as "Girl From Imanema"). Why? They understood that even hackneyed American renditions of their songs were a tribute to—not a mockery of—their cultural contributions.

It is worth acknowledging the existence of shoddy cultural imitation. Unfortunately, Cul-Ap sometimes involves a cheapening of the source culture—as with pu pu platters, chimichangas, and Olive Garden. (Food always offers a great illustration.) Such botched emulation is typically not done out of malice. Rather, it is the result of commercialization run amok. (Most of us don't complain, as—oftentimes—such bungled offerings are quite delicious.) Whether faux Chinese, Tex-Mex, or a hokey simulation of Italian dining, profit is often prioritized over fidelity. The pervasiveness of a hyper-consumerist mentality inures us to such things. Indeed, hyper-consumerism has made most of us indifferent to the commercialization of world culture. This would indicate that out-of-control commercial culture is the problem, not memetic transference across ethnic lines. Such occurrences should make us wary of a societal phenomenon that the Frankfurt School dubbed the "culture industry". {42}

The majority of memetic virality has been due to sincere cultural appreciation; but some of it has been due to the predominance of commercial interests (that is: memetic propagation driven by the profit motive). Admittedly, parsing the positive from the negative is not always straight-forward. But when appreciation is misconstrued as exploitation, we open ourselves up to Cul-Ap-phobia.

We have mentioned a few cases in which Cul-Ap may not have been entirely approved by the wider source-culture. But in some cases, the Cul-Ap is not approved by the wider DESTINATION culture—as with, say, Soviet-era Russians adopting things like blue-jeans and rock music (staples of capitalism—and rebelliousness—from the "West"). Here, there was no power imbalance; there was just a cultural—nay, geo-political—disjuncture; creating a zeitgeist of alterity. In such scenarios, one culture is obliged to hold the other in abeyance—typically for political reasons. Such alterity is unhealthy, as it is usually not limited to exogenous cultural elements; it translates into bigotry (that is: prejudice against THE OTHER based on a systematically-inculcated negative stigmatization).

In evaluating the inter-penetration of cultures, it is prudent to set aside the effect of commercial enterprises. After all, America has exported many things for largely commercial purposes—not always for the better (see mega-churches and fast food chains). Felicitously, though, memetic propagation (a.k.a. cultural diffusion) is not always deleterious. Aside from regrettable instances like Pentecostalism, Facebook, and soda, the U.S. has exported some salutary cultural elements—including jazz, the integrated circuit, and ranch dressing. By interfacing with indigenous sensibilities around the world, such cultural exports have had some happy results. (In Brasil, Jazz gave us bossa nova; in Japan, the integrated circuit gave us Nintendo; and in Mexico, ranch dressing gave us green chili ranch dip.)

It is indubitable that cultural hegemony has had mixed results. Yes, America gave the world basketball and maple syrup; but—alas—it also gave the world cryptocurrency and Scientology. The U.S. is not the only culprit in this respect; there are other guilty parties. Austria gave us Mozart, but it also gave us free-market fundamentalism. France gave us Voltaire, but it also gave us post-modernism. Britain gave us Darwin, but it also gave us tabloid news. {36}

The mother of all mixed blessings has been the internet (thanks to DARPA-net), something that has arguably had more global impact than even the printing press. Some of that influence on all the world's cultures has been salubrious; some of it has been highly dysfunctional. Over the course of the past two decades, expediency, cost, and ease of global communication has skyrocketed. Yet, during that same period, much of social media has become a fetid cesspool of cockamamie ideas and misinformation. When not encountering an endless litany of kvetching, sniping, and mindless invective, many of us spend untold hours wading through celebrity gossip, right-wing propaganda, and other memetic sludge. The balance of social media content is primarily vacuous verbiage and idle banter (a.k.a. "chatting"). {61} In this roiling see in toxicity and inanity, rare is the moment that we encounter a snippet of erudition. {37} In the absence of a thorough understanding of the causes of the social injustices we see all around us, we often end up grasping onto whatever grievance seems to give voice to our plight. The demonization of Cul-Ap accounts for one of those grievances. And, as we've seen, that demonization involves treating appropriation as if it were some sort of IMPOSITION. So let's look a bit more into cultural imposition (Cul-Imp).

The imposition of memes is a problem only insofar as it is a symptom of INSTITUTIONAL (governmental and/or corporate) domination. (This is, after all, how social engineering works.) Problems arise when the propagation of culture is a matter of IMPOSITION (i.e. one group wielding power over another group). This is not the scenario described by "cultural appropriation". Cul-Ap could never possibly be the explanation for oppression / exploitation. So to blame Cul-Ap for structural inequality (or for systemic socio-economic injustices) is to miss what makes oppression oppressive and exploitation exploitative. Gringos cannot possibly oppress Mexicans by eating tacos.

Characterizing Cul-Ap and Cul-Imp is to see incorporation as a means to some sort of HEGEMONY. This is, of course, wrong-headed. The upshot is: Insofar as the promulgation of memes is NOT a function of hegemonic designs, it is not problematic—at least, not in the way anti-Cul-Ap crusaders contend. (Sometimes meme propagation IS problematic; but usually because there is a problem with the MEME.)

There are, of course, legitimate concerns about power asymmetries; as, in any given interaction, such asymmetries often translate to leverage; and leverage is often abused by those in an advantageous position. But it is disingenuous to conflate isolated cases of cultural imposition with cultural erasure. The former can be benign; the latter is always malign. Yet Cul-Ap-phobes would have us believe that whenever one ethnic group adopts a cultural element of another ethnic group, something insidious is afoot...at least when those with more privilege are the adopters and those of the source-culture are marginalized.

In the midst of the putrid vestiges of Jim Crowe in contemporary America, there is one thing of which we can be certain: That soul food is a confluence of myriad cultural influences poses no problem for Afro-American culture.

This goes for children's fare as well as for ethnic cuisine. When G.I. Joe incorporated characters inspired by ninja (Snake-eyes, Storm Shadow, and Jinx), was it derogatory toward Japan's bushido legacy? How about when Marvel Comics introduced Elektra and Silver Samurai? How about when DC Comics introduced Katana and Lady Shiva? As it turns out, the Japanese didn't mind in the least. Why not? Such just-for-fun caricatures of the ninja are not sullying Japanese culture. While it is unfortunate that most Westerners are unfamiliar with the history of bushido (and samurai) culture, nobody is being harmed by content that presents such figures for wide audiences.

While Cul-Ap-phobia is—in large part—the result of ignorance, it is also indicative of skewed priorities. When people are being oppressed, the problem isn't about who's using which memes. To fixate on the adoption of cultural elements in the midst of egregious social injustices is to lose the plot. Memetic transference that might occur in tandem with oppression isn't the problem when there is oppression; it's the OPPRESSION that's the problem. Grousing about gringos serving tacos while Mexican Americans are still enduring discrimination (and facing barriers-to-entry that still exist due to systemic racism) ensures that we will be distracted from society's most pressing problems.

What about famous leitmotifs? Consider the fabled Last Supper—made famous by Leonardo Da Vinci. Surely the well-known painting was based on that final evening, when Jesus gathered his disciples for the Passover feast, right? Nope. Like the early impresarios of Christian lore, Da Vinci was riffing off of a Thracian set-piece that was almost **two thousand** years old—notably: oriented around the god-man, Zalmoxis. (This is described in book four of Herodotus' "Histories"; chapter 95. That was in the 6th century B.C.) Zalmoxis convened a final supper and promised his followers immortality...on behalf of the godhead, Zibel-thi[o]urdos (later Romanized as "Jupiter Urius" by the Chalcedonians). Okay, then. So was THAT original? Nope. The Thracians had appropriated this leitmotif from the ancient Greeks. Zalmoxis, it turns out, was a riff off of **Dionysus**. Known for his commemorative feasts, the Dionysian tradition also inspired several other cultures—from the Dacian "Derzelas" to the Roman "Bacchus"...as well as lore around "Gebeleixis" [alt. "Nebeleizis"] of the Getae. Similar traditions even occurred in Mithra-ism.

Never mind that the men (and woman) depicted in Da Vinci's painting are fair-skinned Europeans garbed in 15th-century attire, gathered in a structure reminiscent of Renaissance Italian architecture. And never mind that the table is set with glass-wear (which would not have been used in 1st-century Palestine). Da Vinci didn't even attempt to make his portrayal resemble a seder conducted by Palestinian Jews during the Second Temple Period. Why not? Well, he was simply re-jiggering an IDEA…in a manner that would resonate with his (Roman Catholic) target audience.

Bottom line: Portrayals of the so-called "Last Supper"—Da Vinci's or anyone else's—are derived from antecedent Greco-Roman (read: pagan) lore. Asserting that the Last Supper is unique to Christianity betrays an ignorance of Christian history.

Declaration of a favorite meme as inherent to a desired time and place is born of conceit. Playing along with such exaltation involves a grave misunderstanding of history; and of how culture works. (It seems the only thing we've learned from history is that most people learn nothing from history.) For those who are taken in by the trappings of ethno-centricity, it turns out the owl of Minerva has cataracts and a broken wing. (Sacred histories are designed to ensure that we view the past through an astigmatic lens.) To justify erroneous claims of cultural ownership, there is always recourse to a "just so story", a custom-tailored narrative that conjures a past that explains the present.

Cul-Ap-phobia is based on a similar myopia. It comes as no surprise, then, that Cul-Ap-phobes become apoplectic the moment they see someone who isn't a member of their ethnic group making use of a meme that they view as a signature feature of their ethnicity; with ORIGINS IN their ethnic tradition. In other words, the meme-in-question is—rightly or wrongly—seen as a cornerstone of their cultural identity; so others' use of it is seen as some sort of trespass. Here, a kind of cultural "ownership" is posited, whereby anyone else's use of it is seen as illicit. ("X is ours now; so we'll assume X has never been anyone else's. Therefore nobody else has a right to X going forward.") It's as if an I.P. for social norms was somehow written in the stars.

This misapprehension stems from a misunderstanding of how culture IN GENERAL works; and of how any given culture—as it currently exists—came to be in the first place. In spite of this, Cul-Ap-phobes persist in their crusade to rid the world of all memetic transference across (perceived) cultural lines. Those duped into joining this cause misconstrue being placated for being empowered.

Affinities

What makes mankind so fascinating is not merely is resplendent variety, it is its commonalities. Even as homo sapiens are wonderfully diverse, it is helpful to discern an underlying human nature; as it reveals that which we all have in common. Anthropology, critical history, and evolutionary psychology all help to shed light on that which transcends ethnicity and culture. As it turns out, certain things (e.g. common courtesy, common sense, moral principles, kin- and kith-ship ties, romantic love, etc.) transcend cultural differences. Pascal Boyer enumerated the universals of human civilization in his landmark work, **Religion Explained**. Such cultural elements can be found in all epochs, amongst all peoples. As such, they attest to the universality of human nature. Tribalistic mindsets impede this endeavor.

While the ancient Greeks spoke of "agape" (universal love), the ancient Stoics spoke of "oikeiosis" (universal affinity). Both were seen as the basis for all moral acts, as the goal is to expand our sphere of empathy—beyond our kin, beyond our kith, beyond our "ethnos" or nation—to all mankind. In other words: Our humanity is the ultimate basis for morality. (What is the opposite of "oikeiosis"? Alterity. Alienation. Abeyance.) In the grand scheme of things, nobody is INHERENTLY a foreigner; as we are all fellow humans. People are only foreign to one another insofar as they are differently habituated due to a series of historical accidents.

Of course, not all affinities are universal. After all, any given person—as a unique entity—has his/her own tastes and sensibilities. Be that as it may, we can all strive to embrace our shared humanity. Our resplendent diversity does not preclude global solidarity. The key is to not be constrained by our tribal affiliations. Affinities, we find, are far more powerful than ethnicities; and often override such demarcations.

But wait. A world where there are no insiders and outsiders? Are these some pie-in-the-sky musings from a starry-eyed idealist? Perhaps. But that doesn't mean we can't use it as our North Star in our everyday life.

Cosmopolitanism asks us—ALL of us—to view society as what Kant called a Kingdom of Ends, whereby we treat all humans as inherently valuable; so recognize the folly of tribal chauvinism ("This is solely for us!") and of exploitative practices ("We lay claim to that as well, even if it was yours.") Cosmopolitanism also asks us to venture outside of our comfort zones and explore the world—exposing ourselves to all that it might have to offer. We soon realize that quibbling over the proper ownership of cultural elements only hampers our ability to foster human solidarity. (I explore this point further in "The Global Pantry".)

An aversion to Cul-Ap involves a kind of in-group bias whereby one correlates affinities with group identity. Here, a proclaimed locus of affinities is taken to demarcate the boundary conditions for the in-group. But there is a snafu in such thinking. For the existence of trans-cultural affinities countermands this (tribal) arrangement. Such shared affinities are seen—by those with a tribalistic mindset—as a kind of betrayal; as ALL affinities are presumed to be a precondition for--even synonymous with--group identity. As a consequence of such errant thinking, there is a correspondence between affinity bias and in-group bias. This is simply to say that these two biases lead people to the same erroneous suppositions; so it all seems to work out. {29}

Under these circumstances, tribalism (of one form or another) seems to make perfect sense: *"This is something WE do; not something YOU do."* So when affinities breach these boundaries, the mechanism for such biases short-circuits. (Note the fear of memetic leakage mentioned earlier—an eventuality that threatens to dissolve the ethnic demarcations on which the group's on-going identity depends.) Hence those who are apt to cry "cultural appropriation!" at any instance of meme-adoption by one ethnic group from another. Such people fail to recognize a simple fact: *Affinities do NOT necessarily correlate with ethnicities.* For, at the end of the day, affinities are not merely functions of enculturation, they reflect something much deeper: a universal human nature.

Only those wed to a tribalistic (spec. an ethno-centric) mindset are apt to see cultural diffusion as something that jeopardizes the parameters of group identity. Hence the Cul-Ap-phobe's insistence that "[insert cultural element here] is something that ONLY WE do." The implication here is: "If anyone else does it; it is to be taken as a slight against us."

Cul-Ap-phobes don't take into account the undeniable power of social / cultural affinities, which--as a consequence of human nature--transcend tribal demarcations. So when they see anyone adopting exogenous cultural elements, it disrupts the scheme by which they discern who's who in a world of wavering identities. In a well-ordered world in which everyone knows their place, and everything has its role in the (purported) "natural order" of things, any discordance will be met with suspicion.

In trying to make sense of such eventualities, we should bear in mind that affinities play a significant role in the emergence of the specific social norms that define any given ethnicity. It's why, for example, so few African Americans are professional swimmers and skiers; why East Asian families prize community over individuality; and why Parisians often come off as snooty. The willingness to disregard this factor shows how racial quotas are a wrongheaded way to address racial injustice. {59}

Taking a prohibition against Cul-Ap to its logical conclusion prompts some unpleasant questions. Shall Levantine Arabs become incensed whenever Ashkenazi Jews—a Turkic / Slavic / Germanic people of Eastern Europe—eat hummus? (If so, we've got a lot of scolding to do.) Yes, Israelis appropriated the savory dish from the indigenous (Arab) population; and that's perfectly fine. What ISN'T fine is the brutal occupation, violent persecution, and indiscriminate slaughter of Palestinian civilians. In addition to the obvious matter of humanitarian atrocities, what's the key difference? One can steal land and property, but not cultural elements. Yes, the theocratic ethno-State, "Israel" has been oppressing and slaughtering Palestinians for the last two generations; but snacking on hummus has had no role to play in their ongoing crimes against humanity.

It would seem that if a liberal, pluralistic society is truly our goal, then there are more prudent ways to handle cultural interaction. As Audre Lorde put it: "It is not our differences that divide us. It is our inability to recognize, accept, and celebrate those differences." Beyond an embrace of diversity, cosmopolitanism is rooted in a celebration of our shared humanity. This amounts to what is effectively cultural xeno-***philia***. Cul-Ap-phobia, on the other hand, prevents us from seeing the humanity in other people; precluding any recognition that cultures meld and ramify over time.

A vibrant culture is a DYNAMIC culture. Indeed, such melding is often synergistic. (My favorite example: The wondrous merging of Hellenic, Persian, and Indian cultures to form the Kushan Empire comes to mind.) We might bear in mind that for any system, dynamism is a sign of vitality, whereas stasis is presage to deterioration.

Cultures merge; but they also diverge…and recombine in surprising ways. Migration patterns are never pre-determined. What determines the metamorphosis of any given culture is largely a matter of historical accident—that is: a matter of geopolitical developments and (conditioned) social affinities. This point is crucial: The history of culture is essentially a record of cultures merging and diverging; coalescing and fragmenting. The question is: Are we to begrudge those who participate in this ongoing process?

We live in tumultuous times. Tribalistic mindsets are more operative than ever; and ethno-centricity is as severe as it's ever been. With so much resentment seething beneath the surface, it's no wonder many end up lashing out in self-defeating ways. When inter-ethnic animus is fomenting beneath the surface, an anti-Cul-Ap crusade is an enticing—yet ultimately counterproductive—way to vent (see the Appendix). Wherefore? We all like to think that the hallmark features of our own group were written in the stars. Little do we often realize that we—like everyone else—are largely defined by a concatenation of historical accidents. How any given culture forms is not fore-ordained. Such indeterminacy is part of what makes culture so fascinating: It is open-ended; and pregnant with possibility. So to describe "cultural appropriation" is to simply describe HOW CULTURE WORKS.

With regards to cultural exchange (whether organic or forced), we might proceed according to a simple maxim: It is not about what was done in past; it is about what we do going forward. Here's the catch: So long as we are guided by human solidarity, multi-culturalism is conducive to the classical liberal tradition. This requires that we recognize that certain things ***categorically transcend*** culture and ethnicity; which is to say that such things are not a byproduct of circumstance. (Contrary to the core dogma of post-modernism, not everything under the sun is a psychical / social construct.)

Losing sight of our shared humanity brings us down a dark road—whereby our basest tribal instincts take over. A civil society is a cohesive society. Contrived indignation over memetic transference across (ostensive) cultural lines only sows division; and requires one to pretend that cultural diffusion is not how culture NORMALLY works. The thinking here is quite simple: Certain memes are to be treated as signature features of tribal identity; and that's that. To transgress this arrangement is to upset what is seen as the natural order of things--thereby throwing a wrench into the tribalists' sense-making machinery.

What's the alternative? The espousal of multi-culturalism is based on cosmopolitanism qua universalism, NOT on cultural—or any kind of—relativism. Cosmopolitanism is upheld by recognizing universal moral principles; so has nothing to do with identity politics or any other depraved touchstone of the Regressive "Left". This entails a rejection of post-modernist mumbo-jumbo. (The right wing's failed assault on cosmopolitan ideals is illustrated by their fumbling attempt to equate multi-culturalism with cultural relativism—thereby associating cosmopolitanism with relativism.) {38} Progressivism dies whenever it attempts to ground itself in relativism (that is: epistemic anarchy) instead of universalism (that is: moral and epistemological common ground). The former requires no intellectual integrity; the latter requires NOTHING BUT intellectual integrity.

Of the post-War epidemic of relativism in America's political and cultural sphere, Isaac Asimov once noted: "There is a cult of ignorance in the U.S. [which stems from] "a strain of anti-intellectualism." He said that such obsequious thinking was "nurtured by the false notion that 'democracy' means that my ignorance is as good as your knowledge." The "anyone's 'take' is just as good as anyone else's" approach to public discourse is not only irresponsible, it is the epitome of cowardice. Relativism does not help us combat tribalism; it only enables more of it. It also invites us to resort to arguments from authority, whereby we ascribe credence to a claim based primarily—or solely—on its affiliation with a given source (in this case, an identity group). Here, credibility is tied to ethnicity; so each group "owns" is proprietary version of the truth. {55}

We must be careful about caring WHO is "right". The key is to not care about the identity of who is right, but rather about what is (objectively) right; and who happens to be saying it. The moment we pretend that credibility is a function of one's demographic profile, we devolve into an interminable ruckus of epistemic bedlam.

Cultural relativism needn't play any role in a pluralistic society. It is a fundamental mistake to conflate multi-culturalism (a noble ideal) with cultural relativism (lots of pedantic balderdash)…or, for that matter, with ANY form of relativism—moral, epistemological, or otherwise. Cultural relativism—like any other kind of relativism—requires one to ignore the fact that there are (categorically) universal principles; and that certain things TRANSCEND culture.

Stating that something is part of someone's culture is not to exempt it from all judgement. Civic responsibility demands that we ascertain which memes most conduce to the kind of society to which we all—as fellow humans—aspire. This attains irrespective of whether the meme is from our own or another's culture. What we want to avoid is cultural chauvinism: the idea that certain memes are better simply because they happen to come from a certain (i.e. our own) culture.

We cannot pick the culture we were born into; but we can choose what we do with that culture. There has never existed a culture that was pre-ordained; or a person that is tied by some ethereal cosmic decree to this or that culture. The idea, then, is NOT to compare cultures wholesale, as if any given culture was destined to be as it came to be. Rather, it is to compare analogous memes—on a case-by-case basis—on their own merits (rather than according to the culture with which they happen to be affiliated by historical accident). In doing so, it helps to bear in mind that there is nothing inevitable—or ineluctable—about the designated culture. It also means recognizing that certain affinities are HUMAN affinities, not merely ETHNIC affinities.

Many Anti-Cul-Ap crusaders seem to be oblivious to this. Standing atop their soapboxes, they have an occluded view of the memetic landscape around them… even as it makes it easier for them to talk down their nose at the rest of us. They refuse to look into the history of a meme; and tend not to care about history IN GENERAL. Such nescience enables them to look at cultural exigencies TODAY, and assume things have always been this way. (Cornrows? Yep, they've been an Afro-American staple since the beginning of the universe!) This is erroneous. For it turns out that we all have a shared nature. (Consider sing-alongs. While it began in Kobe, more than only Nihon-jin enjoy kara-oke[sutora]. Tell Filipinos going to a KTV bar that they are pilfering from the Japanese, and one will be met with shoulder-shrugs.) Some affinities transcend ethnicity because they are a reflection of our universal (human) nature. Therefore we must cease using delimited affinities as a condition for forging human bonds and as a criterion for constraining cultural participation.

More On Narcissism (Individual and Collective)

In ***Robin's Zugzwang***, I discussed how the average American is fed up with the shenanigans of the Regressive "Left". Both political correctness and identity politics have left a bad taste in the mouths of those who might otherwise be open to supporting Progressive policies. Exasperated as many Americans are by the absurdity of ersatz Progressivism, we have seen a migration to the political RIGHT by those who feel lost at sea—abandoned by a so-called "Left" that has jettisoned populism and replaced it with a regime of onerous semantic protocols.

The degree of pettiness with which these gripes are leveled seems to know no bounds. One of the latest proclamations: "non-" is no longer a prefix; it is to now be treated as a new word. Why? Well, you see, some gender non-binary pseudo-activists insist that the HYPHEN in "non-binary" is a sign of bigotry; so it must be treated as two separate words. (Everyone is required to alter the rules of grammar to appease ME.) People are suffering and dying every day due to social injustices; but what we need to do is stop hyphenating the word 'non-binary'. (!)

Wonder why so many are off-put by "Progressivism"? There's your answer. (Memo to all sane people: There is a lot of REAL oppression in the world, and hyphenated words have nothing to do with it.) The point is to see the humanity in those who are androgynous (that is: who's gender identity is neither overtly feminine nor overtly masculine); so to treat them with the full dignity of any other person. Spending our time on frivolous matters does nothing to help those who are marginalized. Being picayune is not a sign of rectitude; it is a sign of pettiness.

We must be wary of the narcissistic tendencies that lurk within all of us. When unchecked, it is tempting to think: "I don't like when people say / do X; therefore X must be WRONG. Consequently, nobody should be allowed to say / do X." This is, of course, the modus operandi of the narcissist.

Alas, rather than pay attention to things that actually have a bearing on civil society, anti-Cul-Ap crusaders insist that we kvetch about the existence of hyphens in hyphenated words. Obsession over formality takes precedence over the concern for morality.

Meanwhile, it's worth bearing in mind that speech codes are blasphemy laws by another name. A society does not inhibit dysfunction by being hyper-censorious; as doing so merely obliges malefactors to MASK their problematic thinking / behavior. Piety is not morality; it is merely a way to keep up appearances in order to stay in the good graces of the powers that be.

While hyphen-gate illustrates the lunacy of political correctness, the question remains: From whence does Cul-Ap-phobia come? Surely decrying "cultural appropriation" is more than just a matter of priggishness.

When taking everything personally, people are more likely to construe anything that fails to support our self-image as a personal attack. This often leads to acrimony; as churlish-ness is always just one step away from tetchy-ness. Indeed, people with frangible constitutions are highly prone to an authoritarian mindset; so are as likely to be petulant as they are to be skittish. How so? Those who lose sovereignty over their own psyche are heavily inclined to need to control their environs (so as to ensure nothing around them disrupts their fragile psychical homeostasis). (Put simply: They are unable to control themselves, so they try to control everyone else.) Hence the common, "HE was the school shooter? But he was always so timid and reclusive!"

Narcissists are unwilling to honor other people's sovereignty over their own lives; they feel entitled to dictate how others think / behave; as they expect the world to bend to their will. If something does not suit them, then it is deemed a threat. To what? To their fragile homeostasis. A frangible constitution is the opposite of the equanimity (as championed by the Ancient Stoics); so is incommensurate with rational thought. This is precisely what lies at the root of political correctness in all its forms—including Cul-Ap-phobia. Neuroticism is, after all, the opposite of mental discipline. {53}

A tetchy disposition can occur not only on the individual level, but on the group level. Those who have been swept up in the fervor of identity politics are often driven by a hunger for tribal retribution rather than by a yearning for human solidarity. Anti-Cul-Ap crusaders—like others who are seized by the identitarian mindset—are looking for a reckoning. They see this as an effective way to promote social justice. But is it?

Not only does narcissism impair our critical faculties; it inhibits our ability to empathize. Civic-mindedness is not based in contentiousness (on either the individual or group level); it is impelled by global empathy—what the ancient Greeks called "agape". For social justice is distributive, not retributive. The idea, then, is to expand our sphere of empathy to the rest of mankind. The identitarian mindset—especially when married with vindictiveness—can only sabotage this noble enterprise, pitting identity group against identity group in a zero-sum game. So, instead of distributive justice (for all), anti-Cul-Ap crusaders opt for retributive justice (directed across ethnic lines). Such resentment invariably leads to self-destructive thinking / behavior. Participants are adjured to enter into any given encounter with an adversarial posture. Interactions between ethnic groups is seen more as a confrontation than as an opportunity. Equanimity is tossed to the wind.

But there's more to Cul-Ap-phobia than neuroses and resentments. This peculiar disposition also stems from a delusive worldview. Many p.c.-mongers and identitarians fashion themselves as experts on matters of which they know little or nothing about. So it goes with Cul-Ap-phobes, who are quick to anoint themselves authorities of ethnicity (simply for having read something on social media—or watched a couple brief videos—about one or another topic). So some knuckle-heads claim that HOOP EARRINGS are uniquely African; and that therefore—in the U.S.—only African Americans should wear them. This is, of course, bonkers. Going back to the Bronze Age, the Egyptians and Sumerians / Assyrians donned hoop earrings. Through the Iron Age, Persians and Greeks donned them. Through Classical Antiquity, the Romans and Goths did as well. And throughout the Middle Ages, so did Celtic, Nordic, Slavic, Turkic, Syriac / Arab, and Indic peoples. Chinese? Yep. Japanese? Yep. Siamese? Yep. In fact, one would be hard-pressed to find an ethnicity that DIDN'T use hoop earrings. {3} Yet the towering conceit of Cul-Ap-phobia is revealed here: "The history of a designated custom began only when WE started doing it. So from here on out, only WE get to do it." {11}

What happens when we apply this onerous precedent elsewhere? Well, the world is on notice: Henceforth, only Croats can wear neckties. (In the 1660's, the French adopted THAT sartorial practice from Croatian fashion; then the Brits got in on the action.) And while we're at it, no more eye-liner or mascara! Why not? Well, you see, the ancient Egyptians were using kohl for eye-enhancement 6,000 years ago. Unless you seek to bring back the society of the Pharaohs, you are doing that ancient culture a disservice by engaging in such cosmetic practices. So why aren't Anti-Cul-Ap crusaders handing out cease-and-desist orders left and right to women shopping at Sephora?

Once more, we see that the logic of anti-Cul-Ap starts to crumble when it is universally applied.

Other Cul-Ap-phobes simply appeal to their own personal impressions of how things are (and preferences for how things should be); as if their own "take" should somehow be the final word on the matter. Little do they realize: Their so-called "lived experience" no more makes them an authority on a subject than admiring my neighbor's hydrangeas last weekend makes me a botanist. (Or were they bougainvilleas?) Conflation of Truth with a given party's truth-claims is a matter of epistemic relativism. Treating one's own personal impressions as objective reality (a.k.a. Reality) is a matter of epistemic narcissism.

We will discuss narcissism later. Here, let's address the role of delusive thinking; as many have misapprehensions about their own heritage. This is due—in part—to the fact that "sacred histories" are embellished historiographies—largely comprised of made-to-order tales—that is: bespoke accounts that are more self-serving than historically accurate. (Those who are LEAST educated on the history of the Levant are the majority of Israeli civilians, who have been fed nothing but outlandish Zionist mythology since childhood.) Alas, ethno-centricity has a strong allure; and dogmatism has its own momentum…for both psychological reasons (path dependency) and social reasons (the need to maintain homeostasis). Such momentum is drastically augmented in cases where it stems from a sanctified dogmatic system. That's why religions maintain such a hold on the minds of supplicants. (One might say that dogmatism has inertia.) As a result, consecrated balderdash is—generally speaking—difficult to dislodge from the minds of hidebound ideologues. Add false certainty and false pride into the mix (always factors when tribal chauvinism is afoot), and disabusing oneself of misconceptions becomes a Sisyphean task.

With Cul-Ap-phobia, this is what we are often up against.

This challenge is compounded by the fact that we are often dealing with those who go out of their way to be offended. As already mentioned, p.c.-mongers make offense-taking their vocation. For those looking for an excuse—any excuse—to claim "offense", there's not much that can be done to assuage their disgruntlement. (Those who are determined to be offended will always find a way.) Trying to appease such bad-faith actors only fuels their narcissism, and encourages more captious-ness. (Grievance farming has become a booming business; and can be extremely lucrative for its most adept practitioners.) Narcissists expect the world to hew to their personal expectations; and they will quickly become verklempt should anyone fail to abide by their demands. And, as mentioned earlier, a tell-tale sign of narcissism is being very, very, very easily offended. ("How dare you do / say anything that *I* find unsettling?") It is from this mentality that we get the chimerical "right not to be offended" propounded by p.c.-mongers.

Those who embrace cosmopolitan ideals rebuff anyone who is calling for meme-sequestration along ethnic lines. In a twist of irony, it is often those same people who endorse race- and/or gender-swapping for the sake of "representation"—as with, say, making Black elves and Latino dwarves in fantasy films in a bumbling effort to enfranchise people of color in the real world. When French game-maker, Ubisoft decided to make the protagonist of their new Assassin's Creed a Black samurai ("Because…won't that help the world's oppressed Black people?"), the world could hear the collective slap of a hundred million Nihon-jin as they face-palmed.

In many cases, altering the demographic profile of classic characters in the name of "diversity" amounts to a kind of cultural vandalism. Such stunts do nothing to empower marginalized communities; and only end up annoying the majority of people. This goes for gender as well as race. {40} Rather than abetting the cause for a truly pluralistic society, such oleaginous posturing undermines it.

When's the last time you heard an anti-Cul-Ap crusader point out the instances of cultural vandalism mentioned in the present book? {56} Bad-faith interlocutors are too busy making unreasonable demands for meme-sequestration to notice the ACTUAL problems with cultural tampering.

People who understand how culture works—and who know the first thing about history—will recognize the demonization of Cul-Ap to be woefully misguided. For in our day-to-day existence, we swim in a sea of appropriated cultural elements—which is simply to say that we exist in a culture that was created by myriad instances of cultural appropriation. It's not that we merely tolerate Cul-Ap in our daily lives; it's that we are completely immersed in it—for better or for worse. It is the proverbial air we breath—and integral part of the social ecosystem in which we operate.

Yet anti-Cul-Ap crusaders insist that memetic transference between ethnic groups somehow undermines any effort to foster equity. Progressives worth their salt are willing to stand up to this gaggle of virtue-signaling grifters, who only succeed in shooting an otherwise noble cause in the foot with a bazooka.

It is worth reiterating: The prevalence of Cul-Ap-phobia is a reminder that Potemkin Progressives' stock-in-trade is moral preening. Non-p.o.c. are expected to grovel in submission to—rather than join in a common purpose with—p.o.c. As they divide their time between pandering and shunning (depending on the target audience), Cul-Ap-phobes end up turning people away from Progressive ideals.

To echo the thesis of **Robin's Zugzwang**: Pandering has no role to play in civil rights activism. Want to help a marginalized community? Don't patronize them. Want to get people to sympathize with one's message? A shaming campaign will probably not win over hearts and minds. Alas, virtue-signaling and shunning are the primary tools of the p.c.-monger. Potemkin Progressives deftly alternate between pearl-clutching and finger-wagging with psycho-neurotic ambidexterity. As they peacock, they deploy condemnation with reckless abandon. And when they engage in identity politics, they do so along demographic lines. For, in their eyes, disparaging certain people based on their demographic profile is the best way to give marginalized communities a leg up.

Here, we should weigh in on the ubiquitous use of "community" in modern parlance. In most cases, the term does not refer to an actual community; it refers to a POPULATION. For instance, when one uses the term "marginalized community" (however defined), one is—in almost all cases—actually referring to a marginalized *population* (however defined)…which is, itself, typically not a distinct community. An actual *community* is a socially-cohesive group of people, which is often multi-faceted (that is: encompassing myriad demographic categories). Meanwhile, a population—defined in terms of a given demographic category—rarely correlates with a single community. Populations are often geographically dispersed, and—rather than falling entirely within a singular community—are scattered amongst different communities. Those communities form as a result of various factors—ranging from geographical proximity to shared customs (within a given context)… or even a shared socio-economic status (ritzy neighborhoods vs. impoverished neighborhoods). There is often a uniform propagation of memes throughout a given community (which is, after all, part of what makes a community a community). However, memetic propagation (that is: cultural diffusion) is not necessarily uniform throughout an entire population.

Within any given population, there may be communal bonds based on certain affinities (which are sometimes the result of a shared demographic profile); but this, in and of itself, does not entail a community. The prime example of this phenomenon is a global ethnic diaspora: a single population that has ramified into various communities as it has dispersed around the world, settling in the midst of indigenous cultural environs. Sephardim in Morocco are not part of the same community as Ashkenazim on Manhattan's upper West Side…even as they are both part of Beth Israel.

In sum: Population is a way of categorizing people; community is a description of social interactions. The former is a way people conceptualize one another in the abstract; the latter is an arrangement that arises from conditions "on the ground". Tribalism (a program based on rigid in-group / out-group distinctions) arises when people strive to bring the latter into alignment with the former (such that there are separate protocols for treating insiders and outsiders) as a matter of course (and often via coercion).

The upshot of this is that the routine usage of "community" in contemporary discourse is somewhat misleading…in that it is often used in lieu of "population". There is a fundamental difference; and it is an important distinction to recognize in public discourse.

Take for example the "Transgender community" (or even the broader "LGBTQ community"). These are populations, not literal communities. In other words, there is not one "Trans community"; there are many communities that include—to varying degrees—Trans people within them. While there may be Trans *social groups*, such groups are embedded within wider communities—none of which are synonymous with the Trans population at large. So we should speak of the Trans POPULATION, not the "Trans community".

The same goes for the "African American community" (an obvious misnomer) and, for that matter, the characterization of any other ethnic group as a "community". America has an [insert ethnic designation] population; but it is not one "[insert ethnic designation] community". Even something as specific as, say, the "Black gay community" is rarely a singular community.

Think of it this way: A community can stand in solidarity; and a population may stand in solidarity; and these two solidarities do not necessarily coincide; nor do such solidarities occur for the same reasons. Populations have factions, each of which has its own interests / agendas. For example, wealthy White gay men often do not commiserate with poor Black gay men. Even as they may all come together in common cause (gay pride), they are often not part of the same *community*. Indeed, racism exists within the gay population…even as homophobia exists within the African American population. Cross-cutting social cleavages within a population entail disparate communities. Demographic categories do not tell the whole story.

With this in mind, we see that the working class is a population in some respects, though a community in others; yet while WASPs are a population, they are certainly not a monolithic community (contrast Harvard square with Appalachia). Meanwhile, we might talk about the bird-watching, scuba-diving, or stamp-collecting community…along with, say, Red Sox nation or Wisconsin Cheese-heads. To what degree communal bonds are salient varies from case to case…even amongst WASPs. It makes no sense to evaluate a culture wholesale—as if it were some unified bloc with clear-cut edges. Yet anti-Cul-Ap crusaders are forced to pretend that cultures are static, with discrete boundaries; and thus definable in concrete ways.

It may be too late to alter the phraseology from "X community" to "X population" in all relevant contexts, but it is important to recognize that the use of "community" in such phrases is often imprecise. I point this out because, unlike entire populations, communities are palpable social entities—each of which has in common a set of social norms / practices (folklore, customs), which exist along with shared concerns, values, legacies, and aspirations. As such, memetics applies to communities more than to populations.

The upshot of all this is that, in everyday life, CULTURE pertains more to a given ***community*** than it does to any given ***population***. While the vast majority of African Americans may share a palpable resonance with, say, soul food, those memes—or any memes—do not propagate uniformly amongst the entire African American population. Why not? Said population is comprised of different communities, each of which has formed due to a unique set of historical contingencies. Certain memes resonate with some communities more than others, which is why those memes are more / less prevalent in different social circles WITHIN that population. Hence the formation of different communities. To disregard this is to miss how and why memes propagate between groups of people.

The proliferation of memes is mostly a matter of epidemiology. Memetic propagation (read: cultural diffusion) follows certain trends, depending on the memetic ecosystem in which each meme is created and transmitted. Said ecosystem determines the virality and trajectory of any given meme. We needn't engage in vector calculus to see how this works; we need only consider the Grand Narrative—what post-modernists dub the "meta-narrative"—that is recognized by the community-at-hand. One doesn't have to take the divergence of the gradient of the curl of a memetic flow to calculate which memes will prevail; as there are only two variables: catchiness and stickiness (that is: how contagious and how memorable any given meme happens to be). {17}

Whatever narrative of the world a community adopts ends up informing the conceptual framework within which it operates. This is the heuristic scheme by which those in the community make sense of things. It is the proverbial lens through which they see the world. Certain memes are more amenable than others, as certain memes fit into the scheme better than others. Virtually everything is couched in those terms.

With regard to causation, there is a recursiveness involved here. The way we think about things impacts the way we talk about things…***and vice versa.*** The positing of CrimeSpeak only hampers our ability to speak candidly, which, in turn, drastically hinders our ability to engage in frank, sober-minded assessment—of ourselves and of others. Policing speech (establishing taboos; limiting expression to what is deemed "acceptable") does nothing to increas the health of a culture.

As social animals, we covet validation from peers, which often leads us to put on airs. Insofar as this is the case, our self-esteem is predicated on how we are perceived by those around us. This is put into overdrive given a culture obsessed with image. The penchant for virtue-signaling—for people of all political stripes—stems from this. This might be thought of as conspicuous consumption—though with memes instead of consumer products. One can telegraph one's stature via the exhibition of tribal signifiers just as much as one can with Coco Chanel. Ethnic identity can be asserted by participating in (i.e. exhibiting) a select bit of cultural heritage…which involves the same socio-psychological mechanisms as broadcasting one's socio-economic status by sporting Ferragamo while driving a Ferrari. In either case, the key is exclusivity. If too many others do it (those outside the "in" club), it will vitiate the semiotic gravity of the signifier. Bentleys are only "cool" if only the socio-economic elite get to have them.

Cultural segregationists proceed according to their baser tribal instincts. Accordingly, they seek to dictate who's entitled to be associated with which cultural elements. Those who transgress the ordained protocols are deemed guilty of "cultural appropriation". Amidst their demands for meme-sequestration, anti-Cul-Ap crusaders end up offering a litany of frivolous grievances—from Scandinavians donning corn-rows to gringos serving tacos.

A sign of how shallow our thinking has become is the daft manner in which certain people articulate themselves. One will notice that some often use a grating style of speech known as "up-talk": an upward tonal inflection at the culmination of an utterance (as if asking a question). Other than simply making the speaker sound ditzy, up-talk is a subtle way to solicit validation…from one moment to the next…whenever engaging in conversation with others. Those who speak in this manner are unsure of whatever it is they are expressing, so are (implicitly) seeking approval at the end of every sentence. Such intonation has the subtext: "I beseech you to validate what I've just said…before I proceed with whatever it is I'm about to say next." Up-talkers (unwittingly) broadcast that they need their interlocutors to show approval of whatever they are saying; as if—with every utterance—their self-esteem is on the line.

The constant craving for validation is indicative of a chronic insecurity. I submit that, so long as this pathology is ascendent, the stage is set for an identitarian mindset; and thus for Cul-Ap-phobia.

To show how earnest they are about what they're conveying, some people will indiscriminately pepper each utterance with linguistic fillers like "seriously" and "literally" (each of which is usually spoken using up-talk, and often involves the opposite of the word's actual meaning). Thus **emphasis** is treated as a surrogate for **gravity**; and **affectation** is treated as a surrogate **sincerity**. Mendacity thereby comes off as audacity; so people ascribe credibility where none exists. Such demotic stylization simulates profundity when there is nothing profound being said.

As a consequence of this mis-calibration, we now live in a nation in which more than a tiny handful of people are so ill-informed and so addled with moral confusion that they can be snookered into voting for a buffoonish con-man (see the Appendix).

Another filler that is sometimes used to seek validation is "…you know [what I'm saying]…" This is an impromptu way for the speaker to check—from one moment to the next—whether or not the interlocutor is ON BOARD with what is being said. (Brits use "yeah?" and the rhetorical "i[s]n'it" at the end of assertions—each of which plays a similar role. Meanwhile, "…di-ba…" plays this role in Tagalog.) Amusingly, such speakers will often insert "…I mean…" as if to remind themselves that they are the authors of their own words ("o sea" plays a similar role in Spanish); and "…honestly…" as if to remind themselves that they should be convinced of whatever it is that they're saying. Statements are often prefaced with "To be honest…" or "To tell the truth…", as if to persuade one's interlocutor that one is worth listening to. {47} Such fillers are the linguistic equivalent of nervous tics; and amount to a plea to "take what I'm saying seriously"…even if the content in no way warrants being taken seriously.

When not simply spouting nonsense, such interlocutors are flooding their interactions with rehearsed talking points and trendy buzz-terms. Listen to the idiotic ramblings of Elon Musk, who—like Donald Trump—can barely make it through a sentence, let alone string together a series of statements into a cogent chain of thought (with anything resembling logical progression).

There are myriad signs that narcissistic thinking now suffuses the public psyche. There are now local news morning shows entitled "Your morning"—so as to leave each viewer with the impression the show is ABOUT YOU. On this count, McDonalds led the way—titling its marketing campaign, "My McDonalds" at the turn of the millennium. Since then, "My…" has been used as a qualifier in countless branding strategies in order to cater to the "it's all about ME" mentality of most consumers. This tracks with the usage of daft phrases like "my truth". It has gotten to the point where many are now unable to mentally process anything that isn't self-centered.

Recent language games reflect the proliferation of narcissism—not just in everyday conversation, but in (ostensibly serious) political discourse. Much of this seems rather mundane, so passes without notice. Nevertheless, subtle changes in phraseology can be quite telling. Consider the commonplace use of "I appreciate you" in lieu of "I appreciate it" when expressing gratitude. Whereas the latter (traditional) phrase pertains to a GESTURE, the former (new) phrase pertains to a PERSON. This transition seems trivial, yet it has interesting subtext: "I want the speaker to express appreciation not for a good deed that I've done, but for WHO I AM."

What's going on here? Many, it seems, are now inclined to make themselves the center of every narrative (see "main character syndrome"). Such people have come to expect others to be thankful not just for what they do, but for the person they fashion themselves to be. Hence the increasing usage of "I appreciate you" instead of "I appreciate it" as a perfunctory expression of gratitude. This may seem trivial; but the upshot of this transition in demotic language is effectively: "It isn't about what I did (on this or that occasion), it needs to be about ME PERSONALLY." Such wording is unwarranted in most situations. If I hold the door open for a stranger, them telling me that they appreciate ME makes little sense; as they appreciate the gesture, not the fact that I exist in the world. (They don't know me; so how could they possibly have an appreciation of me?)

Am I nitpicking here? Perhaps. In contend that this fashionable new locution illustrates how a narcissistic frame of mind has become normalized in everyday speech. Moreover, it diminishes the force of the otherwise profound statement, "I appreciate you"—effectively reducing it to a flippant, "thanks". (The statement that one appreciates another PERSON is far more poignant than simply expressing gratitude for a kind gesture—a distinction that becomes moot when everything is taken personally.) Alas, devaluing the semiotic currency of key terms is the stock-in-trade of p.c.-mongers—as has been done when they equate speech that causes fleeting bouts of discomfiture with "violence" or "assault". In a world where meaning is evanescent, lexical malleability becomes the norm.

Semiotics is, of course, marginally amorphous; but it is now being reduced to something completely vaporous. If words can mean anything, then they mean nothing. But that seems to be the point: Things only mean what I (or you) might want them to mean—at any given time or place—so long as someone finds it suitable. Hence the proliferation of possessive pronouns before "truth" (as if each person was entitled to his/her own version of Truth). {55}

Such semantic dilution is only the tip of the iceberg. There is also a palpably Orwellian engineering of phraseology—a program in which the vernacular is rigged so as to favor the articulation of one sort of thinking over another. There are many examples of semantic dilution—from calling feelings of unease "harm" to calling anything that challenges the tenets of Revisionist Zionism "anti-Semitic". (Being offended is deemed a kind of "injury"; those who are deemed responsible are accused of "assault". Hence what is effectively **semiotic battery** is posited.) Sloppy language enables rent-seekers to pass themselves off as engines of innovation (by conflating wealth *creation* with wealth *extraction*). {57}

The point here is simple: Diminishing the currency of important terms vitiates the semiotic gravity of key terms in our vernacular. Shorn of formal definitions, words and phrases have infinitely amorphous meaning. (Those who are complicit in this may consider heeding the moral of the parable of the boy who cried wolf.) Alas, the debasement of language is often seen as unproblematic so long as it serves an ideological purpose. In a world where we no longer take language seriously, we end up flailing in a lexical miasma. {47}

Many of us have revamped our thinking to accommodate a culture that is being increasingly built around narcissism. Another testament to this intellectually benighted cultural trend is the proliferation of the trendy, new catch-phrase, "lived experience"—invoked whenever a justification for one's position must be conjured out of thin air. (Is there any way to have an experience other than while alive?) Using the most charitable interpretation, "lived experience" refers to one's OWN everyday experience—that is: one's personalized account of simply living in the world, *given who one is*. It is, then, merely an inventory of one's mental content—replete with biases, misapprehensions, misperceptions, misconceptions, etc. (This is to be distinguished from one's "experience" in, say, accounting after having taken the CPA: something that can be assessed objectively.) According to this maximally charitable definition, your "lived experience" is an account of how simply moving through the world AS YOU impacts your psyche. This is all fine and dandy; but THAT is not how the phrase is typically used.

De jure prioritization of "lived experience" is symptomatic of narcissism; and is a recipe for epistemological mayhem. Discursively, it is the ultimate trump card; as recourse to any given person's "lived experience" is treated as a conversation-stopper. It is effectively saying, "You don't know what it's like to be me; so who are you to question what my personal take happens to be? My subjective 'experience' cannot possibly be 'wrong'; so you are not permitted to push back against it." Consequently, any ad hoc invocation of a "lived experience" can be used in any context to curtail further discussion; as nobody can rebut another person's subjective "take". In this sense, the catch-phrase is more an incantation than a justification.

And so it goes: "lived experience" serves as an omni-rationalization for virtually any claim. As it requires no basis in Reality, it can be used by anyone at any time, anywhere, for any reason. The indiscriminate use of this inane locution has recently become commonplace in Regressive "Left" circles. Why? It exempts one from having to back up one's positions with those pesky things known as "facts". This is—in effect—an attempt to elevate personal impressions to the level of empirical evidence. (After all, multi-party corroboration is entirely beside the point when personal impressions are seen as the sole criterion for veracity.) Having invited all comers to participate in such epistemic anarchy, one is at liberty to dwell in one's own universe of pseudo-facts; and then expect all interlocutors to honor those pseudo-facts as inviolable claims. {55}

In discourse, there has never been an instance in which "lived experience" was uttered (when making a valid point) where the speaker could not have simply said, "experience". Appending the "lived" only succeeds in emphasizing that someone was alive during the experience; which is, of course, the only way to actually experience ANYTHING.

Invocation of "lived experience" is effectively saying, "Even if it isn't ACTUALLY true, I feel like it SHOULD be true; and that, my fellow primates, should count for something." The implication is that the world is obligated to honor MY subjective "take" on the matter. "Lack of correlation with Reality is entirely beside the point. You have your 'truth' and I have mine; and that's all there is to it." This essentially serves as a free pass for intellectual dishonesty....which never expires, and can be used for any issue, anywhere, at any time. In practice, "lived experience" is an invitation to indulge in one's own flights of fancy, and to do so in the name of self-affirmation. It thus serves as a license to become unmoored from Reality whenever one finds doing so suitable. "I will not be mollified 'til you honor this assertion." And so it goes: Flights of fancy are treated as statements about the real world. As such, appeal to one's "lived experience" to justify a position epitomizes a sense of entitlement.

The prioritization of subjectivity over objectivity is a recipe for disaster, as it encourages epistemic narcissism. This cast of mind is not just a matter of self-absorption; it entails GLAMORIZED self-absorption. For here, self-absorption is seen as a valiant act; a way of standing up for oneself. Yet this is done at the expense of any concern for equity, which can only be assessed in terms of universal standards. One thereby relinquishes any hope for finding common ground. It is no surprise, then, that the fetishization of personal impressions has led us down a dark road.

We might bear in mind that one is most happy not when one is thinking about "how I feel" (when I'm pleased), but when one is thinking about how others feel (when they're pleased). Fulfillment comes not from what one has managed to do to appease oneself; but from what one has managed to do to benefit the world beyond oneself. This requires taking as a measure far more than one's own satisfaction. By contrast, "lived experience" is entirely about how this or that "sense of things" happens to suit oneself—which is, not coincidentally, the modus operandi of the narcissist. (One might even say that caring loses all meaning if it is limited to just caring about oneself.) "It suits me, and that's all that matters" reflects the attitude of a petulant child, who's purview is limited to his own (oft-erroneous) "lived experience".

In sum: "lived experience" is a way of smuggling subjectivity into discussions about what is ***actually the case***; so the phrase comes in handy in the event that there is no empirical evidence available to support one's desired conclusion. Taken literally, the locution is utterly inane. (Is there any other way to experience something than while living?) Taken seriously, "lived experience" is a license for one to be as divorced from Reality as one wishes…without being called out for being divorced from Reality. This sits well with many. After all, for the relativist, there is no Reality; there is only a bespoke "reality" for you and a bespoke "reality" for me. Beyond that, nothing more can be said.

But what of perspectives? Aren't different vantage points useful?

Well, it depends. Verity is a function of neither appealability nor utility. It is important to listen to marginalized / oppressed people for INFORMATION ABOUT their problems; but we must then heed only well-adjusted, mentally-stable people when trying to figure out solutions. These kinds of people are, of course, not mutually exclusive; yet they are far from one in the same. (The WORST people to provide a candid assessment of the Church of Latter-Day Saints is Mormons. Want to learn about what Scientology is really about; an avid Scientologist is the LAST person one should ask.) Level-headed analysis comes from level-headed people—no matter their demographic profile (that is: so long as they have all relevant information at their disposal).

In the midst of this, we must remain wary of becoming infatuated with our own impressions. People become transfixed by bold statements when they have a vaguely truthful semblance. So they blithely ascribe a chimerical quality to this or that enticing proposition—not because of supporting evidence, but because of an ethereal sense that it is true, or out of a desire for it to be true, or that simply believing X might confer some sort of benefit ("So, hey, I'll just go with X.") Stephen Colbert coined a term for this peculiar phenomenon: "truthiness".

We now live in a post-Truth era, in which it is common for people to operate according to the following protocol: "It feels true to me, therefore I'm going to run with it." (The pragmatic version is: "I find it suitable for my own purposes, therefore I'm going to consider it true FOR ME.") Though staggeringly obtuse, this is often a relatively benign way of thinking about things…until, that is, one then takes it one step further: "…And I expect everyone else to honor this 'truth.'"

I discuss the fetishization of subjectivity in Appendix 2 of **Robin's Zugzwang**. There, I argue that relativism provides the epistemological and moral foundations for both political correctness and identity politics…all while enabling right-wing propaganda to find purchase in the minds of a gormless electorate (see the Appendix to the present book).

We have already talked about the role that neurosis and ignorance play in people's aversion to Cul-Ap. A combination of narcissism and relativism underlies much of the hysteria surrounding Cul-Ap. Indeed, Cul-Ap-phobia requires one to be both self-absorbed and oblivious to—or in complete denial of—universal moral principles. The latter follows from the former.

The exaltation of subjective "experience" feeds into our most narcissistic tendencies; as one can make anything all about one's own feelings on the matter. Hence one is invited to pretend that one's personal take holds the same weight as—**or even more weight than**—hard evidence. After all, who needs facts when we are basing our entire epistemology on sentiment? And who needs substantiation when all anyone is looking for is validation? In this scheme, everything is personal; so "lived experience" is the ultimate standard for legitimacy.

It makes sense, then, that it is no longer enough for others to appreciate my good deeds; I need everyone to appreciate ME. (I am entitled to plaudits simply for being myself.) Hence the use of "I appreciate you" instead of "I appreciate it" whenever the speaker wants to express gratitude for a kind gesture: He/she has been trained to cater to the narcissism of all interlocutors.

As a result of all this, we are admonished to remain within the memetic cordons that have been erected; and to "stay in our own lane", refraining from heterodox expression in the event that a skittish passerby's psychical homeostasis is at stake. (This is effectively the polar opposite of the Stoic ideal envisioned by Seneca the Younger.) We are thereby adjured to vilify anyone who neglects to work around MY—or any given bystander's—peccadillos.

A similar mentality underlies the demand that nobody should be allowed to do / say anything that one finds unsettling. "If it triggers me, the rest of the world must be prohibited from doing it" conveys a sense of entitlement that stems from narcissism. A repercussion of the normalization of narcissism is the incentivization of a hyper-captious disposition. As a matter of course, such a person is apt to catastrophize every bout of discomfiture—as if unease were indicative some sort of internal calamity

We are often stymied by miniature cataclysms of our own making—a point made by the ancient Stoic philosophers. {53} It is not what happens to you, but how you react to it that matters. This crucial point was made by Epictetus almost two thousand years ago. "Our distress does not stem from events themselves, but from our interpretation of them." (Put another way: Offense is taken, not given.) We cannot always control what happens to us; but we can control how we respond. Having sovereignty over our own minds is not only the basis for (Kantian) autonomy; it is the surest antidote to narcissism.

Each of us has the ability to choose how to (mentally) process the things we experience as we contend with an oft-beguiling world. {39} It is a cop-out to always blame bystanders for our own psychical turmoil. This does not let malefactors off the hook; it simply enables us to identify who the malefactors ACTUALLY ARE.

So what of circumstances that elicit distress? In the final analysis, we find that many of those miniature cataclysms are of our own making; and would not exist but for personal idiosyncrasies and hang-ups for which others are not responsible. There is nothing revelatory in pointing out the simple fact that our impressions of things are often as much about our own psychical quirks as they are about the things themselves; as personal impressions are mediated through a mental process that is, after all, quirky in ways that are unique to each person. Always blaming the world for those quirks—and the internal repercussions of those quirks—is not only narcissistic; it is foolhardy.

While considering the p.c.-monger's penchant for catastrophization, we might note the symbiosis between emotional instability and self-absorption. (This explains the concomitance of histrionic personality disorder and narcissistic personality disorder.) It turns out that interminable skittishness is prevalent in a culture that plays into deep-seated insecurities. This leads to needless acrimony; as it is a small step from skittishness (pearl-clutching) to peevishness (finger-wagging). {43}

Given these fraught conditions, every encounter is a skirmish waiting to happen. Honest interlocutors are forced to navigate a veritable mine-field of taboos—each of which is posited in an ad hoc manner in an (oft-vain) effort to appease the adjudicators of good form. While participating in public discourse, we are obliged to walk on eggshells so as not to elicit the ire of the p.c. constabulary. It's as if the agora has been rigged with a lattice-work of incendiary tripwires. Consequently, we all find ourselves perpetually in danger of running athwart of those who have taken it upon themselves to police everyone's speech for minor indiscretions.

In his essay, "The Prevention Of Literature" (written at the end of 1945), George Orwell noted that "even a single taboo can have an all-round crippling effect upon the mind; because there is always the danger that any thought may lead to the forbidden thought." His point is that restrictions on acceptable thinking / language are a slippery slope. We mustn't underestimate the relation between thinking and behavior. Constraining one invariably hinders the other.

Cul-Ap-phobia is the result of a puritanical, authoritarian mindset; though—admittedly—the authoritarianism of political correctness is far more discursive than it is physical. (Instead of a boot on our neck, it is an albatross around our neck.) In an attempt to engage in critical deliberation, we wind up tip-toeing around gratuitous linguistic strictures…while being incessantly pelted from every direction with the latest "woke" buzz-words. It becomes very difficult to conduct serious discourse amidst this relentless barrage of vapid jargon.

A sign that cult activity is afoot is the gratuitous use of insider lingo. Lo and behold, p.c.-mongers have lifted some of their fatuous terminology from New Age vernacular. Consequently, a panoply of inane locutions can be heard whenever cloying theatrics are afoot. (We routinely encounter usage of terms like "empowerment" and "holding space".) To stay in the good graces of the p.c. constabulary, we are expected to treat vacuous verbiage as sage exposition.

In Regressive "Left" circles, a preoccupation with etiquette has only served to distract us from a focus on moral principles. A deontic is impossible when we are concerned with adherence to social norms. Politically, this can leave us with the impression that we are attending to social justice when we are, in fact, doing nothing of the sort. Even as the preponderance of attention is devoted to matters of propriety, a thin veneer of Progressivism is maintained. As a result, we end up obsessing over formality rather than considering basic morality. In the process, we find ourselves facing a new quandary: Who, exactly, shall adjudicate these matters?

Who Are The Arbiters Of Memetic Transference?

The (self-appointed) impresarios of cultural ownership fashion themselves as governors of the memetic ecosystem. They issue edicts with reckless abandon; and do so as if they were simply serving as sentinels of cultural integrity. On what do they base each decree? Their own (dubious) impressions of a chimerical cultural ownership; and beliefs of what everyone else should consider sacrosanct.

When hubris is passed off as something laudable, many are duped into playing along. (Think of those who are foolish enough to allow a pair of grifters to fleece them whilst nibbling on hors d'oeuvres during a **Race2Dinner** session.) Just as race-hustlers sow—then monetize—resentment, anti-Cul-Ap crusaders stoke acrimony rather than foster comity. While the former keeps them in business, the latter would solve the problem off of which they profit. So it is no surprise which of those dispositions they encourage.

Once identity politics takes over, we find ourselves in a world where literally anything can become racially charged. (If a non-p.o.c. passerby smiles at a p.o.c., we are expected to believe that it is racially motivated; if a non-p.o.c. passerby NEGLECTS to smile at a p.o.c., it is a sign of racial bias. Either way, racism MUST be afoot.) The proposed solution to this predicament is to engage in counter-racism—as if one could somehow nullify racial prejudice in one direction by being racially prejudice in the other direction. It is imperative that we recognize the folly of trying to combat racism with racism-in-reverse. (It seems to somehow still escape some that one doesn't fight bigotry by BEING bigoted.) The mistake is to assume a negative feedback loop when one is actually creating a positive feedback loop. Counter-bigotry fuels the original bigotry; as alterity feeds upon alterity.

In the attempt to dampen bigotry, one exacerbates it. For the impresarios of political correctness / identity politics, this is BY DESIGN. (It is predictable that problems will arise when people profit from the problem they purport to be solving.) Antipathy—on both the individual and tribal level—is recursive; which means that it operates as a positive feedback loop. Alterity no more paves the way to comity than inebriation paves the way to sobriety.

The Bacchanalia of virtue-signaling indicative of ersatz Progressivism is intended to obfuscate a complete lack of virtue. This is often accompanied by emotive ejaculation—whether in the form of contrived fluster (pearl-clutching) or contrived indignation (finger-wagging). This phony pathos—sometimes called "bathos"—has parallels in other contexts, whereby over-compensation is employed to elide deficiency. Consider how mediocre singers compensate for their lack of vocal talent with a mawkish stylization known as "cursive singing", whereby a surfeit of maudlin affect is used to make up for the fact that they have limited crooning capabilities. Such gimmickry is obsequious; yet it enables the singer to seem fervent in their delivery of the lyrics. To the untutored ear, such affect comes off as some sort of artistic attainment. {41}

There are many analogies to such over-compensation. {39} In melodramatic novels, overly-flowery language is used in lieu of genuine eloquence to enrapture the reader (think of the "purple prose" in Harlequin romance); bad acting is characterized by the promiscuous use of affect (think of the "over-acting" indicative of telenovelas); artificial flavoring is used in junk food to create the illusion of culinary prowess; and excessive amounts of CGI is used in cinematography to keep the audience bedazzled when there is a deficiency of quality writing. In each case, many cannot tell the difference between authenticity and gimmickry. People are tantalized; and that is treated as a dependable barometer for quality.

It is easy to bamboozle those who are accustomed to cheap satisfaction—something that is entirely subjective, so not to be confused with objective well-being (eudaimonia). The trick is to exploit the desire for titillation…and meet expectations for immediate gratification (a subjective state that is often misconstrued as a boon to well-being). Hence the normalization of shallow thinking. The incessant over-stimulation of our lizard brains has elided this out-of-control problem—creating an ephemeral sense of fulfillment. Such appeal is analogous to a drug-induced dopamine rush. The effect is a ravenous appetite to sustain the "high"; which invariably leads to dependency…and thus addiction.

In an era governed by auto-tune, photo-shop, and other filters, not only are most people unable to tell the difference between artificial and authentic; most people *no longer care* that there is a difference. {42} Phoniness and superficiality are no longer detractions; they have become an attraction. This is the natural consequence of an epistemology in which the distinction between subjectivity and objectivity have become blurred. As we allow ourselves to be hypnotized by spectacle, critical thinking goes to the wayside.

The inability to discern profundity from fatuity paves the way for an orgy of charlatanry. We find ourselves in a world where click-bait governs the public's allocation of its (fragmented) attention. The corporatization of the online world has led to the degeneration of public discourse. Today, any bozo with social-media savvy can find a forum to ply his trade—spewing invective while peddling an endless cavalcade of harebrained theories.

Much of this dysfunction has been exacerbated by our everyday existence—

largely ensconced as it is within an online ecosystem. There has come to exist a (debilitating) positive feedback loop: stunted attention spans begets social media usage...while social media usage begets stunted attention spans. (Consider something like Blackstone-backed "CocoMelon", which is severely impeding children's cognitive development under the guise of keeping them "engaged" and "amused". Frequent jump-cuts train our minds to be averse to sustained focus—as attention flits from one titillating moment to another.) Under such circumstances, impetuosity supplants deliberation. Shallow thinking and mental passivity become the norm; which, by the way, is exactly as the power elite want it. An epidemic of pliable minds entails a population that is much easier to manipulate.

Online, people are looked at, yet never really seen. People talk a lot, yet don't really say much; hear a lot without really listening. Mercurial minds are only willing to process fleeting impressions—moment to moment. Many are now at the mercy of caprice. Authenticity is a moot point when visibility is the sine qua non of online engagement. Instead of fostering meaningful connection, most social media (Facebook, Instagram, Snapchat, Tiktok, Twitch, etc.) fosters anxiety and isolation. People's lives become a stage-managed series of photo-ops rather than organic moments. People are not only alienated from each other; they are alienated from humanity itself—their own and everyone else's. We fixated on appearances rather than substance; presentation over deliberation. On social media, we're posting about everything without truly saying anything; and we're listening to everything without truly hearing anything; and we're looking at countless images without really seeing anything.

With all this superficial connectivity, we get ephemeral social connection without deep human connection. (Some of the most hyper-connected people online are the loneliest people on Earth.) Under such circumstances, insecurity abounds and vapidity reigns supreme. This sets the stage for the social dysfunction we now see all around us. {37}

It is no wonder, then, that so many have succumb to the allure of identity politics. One need only follow the prescribed choreography, no erudition or critical reflection required. Social cachet can be garnered by simply adhering to the catechism du jour. To earn approval from compatriots, one need only stick to the assigned script. (Those who have the temerity to stray from the assigned script are summarily vilified.)

All this has dire consequences for the public discourse. Whenever hearing (what passes for) "debate" on pressing matters, audiences are apt to mistake gotcha-moments for having made a good point; publicity stunts for meaningful acts; snazzy rhetorical gimmickry for scintillating insight. Credulous audiences are apt to misconstrue a smooth delivery of canned statements as oratory prowess. Sophistry is seen as sound argumentation. Catchy platitudes are considered pearls of wisdom. Sensational punditry is confused for serious journalism; stridency for sagacity. The projection of (unearned) confidence is perceived by some as a sign of credibility. Meanwhile, per the Dunning-Kruger effect, confidence is often inversely proportional to erudition: People are convinced they have knowledge of things about which they are completely ignorant. Alas, the combination of confidence and incompetence is sadly commonplace. (In corporate parlance: "upper-management material".) Hence the proliferation of billionaire imbeciles. {21}

In Part 1, we saw how political correctness and identity politics are not only incommensurate with Progressive ideals, they are diametrically opposed to those ideals. This becomes apparent with Cul-Ap-phobia—what with all the hubbub over who "owns" which cultural elements. Where do we draw the line? Blowing out candles on a birthday cake? Thank you, ancient Greeks (a tribute to Artemis). Using ketchup as a condiment? Thank you, Chinese (from the Manchu "koe-chiap"). Making a pinky-swear? Thank you, Japanese (the "yubikiri", coined by the Yakuza). Nobody on Earth sees the adoption of such memes as problematic. Indeed, the memetic origins of MOST customs pass without notice. After all, a group's ethnic identity does not hinge on every one of their customs.

Of course, there's nothing sacred about candles, condiments, and pinky-swears. In some cases, though, a meme is a ***signature feature*** of this or that ethnicity; so is seen as sacrosanct. However, it does not follow from the fact that a certain meme is a source of ethnic pride that nobody of any other ethnicity should ever make use of it in their own lives. Cultural elements have a past and a future, and much of that involves transmission between ethnic groups. (Yuletide traditions weren't always about Christmas; and—for the vast majority of educated people—Christmas is now no longer about Christianity.) As we'll see shortly, what was once sacred may now be quotidian.

Upon a survey of the world's cultural exchanges over time, we find that the integrity of a culture does not require its participants to stake their claim on a particular meme. Maintaining cultural integrity simply requires honesty.

As usual, the problem with parochialism is that groups of people anchor their self-esteem in the esteem accorded to certain cultural elements. Sanctified memes are taken as proxies for DIGNITY. So to critically evaluate those memes, the thinking goes, is to derogate the people who covet them. According to this thinking, sanctified cultural elements are rendered the basis for the humanity of those who do the sacralizing. This is based on a "post hoc ergo propter hoc" mis-step: mistaking what we now happen to associate with WHO WE ARE for something we own. We thereby set ourselves up to be offended.

This is a reminder that with political correctness, everything is taken personally; and, as a consequence, objectivity goes completely out the window. Most p.c.-mongers deign to vanquish the inequities of society with a strict regimen of enforced propriety—as if all the ills of the world were attributable to breaches of etiquette. In doing so, they confuse propriety with probity.

It is one thing to be smitten with etiquette; it is quite another thing to WEAPONIZE etiquette, railing against anyone who refuses to color within the lines. In this daft scheme, good form masquerades as moral principle. The strictures of political correctness are simply blasphemy laws by another name. In fact, the program has all the trappings of cult activity—replete with an Inquisition.

So the question remains: What is one to do in the event that one wants to explore other cultures; and—as it were—try things on for size? It seems that, so long as this is done out of good will, one's primary obligation is to give credit where credit is due. So we come back to the issue of proper attribution. The Hmar invented the bamboo dance…which was soon adopted by the people of Mizoram and Assam. The craft eventually migrated all the way over to northern Luzon (in what is now the Philippines)…though, today, most Filipinos have no idea what its actual origins might be. What are we to make of this? It's not as though Filipinos are exploiting the Hmar people, or intend to disrespect Hmar culture. The adoption of the bamboo dance is simply a reminder that it is important to give credit where credit is due. Reggaeton? While it was popularized by Puerto Ricans, Dominicans, and Cubans, it originated in Panama. Carnival? Best known in Brasil and Colombia; but it originated in Trinidad.

Ok. But what about flubbed attempts to simulate a culture? Surely we might take issue with those who engage in cheap caricatures; or are far too cavalier with others' heritage. Indeed. But botched emulation is not degradation. Rather, it is merely a bumbling attempt to pay homage. While perspicacity is important, a deficit of perspicacity isn't an attack. Even as Anglo-Saxons may bungle Latin American cuisine, the results are—at worst—simply creating mis-impressions about what such cuisine REALLY IS. This is often a consequence of the proliferation of lazy stereotypes in pop culture. Hence the mis-characterization of chimichangas as "Mexican". When most people think of Chinese food, the first things that come to mind are General Tso's chicken and fortune cookies—neither of which is genuinely Chinese. Such misapprehension abounds with several ethnic associations. (Italy? Pasta. Sweden? Meatballs. Netherlands? Windmills. Germany? Lederhosen. Russia? Movie villains. Romania? Vampires. France? Where do we even begin?) As it happens, Netherlands is about more than women in Klederdracht frolicking through fields of tulips; Russia is about more than drinking vodka while playing chess; Jamaica is about more than smoking reefer while listening to reggae; and Scotland is about more than playing bagpipes while wearing a kilt. Yet, for better or worse, these puerile caricatures have taken up residence in the (uncultivated) minds of many Americans.

Appreciating an element of a culture—even in a clumsy way—is not the same as indulging in cheap caricature of that element; and is certainly not the same as DEROGATING that element. Those who prosecute this ersatz transgression fail to see that there is a difference between naively being hokey (trying something on for size, just for the fun of it) and derisively engaging in mockery (demeaning others simply because they are different). Make no mistake: In the midst of all this, ill will DOES exist. It makes sense to decry mockery; as mockery is mean-spirited. Be that as it may, it is worth repeating: There is a fundamental difference between botched emulation and intentional derogation; and an even more fundamental difference between appreciation and exploitation. This difference must be acknowledged if we are to call out instances of ill-will. Looking for Cul-Ap around every corner will not help us make these important distinctions.

Unfortunately, when Cul-Ap-phobes hear about instances of (alleged) "cultural appropriation", their minds immediately jump to some sort of cultural EXPLOITATION. Such thinking is erroneous. When it comes to cheap knock-offs of ethnic markers, the problem is not the adoption of an exogenous cultural element; it's that no sincere appreciation is involved. The issue, then, is attitude. "Hey, look at this! Isn't it amusing / weird," is not so much a case of cultural appropriation as it is simply ***being a jerk***. There is a crucial distinction to be made between a desire to partake in something and a desire to ridicule it.

Even as there is nothing inherently demeaning or exploitative about cultural appropriation, we should be mindful of the fact that virtually ANY act can be done in a way that is demeaning and exploitative. Such contingency does not entail that ALL CASES of the act are iniquitous. (Depending on the social context, smacking a woman on her derriere can be either terribly rude or wonderfully erotic.) We encounter semiotic disparity with many modes of expression—from table manners to physical gestures—***as they exist in different cultural contexts***. (A KKK celebration in the Philippines is different from one in the United States.)

As we saw in Part 1, while a Nazi hakenkreuz and a Hindu swastik[a] have a superficial resemblance, one is reprehensible while the other is beautiful. In other words, even as they are visually similar, there is no semiotic parity whatsoever. How can we be so sure? CONTEXT. Without context, gestures are shorn of all meaning. Case in point: In the vast majority of situations, sneaking up behind people and dumping a large container of ice-water over their heads would be considered one of the rudest things one could possibly do. In American football, though, doing this to the coach of a team that has just won an important game is considered high tribute. Context matters. (Again, consider spankings.) Common sense tells us that effrontery only makes sense after having considered MOTIVES. Just as actions-in-general cannot be understood without taking into account intentions; without factoring for INTENDED meaning, semiotic analysis is senseless.

Alas, when an obsession with formality trumps concerns about morality, common sense takes a back seat, and we lose sight of what truly matters—to wit: whether or not one is coming to an exchange in good faith. (In a world fixated solely on optics, splendid decorum often masks bad faith.) The pre-occupation with "how things appear" (alt. "leaving a good impression") tends to divert our attention from underlying principles.

Elementary semiotic analysis makes plain that, across cultures, superficial resemblances do not necessarily bespeak the same motivations. In fact, one of the many problems with political correctness is that we are all obliged to pretend that such distinctions don't exist. This seems plausible. After all, many of us are inclined to impute our (eminently fallible) personal take on a phrase or gesture to the speaker / actor…as if our subjective states somehow dictated an objective reality for the rest of the world. This is the quintessence of narcissism; and we are all prone to this pitfall.

In evaluating potentially problematic cases of Cul-Ap, it is important to bear in mind that mere participation is neither exploitation or derogation. We are right to be wary of any failure to give marginalized ethnic groups a voice. This is especially so when those groups have been historically oppressed…and are only recently being given recognition as equal members of society. Cul-Ap does not preclude us from pursuing this noble aim. To wit: Trying a meme "on for size" does not deny those in the source-culture a voice. There is nothing wrong with being curious… or inspired…or playful.

There is, of course, a different semiotic protocol for things that are part of a HALLOWED tradition…rather than, well, just part of a given community's general, workaday tradition. When Cul-Ap is done too cavalierly, the adopter accords insufficient gravity to a cultural element that warrants more reverence. So the question remains: How are we to treat memes that are considered SACRED by the source culture?

It is entirely possible to, say, make use of architectural styles from other cultures in respectful ways—whether the Mongolian "yurt" or the Apache "wigwam". Yet there seems to be an additional factor when sanctification is concerned. Consider the migration of the pagoda from Gopala Nepal to Tang China to the Khmer Empire…onward to Dai-Viet, Siam, and Burma; as well as to Goryeo / Joseon and Kamakura Japan. The question arises: To what degree shall we curtail further propagation of the pagoda beyond its role as a consecrated Buddhist structure? This is a difficult question to answer. So long as the intent is not to mock, it would seem that the world is one's oyster.

But the question remains: Is the calculus different when it comes to the sacred? Perhaps. This is especially concerning when exogenous commercial interests are involved. To elucidate what is at issue, let's consider what is arguably the most sacred—and well-known—SYMBOL in human history: the cross. During the past two or three generations, many people who don a crucifix (typically as a talisman affixed to a necklace) are not formally Christian; as least not doctrinally speaking. Of course, devout Christians have traditionally taken this symbol very seriously; yet few are outraged when non-Christians use it as an accessory—that is: for purely aesthetic purposes. Is this particular fashion choice an instance of Cul-Ap? Yes. Is it problematic? Not necessarily. In secular iconography, crosses are now ubiquitous, oftentimes simply due to the fact that many think that they look rather nifty. Piety has nothing to do with it.

A similar thing occurred with the **yin-yang** (appropriated from Buddhist iconography for purely aesthetic reasons) and the **onkara** (the deva-nagari ligature for "om"; appropriated from Hinduism for a variety of spiritual reasons that often have little to do with the source culture). Indeed, sacred symbols sometimes come to be treated as casual accessories, as anyone knows who has donned a *fleur-de-lis* (originally the Frankish symbol for the divine right of kings). So, yes: The Boy Scouts of America are guilty of ripping off the Holy Roman Empire. Shall we be incensed by this?

The moral of the story is that the sacred for some isn't always sacred for everyone. This needn't be a problem. For even hallowed folklore is invariably the product of Cul-Ap. So to eschew Cul-Ap denies the very basis for the culture one deigns to protect. Cul-Ap, it turns out, is generally benign; and oftentimes even salubrious…even when it involves sacred traditions. For EVEN THEN, Cul-Ap was likely how those traditions came to be in the first place.

That's not to say that it's fine to be supercilious when it comes to someone from one ethnic group using a meme that is considered sacred by another ethnic group. It is simply to say that we should modulate our response according to what is most conducive to the commonweal. It makes little sense to be irked by people donning crucifixes…or yin-yangs, or onkaras, or even the occasional fleur-de-lis… for purely cosmetic reasons. This becomes obvious once we recognize that our primary concern should be the (continued) existence of systems of oppression / exploitation / marginalization. Even so, bickering about "cultural appropriation" does absolutely nothing to dismantle iniquitous power structures.

When it comes to the profit motive, nothing is sacred. But appropriation is not the same as commodification. When corporate interests appropriate culture, it is problematic **because of the corporate interests**. When a gringo eats a taco, it's just a matter of someone enjoying a tasty treat that originated in a culture other than his own.

Yes, there is a problem with the commercialization of culture. For when corporate interests are the engine of cultural formation, cultural elements are reduced to mere kitsch. Treating cultural elements as commodities makes a culture ripe for exploitation. We can all agree that consumerism should not be the main driver of cultural engagement. A people's heritage shouldn't be for sale; and the value we place on cultural elements should not be determined by how much we can line our pockets. By putting a price-tag on culture, we cheapen it. {48}

We shouldn't lose site of the fact that there are dubious motives all around us. We must grant the fact that appropriation is ***not always*** a matter of appreciation. If a man who isn't Sikh is donning a Punjabi turban for no reason other than to mock the sartorial practices of Punjabis, we can indict such a person for being a jerk. So, in the event that a non-Sikh opts to don a dastar, we might consider his reasons for doing so. The question must always be posed: What are the motives? To wit: Is it to pay tribute or is it to poke fun?

With this concern in mind, we might ask: Why is it not okay for "Westerners" to display a Siamese Buddha on the mantle-piece of their parlors, yet perfectly fine for Thais to bedeck their shopping malls with Christmas decorations? For Buddhists, the former is sacred; for Christians, the latter is sacred. Yet here we are. After even a cursory survey, we find that the strained logic of Cul-Ap-phobia collapses under the weight of such contradictions.

To reiterate: When adopting an exogenous cultural element, proper attribution is warranted. Virtually everyone agrees that Americans drinking bubble tea and Taiwanese drinking milkshakes is perfectly fine…so long as the cultural origins of each are recognized. Both cultures are better off for having appropriated from one another.

Like most other things, cultural appropriation can be done either scrupulously or unscrupulously. It is therefore important to distinguish between acclaiming and japing; and to always give credit where credit is due. This means cultivating a thorough understanding of the topic before being clocked over the head with the next meme embargo.

Again, we should take note of the selective outrage (read: hypocrisy) involved with anti-Cul-Ap crusades. There is a certain hypocrisy to denouncements of "cultural appropriation"; as we are notified that it is only problematic when OTHERS do it. Anti-Cul-Ap crusaders fail to recognize that one does not indemnify oneself against charges of ethno-centricity by simply claiming a given ethnic identity; nor does anyone's ethnicity exempt them from moral responsibility. The willingness of anti-Cul-Ap crusaders to blithely mis-represent aspects of a culture's heritage—whenever it suits them—attests to the hypocrisy of those same people. {15}

Ok. But what about power asymmetries? Doesn't the DIRECTION of adoption matter? To wit: Isn't there a problem with those with more power make use of the customs cherished by those with less power? Answer: Maybe, but not necessarily. In his book ***Culture And Imperialism***, Edward W. Said addressed cultural IMPOSITION, not cultural appropriation. In the event that imperialism is afoot, Cul-Imp is often done in order to control the narrative; and to establish social norms that are amenable to prevailing power dynamics. By dictating people's ways of thinking and acting, one can ensure their abiding capitulation to incumbent power structures. In sum: Cul-Imp is a method of control—which is to say that it is a means of asserting domination; as it forces others to adopt the practices / mores / dogmas of those in power.

To suppose that Cul-Ap is involved in structural inequalities that exist along racial lines is to show that one does not understand WHY those structural inequalities exist. While it is true that some inequities persist along ethnic cleavages, it is important to stay vigilant of the current interplay between culture and power… which often does not correspond to how thins were in days gone by. Vestiges of past inequalities remain; but present exigencies must be taken into account.

Understanding the interplay between culture and power helps explain how systems of power orchestrate the conditions that serve to maintain that system. In short: Those in power use that power to protect that power. {18} That said, prohibitions against Cul-Ap do nothing to subvert incumbent power structures. (To repeat the example: The problem with the ongoing persecution of Palestinians by Israelis has nothing to do with the fact that the latter eat hummus. Judeo-fascists do a lot of horrific things to Arabs; eating an Arab dish isn't one of them.) It is oppression with which we should have qualms, not any cultural transmission that may have occurred concomitant with said oppression. Regarding a subjugated people adopting the culture of imperialists, one might ask: Does a single Filipino for a moment lament the fact that their country ended up adopting American lingo, American pop music, American cuisine, and American clothing fashion? The mere suggestion is laughable.

When the Spaniards or Americans or Japanese were occupying the Philippines (and routinely massacring innocent civilians), would it have occurred to any Filipino to complain when some of the occupiers / oppressors started snacking on balut? No. Why not? (It turns out anyone can eat a half-formed duck embryo.)

Were there power asymmetries involved in this dynamic? Yes. But shall Cul-Ap be implicated in the iniquities visited upon the indigenous population of the Philippines?

With power invariably comes the abuse thereof. Those in a position to do so can abuse their power in various ways—from marginalization to outright persecution. Another abuse of power might be cultural engineering. But this is not to be confused with the appropriation of elements from the subjugated population's culture—an act that has very little to do with controlling others. Cul-Ap is not Cul-Imp; nor is it necessarily exploitative. Of course concerns about power asymmetries are entirely valid; and should be addressed decisively. Yet none of the problems arising from structural inequalities along ethnic lines are addressed by demonizing Cul-Ap.

So what, then, of the (perfectly valid) concern about imperialism? Imperialistic agents engage in both imposition (ON others) and/or an expropriation (FROM others). This entails the domination / exploitation (OF others). But Cul-Ap does not involve either of these; as it is either a matter of engagement (WITH others)... or of simply leaving others to themselves.

The other form of appropriation IS of concern—namely: that by which one seizes CONTROL OF the object (rather than simply SEIZING it). Yet this has nothing to do with what is often referred to as "cultural appropriation"; as Cul-Ap is no more about **taking control over** than it is about simply **taking**. (Both are forms of expropriation.) For cultural appropriation is merely a matter of cultural participation. It certainly has nothing to do with either controlling or seizing anything. Cul-Ap is about SHARING, not about usurping SOVEREIGNTY.

As discussed, in order to make their indictments seem coherent, Cul-Ap-phobes are forced to construe "participating in" as some kind of "control over". In other words, they view mere participation as some sort of predatory—even hegemonic—activity. To repeat: This involves the confusion of appropriation with expropriation; participation with exploitation.

A sign of the speciousness of the anti-Cul-Ap crusade is the recent emergence of the pejorative, *"culture vulture"*. This inane locution makes it seem as though some sort of predation (read: cultural expropriation) were at issue whenever cultural appropriation occurs. This contentious term is bandied about as though there were dastardly villains scavenging the social landscape—and now, DIGITAL landscape—for cultural elements to seize for their own selfish purposes. What is basically just cultural diffusion is depicted as a kind of strip-mining operation.

In the final analysis, the problem with "cultural imperialism" would be the IMPERIALISM. When unconnected to imperialism, then, cultural globalization is not necessarily a matter of domination / exploitation. When group A adopts a cultural element from group B, A is not dominating / exploiting B. However, Cul-Ap-phobes suppose that the propagation of memes is INHERENTLY imperialistic—as if epidemiology somehow translated to hegemony. This is an utterly spurious proposition.

Antonio Gramsci conceived "hegemony" as the control that those in power wield with impunity over a subdued / marginalized population. He held that this was largely a matter of controlling the *culture*. This should be contrasted with Cul-Ap, which has nothing to do with imposing anything on anyone, or trying to govern their lives (spec. their thinking and behavior). After all, being able to dictate social norms and/or habits of thought translates to the ability to—as Noam Chomsky put it—"manufacture consent" amongst the rabble vis a vis the system of domination / subjugation.

Cul-Ap is about making use of exogenous cultural elements, not wielding control over people. Ironically, it is the Cul-Ap-phobes who design to control others by fiat—issuing permissions from on high as to who is and isn't permitted to participate. They proceed as though being super-duper condescending is the magical tonic for socio-economic elitism.

Bespoke Temporal Framing (A Reprise)

It is worth revisiting the matter of arbitrary timelines—specifically with regard to the complexities of cultural origins, and our proclivity to use self-serving time-frames when positing those origins. As we have seen, proper attribution is not always as straight-forward as the arbiters of cultural transference like to think. In Part 1, we discussed the **terms by which** meme-sequestration is carried out often depends on *where one begins the timeline* (for the cultural element at hand).

Resisting the temptation to employ a self-serving time-frame is no easy thing; as we all have the tendency to delimit our purview to that of our own community (however defined); such that our only concerns are the concerns of the in-group. We are all inclined to espouse one or another "just so" story—an etiological myth that justifies our current positions. In other words: The fracas over the adoption of exogenous cultural elements stems from a temporal conceit…both on the part of the accusers and the accused.

While this misses how cultures form, it is largely attributable to a general lack of awareness of history. Much of the hullabaloo over Cul-Ap has to do with misapprehensions about the origins of a given piece of cultural heritage. Yes, more people should be aware that Elvis Presley's "Hound Dog" was lifted from a Black singer: Big Mama Thornton; and that the rest of his repertoire was made possible by trailblazers like Chuck Berry and Little Richard. Then again, Big Mama Thornton was performing a song that had been composed by…two Jewish men. Where, then, are we to place the alleged memetic contraband?

Elvis' incorporation of an African American idiom does not mean that such musical appropriation is morally dubious. We might note Little Richard's words about Presley: "He was an integrator; he was a blessing; [as he] opened the door for Black music" into the mainstream. As is often the case, cultural transference goes both ways—a fact demonstrated by Black artists like Shaboozey vis a vis country-western. This is a reminder that virtually ALL music is hybridized music.

Cultural transmission is—more often than not—a matter of cultural EN-

RICHMENT. As Little Richard pointed out, memetic transference brings people together. The key, then, is not proscription; it is ***proper attribution***. One of the greatest composers of the 20th century, Keith Jarrett incorporated jazz, blues, gospel, country-western, AND classical into his repertoire. To the observation that he was appropriating musical styles from other traditions, he would likely have said, "You're damn right I am. After all, that's how it works!" (The important thing is that he gave credit where credit was due.) It would have made no sense for the Germans to be irritated that Jarrett sometimes riffed off of Bach.

To the anti-Cul-Ap crusader, we might pose a few questions: When the Catalonian musical artist, Rosalia hybridizes Flamenco and hip-hop, is she engaged in memetic theft from Andalusian Roma and African Americans? How about when Bosnian / Kosovar musical artist, Dua Lipa incorporates disco and R&B into her repertoire? How about when ANYONE engaged in ANY music ANYWHERE, and their influences are not from their own culture?

Ben E. King offers yet another case study. He incorporated Gospel and Latin-American music—as well as classical German orchestration—into his repertoire. Cultural hybridization involves (what is effectively) memetic imbrication—as is the case with creolization (linguistic), syncretism (religious), and "fusion" (both culinary and musical). In other words, such hybridization routinely occurs with languages, creeds, cuisines, and musical idioms—as well as with attire, architecture, folklore, and virtually anything else. This is not a bad thing.

When considering creole languages, syncretic religions, dishes that borrow from exogenous ethnic recipes, and virtually any other form of cultural hybridization, we are reminded that the cordoning of cultures countermands the metamorphosis of which EVERY culture is a manifestation. Cultures are inherently dynamic, not static. They interact with one another in an on-going process of interpenetration—affecting each other along the way. Depending on a variety of factors, influences may be unilateral or reciprocal. In any case, attempting to freeze any given culture at a certain time and place is to betray the very process that made it what it currently is.

As already mentioned, "Christmas" is the end of a long line of cultural appropriation centered around the winter solstice—going back to at least the Roman "Saturnalia". Yet its pagan origins are elided by those who now claim the auspicious occasion as uniquely their own. The same goes for Easter. Indeed, celebrations of the vernal equinox go back to the 2nd millennium B.C. with the Babylonian / Assyrian festival, "Akitu[m]". Another of the oldest versions of this was the Persian (Zoroastrian) "Nowruz". "Zag-muk" [beginning of the year] was a Babylonian festival in December that lasted 12 days. {45} It celebrated the triumph of the godhead, Marduk over the forces of Chaos, symbolized by the aquatic serpent, Tiamat. (Yes: It was originally "the twelve days of Zagmuk"!) Meanwhile, the most important festival for the Etruscans was the "Ambarvalia" in May; and was dedicated to the mother goddess, Dia. In Christendom, the holiday was based on the Roman festivals of "Floralia" (alternately: "Cerealia", a revamped version of "Ambarvalia"). It bears worth repeating: The ROMAN winter solstice celebration included several leitmotifs that were later adopted by Christ-mas-tide revelers…replete with decking the halls with wreathes of evergreen.

Is it that surprising that Christians also adopted pagan practices for their spring equinox celebration (that of their Messiah's re-birth)? Not at all. Throughout ancient times, there were various celebrations of re-birth during spring-tide. In the Hindu Kush, Sindhis celebrate "Chetri Chandra" at springtide. In Ireland, the Gaelic "Beltane" was clebrated throughout the Middle Ages. Yet how many times do we hear Hindus or Druids complaining that Christians are using predominantly pagan rituals in their celebration of their savior-god's revitalization? This is, of course, precisely the point: The fact that bunnies, Easter-egg hunts, and tasty chocolate candies have come to be associated with Pauline soteriology reminds us that memes usually have highly idiosyncratic genealogies.

Never mind Christmas and Easter. Roman Catholicism ITSELF is based almost entirely on pagan traditions. "Ash Wednesday" was a repurposing of the Norse "Day of Odin", where Vikings placed a small smudge of ash on their foreheads to ward off bad fortune. "Lent" has roots in Assyrian tradition, with the forty-day fast dedicated to Damuzid (a.k.a. "Tammuz"). Even Valentine's Day (ostensibly a tribute to the fabled martyr, Valentinus of Terni) has pagan roots. The Roman Catholics—under the direction of Pope Gelasius—appropriated that auspicious occasion from the Roman feast of Lupercalia: a celebration of fecundity (spec. female fertility). And it turns out that EVEN THAT had been appropriated from another culture: the ancient Arcadian festival of Lykaia.

In sum, the only way complaints about Cul-Ap seem to hold water is when we limit our framing…such that the ORIGINS of the meme-in-question are placed precisely where we want them to be on the historical timeline; and NO EARLIER.

Aside from strategically delimited temporal framing, we also tend to constrain our purview to our own ethnic heritage. It bears worth noting that cultural diffusion often occurs in places we don't realize. The tale of Robin Hood is a prime example. This folk-hero was made famous by ballads from the 15th century like "Robyn Hode And The Munke"…as well as various versions of the "Gest" of Robyn Hode. Later, he was dubbed Roger Godberd (the noble vigilante of Sherwood Forest) by some; Robert of Loxley by others; and Fulk Fitz-Warin by still others. All those were all English versions of the folklore; and they may or may not have been based on an actual person.

The tale is a timeless one: A noble thief takes from the rich and gives to the poor. But where, exactly, did this idea originate? It's hard to say. Who might have taken it from whom? It's hard to say. The idea clearly has universal resonance, so may well have emerged in different cultures spontaneously; which is to say: independently (that is: not due to memetic transference). The appeal of this story is understandable: A philanthropic mercenary mets out economic justice--righting wrongs in an unjust society. Vigilante justice is a universal theme; as attested by the proliferation of this familiar plot.

Around the world, there ended up being…

a *French* version: Louis Mandrin

a *Scottish* version: Robert Roy MacGregor

an *Irish* version: Redmond O'Hanlon

a *Dutch* version: Kobus van der Schlossen

a *German* version: Johannes Buckler (a.k.a. "Schinderhannes")

an *Estonian* version: Rummu Jüri

a *Lithuanian* version: Tadas Blinda

a *Slovak / Polish* version: Juraj Janosik

a *Russian / Cossack* version: Stepan Timofeyevich Razin (a.k.a. "Stenka")

a *Georgian* version: Koba

an *Abkhazian* version: Abrskil

a *Ukrainian* version: Ustym Yakymovych Karmalyuk (as well as a Yiddish variation: Hershel of Ostropol)

a *Bulgarian* version: Hitar Petar (the Macedonian variation of whom was Itar Pejo of Mariovo)

a *Romanian* version: Iancu Jianu

a *Turkic* version: Koroghlu

an *Ottoman Turkish* version: Hekimoglu Ibrahim

a *Tamil* version: Koose Muniswami Veerappan

a *Sinhalese* version: Deekirkevage Saradiel

a *Chinese* version: Song Jiang

a *Japanese* version: Ishikawa Goemon (a.k.a. "Gorokizu"; as well as Nezumi Kozo, inspired by the legendary figure, Nakamura Jirokichi of Edo)

a *Korean* version: Hong Gil-dong (loosely based on the historical figure, Im Kkeok of Yangju)

a *Swahili* version: Fumo Liyonga

a *Mexican* version: Jesus Malverde as well as Joaquin Murrieta Carrillo

...to mention examples from two dozen cultures. Some of these tales were based on real people (though partially apocryphal); some of them were entirely fictional. It is, of course, entirely possible that a few of these tales emerged independently of the others; especially when they were inspired by historical figures. However, in other instances, the tale as it came to exist in one culture was likely an adaptation from another culture's version. (Great idea. Let's make our own version of that.) {19}

In any case, over the centuries, this well-known theme has clearly transcended cultural differences; as it resonates with all people, regardless of ethnic sensibilities. Wherefore? The tale says something about our shared humanity. Indeed, it is a legend that speaks to us...even if we need to couch it in terms of our own cultural heritage. So—like other themes with universal resonance—the Robin Hood theme has an appeal for ALL homo sapiens, irrespective of geography, era, or culture. The question arises: Was it an objectionable thing in the cases where one culture may have adopted the theme from another culture—adapting it to their own sensibilities and making it their own?

This would be a rather strange indictment.

When we regard instances of cultural diffusion, we might ask: In the cases of folkloric cribbing, who cribbed from whom? This might be historically interesting, but it is morally irrelevant. Sometimes mythemes emerge in different places / times independently; sometimes they are coopted from exogenous sources. Either way, insofar as any given motif qualifies as a mytheme, there is something about it that resonates with all humans—be it a rags-to-riches story or a holy trinity.

Robin Hood is a reminder that in most cases, the result of Cul-Ap has been salutary. Moreover, the myriad incarnations of this legendary figure illustrates that there does not exist any meme that is INHERENTLY part of a singular meme-plex–that is: inscribed on a particular culture for all eternity. Memes know no such exclusivity.

There are no more cultural essences than there are racial essences. There are only trends within social groups; just as there are only phenotypic tendencies / pre-dispositions within haplo-groups. And there is no necessary correlation between a given cultural element and a certain ethnic group. Such correlations were not written in the stars.

Alas, misconceptions about cherished cultural elements abound. During one of my sojourns overseas, a Scandinavian man expressed befuddlement when I mentioned that some Black people in the United States would have qualms with his corn-rows. Upon stating (correctly) that his ancestors had been donning that particular hair-style for much longer than African Americans' ancestors, I notified him that many Americans didn't know much about the Vikings beyond the apocryphal horned hats and row-boats adorned with wooden shields. This was a stark reminder that demands for cultural segregation (meme-sequestration along ethnic lines) are predicated on ignorance. (Alas, priggishness and nescience often go hand in hand.) We discussed the fact that corn-rows, Bantu knots, AND dreadlocks actually go back to Pharaonic Egypt…and continued to proliferate through centuries of Greco-Roman culture. {11}

I told the Scandinavian that I shared his dismay; then notified him that, in the United States and Great Britain, there are certain people who go out of their way to be offended by something—ANYTHING—that might get them some attention. The "trick", I explained, is to pretend that by grousing about such matters, they somehow give succor to those who have been historically disenfranchised. Upon hearing this, the Scandinavian was understandably flabbergasted. He was morbidly curious, so inquired: What other frivolous grievances exist (regarding the purported outrages of "cultural appropriation")? I mentioned White girls wearing hoop earrings and anyone who isn't Japanese making sushi. He was aghast that anyone might have compunctions with such things. We agreed that such grievances aren't a matter of civil rights activism; it is idiocy. (I bid him adieu, and was reassured that writing the present book was a good idea.)

There are, of course, legitimate concerns about MIS-representation. But there is nothing *inherently* dishonest about adopting an exogenous cultural element. The Brits got the Waltz from the Viennese; and the Spaniards got the fandango from the

Moors; yet neither Austrians nor Andalusian Arabs seem to be bothered. (One must wonder: Do even CUBANS want only Cubans dancing the salsa?) According to anti-Cul-Ap crusaders, such cultural transmission is a kind of annexation—as if adoption was tantamount to expropriation. Some use the pejorative, "culture vultures" to deride the alleged culprits of this imagined transgression. But Cul-Ap is not a matter of picking at dead flesh; it is a matter of harvesting the ripe fruits of human activity…and SHARING them. Adopting an exogenous cultural element is not a matter of predation.

Never mind that. Anti-Cul-Ap crusaders insist that "cultural appropriation" be seen as a kind of resource-extraction. They thus characterize Cul-Ap as some sort of HEIST. As such, the adoption of exogenous cultural elements is seen as a grave social injustice in every feasible scenario. What they fail to consider is where such unwarranted compunction leads when taken to its logical conclusion.

If we hew to the (contorted) logic undergirding calls for cultural segregation, whenever Marshall Mathers (a.k.a. "Eminem"), Nora Lum (a.k.a. "Awkwafina"), or Audrey Chu (a.k.a. "Nuna"), they are guilty of some sort of sin. (That would go for Harry "Mack" McKenzie as well.) When Jamie Oliver makes Jamaican cuisine, he is guilty as well. To the extent that a puritanical, authoritarian mindset is given a sheen of Progressivism, such claims come to seem plausible to biddable audiences. But to reasonable people, such grievances are just plain absurd.

Alas, in spite of all this, Cul-Ap-phobia continues. But WHY? Across the U.S. and the U.K, grievance-harvesting has become somewhat of a cottage industry; and a surefire way to get lots of attention online. In terms of social aggrandizement, it has proven to be a bonanza for clout-chasers. The rest of us are urged to heed their admonitions. Accordingly, the masses are told that, while we need to get to work on promoting social justice, we can't make any REAL headway unless we prevent anyone who isn't Brazilian from doing the Samba. We're also asked to believe that a non-Argentine teaching Tango classes or a non-Cuban teaching Rumba classes is somehow an infringement on the respective source-cultures. (And don't forget: To be for queer rights, one must now be against hyphens!)

This is what being utterly ridiculous looks like.

Such derangement seems to have no limits. I once heard a commentator say that the "fade" (haircut) was invented by African Americans. (The "fade" goes back to at least 1855, when Serbian barber, Nikola Bizumić invented adjustable hair-clippers. Leo Wahl patented electric hair-clippers—with variable-length attachments—in 1919.) The "fade" works on any hair—a fact demonstrated by soldiers at every military base on the planet. Not finished with his tirade, said commentator then stated that a crowd swaying back and forth—at, say, a sporting event—is somehow uniquely Black. Therefore non-Black audiences should refrain from doing so. (He seems to have had in mind a distinct swaying style that became popular in 2009 with the song, Swag Surfin'.) Conclusion: Black people invented swaying; so when White crowds sway in this manner, they're "consuming Blackness".

This is what paranoid schizophrenia looks like. {3}

As we've seen, the rational proffered by Cul-Ap-phobes is riddled with myriad absurdities and incongruities. There is now rap music in virtually every country on earth, performed in virtually every major language. So we might ask: Is this a bad thing? If we apply the logic of Cul-Ap-phobia to everyone on the planet, then the answer is: yes. But it's NOT a bad thing.

Seeing as how Vikings were donning them first, shall anyone who is not Scandinavian refrain from donning cornrows? If so, there are going to be a lot of displeased Black folk. But, of course, such a prohibition would be absurd. Again: It is not that most Americans are poorly informed; it's that they are—by and large—stupendously MIS-informed.

Those who have become drunk on Cul-Ap-phobia are effectively calling for cultural segregation—basing such calls on specious claims of cultural ownership. This is a recipe not only for tribalism along ethnic lines, but for endless tribal animus. To repeat the point: Ethno-centricity is a death-knell for cosmopolitanism. Cultural segregation serves nobody. It's just an excuse to cavil. But caviling is now a booming business; and is a surefire way to gain oodles of attention online. Unfortunately, this often involves reverse victimization, whereby the bully fashions himself as the victim. {34}

This is not to say that all Potemkin Progressives are mendacious. Many are simply naive; which is simply to say that they are rubes. Put another way: Those who are taken in by the trappings of ersatz Progressivism don't necessarily have an ax to grind; they are dupes; as they have been snookered into participating in a crusade they've been told will somehow help those who are marginalized. It will do no such thing.

Here's what they miss: Appeasing society's tetchiest people is not the Holy Grail of civil rights. Quite the contrary, it is a surefire way to ***fetter*** civil rights. Potemkin Progressives who inveigh against the bugbear, "cultural appropriation" fail to realize that a meme-sequestration regime is antithetical to liberal democracy.

Where does this leave us? Rebuffing political correctness requires us to resist our narcissistic tendencies. Rebuffing identity politics requires us to resist our basest tribalistic instincts (which includes building up a resistance to the allure of collective narcissism). Both rebuttals are required when pursuing Progressive ideals.

Falling into a Reactionary mindset is tempting, as it allows us to succumb to a panoply of enticing dysfunctions--from narrow-mindedness to short-sightedness. Sure enough, Cul-Ap-phobia is the result of insecurity, myopia, and conceit; but above all, it is the result of intellectual laziness. Alarmism about the appropriation of cultural elements diverts focus away from issues that actually matter. Instead of hemming and hawing about sports fans swaying in the bleachers, we're much better off maintaining an emphasis on basic human decency.

The captiousness exhibited by Cul-Ap-phobes stems from the vile cocktail of neuroticism and self-absorption. This accounts for the intermittent alternation between fluster and bluster of p.c.-mongers. Such thinking is based on what Jean-Paul Sartre referred to as "bad faith"—a psychological condition stemming from an abdication of freedom—whereby one allows oneself to be at the mercy of circumstance.

Fixated, as they are, on subjectivity, the martinets of p.c. end up languishing in what Sartre dubbed our own (situational) "facticity". Here, one becomes preoccupied with the "felt sense" of one's psychical state at any given moment, subordinating one's "identity" to one's perceived role in the world—as if casting oneself as the central player in the movie that is the world. (The role in which one casts oneself is often a function of social pressures.) In doing this, one ends up severely compromising one's autonomy. Winding up in the thrall of one's subjectivity, one abdicates one's freedom. This leads to frangible constitutions; as a strong attachment to our role in the world makes us more prone to the illusion that our identity is under attack.

Says the promulgator of p.c. protocols, "If you do something I don't like, you have HARMED me; you have INVALIDATED me; you have ERASED me." The narcissism here is plain to see. This is main character syndrome in its most naked form. (Bear in mind, the narcissist sees a failure of others to placate / validate him as a kind of ***assault***.) One's self esteem is tethered to one's image. Kierkegaard saw this as a source of despair from having witnessed how complacent people could be within the candy-coated prison of their character defenses—a prison that is largely of their own making. Such misapprehension explains why people often allow rapacious careerism to take precedence over the pursuit of genuine fulfillment. (It is a matter of confusing a narrow conception of "success" with eudaimonia.) While oft-unacknowledged, there is a difference between making a good living and making a good life. In Sartre's terms, by languishing in one's own facticity, one becomes too self-involved to recognize one's potential to be truly autonomous. {62} By putting oneself at the mercy of social pressures, one's self-esteem is based entirely on how well one plays the role that one has been assigned. {39}

The self-absorption of the narcissist, though, operates at the level of the individual. Even as his psyche is addled with insecurity, he compensates with an over-inflated view of himself. It's not merely that he's the center of his own universe; he is the center of THE universe. ("It's my world; everyone else just lives in it.") The narcissist's thinking proceeds as follows: "Everything others do must be assessed based upon how it makes ME feel." {43} As Sartre saw it, insofar as one engages in "bad faith", one's self-esteem is built on quicksand. For such "bad faith" is not only being dishonest with others; it is being dishonest with oneself. This depraved state involves some combination of delusion and neuroticism—that is: an inflated sense of self-importance along with a siege mentality (read: a "woe is me" attitude). Both are tell-tale signs of a narcissistic personality.

According to Sartre, the way we emancipate ourselves from this debilitating condition is by transcending it—a feat that requires an ample amount of self-discipline. Therein lies the rub. It takes gumption to realize our potential to be truly autonomous. The problem is that, for many, rather than a source of empowerment, such potentiality is a source of ANXIETY. It makes sense, then, that those with fragile constitutions invariably succumb to narcissistic tendencies. They do so out of timidity. (This is a reminder that there is something craven about conceit.) Under such circumstances, one is able to affirm only one's own "facticity"; one's subjectivity is seen as all there is to existence. (Note that this is the opposite of Stoicism.)

And so it goes: "bad faith" involves shying away from one's capacity to TRANSCEND one's "facticity"—failing to get beyond one's own subjective experience, thereby defaulting on one's freedom. It is this debilitating mentality that underlies a preoccupation with propriety (read: political correctness). The irony is that the bad-faith actor is not merely **lying** to himself, he is **short-changing** himself. In trying to puff himself up, he ends up not giving himself enough credit. {62}

Narcissists are unwilling to take responsibility for their own psyches. The narcissist and the p.c.-monger effectively say the same thing: "YOU are responsible for ameliorating MY psychical problems. Therefore you are implicated in—and thus culpable for—any distress I might experience." Adopting this posture has certain utility for those lacking self-respect and/or mental discipline. Going out of one's way to feign "offense" is a way to accrue social cachet; and to justify an inflated view of oneself (hence individual narcissism) and/or one's tribe (hence collective narcissism). The former is the basis for political correctness; the latter is the basis for identity politics.

The upshot of all this is that people remain ensconced in their own memetic bubbles. They put on airs (so as to telegraph to fellow travelers that they're with the program); and, meanwhile, are susceptible to harebrained ideas (e.g. cultural segregation is the best way to protect marginalized communities from exploitation). The idea is to keep up appearances (so as to appease the constables of p.c.); and so skate by without having to bother with rectitude.

It's worth noting: A significant reason **performative morality** —replete with mock devastation and contrived indignation—has become normalized is that social media has made social interaction performative. After all, it is much easier to engage in pearl-clutching and/or finger-wagging in a virtual space; as one operates at a safe remove from ACTUAL human interaction. {37} So we shouldn't be entirely surprised when we are bombarded with frivolous indictments from a brigade of sanctimonious cultural impresarios, scolding us for saying / doing something they find unsettling.

A penchant for manufactured vexation has made offense-taking somewhat of an avocation for aficionados of p.c. With all the pique, one would think the grievance at hand pertained to some sort of cultural ASSAULT. But nothing could be further from the truth.

This is nothing new. Grifters have ALWAYS plied their trade by concocting pseudo-problems that are in need of solving. They do this so that they may then congratulate themselves for solving them; and cash in on the alleged "solution". (As **Race2Dinner** demonstrated, all this activism is merely ceremonial—a kind of exhibition that is done primarily for social benefits. See **Robin's Zugzwang**.) In a world where "lived experience" is treated as the ultimate standard for legitimacy, the mere pretense of morality suffices.

Those smitten with "lived experience" are reticent to concede that—at the end of the day—they REALLY DO acknowledge objective reality; even as they protest that there's no such thing. They refuse to admit that when they're aloft in a plane, it's not their "lived experience" of flying that keeps it in the air. But deep down, they know that their personal take on the matter is rather beside the point; as aerodynamics is unaffected by their subjectivity.

It's not that such people don't care about facts per se; it's that they manufacture "facts" to suit their own interests. For them, "fact" is simply a euphemism for a proposition they happen to fancy. Anything that doesn't comport with their preferred scheme is not considered a "fact"; it's just something that others say…which must be summarily dismissed as "wrong". Where actual evidence points is beside the point; as they are caught in a cycle of inexorable confirmation bias. This is a reminder that, given the right psychological conditions (staunch vested interests; ingrained mental habits; deep emotional investments), people will only hear / see what they WANT to hear / see.

(Here, it's worth noting that **political** Stockholm Syndrome is not merely about credulity; it stems from a high degree of insecurity. While fervent ideological commitments demonstrate how impregnable ideological echo-chambers can be, there are circumstances under which people are determined to believe certain things out of sheer practicality. As with **conventional** Stockholm Syndrome, this is a coping mechanism; as well as a defense mechanism. We are reminded that this syndrome operates on the group level as well as the individual level; as—throughout history—we have seen the subjugated come to adore—and even revere—their subjugators.)

When relativism takes hold, the attitude is essentially: "I have constructed my own (bespoke) 'reality' on which I have come to depend; so don't you dare meddle with it. In fact, I insist that you recognize it as perfectly legitimate…lest I feel slighted. I have staked my claim—nay, my very identity—on this being the case; so for anyone to upend it is tantamount to a personal assault."

The narcissist asserts his "truths" by fiat. If anyone has the gall to know otherwise, the narcissist will quickly become incensed; treating any dissent as some sort of assault on what they deem to be sacrosanct. Such subjectivism-on-steroids is the crux of epistemic narcissism. For those who come to depend on their custom-tailored "reality", defense mechanisms are put in place. Not acceding to their preferred scheme is seen not merely a matter of disagreement; it is seen as an assault on **who one is**.

In a nutshell: Invalidation is seen as a personal affront. These are the waters in which p.c.-mongers swim.

It would be copacetic if such people simply retreated into their own wonderland and left everyone else to their own devices. However, many are inclined to demand that the rest of the world play along. "It's not enough that others allow me to indulge in my own fanciful 'reality'; I expect everyone else HONOR it, and act accordingly." Failure to accede to these expectations is seen as some sort of personal insult.

Narcissists make grand proclamations about right and wrong; yet their rationalizations have little—if any—grounding in objective reality (a.k.a. Reality). After all, they are only concerned with their own "lived experience". To make matters worse, they insist that everyone else honor said experience—as if a given party's subjective claims could be used to justify ethical obligations / restrictions on the rest of the world. (To reiterate the point: Those who cannot control themselves often try to control others.) This comes from a mixture of insecurity and resentment—tragically commonplace amongst Reactionaries of all stripes.

This brings us back to the blinkered thinking at the root of Cul-Ap-phobia. In Germany, when a Kraut purchases a döner kebab from a Turk, who is benefiting from whom? This simple—nay, scrumptious—inter-ethnic transaction results from the meeting of two cultures, creating a culinary synergy (with, it might be added, felicitous outcomes for everyone involved). There is nothing sinister about this. Throughout human history, everywhere in the world, memetic constellations drift into one another; which is simply to say that as people in different cultures interact, the cultures THEMSELVES intermingle; and do so for a panoply of reasons.

No culture exists in a vacuum; and no culture has distinct boundaries. {36}

What lesson are we to take from this? At the end of the day it is our humanity, not our ethnicity, that should bind us. To recognize this tenet is not an impediment to cosmopolitanism; it is a **precondition for** cosmopolitanism.

As far as social injustice is concerned, there are serious matters of socio-economic inequality—not only across the U.S., but around the world. Proscribing cultural appropriation will do absolutely nothing to resolve it. Marginalized communities aren't marginalized because too many people are adopting their cultural practices; they are marginalized because of tribal chauvinism. The adoption of cultural practices is attributable to ethnic open-ness; whereas tribal chauvinism is attributable to ethno-centricity.

To questions about how a culture may be enhanced in one way or another, the aspiration must always be toward "bildung"—that is: culture based on what the ancient Greek philosophers dubbed "arete". This is simply to say: a culture that prioritizes erudition and good will. Cultural appropriation is a good way to do this; as the sharing of key cultural elements is a way of bringing people together across ethnic lines.

What does this have to do with American politics? The "woke" wing of the Democratic party—inexorably histrionic and pathologically captious—has become an overwrought caricature of Progressivism. It is in these circles that we find a high incidence of Cul-Ap-phobia…amongst other manifestations of identity politics and political correctness. (Meanwhile, much of the rest of the Democratic party—corrupt to its core—is simply a clan of corporatists with quasi-populist pretenses. The party is now home to a battalion of p.c.-mongers, Neoliberals, and Neocons. Hence the exaltation—within the party leadership—of corporate lackeys like Rahm Emanuel.)

So it has gone: Many would-be Progressives—eager to show the world how "with it" they are—feel obliged to comply with all the latest p.c. ordinances…as if they had been issued from a glimmering citadel of rectitude. ("Look, everyone! I said 'LatinX' instead of 'Latino'!") From the precincts of the Regressive "Left", we are treated to an alluvion of cloying lip-service…with almost no ACTUAL Progressive policies. Corporatism persists, unabated…even as the optics is meant to be flattering. {63}

Those who don't want to lose their hall-pass must abide each and every edict. Any false step is sure to elicit stern obloquy from the constables of p.c. Few want to risk ostracism from the hallowed ranks of the Democratic establishment; so anyone who dreads being labeled "right-wing" acquiesces.

Cul-Ap-phobes are part of this charade. As with other aficionados of p.c., they become apoplectic the moment they encounter any breach of etiquette. So they end up hawking material that is antithetical to their purported ideals. Yet they are adept at mouthing enticing platitudes; so often come off as valiant defenders of those who are exploited / disenfranchised. But here's the thing: Fancy rhetoric no more enfranchises marginalized communities in America than it provides healthcare to the poor or protects families from bombs in Palestine.

Such counterfeit "Progressivism" is tremendously off-putting the average American, driving otherwise reasonable people even further to the right. When met with such rigamarole, the average Joe throws up his arms and says, "To hell with this silliness." He feels as though he has no recourse but to run into the arms of a G.O.P. that shares his revulsion of the litany of outlandish p.c. protocols. Republicans may be every bit as corrupt as the Democrats, but at least they don't look down their nose at him and call him an idiot for not playing along with their reindeer games.

So much of public discourse is governed by a covey of pompous scolds…who alternate between pearl-clutching and finger-wagging as the need arises. Practitioners of this odious craft evince a pretentious humility; then expect to be accorded bounteous accolades…as they bask in all their virtue-signaling splendor. The trick is to pass their hubris off as humility, whereby obduracy can be seen as a kind of valor. (After all, the art of pearl-clutching is what amounts to ostentatious demureness.)

A divisive approach to social interaction between ethnic groups is worse than futile. The identitarian mindset is, at root, tribalistic; and therefore antithetical to the most fundamental principles of cosmopolitanism. Moreover, demands for political correctness are far more debilitating than beneficial…not to mention illiberal. At root, a regime of political correctness is authoritarian and puritanical. By upholding p.c. protocols, we are obliged to become insufferably captious—precluding any chances of human solidarity.

Generally speaking, a frangible disposition translates to an irritable disposition. So it comes as little surprise that an obsession with political correctness creates all kinds of un-necessary aggravation…without solving any structural problems. (Good will is difficult to engender in the midst of chronic aggravation.) The best that might do is bring about fleeting bouts of gratification…before inducing the next episode of perturbation. And round and round we go, chasing a psychical homeostasis that is forever out of reach…while incumbent power structures remain unaffected.

As we survey the vast memetic panorama of today's globalized society, we find that elements of one culture routinely intermingle with elements of various other cultures in unpredictable ways. Someone at one location on the planet will invariably encounter a meme from another location on the planet, and—if it strikes their fancy—will incorporate it into their own memetic repertoire. In doing so, sometimes they'll recognize that it is an exogenous cultural element; sometimes they won't. Over time, they make it their own, often with little regard for its origins. Few who play chess think of it as partaking in medieval Persian culture. And none of those who deck the halls with boughs of holly consider themselves to be partaking in the pagan traditions of ancient Rome. Why not? Nobody takes umbrage with THEIR OWN Cul-Ap; as they blithely disregard the provenance of whatever they're doing that they consider to be endogenous to their culture. Hence grievances about "cultural appropriation" can't help but be highly selective.

Those who have compunctions with Cul-Ap *qua **Cul-Ap*** cavil about imagined improprieties (in one context) even as they invariably partake in analogous improprieties (in virtually every other context). As we saw earlier, there is a special kind of in-group bias that involves the treatment of affinities as tribal demarcations. To flout said demarcations is seen as a betrayal of the tribe. Trans-cultural affinities are seen as a kind of thought-crime. Indeed, there is something Orwellian about all this. Whenever encountering these Cul-Ap-phobes, we might wonder: To comply with their proposed ordinances, what would they have us do?

While navigating the world's roiling memetic ecosystem, it's as if everyone were obliged to seek approval from an officially-appointed meme-adoption adjudicator (presumably located at the local Ministry Of Culture) before engaging in any activity that might be construed—by someone, somewhere—as "cultural appropriation". The message: Be careful what you do; because if others did it before you did, you're guilty of having illicitly adopted a meme. (For how many things this would disqualify from contemporary culture, see my essay on "Mythemes".) We might note that "unauthorized use of meme" is an indictment one would only expect to encounter in a totalitarian society.

But what of SOME restrictions on cultural diffusion? At what point do such strictures become a matter of cultural segregation? It makes sense to dissuade mockery; yet we get into shaky territory if our criterion for opprobrium is offense-taking. Anyone can claim to be offended by anything. In any case, taking offense often reflects the hang-ups of the offense-taker more than it does the iniquity of the purported offender. One party's subjective experience mustn't be treated as license to make demands on all bystanders.

Offense-taking comes in handy as a discursive redoubt. Whenever "I feel offended" is wielded by an interlocutor in an offensive maneuver, it is done in a last-ditch effort to stand one's ground when no argument is available to support one's position. For lack of anything intelligent to say, one can simply claim "offense"; then avoid conceding that one has no solid grounds for taking the stance that one has taken. This is a very enticing proposition for those who have nothing erudite to contribute to the public discourse (yet nevertheless yearn to be noticed).

Anti-Cul-Ap crusaders insist on bickering the moment one of their protocols is breached. This manufactured imbroglio becomes especially acrimonious whenever we're dealing with a cultural element associated with the Orient (read: non-Christian, non-White precincts of the globe) in the event that it crops up in the Occident (read: White Christendom). The grievances of Cul-Ap-phobes, then, are based on a false dichotomy—involving what is effectively the fetishization of "the West". Power asymmetries matter when evaluating instances of memetic transference. Indeed, we should always be wary of exploitation when those with more power leverage their power in order to—as it were—lord it over others. But when Cul-Ap is concomitant with exploitative activity, it is the ***exploitation*** that is the problem, not the Cul-Ap ***per se.***

As we saw in Part 1, the meme-sequestration regime prescribed by Cul-Ap-phobes is based on an ignorance of world history; not to mention a fundamental mis-understanding of how culture-in-general works. Anti-Cul-Ap crusaders demand that we all pretend CURRENT semiotic schemes were AS IS since the beginning of time. This obliges us to ignore—or even elide—the genealogy that yielded any given meme's current semiotic incarnation. Such an ornery posture stems from temporal conceit; as it asks us to suppose that the way things are NOW is the way they've always been. (African Americans often don dreadlocks? Well, then, that's the way it must have been ALL ALONG. Proceed accordingly!) Such obtuse thinking is the hallmark of parochialism (i.e. the opposite of cosmopolitanism); and—rather than fostering comity across ethnic lines—only succeeds in amplifying ethnic alterity.

Examples of this myopic worldview are legion. Take, for instance, the vibrant prints created by the renown Lebanese clothing designer, Alfred Shaheen; who, it might be noted, lived in Hawaii for much of his life. He has been castigated by a coterie of Cul-Ap-phobes. Why? Well, you see, he had the audacity to incorporate Polynesian—as well as Indian—patterns into his eccentric outfits. The patterns he used paid homage to some of the world's most beautiful cultural achievements; yet he was besmirched for his efforts.

Shaheen wasn't using the patterns as a gimmick (which would have been a problem); he was honoring a cultural legacy (presumably a good thing). He wasn't trivializing the patterns in a gambit to monetize them (which would have been a problem); he was expressing a deep and profound aesthetic appreciation for them (presumably a good thing). He wasn't taking credit for others' sartorial attainments and passing them off as his own (which would have been a problem); he was paying tribute to another culture's contribution to the world of fashion (presumably a good thing). Indeed, everything he did was laudable.

Never mind all that, though. Anti-Cul-Ap crusaders have seen fit to engage in carping—and, of course, calumny—against the late Shaheen; and those who continue to celebrate his wonderful sartorial achievements. To get their campaign of obloquy to seem to have an iota of merit, they conflate memetic adoption with some sort of exploitative enterprise. They can then thank themselves for sticking up for the Polynesians of the world. (Petulance seems justified when one is self-righteous.) Appreciation as exploitation? Such legerdemain is used to rationalize a program of contrived indignation; thereby telegraphing to compatriots that they are somehow "woke". So far as they can see it, being churlish is the optimal way to showcase their unimpeachable moral intrepidity.

It might be noted that whenever presenting a new outfit, Shaheen gave full credit to the source-culture; as the entire point was to celebrate it. But no matter. Those who make a sport out of being "insulted" feel justified in claiming "harm" or "injury"…in some ethereal sense that only THEY seem to understand. The contention is that they are harmed / injured whenever anything causes them even the least bit of psychical discomfort. In doing so, they can assert victim status. Victim of WHAT? Of "cultural appropriation"…re-conceptualized as "assault" or "theft" or "violence" or "oppression".

There is something palpably Orwellian about the faux outrage expressed by the more unctuous Cul-Ap-phobes. This is a feature, not a glitch. Indeed, the excoriation of Shaheen (and those who have donned his outfits) is straight out of the Cul-Ap-phobia playbook—replete with demands for piety; and, of course, shunning for heresy. Alas, such hyper-censorious-ness is indicative of p.c., which sees the clutching of pearls as a valiant act.

Think all this is a tad bit nutty? You'd be correct. Like p.c.-mongers in general, anti-Cul-Ap crusaders make a sport out of being "offended". Their puritanical mindset is misconstrued as a sign of rectitude. Make no mistake: There is a method to their madness; as each blasphemy law serves an important purpose. By feigning "offense", participants in this charade can accuse their targets of some irredeemable transgression—be it "assault", "theft", "violence", "oppression", or some form of exploitation. Why? So that they can then claim to feel "unsafe". Unsafe from what, exactly? Well, from the perils of being "offended".

Is there any assault / theft / violence / oppression / exploitation ACTUALLY occurring? Of course, not. But that's not the point. It is the INDICTMENT ITSELF that does all the work. The idea is to engage in maudlin theatrics whenever experiencing a fleeting moment of discomfiture…as a result of whatever made-to-order transgression can be conjured from the aether. (They're standing up for cultural integrity, after all.) Benefits to the source culture? Zero. But no matter: They have seized the opportunity to virtue-signal. And that is all they're really interested in. After all, the fundamental maxim of political correctness is quite straight-forward: The rest of the world is responsible for ensuring that *I* never feel the least bit unsettled by anything. Ever.

Other than stemming from a high degree of narcissism, this tendentious orientation is antithetical to the spirit of pluralism. In learning how to get along with others, one of the first things we learn as children is that there is no "right" not to be offended. Things don't always go our way, or hew to our sensibilities. To construe a sense of unease elicited by X as an indication that X is INCORRECT is an elementary mistake. Yet p.c.-mongers seem to have never learned this lesson. Hence the programatic demonization of Cu-Ap.

In witnessing these oleaginous proceedings, it is difficult to say what motivates any given anti-Cul-Ap crusader. It is certainly not human solidarity; as they aim for division at every turn. Some are simply hungry for attention. Most are seeking some sort of validation. ALL of them are one or another combination of egregiously mis-informed, horribly insecure, and tremendously dishonest...with some neuroses and histrionics thrown in for good measure.

This is all part of the grievance-industrial-complex, fueled by an abiding p.c. mania propounded by platoons of Potemkin Progressives. (Again: Cul-Ap-phobes' only contribution to the public discourse is some combination of pearl-clutching and finger-wagging). Their charge is to cavil about imagined crimes...while ignoring anything that might actually promote the Progressive cause.

There are myriad contexts within which we might appraise the moral status of Cul-Ap. In Part 1, we explored literary influences across cultures. Let's consider some more. My contention is that we should be grateful that Chaucer (an English writer) riffed off of Boccaccio (an Italian writer). The Canterbury Tales are, in part, a literary appropriation of the Decameron. And to that, we should say, "Bravo!"

Shakespeare lifted his plays from myriad sources—most of it not from his native England. And thank god he did. The bard from Stratford-upon-Avon did not have to be a Moor himself to write the compelling Moorish character (Aaron)—a man who was romantically involved with a Gothic queen (Tamora). Why not? "Titus Andronicus" captures a universal theme: the tragedy that lurks behind all vengeance—irrespective of ethnic background. The fact that the play's key characters are Roman, Arab, and German reminds us that human nature transcends tribal affiliations. As is the case with ALL great literature, the point is to put oneself in another's shoes. The same cosmopolitan spirit undergirds ANY Cul-Ap that is done in good faith: wanting to walk in the shoes of those who come from another walk of life. In the end, we're all human. Shakespeare recognized this, which is why his stories were not limited to his fellow Englishmen.

So why all the fuss over Cul-Ap NOW? Well, there is good reason for the concern—broadly speaking. We are now more cognizant of—and thus sensitive to—power disparities between ethnic groups, and the incidence of domination / marginalization / exploitation concomitant therewith. Be that as it may, it is possible to get carried away with establishing prophylaxes against social injustices. When we encounter some of the more obstreperous caviling on the matter of Cul-Ap, we find that there is typically some sort of neurosis (regarding cultural transmission) involved. Hence the neologism: Cul-Ap-phobia. We soon come to find that many Cul-Ap-phobes are simply looking for something—ANYTHING, no matter how frivolous—to complain about. This is in keeping with the social pathology known as "political correctness". Others are downright racist THEMSELVES—as with those who castigated Awkwafina for using a "blaccent".

The mantra of identity politics amounts to something rather anti-social: Instead of celebrating cultural diffusion, we should be wary of it...at least in the event that one ethnicity opts to emulate another. This is a message from which genuine Progressives recoil; as it is an explicit repudiation of cosmopolitanism. Rather than embracing our shared humanity, it admonishes us to ignore it in favor of a divisive framing. It prescribes a way of seeing the world based explicitly on demographic categorization schemes. This is incongruous with the cosmopolitan ideal.

Some Possible Problems

It might be noted that there are social phenomena that are, indeed, highly problematic; yet have nothing to do with Cul-Ap—namely: people of one ethnicity PRETENDING TO BE someone from another ethnicity (invariably according to a commercially viable stereotype). This is sometimes referred to as "X-fishing", where X is the ethnicity being simulated. (There is a crucial distinction to be made between simulation and emulation.) The most notorious examples of this are blackface, brownface, yellowface, and redface. But that's not Cul-Ap. Done in good faith, Cul-Ap is not a cheap caricature. It doesn't chide others; it engenders human solidarity.

When our shared humanity is front and center, compunctions with cultural diffusion seem to evaporate. The Roma are some of Europe's most marginalized people; yet they don't hem and haw when everyone else engages in Flamenco dancing (which originated when their community intermingled with the Moors of Andalusia in the Late Middle Ages). Yes, they are slightly annoyed with women dressing up as "gypsies" for Halloween; but this is primarily due to the ignorance most of us have regarding their ongoing plight as an oft-rebuffed ethnic minority. Still struggling to dispel antiquated stereotypes (itinerant beggars, eccentric fortune-tellers, and roving pick-pockets), the last thing they need is more of us snickering as we engage in cheap caricatures. (In film, it is a mixed bag. While there was a romanticized portrayal of Roma with Grizelda in Disney's "Hunchback Of Notre Dame", the portrayal in "Snatch" was not quite as flattering.)

Aside from trafficking in stereotypes, grievances about Cul-Ap worth taking seriously fall into two basic categories: either **(A)** improper—or complete lack of—attribution; or **(B)** according insufficient gravity to a cherished meme (i.e. one that plays a prominent role in a ethnic group's heritage). Let's briefly look at each:

is a matter of giving credit where credit is due. Shall we indict Elvis Presley for re-doing Big Mama Thornton's "Hound Dog"? Yes and no. The sin wasn't the Cul-Ap; it was the lack of attribution. With respect to the first (White) practitioners of rock 'n roll, credit is due to Chuck Berry and Little Richard. But, then again, even those (Black) men were influenced by an exogenous culture—namely: hillbilly / country music; as well as the folk music (Afro-American and WASP-oriented) that predated them. And as for "Hound Dog"…it's worth repeating: the song was written by two Jewish men.

involves a flippant use of a meme that has been sanctified in some way by those in the source culture. For example, one might cavalierly don a piece of clothing that commands a deep meaning for those hailing from a certain tradition—treating the item as a nifty yet dispensable accessory. This grievance pertains to those who heedlessly partake in an exogenous cultural element without regard for the role it plays within its native habitat. When we engage in Cul-Ap merely to attract attention, or to make a profit, or to get a laugh, we are—at best—being petty. Otherwise, we're just being jerks.

The qualm with neither (**A**) nor (**B**) is with Cul-Ap per se. Rather, the issue is whether or not the Cul-Ap is being done in good faith. Felicitously, such (legitimate) grievances can be remedied in relatively straight-forward ways. Give credit where credit is due; and avoid mawkish participation. In other words, give appropriate recognition and don't be disrespectful. It's not rocket science.

We might think of it this way: The problem with people being ignorant is ignorance. The problem with people being shallow is shallowness. And mischaracterization is always wrong because it is dishonest. Nobody likes to be caricatured by bystanders who do not have a full understanding of them. Recognizing this prompts a call for common courtesy, not for cultural segregation.

When considering these matters, it's helpful to bear in mind that cultural sharing is not a zero-sum game. Often, EVERYONE benefits when Cul-Ap is done in good faith. Little Richard himself observed of Elvis that "he was an integrator. Elvis was a blessing." How so? He correctly noted that the white-male- dominated American music industry "wouldn't let Black people through. [Elvis] opened the door for Black music." There is a lesson to learn here. Cultural integrators bring people together by elucidating shared sensibilities; by exploring affinities that may have otherwise gone un-noticed. By engaging in Cul- Ap, they enable us to see the humanity in those who are different from us.

So are we to begrudge artists for stylistic preferences culled from cultures other than their own? We might pose this question as follows: Was Eminem a good thing or a bad thing for rap? Dr. Dre provided us with a decisive answer.

Alas. Cul-Ap-phobes decry all trans-cultural adoption—as with, say, the Chinese-American performer, Audrey "Nuna" Chu adopting a certain musical idiom pioneered by African Americans (R&B); or the British chef, Jamie Oliver preparing his signature "punchy jerk rice" (a Jamaican flavor). In considering such cases, what we discover is that there is no trans-cultural appreciation without some form of trans-cultural participation.

As I hope to have shown in the present book, when it comes to culture, EVERYTHING is—effectively—a remix. When transmitted between cultures, cultural elements invariably undergo some sort of metamorphosis—salutary mutations that result from (what is effectively) memetic synthesis. Rarely is this by design.

It is the result of a process of human interaction across cultural lines—something we should ENCOURAGE. Meanwhile, entire cultures THEMSELVES undergo a metamorphosis—part of which is due to cultural hybridization. In terms of memetics, we behold an organic process by which a new meme is grafted onto an older, extant meme—yielding a novel meme. This is how ANY culture is formed from constituent elements.

The re-purposing of cultural elements has recently been given the name "remix culture". This has generally been considered to be a matter of *innovation*; and thus a salutary development—be it in music, dance, literature, architecture, the culinary arts, the visual arts, or clothing design. But cultural hybridization is what culture IS—indeed: what it has ALWAYS BEEN. Culture could not possibly be anything else. Lukes put it well: "The idea that cultures are wholes, rather than clusters or assemblages of heterogeneous elements with varying origins, is a systematic exercise in the reduction of complexity based on mythical thinking" (ibid.)

Cultures are man-made memetic ecosystems, each with its own social climate—that is: with a unique—and fluctuating—set of environmental conditions (from geo-political exigencies to the commercial trends). As such, cultures are concatenations of variegated elements originating from different places and times under different circumstances…for a variety of reasons which are not immediately obvious to the adopters.

The problem with demonizing Cul-Ap, then, is how one is to precisely demarcate the source-culture for any given meme. For memes percolate up from the burbling stew that is the meme-o-sphere, crystalizing here and there (due to one historical accident or another). Memes then shift from one cultural context to another in response to subsequent accidents of history. It's contingency ALL THE WAY DOWN.

A memetically-quarantined culture is a stagnant culture. Worse: Demanding that everyone "stay in their own lane" is tantamount to a mandate for cultural segregation. We might note that such an attitude is nothing new: Progressives have always had to contend with Reactionaries who have insisted everyone "know their place".

This is an unreasonable request in a globalized world—a world in which people are eagerly interacting with one another, seeking to embrace anything that is new and appealing. This should remind us that culture is amorphous—with blurry edges. It mixes with other cultures and undergoes a metamorphosis—sometimes for the better, sometimes for the worse, but usually in utterly innocuous ways. The result is that what many might perceive as an *emblematic* element of a particular culture is really not what they fancy it to be. It's just another meme in a long line of memes.

Those of us who value progress celebrate novelty; they don't shy away from it. And those who value pluralism celebrate inter-ethnic collaborations. In the 1970's, Spyro Gyra brought together WASPs, Latinos, Jews, and African Americans—each of whom brought their own cultural sensibilities—not to mention their own unique flavor—to the band's music. Such developments should be applauded by musicians of all stripes.

It helps to assess cultural formation—and subsequent calcification—from a temporal perspective. Cul-Ap is an on-going process. It has no discrete beginning; and it is forever open-ended. Using "cultural appropriation" as an indictment only makes sense if we take a snap-shot at a specific place and time; and pretend that it represents a timeless truth; some immutable exigency that we tamper with at our peril. When it comes to our most hallowed cultural elements, this impression is tempting but erroneous. Upon recognizing this, we find that Cul-Ap-phobia is based on a misconception of what cultural elements are and how they work. As I showed in Part 1, the notion of meme-ownership (by a delimited group) is a dubious one. For to lend it credence, one is forced to disregard how the meme came to be as it is in the first place. This invariably obliges us to posit arbitrary (read: self-serving) timelines, which are used to create the official origin story for any given cultural element.

"Dreadlocks, you say? Oh, well that began with African Americans!" One may as well contend that Catholic schoolgirls invented pigtails. As discussed earlier, dreadlocks had been used by Native Americans, Indians, and Norsemen for centuries before they became a staple of Afro-American culture. And they were used in ancient Egypt, Greece, Mesopotamia, and Persia long before even that. It almost makes one wonder who in the world HASN'T donned them at one point or another. So who owns the dreadlock? Well, nobody. And everybody. One could just as well ask who owns nose rings, braided hair, or lipstick.

Such gratuitous acrimony is a reminder that cultural segregation divides us. By stark contrast, Cul-Ap–done in good faith—highlights our shared humanity. This is especially so when it comes to artistic expression. The cosmopolitan ideal doesn't merely allow for the latter; it demands it.

Human solidarity entails going beyond the provincial mindset of constrained ethnic commitments. We might ask: How many who have contributed to the Western canon in the past four centuries have borrowed from Cervantes…often without having cited the iconic Spanish author? That Don Quixote was composed in Spanish is important; but it is not a BOUNDARY CONDITION. ***Creativity transcends ethnicity***. It has always been that way. The ancient Romans riffed off of the ancient Greeks. The ancient Jews riffed off of the ancient Assyrians. The earliest Christians riffed off of virtually everyone they encountered; and the first Muslims did the same with antecedent Syriac motifs.

The world is festooned with such examples. We typically think of kefir as coming from Russia, but it was actually started by the descendants of the [k]Hazars—namely the Karachai and Balkars. So it was originally Turkic, then re-branded a staple of Russian culture. Even India has a version of the delicious yogurt beverage: lasi. And another version eventually cropped up in modern Turkey: ayran. Shall we begrudge everyone on the planet, throughout all of history, for having engaged in some sort of Cul-Ap? Of course not. But why not?

In Part 1, I called out the self-appointed arbiters of cultural transference for betraying the spirit of cosmopolitanism. (Who shall be the official arbiters of meme-allocation? It seems that it's anyone who feels like anointing themselves the representative of an entire ethnic group. It's a game that anyone can play.)

It is worth noting that the inverse of Cul-Ap-phobia is a fear of cultural contamination. Both neuroses stem from conceit; as both involve delusions about maintaining (a chimerical) purity. This is one of many forms of Reactionary thinking. Totalitarian regimes are against their closed societies adopting exogenous cultural elements for fear doing so might taint what they see as an ethnically-pristine domain.

Says the Cul-Ap-phobe: Who is better positioned to ward off those irritating bugaboos than a cadre of persnickety litigators—charged with routinely monitoring who is using what memes? (We might note that one thing that INGSOC was missing was a Ministry of Cultural Purity.) Whether it's alarmism about cultural appropriation or about cultural contamination, we are forced to contend with these commissars of culture. Both kinds mandate a regime of cultural segregation—though from opposite perspectives: one to prevent memetic egress, the other to prevent memetic ingress. For the Cul-Ap-phobe, such egress is not seen as sharing; it's seen as a kind of theft. And such ingress is not seen as pluralism; it's seen as a kind of infection.

As discussed previously, the notion of cultural purity is illusory; as all culture is derivative—the result of a long process of Cul-Ap from different sources at different times for different reasons, going back to time immemorial. To find a culture that did NOT form from Cul-Ap, one would be forced to go back to the Sumerians.

Recall the example of spring-tide. The Assyrian celebration of the vernal equinox, Akitu[m]—dating from the Iron Age—made its way into the Aramaic (then Syriac) vernacular. It makes sense that this occasion was later designated for Passover in Judaic lore—that is: during the month of "Nisan[u]" (an Assyrian term based on the Sumerian term, "nisag", meaning "first fruits" or "rebirth"). Adapted from the Babylonians during the Exilic Period, the Aramaic was later rendered in Classical Hebrew as "Arah Nisanu". It is now simply known as "Aviv" ("abib" was early Semitic for the first ripening; i.e. rebirth). {32}

Meanwhile, the ancient Persian holiday, Nowruz—also dating from the Iron Age—was appropriated by most of the world's Turkic communities—each of which made it their own. There also came to be Afghan, Georgian, Albanian, Kurdish, and Bengal versions. Later on, practitioners of the Baha'i Faith adapted a version for their creed. What we find, then, is a veritable Saturnalia of cultural appropriation across the globe. According to the anti-Cul-Ap crusader, though, every one of these communities is "guilty" of Cul-Ap.

We must ask ourselves: Is this something we should condemn?

No sane person would answer in the affirmative. If Jews, Christians, and Muslims were forced to jettison every part of their religious tradition that had pagan origins, there would be almost nothing left. And if the United States purged itself of every cultural element that originated in a foreign land, there wouldn't be much left. (Apple pie? Nope. Brought overseas by the Brits, the Swedes, and the Dutch. Cowboys? Nope. That's from Mexican vaqueros. Baseball? Nope. Started as rounders in Ireland.) If we were to eliminate anything that was culturally appropriated, the only parts of Americana remaining would be investment banks, insurance companies, and lawn darts.

On a global scale, if we were to negate all Cul-Ap going back to the Iron Age, human civilization would be still be comprised of the Maya / Aztecs (in Meso-America), the Celts (in Europe), the Copts (in Egypt), the Mycenaeans (in Greece), the Assyrians (in Mesopotamia), the Achaemenids (in Persia), the Vedic peoples (in India), and the Zhou Chinese (in the Yellow River Valley): **all of them culturally segregated for the rest of eternity.**

As mentioned earlier, we like to believe that OUR OWN sanctified memes are unique to us; scoffing at the idea that they might be derivative. We insist on seeing novelty where it doesn't exist; then decry Cul- Ap the moment we disapprove of an isolated instance of memetic transference. Consider the twelve days of Christmas. "Zagmuk" was the Sumerian celebration of the winter solstice. It was comprised of 12 days. As the tale goes, the primary god, Marduk was slain...and was then resurrected on the spring equinox. (This should sound rather familiar.) That was during the Bronze Age. {45}

A rudimentary knowledge of history is all that is needed to disabuse Cul-Ap-phobes of their peculiar gripe; as the gripe only seems credible to those who have not thoroughly thought through the matter. I submit that a basic understanding of how culture-in-general works is all that is needed to attenuate this neurosis. Ranting about Cul-Ap, one may as well grouse about the fact that all the world's peoples happen to breathe oxygen.

How, then, shall we think about memetic transference?

Consider "cumbia". Since this dance style eventually migrated to other Latin American cultures from Columbia, do all other Latinos owe a debt to Colombians? Perhaps. But wait. Cumbia is essentially just a Latin take on belly dancing...which was popularized by Arabs, Turks, and Persians during the Middle Ages. Even THEY were not the originators, as the dance style likely originated in Pharaonic Egypt. (In Arabic, the style is referred to as "raqs sharqi", meaning "Oriental dance". In typical Latin American fashion, it was rendered a partner dance.) As it happens, belly dancing also led to "flamenco" dancing (also a partner dance) in Andalusia— first amongst the Romani, before eventually catching on with Spaniards. So what are we to make of all this? Is there something villainous afoot?

Let's answer that (absurd) question by posing another question: Shall the Belgians and Swiss thank the Aztecs for chocolate? (The name derives from the Nahuatl "cacahuatl".) If so, they presumably owe a massive debt to all Meso-Americans. Bear in mind that when Coenraad Johannes van Houten created Dutch cocoa, he was engaging in Cul-Ap. After all, he co-opted a hallmark of Native American culture from a people. Was Coenraad being iniquitous? Don't be ridiculous. His adaptation was largely the consequence of him sharing the same planet as Native Americans.

When Morgan Bullock (an African American from Richmond, Virginia) pursued her passion in Irish Dancing, it is disingenuous to contend that she was pilfering from the Celtic legacy. She wasn't extorting Irish culture; she was paying tribute to it. Indeed, the DANCING may have been Irish, but SHE didn't have to be.

The question remains: Might it be said that Morgan was "appropriating" something from an exogenous culture? Sure. Should the Irish feel slighted by this? That would be a peculiar reaction to what she was doing. It would be like begrudging Yo-Yo Ma for performing a concerto on his cello that had been composed by Bach for the harpsichord.

Cul-Ap sometimes involves black dancers performing Irish dances; and sometimes it involves Chinese musicians performing German music.

Perhaps Morgan will adapt Irish Dancing to hip-hop, creating a novel (hybridized) style...as occurred with belly dancing (Middle Eastern) to flamenco (Andalusian) to cumbia (Colombian). Appropriation is—after all—the engine of emerging culture. That's how older cultures got there themselves. We mustn't begrudge these cultural mavens for doing what our progenitors did in the first place.

Demanding that Cul-Ap be proscribed is opposed to the cosmopolitan spirit. Indeed, to have a problem with Cul-Ap is to have a problem with CULTURE ITSELF. Memes propagate across cultural lines because no meme is tied to any given culture by some immutable law of the universe. It's why the British don't take umbrage when Americans say, "It's as American as apple pie." (The pie is originally from England; though apples originated in Kazakhstan.) And it's why Americans don't take umbrage when culinary maestros from Africa or Asia create their own ethnic variation on the scrumptious dessert. After all, EVERYONE loves apple pie.

The indemnification of memes would not preclude exploitation; it would simply divert our attention away from structural inequalities (which ACTUALLY account for the more privileged exploiting subalterns) toward the breaching of token formalities. Consider that the Muslims of Andalusia contributed to the development of flamenco by merging belly-dancing with Romani dance. Cul-Ap no more contributes to marginalization than the Moors were short-changed when Colombians inaugurated their famous spin-off of flamenco: cumbia.

In sum: If our aim is to eradicate social injustice, tantrums over Cul-Ap only end up being a distraction. It is no secret that there are far more important things to concern ourselves with than who "owns" apple pie...or chocolate...or belly dancing. We live in a world with massive structural inequalities, in which certain communities are marginalized...and oppressed...and exploited. Socio-economic injustices run rampant throughout society. So we might ask: At the end of the day, does it really matter whether this or that teenage girl celebrates a "quinceañera" (a Meso-American tradition for girls who turn fifteen) or a "sweet sixteen" birthday (popularized by WASPs)? Answer: No. Heck, she may as well do both! And we may as well throw in a Bat Mitzvah-style candle-lighting ceremony while we're at it.

In what other contexts might we illustrate the salutary nature of Cul-Ap? Let's look a bit more at our treatment of ethnic cuisines. By seeing how culinary practices have affected one another, we might shed light on how best to think about the adoption of exogenous cultural elements.

The Global Pantry

Sharing food is a time-honored way to engender comity between different communities. Indeed, "breaking bread" with one another is one of the oldest ways to forge bonds with wayfarers. Our shared humanity is exemplified by EATING together; and this is especially so when we treat each other to cherished recipes from days of yore. Amicable culinary transmission is yet another reminder that (cordial) trans-cultural exchange serves to attenuate alterity. In this sense, sharing in our daily bread is one of the first steps in eliminating the marginalization of minority communities…who are often seen as "other" by those in a position of privilege.

Those from different tribes "breaking bread" with one another reminds us that Cul-Ap fosters some of the most profound connections between ethnic groups.

It should be uncontroversial, then, to note that one does not have to be Mexican to eat fajitas any more than one has to be Swiss to eat Emmentaler cheese. (Swiss cheese isn't actually Swiss.) Today, many cuisines are drawn from what is effectively a global pantry. Behold a process in which culinary practitioners use ingredients from around the world. Most chefs do this at their own discretion; and with phenomenal results.

There is nothing sinister going on here. For it is just humans in one place appreciating things traditionally used by humans in another place. In viewing this phenomenon, we may wish to bear in mind that…

Chervil is originally from **France**.
Dill is originally from the **Slavic region**.
Dukkah and **thyme** are originally from **Egypt**.
Tahini is originally from **the Levant**.
Cumin is originally from **the Eurasian Steppes**.
Rosemary is originally from **Mesopotamia**.
Saffron is originally from **Persia**.
Turmeric and **mustard** are originally from **India**.
Ginger and **coriander** (a.k.a. "cilantro") are originally from **China**.
Basil and **lemon-grass** are originally from **Southeast Asia**.

Yuzu-kosho and **kimchi** are originally from **Japan**.
Sambal is originally from **Java**.
Nutmeg, **mace**, and **cloves** are originally from the **Bali / Maluku**.
Paprika, **vanilla**, and **chocolate** are originally from **Meso-America**.

When it comes to the culinary arts, these are just INGREDIENTS, not marks of divine ordinance. But this inventory illustrates the point well. (Such items have been culled from various flora, which—surprise, surprise—tend to grow in some places rather than in others.) The point is that we all partake in an exchange of elements in order to create our own unique dishes. It's ALL culinary hybridization.

"Hold on there!" the Cul-Ap-phobe protests. "Using herbs from faraway lands is not cultural appropriation. Ingredients themselves are not cultural elements." True. The point here is simply that, in everyday life, we routinely use things that are not originally from our own country…often without realizing that that's the case. Technology is another illustration of this (also not a cultural element, yet certainly something that affects culture). {61}

To recognize the fatuity of decrying Cul-Ap whenever signature elements of "ethnic" cuisines intermix, one need only concede that every ingredient that has ever existed originally came from SOMEWHERE…and then acknowledge that recipes are essentially just a certain combination of ingredients with a prescribed mode of preparation.

Apples originally came from Kazakhstan / Kyrgyzstan—likely planted by the Uyghurs in the Early Middle Ages. That was coupled with crusts by the Franks in the Late Middle Ages. So are we to suppose that apple pie is best characterized as a fusion of medieval Turkic and Germanic cuisine? {64} What in heaven's name is an American Cul-Ap-phobe to do?

Let's suppose, then, that apple pie is heretofore off-limits to WASPs. Perhaps we could just have some yogurt instead. Well, only if you're GREEK; as "oxygala" (rendered "xynogala" in modern Greek) was originally Hellenic fare. Ok. Well, then how about some custard? Sure, such a choice is permissible; but only if you're FRENCH.

What about just having a cookie? That's fine…if you're PERSIAN, that is. Everyone else is outta luck.

According to this logic, the entire planet is complicit in some perfidious scheme of culinary cooptation. So far as anti-Cul-Ap crusaders are concerned, anyone using fennel, parsley, sage, marjoram, or oregano—who does NOT have ancestors from the Mediterranean basin—is engaged in a memetic heist; and so must be excoriated. The same goes for those using nutmeg, mace, or cloves who don't have ancestors from the Maluku islands of Malaya. Heaven forfend you happen to prepare a vanilla or chocolate dessert without paying tribute to the Aztecs, sip a coffee without paying tribute to the Abyssinians, or drink some beer without paying tribute to the Egyptians. And be careful not to ever use sambal without first securing permission from the world's Indonesians.

Sound ridiculous? It should. Because it is. (Imagine if Cajun food was limited to resteraunts in New Orleans.)

Willful ignorance is required to not realize that memetic transference is part of the natural course of cultural evolution from one epoch to the next—whether with food or anything else. Yet those who are determined to demonize Cul-Ap persist, heedless of how culture actually works. We come to find that cultural FORMATION is invariably the product of cultural DIFFUSION.

A survey of ingredients isn't just an illustration of where anti-Cul-Ap crusaders go awry, it serves as a useful metaphor. Just as ingredients constitute a certain CULINARY recipe (subject to alterations), cultural elements comprise an overall CULTURAL recipe (subject to alterations). In analogous ways, memes comprise a meme-plex; tenets comprise an ideology; sacrosanct dogmas comprise a holy creed; etc. Such things are rarely set in stone. Over time, they are open to modification as the need arises. Moreover, constituent parts migrate from one place to another—sometimes by design, often by sheer accident of circumstance.

When it comes to assessing how cultural interaction influences the dietary habits—and preferences—of respective peoples, indigenous botanical exigencies are historically relevant. (Friendly neighborhood reminder: bordeaux comes from the soils of Bordeaux, burgundy comes from the soils of Burgundy, and cognac comes from the soils of Cognac; yet the palate for wine seems to be universal.) Geographical origin does not translate to memetic ownership along ethnic lines. In terms of permissible adoption of exogenous cultural elements, such exigencies are entirely beside the point. One certainly does not need to hail from Champaign to drink bubbly on festive occasions. (Memo: shiraz did not originally come from Shiraz; it originated in the south of France. Shall we rebuke Persians for making it?)

To those who insist that the provenance of a cultural element should dictate who's entitled to adopt it, we may continue to pose some more awkward questions. Shall we begrudge the French for croissants? For it turns out that flaky style of bread was derived from the Austrian kipferl (alt. "kifle"). The adjudicators of cultural transmission would not have allowed those delectable pastries to make their way out of Austria—let alone out of Europe—what with their meme embargoes and demands for cultural segregation. It makes one wonder: Is there such a thing as culinary exploitation? Why aren't the Viennese up in arms over Parisian croissants?

How much of our most celebrated culinary traditions emerged as a result of culinary appropriation? Consider soul food: a hallmark of Afro-American culture. Notable staples of this cuisine include grits, cornbread, hushpuppies, and pecan pie. All four were appropriated from Native Americans. Chicken and waffles? Dutch. Mac and Cheese? British. Pork and beans? Portuguese. Even fried chicken (likely due to Scottish influences) is the result of culinary appropriation. Much of the rest was—as is the case with many other cultures—the result of a gradual melding of different ethnic groups…which found themselves in close proximity…as the result of a sequence of historical accidents. Due to geo-political exigencies in Louisiana, jambalaya resulted from the merger of French, Spanish, and Caribbean culinary practices. Meanwhile, gumbo was a merger of French, West African, and Native

American (Choctaw) cuisines. While distinctly Afro-American, it turns out that soul food is a smorgasbord of Cul-Ap.

It was, of course, inevitable that some indigenous African fare (okra, sesame, yams, black-eyed peas, and jollof rice) would be incorporated into the culinary repertoire—largely due to Bantu, Hausa, Yoruba, and Igbo influences. ("Okra" derives from the Bantu "ki ngombo"). Barbecue was pioneered by Native Americans, though the African diaspora later created its own version; and the preparation was soon adopted throughout the antebellum South. Collard greens began in Dalmatia and Anatolia, yet eventually made their way to the Swahili Coast (as "sukuma")… and then to West Africa. The rest was history.

It would be insane to begrudge African Americans—a long-subjugated people—for adopting some of the culinary practices of their subjugators. As already mentioned, when significant power asymmetries exist, cultural IMPOSITION—rather than cultural appropriation—often occurs. Colonizers often impose their culture onto the colonized in a move that is more a matter of hegemony than of comity. But it is the SUBJUGATION that is the problem, not memetic transference. To reiterate: It is a mistake to conflate Cul-Ap with Cul-Imp.

Much of the cultural migration we encounter around the world has occurred because of commerce. When the Japanese adopted "concha" from the Portuguese, rendering it "melonpan", was this some sort of trespass? Probably not any more than when the Portuguese started eating sushi. Meanwhile, curry ended up becoming a big hit in Japan (as with currypan), with a distinct style that barely resembled the Indian version. Do Indians hold this against the Japanese? Nope. And wouldn't you know it: The Japanese are perfectly fine with Indians eating sashimi.

Culinary styles that were, at one point, the signature trait of a particular culture end up migrating across cultural lines. Such memetic dispersion is only natural—which is why fajitas, quesadillas, and chimichangas have become ubiquitous throughout the Occident…in spite of the fact that they happen to be Anglicized offshoots of Mexican fare (a.k.a. Tex-Mex). Stylistic choices affect one another, whether it's food or clothing or anything else. Something may originate in one place, and come to be associated with later adopters. Even thought coffee beans originated in Abyssinia, they were later made popular by the Javanese in Dutch Indonesia (hence the colloquialism, "Java") and by Latin Americans. In spite of this, no Ethiopians seems to be bothered; even as Juan Valdez is not paying tribute to the Aksumites. This is sometimes a matter of manufactured legacy. The Slavic dumplings now commonly known as pierogis were brought to Eastern Europe from the Far East by the Kievan Rus in the 13th century; yet the Poles now lay claim to them (as "varenyky") by associating them with the folk-hero, Jacek of the Odrowaz (a.k.a. Saint Hyacinth). Russians now eat "pelmeni".

What of the fixation on cuisine exhibited by "foodies" who've become afflicted with Cul-Ap-phobia? Their first mistake is to suppose that they have identified a phenomenon that is unique to the Occident. Since the Middle Ages, turmeric and cumin have commonly been used in Arab dishes. Are we to suppose, then, that Arabs are somehow guilty of illicit Cul-Ap from Indians? (Arabs adopted Indian numerals as well. Is that another travesty?) Ever put mustard on your hot dog? Well, then, you're ALSO stealing from the Indians. Enjoy Bavarian cream? It turns out that the delicious confection is off-limits if you're Bavarian. Why? Well, you see, the desert was mis-named after being developed by a French chef (Marie-Antoine Carême). Where's the outrage?

To further illustrate the neurosis involved with Cul-Ap-phobia, let's consider a recent case of umbrage. Some of the more vociferous Cul-Ap-phobes have criticized the renowned chef, Rick Bayless for his expertise in—and passion for—Mexican cuisine. Why? Well, you see, he is WHITE. The irony here is mind-bending; as anyone who levels such a criticism is racist. This holds whether or not the target of opprobrium happens to be from a marginalized ethnic group. Bigotry is bigotry, regardless of who's doing it and to whom it is aimed. Bayless is a champion of Mexican culture, not a thief. (If only MORE gringos had the appreciation that he exhibits.) Yet according to the logic of Cul-Ap-phobia, Bayless's contributions are to the DETRIMENT of Mexican culture. Welcome to the wacky world of Cul-Ap hysteria. Once again, cosmopolitans are forced to contend with a cadre of officious schoolmarms who, pretending to know anything about international cuisine, are determined to tsk-tsk-tsk their way to some "woke" panacea; and end up sending themselves into paroxysms of contrived indignation. They engage in their crusade even as they sprinkle some basil onto their dinner...without having thanked those of East Asian descent. After all, Cul-Ap is only iniquitous when OTHER people do it.

The logic here can become so convoluted that an obnoxious commentator once indicted a novel chickpea-based stew in which turmeric was used as an ingredient. Wherefore? Because many curries also use turmeric. (!) Therefore said stew could be obliquely considered a kind of curry...even though it did not contain the key element of curry: **curry leaves**. The commentator's conclusion: Said stew was—IPSO FACTO—a case of illicit cultural appropriation from Indian culture.

This is bonkers.

The upshot of such a bizarrely censorious attitude is actually quite simple: Limit your diet to only the things that your ancestors likely ate...centuries ago. (Non-Belgians who enjoy eating Belgian waffles are on notice!)

But suppose, for a moment, we actually attempted to do this. We regret to inform all mankind: If you aren't English, marmite is forever off-limits to you. Meanwhile, if you ARE English, you're stuck with mutton and haggis for all eternity. (On second thought, haggis is Scottish, so that's off-limits as well!) It seems not to occur to anti-Cul-Ap crusaders that virtually everyone on the planet engages in culinary appropriation on a daily basis; because that's how FOOD works. Rare is the recipe that does not involve the cooptation of ingredients and culinary motifs from other ethnic traditions.

We already know that vanilla and chocolate were developed by Maya and/or Aztecs; so for those who aren't indigenous to the region, don't get any ideas. And what of broccoli? This nutritious delight is a vegetable from Sicily; and did not become a part of the American dietary repertoire until the 19th century. (That's right.

The Founding Fathers did not know what broccoli was.) Are we now ALL guilty of purloining Sicilian cuisine?

The migration of food is but one indicator of cultural diffusion. This includes not only culinary practices / styles (a.k.a. "ethnic cuisine"), but—as we've seen—the ingredients themselves. Consider the fact that, before the 16th century, there were no potatoes in Ireland. (!) Many forget that these starchy tubers were imported from North America. The same goes for corn (maize) and baked beans. (So if you're not Native American, you're barred!)

What many around the world now take for granted during regular meals had origins that are rarely acknowledged.

Food is a reminder that calls for cultural segregation are indicative of hyper-provincialism. Undergirding such censure is a myopic way of seeing the wider world—a mentality that hampers efforts to forge human solidarity across ethnic lines. Never mind the fact that the cultural elements anti-Cul-Ap crusaders purport to be "protecting" were—in almost all cases—THEMSELVES appropriated from antecedent cultures. The declaration is: "Now that these memes have been declared OURS, nobody else shall be permitted to adopt them ever again!" So much for "as American as apple pie." (Again, apple pie was British as well as Swedish and Dutch before it was American. It was Frankish before that; and it was Turkic before that.) {64}

To condemn Cul-Ap would be to negate virtually everything that is now considered "American" (including apple pie); and to forestall America's continued cultural evolution.

There are endless examples that illustrated the errency of an anti-Cul-Ap crusade vis-a-vis food. Those who hem and haw about non-Japanese people eating sushi typically do not even understand what the term MEANS. As it happens, the moniker is short for "sushi-meshi", which simply means soured rice. But wait. The raw fish content with which "sushi" is primarily associated is actually "shashimi"; while the accoutrements (such as the seaweed wrap) are generally referred to as "neta". So is it the RICE with which these kvetchers are concerned? Or is it the use of seaweed wrap? Or is it the use of raw fish? And does this vague prohibition include the dish's predecessor, "funa-zushi", something that simply involves fermented fish ("nare-zushi")...which, as it turns out, can be found everywhere on the planet? Would a prohibition against non-Japanese people serving sushi include its variants like "ura-maki", "maki-zushi", and "maki-mono"...none of which are exclusively Japanese? What are we REALLY talking about here? Who draws the lines? Can NOBODY eat uncooked seafood outside of Japan? If so, does it need to be consumed separately from seaweed? Or is the rule that it just can't be WRAPPED IN the seaweed? (And when non-Japanese diners do eat such things, can they do it while watching Gundam?)

But wait. What of Japanese cuisine that was ITSELF culturally appropriated? As it turns out, "tempura" was taken from the Portuguese. So shall the Japanese ALSO be indicted for illicit Cul-Ap? (By the same token, we might ask: When Scandinavians eat hummus, is there a reason for the Lebanese and Palestinians to be thrown into a moral panic?)

The repercussions of enacting strictures against Cul-Ap are rarely considered—especially if those strictures were to be applied consistently (which is to say: applied to everyone). Such repercussions of are, of course, not at all what anti-Cul-Ap crusaders intend; but it is an unwillingness to take the proposed mandates to their logical conclusion that exposes the flaws in their reasoning.

Going back centuries, mandates for memetic sequestration along ethnic lines would have precluded much of the cultural efflorescence that has led us to where we are today. So what are we to make of culinary appropriation? We're all doing it...even when we don't realize it.

And that is what often ends up broadening our horizons. I have prepared bratwurst at a home in Hamburg, Germany; thali at a home in Gujarat, India; and chicken adobo at a home in the Philippines. In none of these cases was I notified: "Remember, you're not allowed to do this on your own." The same goes for having made pastels at a home in Brasil, pelmeni at a home in Russia, and khao soi at a home in Thailand. I suspect that if I ever had the pleasure of preparing injera at someone's home in Ethiopia, the story would be the same. "By all means: Try this when you get back home!"

Upon surveying the world's resplendent variety of cuisines, we are reminded that Cul-Ap is--more often than not--salubrious; so is welcomed across the planet. It's why Indians now eat biryani (Persian); why Thai people now eat satay (Indonesian); why the Japanese now eat kimchi (Korean); and why everyone now eats ramen (Japanese)

In the end, we are all participants in a grand human jubilee.

Learning Opportunities

So we arrive once more at the perennial question: When striving to foster social justice, on what shall we focus? I submit that, whatever the answer (to what is, admittedly, a complicated question), token formalities should be the least of our concern; as a fixation on propriety only sidetracks a cause purporting to be "Progressive". Not only does it serve as a distraction; it ends up coming off as elitist and out of touch. {60} While it is an intractable task to provide an exhaustive account of what should take precedence over what; we can at least procure a rough hierarchy of priorities. Decorum surely falls low on the list. So what role might a proscription against Cul-Ap play in this noble enterprise?

In proceeding with this inquiry, it is worth speculating. Were we to mandate cultural segregation for everyone on Earth, what would the repercussions be? Only Italians can wear a fazzoletto? Only Russians can perform The Nutcracker? Only Ethiopians can bake injera? Gosh-golly. While we're at it, we may need to clarify whether the plait donned by women the world over is really a **Dutch** braid or a **French** braid. Who appropriated whose culture THERE? (Either way, be careful which hairstyle you use.) Taking the anti-Cul-Ap crusade to its logical conclusion, we quickly find how silly it becomes.

When it comes to Cul-Ap, the salient issue is proper attribution—something, it turns out, Cul-Ap-phobes often know (or care) very little about; contrary to their own claims. Trans-cultural adoption is about giving credit where credit is due; and that requires one to know something about world history (how cultures have interacted over the course of centuries). Such inquiries can be tremendously edifying. Alas. The self-appointed adjudicators of meme transference are not interested in edification; as they are too busy with "call out" culture to concern themselves with such quixotic endeavors as, say, generating awareness and forging global human solidarity.

They would much rather segregate cultures than appreciate them.

Again, the question arises: Can one purloin a cultural element? As discussed earlier, barring intellectual property (which is simply a legal construct, which pertains to a delimited realm of ideas), memes cannot be pilfered. And so it goes:

Where Cul-Ap-phobes see some sort of memetic heist, cosmopolitans see cultural enrichment. The latter recognize that instances of memetic cross-pollination are often a salutary development for mankind; not something to be denounced.

A cordoned-off culture is an insular culture. As such, prescribing a regime of meme sequestration is antithetical to the cosmopolitan ideal. Cosmopolitanism is predicated on an (unabashed) embrace of our shared humanity; which—by definition—transcends ethnicity. It is therefore unconstrained by this or that historical accident. After all, any and every cultural demarcation—as with national affiliation—is an accident of history. While such demarcations serve a practical purpose in everyday life, they do not entail some eternal cosmic law—as if discrete boundaries written in the stars—to which we must all accede. So go ahead, weave your hair however you'd like; make whatever music you'd like; and—while you're at it—treat yourself to some apple pie.

A pluralistic society cannot exist in the midst of memetic cordons. Decrying "cultural appropriation" accomplishes nothing (barring, perhaps, stirring pointless resentment). In a misguided attempt to uplift marginalized communities by "protecting" their cultural heritage, such interlopers end up amplifying alterity. Once more, we are reminded that the aim of Cul-Ap-phobes is the segregation—rather than the appreciation—of cultures.

As we have seen, that's how something as simple as FOOD works. The same goes for etymology; because that's how LANGUAGE works. The same goes for religious beliefs; because that's how DOGMATISM works. Etc. Memes that subsist, subsist because they propagate; and they propagate because they resonate with different people at different times and places…for any number of reasons. We are all human, which means that accident of birth does not make any of us exempt from this all-encompassing dynamic. More to the point: We are all a part of a global memetic ecosystem, so we are all complicit.

The key, then, is to recognize the malleability of culture…IN EVERY INSTANCE.

Memetic transference across cultural lines—which THEMSELVES are fuzzy, and perpetually fluctuating—is a function of socio-psychical resonance. Such resonance is, in part, explained by our shared humanity; but it is also dictated by historical contingencies (incumbent power structures, exigent social norms, prevailing sensibilities, etc.) This cultural gradient exists simply due to the fact that certain people, under certain circumstances, have affinities for some memes rather than others. Some people like curry (many of whom are not Indian); others don't. And that's fine. Begrudging people for their culinary choices (i.e. when those choices happen not to coincide with their ethnic identity) is antithetical to the spirit of cosmopolitanism. Would we do the same with literary choices? Musical choices? Sartorial choices?

Human interaction entails memetic transference. Whenever in close proximity, cultures do not ABUT; they BLEND. Their boundaries are rarely distinct and static; they are blurred and fluid. Consequently, demarcations become fuzzy…and even illusory. Now that we live in a globalized world, such proximity is not limited to geography. And that's wonderful. Thank heavens for memetic dispersion—be it musical, literary, culinary, sartorial, mythological, or anything else.

What about architecture? As one might expect, we find a treasure-trove of examples that illustrate the thesis of the present book. During the Renaissance, certain elements of Europe's gothic architecture—specifically, the signature pointed arch—was heavily influenced by Islamic structural design. Shall we consider this an instance of the Occident illicitly appropriating a meme from the Orient? Is Alhambra in Grenada a tribute or a desecration?

But wait. As it turns out, the pointed arch that is so often associated with Islamic architecture was itself appropriated from antecedent Sassanian (Persian) architecture...which had actually been pioneered by the ancient Assyrians in THEIR architecture during the Bronze Age. Meanwhile, the Byzantines made use of this distinct structural feature long before the Muslims adopted it—as attested by the Karamagara bridge in Cappadocia c. 500. Shall we consider this a case of serial memetic theft?

That's not all. The signature "horseshoe arch" typically associated with Islamic Andalusia was, in fact, lifted from the antecedent Visigothic design. Are we to suppose, then, that the Moors are indebted to the Goths? And what of the Turks' adoption of Baroque (spec. Rococo) motifs? Memetic transference brought THAT aesthetic from Italy to France to Spain...and even to Russia. It was a spree of unbridled Cul-Ap from Anatolia to Iberia...and all the way up to Saint Petersburg!

There are myriad examples of this in architecture. The medieval European structures known as "cloisters" were based on the "peristyles" of ancient Rome: private gardens surrounded by colonnades. The Romans had adapted this structural feature from ancient Greece...which, in turn, had antecedents in ancient Persia. We might also note that the word "paradise" derives—via Latin and Greek—from the Old Persian (Avestan) term for a walled-in garden: "paridayda" / "fairi-daeza" (which yielded the Arabic term, "firdaus", a moniker used in Islamic lore to describe heaven). Are Christian monasteries—and the Koran, for that matter—to be prosecuted for illicit Cul-Ap? Is Cambridge University guilty of appropriating an architectural motif from Iran?

Tracking the cross-currents of culture is like tracking the winds. And trying to predict how one culture will interact with another is comparable to predicting the weather. In either case, one is contending with highly-complex, open systems... which, when they meet, are bound to inter-penetrate in idiosyncratic ways. Memetic zephyrs impinge upon a given locality, and do so in surprising ways. This is the case whether we are talking about architectural motifs or literary motifs. It is the case whether we are talking about hallowed folklore or iconography. It is the case whether we are talking about musical styles, or dancing styles, or clothing styles, or culinary styles, or anything else. It is asinine to begrudge anyone who opts to participate in this on-going dynamic.

Cosmopolitanism entails that one eschews Exceptionalism in all its grotesque forms; and recognizes that one's own culture is—in the grand scheme of things—nothing ontologically special. There is no divine ordinance. All cultures are a concatenation of social constructs; and all social constructs are accidents of history. No singular culture was determined by some sort of Providence; and no memetic ownership was written in the stars. So it is important that we come to any evaluation of cultural exigencies not as members of any particular tribe, but simply as fellow humans.

In the early 1930's, the renowned social anthropologist, Ruth Benedict noted that "there has never been a time when civilization stood more in need of individuals who are genuinely culture-conscious, who can see objectively the socially conditioned behavior of other peoples without fear and recrimination" (**Patterns Of Culture**, p. 10-11). Benedict's approach was to evaluate the world's widely-variegated cultures NOT through the lens of one's own culture, but from an impartial perspective. As Edward Said would four decades later, she rejected the Occident-centric way of seeing the world. Surely, both Benedict and Said would have recoiled at the thought that people would one day vilify those engaged in Cul-Ap; and do so in the name of social justice.

In order to make their case, those who decry "cultural appropriation" need to point to a scenario in which Cul-Ap occurred between a purported source culture (A; i.e. the alleged victim) and a destination culture (B; i.e. the alleged culprit); then show that there was harm done to A—or members of A—as a result of said Cul-Ap. One would find that the only injustice is that of B not giving proper attribution to A (with regard to the element in question). This problem cannot be explained by Cul-Ap PER SE. Rather, it implicates those engaged in the Cul-Ap who happen to be ignorant or dishonest.

Granted, Cul-Ap may sometimes be concomitant with (actual) exploitation / derogation. However, in such cases, the Cul-Ap accompanies, but does not FACILITATE, said exploitation / derogation. More often than not, when members of B seek to dominate or marginalize members of A, the members of B force members of A to adopt cultural elements of B. In other words, they do the OPPOSITE of Cul-Ap—which is to say that they impose rather than appropriate cultural elements.

It is important not to construe participation in a cultural phenomenon as annexation of that cultural phenomenon. Alas. For the Cul-Ap-phobe, any non-Japanese person who creates manga isn't respectfully partaking in a celebrated Japanese art-form; such a person is PILFERING it. Cul-Ap-phobes seem not to understand that cultural appropriation done in good faith is synonymous with cultural appreciation. And that cultural appreciation is a salutary thing—nay, a prerequisite for cosmopolitanism; and an integral part of living in harmony in a pluralistic society.

But what about jerks? It's no secret that sometimes Cul-Ap is done flippantly; with complete lack of consideration of cultural exigencies; and sometimes even with a jeer. When that is the case, it is often done to patronize or demean members of the source culture. In such cases, the Cul-Ap is done for the sake of mockery. This may be done as a result of contempt and/or heedlessness. In other words: Cul-Ap is done out of ill will. What should be indicted, then, is the ill will; not the Cul-Ap.

Here's a simple rule for all human interaction: Don't be an asshole.

While we are right to be concerned about ill will when it comes to any interaction between ethnicities. Yet, as we've seen, there is often a misdiagnosis of things as having to do with Cul-Ap when something else is the problem. Consider the mascots for sports teams. The reason the Cleveland Indians are now the Guardians and the Washington Redskins are now the Commanders is that such a cartoonish treatment of an ethnic identity (Native Americans) is unfilial—a flouting of civility. (Presumably, a similar alteration is forthcoming for the Atlanta Braves and Kansas City Chiefs.) Of course, such symbolic gestures do little to solve the underlying problem. (Washington D.C. is not less violent because the Bullets are now the Wizards.) To make matters worse, professional leagues are a commercial enterprise. Turning a group's cultural hallmarks into KITSCH is one thing; but to do it in order to fill the coffers of large corporations is another.

When driven by the profit motive, cultural exploitation is especially problematic. However, not all Cul-Ap is of this nature. So to pretend that Cul-Ap is inherently exploitative is disingenuous. When Canadians celebrate "Caribana" and "Cari-fiesta" each year, are non-Caribbean-born citizens obliged to refrain from participating in the festivities—that is: from Caribbean dance, Caribbean song, Caribbean dress, and Caribbean food? Are we to suppose that non-Caribbean-born citizens are only permitted to participate in Caribbean culture that day? At any given time and place, how do we know what's off-limits to whom? And under what circumstances? What are the criteria by which we determine the existence of Cul-Ap; or, in the cases where we agree it exists, the criteria by which we ascertain whether or not it should be permissible?

As already mentioned, a key factor in the grievance against Cul-Ap is an asymmetry in socio-economic power. Anti-Cul-Ap crusaders hold that if those who are more powerful force their memes upon those who are less powerful, the meme-adoption must be forgiven; as it is a matter of subjugation. If, on the other hand, the more powerful adopt memes from the less powerful, something iniquitous is afoot.

All reasonable people agree that when colonizers take over a region and impose their culture on the colonized, the latter's use of exogenous cultural elements is no sin. After all, they are typically INCURRING rather than deliberately APPROPRIATING the memes of the imperialists. The meme adoption wasn't their choice. So, as victims, members of the destination culture should be given a pass. The culprits are those of the SOURCE culture.

However, this standard becomes less clear in other scenarios. Consider all the elements of British culture that are of French provenance due to the Normans having conquered England in 1066, and ruled there well into the 13th century. (Modern English is more influenced by Norman French than by either German or Old English.) What if the Normans had never exercised any cultural—or political—influence over England; and English Francophiles had, instead, voluntarily adopted French memes during the High Middle Ages? According to the logic of Cul-Ap-phobes, that would make the appropriation of French memes illicit. Does this criterion make sense? Or…perhaps the meme adoption would be permissible in such a scenario simply because there would not have been a significant power asymmetry. But what if the English were significantly more powerful than the French during the relevant period in history? Would THAT change things?

We encounter similar questions when it comes to bigotry. Can a member of a marginalized community be bigoted against members of a dominant community? There's no doubt that power asymmetries play a role in how / why bigotries form, and how much harm those bigotries can do. But is bigotry PER SE solely a function of power asymmetry? The answer is no. When the oppressed are bigoted against anyone who falls within the same demographic category as their oppressors, it may be more benign; but it is still bigotry. {46}

Cul-Ap transpires in several media: song, dance, attire, literature, architecture, cuisine, etc. Tracing the genealogy of any given meme is not always straight-forward. As discussed in Part 1, there are many illustrations of how iconography undergoes a semiotic metamorphosis as it migrates from culture to culture—from the caduceus to the swastika. Another example discussed was the hexagram. For much of the 19th century, it was used for the emblems of slave patrols in the antebellum South. That was the basis for the earliest sheriff badges across the United States. (After the second World War, the shape was gradually adjusted—giving the star either five points or seven points instead; or even transitioning to a shield.) When Kabbalists began using the hexagram (as the "Star of David") in the Late Middle Ages, the Japanese had already been using it for centuries (as the Kagame crest). Granted, medieval practitioners of Kabbalah didn't "appropriate" the hexagram from Shinto practitioners any more than racist Americans "appropriated" the hakenkreuz from Hindu / Buddhist iconography; but the occurrence of such symbols across distant cultures illustrates how certain memes (esp. those with some kind of resonance) crop up in different places at different times for different reasons.

Something as simple and catchy as a hexagram may well emerge spontaneously in various cultures—each occurring independently of one another. Surely, Hindus in India made use of the hexagram for some of the same reasons they made use of the swastik[a]: it's very cool looking. But there are also instances where one culture adopts a meme from another culture because they find it rather nifty—thereby making it their own. Hence the Nazi hakenkreuz (likely adapted from the Old Norse symbol for Thor's hammer). In such cases, exogenous cultural elements are often re-conceived as endogenous; as nobody likes to think of auspicious items in their cultural repertoire as derivative. As mentioned earlier: When it comes to appraising our own culture, we like to see novelty where it doesn't exist. Consequently, we are apt to deny Cul-Ap when WE do it; even as we are quick to notice it when others do it.

Those who want cultures to be memetic silos are countenancing the most extreme form of parochialism. But, for anti-Cul-Ap crusaders, cultural segregation is precisely the point; and feigning offense is their stock in trade. Anyone familiar with the cosmopolitan ideal knows that it is difficult to embrace our shared humanity across cultural divides if one is pilloried the moment one dares to sample an exogenous meme. (The idea: Appreciate others' cultures; but you are obligated to do so FROM AFAR.) A cosmopolitan outlook is predicated on a recognition of universals; which is simply to say that it is based upon that which transcends all cultural divides. Meanwhile, cultural segregation represents everything that cosmopolitanism is against.

There is nothing written in the stars about this or that culture, let alone about ownership of any one of a culture's signature elements; as any given social norm is the product of a long sequence of historical accidents. Such things cannot possibly define our humanity; for there is nothing accidental about being human.

Irrespective of circumstance, we all have access to the better angels of our nature because we are all human–irrespective of culture. As such, parochialism–whereby one circumscribes one's sense of humanity according to this or that cultural affiliation–is not consummate with a sincere embrace of universals. Such an outlook is inimical to cosmopolitanism.

A genuinely cosmopolitan zeitgeist demands a broader perspective. (Think of it as a nominally meta-cultural perspective—a variation on Rawls' socio-economic "original position".) This entails a vantage point that urges us to see past our own memetic orbit, to venture beyond the confines of our assigned cultural boundaries, and thereby expand our horizons. After all, those boundaries are nothing more than an accident of history. Human solidarity demands nothing less. Such solidarity is possible only because we are capable of rising above the warp and woof of the social constructs that govern our daily lives.

Any given feature of a given culture—as with any given part of a dogmatic system—is not inextricably tied to a particular ethnic group. As with any social norm, a custom emerges when, where, and how it does by historical accident. This is why criticizing an element of a given culture—or of a given religion—is entirely disconnected from bigotry against whatever group might happen to espouse that element. Memes are not people. One can no more be racist against a social norm than one can be racist against a recipe for casserole (which may or may not happen to be affiliated with a certain community). In fact, suggesting that such criticism is somehow "racist" is ITSELF born of racism. (The ironies never end.)

Criticizing a dubious practice that inheres in a particular culture as actually a civic responsibility. For it is based on the fact that we are all fellow humans; and so are ultimately subject to the same moral standards...whether we acknowledge it or not. Our shared humanity is what gives us all access to universal principles: standards by which any practice—regardless of when or where it occurs, or how much it is sacralized—can be evaluated. Objective morality is unconcerned with the myriad idiosyncrasies of communal consecrations. We are all human, so we all have recourse to the same moral compass.

More to the point: The humanity of a given person / group is not dependent on any particular social norm. We are far more than an agglomeration of the conventions we countenance–whatever those conventions might happen to be. For our humanity transcends the memes we espouse. What makes us human is not some historical accident—even one that has been sacralized for eons. Meanwhile, the memes we adopt—and opt to retain—are NOTHING BUT a historical accident.

Such affinities are, after all, up to us to embrace or discard; and do so according to that which transcends our memetic proclivities.

As Johann Gottfried von Herder pointed out, mankind is not divided into distinct races with any inherent differences that really matter; mankind is divided by CULTURES, all of which are adopted after birth...and, of course, BY ACCIDENT OF birth. And over time, cultures meld. How so? Well, mediated as they are by human interaction, they CAN'T NOT meld.

Cul-Ap-phobia is the lifeblood of cultural segregation—impelled, as it is, by a fever-dream of cultural puritanism. Like most of those obsessed with political correctness, anti-Cul-Ap crusaders are puritanical, authoritarian, and hyper-censorious; which is simply to say that they are Reactionary: the antithesis of the astute cosmopolitans that they fancy themselves to be. Being, as they are, the constables of enforced parochialism, we are notified that we are morally obligated to accede to their decrees.

Quite the contrary: Progressives are often morally obligated to repudiate said decrees.

In the final analysis, we find that nothing was pre-ordained to be a part of any given culture. There is no cultural destiny. It's all open-ended. So a culture—as it happens to exist NOW—is merely a stage in an on-going process. On the way to where? Nobody knows. What will become of this long, meandering metamorphosis? Only time will tell. But that's part of the fun of it. We're all just trying to evolve; and part of that is adapting our meme-o-sphere to new developments. As fellow humans, we find that certain memes are good for everyone, others are bad for everyone; and ANYONE can point this out. For the only credential required is, well, being human.

So what are we to make of those who design to cordon off a specified culture, as if it could be discretely defined? As I hope to have shown, any demarcation between one culture and another is interminably blurry, and perpetually in flux; and—in any case—an accident of history. So the exact position of the border between THIS culture and THAT culture is oftentimes illusory.

Cultures are dynamic agglomerations that are ever-evolving, not static wholes meant to be preserved as-is for all eternity. Moreover, since before recorded history, ethnic identities have always been amorphous; and don't depend on any given meme for their continued existence. Such is the nature of memetic exchange: the lifeblood of all human interaction. As a result, embracing our shared humanity requires us to break out of our parochial mindsets; to not be hung up on what we—or others—happen to have inherited *by accident of birth*. The point, then, is to look beyond the cloistered precincts of our own cultural milieu; and survey–with a sense of awe and wonder–the vast, global meme-o-sphere. Only then can we recognize the world–in all its glorious variegation–as our common home.

Anti-Cul-Ap crusaders often fashion themselves as the official adjudicators of cultural ownership; and thus the arbiters of meme-transference across (what they see as) eternally demarcated, static cultural boundaries. This is based on a grave misunderstanding of what culture is. Any given culture is an amorphous unity of elements that is perpetually in flux (rather than as a rigid assemblage of disparate fragments, held in stasis). Each element melds with the others in organic ways—blurring the boundaries between them. Cultures are, after all, dynamic; not static; and don't subsist by being hermetically sealed off from the rest of the world. Every extant meme has been adapted to occupy a place in the grand memetic repertoire; playing a role the significance of which changes over time.

It bears worth reiterating: Cultures are amorphous: more like a swirling kaleidoscope than a static mosaic. Here in the U.S. (and Canada), we are steeped in a roiling memetic soup; and that's a good thing.

Those who are affiliated with a given culture often stammer and stumble through the fluctuating memetic environs in which they find themselves, interacting with exogenous cultural elements as the occasion arises; and they are able to do so without losing their cultural identity—as with, say, Jewish Americans ordering out for Chinese food while playing mah-jong. Unless one is a religious fundamentalist, one recognizes that one doesn't need to relegate oneself to a memetic cordon in order to maintain one's "minhag". In the meantime, nobody of Chinese heritage feels as though their culture is being pillaged when someone who isn't Chinese partakes in one of their signature games while indulging in General Tso's chicken.

Guidelines For Fostering Healthy Cul-Ap

As we've seen, there are valid concerns about Cul-Ap—specifically when it involves mockery, any kind of exploitative activity, the perpetuation of stereotypes / stigmas, lack of proper recognition, or the downplaying of cultural significance. But what about all OTHER instances of Cul-Ap?

In trying to navigate the labyrinthine logic of Cul-Ap-phobia, I am left with questions about my own conduct. Is wearing the Buddhist necklace my Thai friend gave me unseemly because I am neither Thai nor Buddhist? Am I guilty of Cul-Ap every time I put it around my neck? This seems to be tantamount to asking: Shall I refrain from aspiring to be—in the words of Thomas Paine—a citizen of the world? The important thing, it seems, is that I appreciate what the necklace means in ancient Siamese culture; and—in particular—to my Thai friends. So long as I have an understanding of its significance in Theravada Buddhism, it would seem that—as a fellow human—I am edified by embracing this hallowed talisman.

Felicitously, I am put at ease the moment I realize that the arguments against Cul-Ap are entirely specious. In leveling charges against those of us who make use of memes from beyond their own culture's purview, anti-Cul-Ap crusaders may as well impugn someone for illicitly annexing the oxygen she breathes when it has wafted from foreign lands. Mankind shares this planet, and remains in awe of the same night sky. There is no reason to balk at the chance to share in the fruits of mankind's magnificently diverse cultures. The human family is a widely variegated mosaic of cultural spaces, each melding into the other over time. This is a GOOD thing.

As we have seen, much of what is derisively labeled Cul-Ap is, in fact, simply people trying to interact with—and appreciate—other cultures. Sometimes, this means putting on someone else's hat (that is: trying it on for size). And sometimes doing so leads to the conclusion: "Gee-wiz, that's a great idea. I think we might start doing that too."

When people make use of exogenous cultural elements, the results are usually favorable to everyone involved. Affinities are developed, bonds are formed. Be that as it may, there are–from time to tome–instances of impertinence. This can happen in various ways. A lack of appreciation for the virtues of the material's source; and a lack of proper attribution. These are the two most common problems. A recent example—one of many in dunderheaded Hollywood casting choices—was Dreamworks' decision to cast a White actress (Scarlett Johansson) as the protagonist in the Japanese anime classic, "Ghost In The Shell". (Hollywood then doubled down, and cast a White actor in "Death Note".) This was somewhat of a travesty, just as when ANYONE disregards the ethnic origins of a story; or is disingenuous about the ethnic identity of the story's characters. {30} (Still no word yet on whether anyone is planning on casting a gender-fluid Asian midget as Tevye the milkman in Fiddler on the Roof.) The irony here is that it is primarily Cul-Ap-phobes who endorse such mis-representations.

At Disney, movie producers who chortled about inclusivity turned around and used CGI dwarves in the Snow White remake…instead of using ACTUAL ACTORS (specifically: those with dwarfism, who already had limited casting opportunities). Is this idiocy or perfidy? One must wonder.

This is what happens when the identitarian mindset short-circuits.

To reiterate: Cul-Ap plays no role in social injustice; and certainly has nothing to do with continued existence of bigotry in our midst. Vilifying those who engage in Cul-Ap not only does nothing to solve the problems we say we want to solve, it serves to exacerbate extant tribal divisions. Rather than replacing alterity with comity, it simply couches the alterity in different terms.

If one wants a prime example of Cul-Ap gone awry, look no further than the hokey "New Age" American appropriation of (Indian) yoga—suffused, as it is, with oodles of faux spirituality and an ever-shifting glossary of inane jargon. Notable is the utterly daft use of "namaste" as a kind of profound utterance; as if it were some deeply spiritual incantation (as opposed to what it actually is: the Hindi word for "hello"). {27} Again, we find that Cul-Ap is problematic primarily when it is done out of ignorance.

There is a valid concern about those who are mendacious enough to adopt a meme from elsewhere, then pass it off as their own. In such cases, the problem isn't the adoption per se; it is the dishonesty. Incorporating "exotic" ingredients is not some sort of "cultural theft". It is, in fact, the way that the culinary arts have worked since time immemorial. Any given item is invariably going to be a novelty to someone somewhere at some point in time; as every place on Earth has social norms from one historical period to the next (of which certain things are NOT a part). It is no crime to find something "foreign" if it is, indeed, unfamiliar. After all, what is and isn't familiar is a matter of historical accident.

The key is how people treat—and react to—such encounters. It's a choice we all have: Do so either with conceit and superciliousness…or with an open mind and open heart. A genuine appreciation for the new meme's origins makes Cul-Ap MORE appealing; not less. If we're truly concerned about empowering marginalized communities, unabashed cosmopolitanism is what matters. This means giving credit where credit is due (that is: according respect wherever it is warranted), and embracing what historian Iriye Akira referred to as "cultural internationalism".

Make no mistake: odious cases of Cul-Ap do exist. They often involve efforts to erase an ethnic exigency or simply a blatant disregard for the cultural legacy of the material. (There is a difference between the failure to give credit where credit is due and deliberate elision of the origins of an idea. One is careless, the other perfidious.) For example, some Israelis rebranded the Lebanese-Palestinian chickpea-based mezzeh item, "[k]Hummus" as Israeli–a semiotic maneuver that was concomitant with the (attempted) erasure of an entire PEOPLE. (As it happens, cultural cleansing often accompanies ethnic cleansing.) However, the problem in such a case is obfuscation, not appropriation. The sin lay not in eating hummus, but in denying where it came from.

Hummus was not an isolated incident. As it happened, halva, tahini, z'hug, falafel, shawarma, and pepitas were all co-opted from Arab cuisine and dubbed "Jewish" by Levantine and Maghrebi Jews. Such items are now considered staples of "Israeli" cuisine by those who don't know any better. Here's the point: Such Cul-Ap is a wonderful thing…so long as the origin of the culinary items is not elided.

Another odious form of Cul-Ap is what amounts to cultural VANDALISM–as when the "Hare Krishna" cult mal-appropriated Hindu motifs. This can be a matter of desecrating another tradition's artistic achievements–as when Hollywood adapted the manga, Dragon Ball into the risible film, "Dragonball Evolution": a mawkish American rendition of a Japanese classic (done for purely commercial purposes). The film was produced with complete disregard for the material's cultural legacy, and unconcerned with the artistic merits of the source-material. Yet we heard nothing but silence from those who threw tantrums when an Asian dared to pen a parable about the evils of slavery.

Regarding anti-Cul-Ap crusaders who's motives are not duplicitous, it can be said that their misgivings about Cul-Ap are gravely misplaced. Though concerns about degradation are valid, censuring (allegedly illicit) appropriation based on ethnic identity is not an effective way to mitigate such regrettable occurrences. One cannot mitigate ill will simply by proscribing it.

We might remind ourselves that even those from WITHIN the culture-in-question are capable of mal-appropriating an element of that culture. One does not have to hail from a different culture to pervert an artistic masterpiece—a literary or musical work—or to desecrate a sacred artifact. So clearly it is not the Cul-Ap PER SE that is the problem in such cases.

One way to look at the issue is as follows: Appreciation is the opposite of resentment. The former begets comity; the latter begets enmity. Whenever Cul-Ap-phobia is operative, we find people sowing resentment and suspicion. Meanwhile, being "cultured" stems from appreciation. It involves a celebration of the world's resplendent variety of cultural offerings.

Even as we celebrate, we should be prudent. Given that Cul-Ap does not (automatically) entail a kind of derogation of the source-culture, we might wonder: What are the things with which we should be concerned? When it comes to adopting cultural elements that are clearly from outside one's own culture (for the time being), there are two basic conditions of basic decency that should be honored:

ONE: Give credit where credit is due. It is a matter of common courtesy that the source-culture of the element-in-question not be mis-characterized; and that there be proper attribution in the event that something is being adopted from another culture (at least to the degree that a distinct source-culture can be designated). It is, of course, routine for prideful peoples to be reticent to acknowledge that cherished elements (elements that often buttress their own identity) were lifted from other cultures. But recognition of actual history (i.e. cultural legacies) poses no problem for those who are honest about the origins of their own heritage. {14}

TWO: The adoption should in no way lend credence to--or enjoin--real exploitation. That is to say: It should not be done in a way that adopters are apt to benefit to the detriment of the integrity of the source-culture. It is reasonable to suppose that those who use an exogenous cultural element as a GIMMICK may not be acting in good faith. As we have seen, commodifying cherished cultural elements cheapens them. The only acceptable reason to employ gimmickry is for satire (i.e. for didactic purposes), where the aim is to bring attention to an important issue. By making use of cultural elements for dubious reasons, one is betraying the spirit behind them. THAT is the problem.

Put briefly: All participation should be done in good faith, with proper attribution. Cul-Ap should never be done to denigrate. In viewing cultural elements that happen to be foreign, we must never lose sight of the fact that humanity transcends culture. Even amidst the world's motley assortment of cultures, mankind is one.

It goes without saying that Cul-Ap is not inherently salutary. Recognizing this fact is simply to say that there can be perfidious forms of Cul-Ap. Be that as it may, the problem in such instances is the perfidy, not the "appropriation". For Cul-Ap is not inherently defamatory; it is the ill-will of the people engaging in it that make such cases objectionable. In and of itself, meme-adoption is a morally neutral act; which means that "cultural appropriation" is categorically amoral. Every culture has done it. Every culture continues to do it.

Again, we should be reminded of the captiousness—endemic to p.c. in general—that animates Cul-Ap-phobia. The prospect that someone, somewhere might claim to be "offended" / "insulted" is the eternal, ever-present hobgoblin of p.c.-mongers…who insist that any given person's (purported) discomfiture entails that certain guidelines (read: formalities) must be mandated for any and all bystanders who could feasibly be blamed for eliciting said discomfiture. Thus one party's subjective state can be used as justification to impose obligations / restrictions on others—especially on those who can be blamed for whatever psychical turmoil might be experienced by anyone who is especially prone to, well, psychical turmoil.

In the event that ill will IS involved, we must bear in mind that bad faith is opprobrious regardless of the context. The fact that the same act can be done with good will proves that it is not the act itself that is at issue. The same "cos-play" can be done from a place of admiration or of derision. But even if it is done out of spleen, we must ask: Is acerbic mockery—even the most offensive kind—to be permitted in a free society?

Bottom line: We needn't resort to frivolous indictments of Cul-Ap to denounce perfidy. Instances of Cul-Ap that involve dubious motives are not indictments of Cul-Ap; they are simply reminders that anyone can have dubious motives when doing, well, ANYTHING. The solution, then, is not to proscribe Cul-Ap; it is to ensure that Cul-Ap is done with a modicum of common courtesy. As I hope I have shown, once we deign to forbid all instances of Cul-Ap, we miss what makes any culture WHAT IT IS; and end up devolving into absurdity.

The issue to address, then, is that of proper attribution / recognition. To illustrate this point, let's look at an example to which many can relate. In the United States, White people have been doing the well-known dance known as the "Electric Slide" since the late 1980's. Most of them haven't the faintest idea that the song, "Electric Boogie" (originally by Bunny Wailer in 1982; later re-done by Marcia Griffiths) and accompanying choreography come from Afro-American culture. (The dance dates back to 1976, when African Americans started doing it at backyard barbecues and neighborhood block parties.) Such nescience can be attributed more to heedlessness than to perfidy. (Amusingly, the line dance came to sometimes be referred to as "the hustle" in the mid-West; and was often done to the song, "Now That We Found Love" by Heavy D & The Boyz.) Here, Cul-Ap is not the problem. As is often the case, a lack of recognition of the cultural origins is at issue. Such dereliction is remedied not by cultural segregation, but by generating awareness. In other words: The answer is more cultural INTERACTION; and—invariably—more cultural MIXING.

The little-recognized provenance of the Electric Slide is not an anomalous phenomenon. Such oversight is a reminder that Cul-Ap is part of the natural process of memetic transference between ethnic groups. In music, this is illustrated by the Afro-American basis for jazz, the blues, R&B, rock 'n roll, and—for that matter—most pop music. All of it is a matter of diffusion / absorption, not annexation / deracination. (Recall Little Richard's words about Elvis.) That Britney Spears owes a debt of gratitude to Chuck Berry isn't the problem; that many of her fans are unaware of this debt of gratitude is.

In the meantime, White people doing the Electric Slide in no way infringes on African Americans' ability to do the same.

We are all engaged in an on-going process of Cul-Ap—a process in which each of us partakes at our own discretion. For, in a civil society, cultural participation is a matter of personal prerogative. The question is not whether or not we're doing it; it's whether or not cultural appreciation is involved. Unfortunately, for many, sincere appreciation plays little role.

Yet a dearth of cultural appreciation is not solely due to a failure to acknowledge history (spec. the memetic genealogy that spawned the cultural element we've embraced). Being "cultured" involves other things as well. It primarily means being relatively well-versed in the landmark artistic achievements of global society—musical, sartorial, architectural, theatrical, and all the rest. After all, aesthetic value (which is universal) transcends cultural demarcations (which are circumstantial). Memetic transference across cultures is inevitable, as memes are—by their nature—viral. This is the case whether the memes are culinary or literary or anything else. To fail to understand this is to fail to understand how culture works. This even goes for something as basic as language. Heck, it goes for every social norm on the planet...even a silly dance performed at wedding receptions. Shall we begrudge those who want to partake in the bountiful cultural smorgasbord of humankind; or shall we delve in? For anyone who values cosmopolitan ideals, the answer is obvious.

It is important to take into account power asymmetries whenever assessing possible instances of social injustice. Indeed, socio-economic inequality disproportionately impacts historically oppressed / marginalized marginalized communities. (Such disproportionality explains why it makes sense to have a Black Chamber of Commerce, but not a White Chamber of Commerce.) But the vestiges of Jim Crowe will not be eradicated by preventing White people from doing the Electric Slide.

More than just undermining the integrity of public discourse, crowding the discourse with petty grievances gives Progressivism a bad name...while providing right-wing polemicists with fodder to assail their political adversaries. Potemkin Progressives—anti-Cul-Ap crusaders included—sabotage the Progressive movement by introducing a skein of frivolous indictments, thereby shooting an otherwise noble cause in the foot. They persist in their misguided efforts because they find that an anti-Cul-Ap crusade—replete with a profusion of tendentious rigamarole—provides them with a perverse satisfaction.

While anti-Cul-Ap crusaders—and all the other identitarians of the Regressive "Left"—are sitting atop their high horses feeling good about themselves, the rest of us will remain down here on the ground; and continue trying to solve the world's actual problems.

Concluding Remarks For Part 2

I opened this book with a passage worth repeating: When harmonious, a culture might be thought of as a mellifluous memetic fugue. Yet even the most ordered cultures are a hodge-podge of elements culled from different places at different times for different reasons—usually by sheer happenstance. Cultures are rather messy things; and that is what makes them so fascinating. (A wonderful book on this topic is Felipe Fernández-Armesto's ***A Foot in the River***.) Any given culture is not some timeless blueprint inscribed into the fabric of the cosmos; for it could easily have been other than it now is; and it STILL CAN be something other than what it currently happens to be.

This all occurs due to memetic transference across cultural lines.

So what's all the fuss? The sort of "appropriation" against which Cul-Ap-phobes inveigh is seen as a form of oppression and/or exploitation—as if those engaged in Cul-Ap were participating in a meme-procurement racket. To equate meme-adoption with an oppressive / exploitative enterprise is to censure what—it turns out—is the basis for human bonding (whether it be within or across cultures). This holds true even in the case of power-asymmetries.

Due to the fact that cultures have fuzzy boundaries, proscribing Cul-Ap becomes an Sisyphean task. Where cultures begin and end is not only indeterminate, but perpetually in flux. Each culture is comprised of a fluid amalgam of myriad elements, any one of which might be shared with various other cultures. As the numerous examples provided in this book attest, any given meme probably has a history that does not immediately announce itself.

Myriad things that are now found in the Muslim world were appropriated from non-Islamic cultures. The "shura" council (a term used as the title of Surah 42 of the Koran) is an adaptation of the Turkic "khurultay"...which was itself taken from the Mongolian "Khooraldai"...which was Tengri-ist before it was Islamic. This reminds us that cultures often blend into one another—nay: SEEP into one another. So navigating the interlaced border between MY culture and YOUR culture is a byzantine task.

According to Anti-Cul-Ap crusaders, the problem with the appropriation of exogenous cultural elements is that ***by simply engaging in*** such an act, one is according insufficient respect to the source-culture. The idea is that to engage in Cul-Ap is to evince an intolerably cavalier—even disrespectful—attitude toward others' cultural identities. Yet not all people who participate in meme-transference across cultural lines are heedless of the source- culture; and—in any case—most of the ACTUAL instances of derogation ***do not involve Cul-Ap***. Cultural transference stems from affinities; and exploitation rarely involves an effort to forge affinity.

What is also lost on anti-Cul-Ap crusaders is that having (actual) respect for culture involves respecting how cultures emerge in the first place. To be respectful of culture QUA CULTURE, one must acknowledge the process that created it.

The anti-Cul-Ap crusade is as much about moral preening as it is about caviling. Having indulged in an ample display of kvetching, the anti-Cul-Ap crusader can then pat himself on the back for—in his own eyes—having valiantly expunged a raft of chimerical social injustices from society. It's as if by denouncing selected instances of cultural diffusion, he has made the streets safe for ethnic minorities.

Most of those taken in by anti-Cul-Ap hysteria—and by p.c.-mania in general—are determined to be offended for any reason, at any cost. Participants in this charade wear their contrived "offense" like a badge of honor. It soon becomes plain to see that the anti-Cul-Ap crusade is more about theatrics than it is about ethics. Participants in this charade are eager to find an excuse—ANY excuse, no matter how fatuous—to claim "offense" in a gambit to telegraph their "woke" bona fides to like-minded ideologues. Such pretense becomes de rigueur when p.c. governs public discourse. One has done nothing to bolster the commonweal, but at least one has gotten some attention.

Such posturing involves no rectitude. For an obsession with etiquette does nothing to engender probity; it simply obliges everyone to—well—keep up appearances. Being principled, it should be noted, means not being at the mercy of social pressures.

But does it make sense to show respect for all cultural elements? Promiscuously-allotted "respect" is an empty gesture. Shall we simply go ahead and show "respect" for virtually ANYTHING by dint of the fact that it happens to be a cultural element somewhere? Are we to show "respect" for the burka / niqab? (Hint: It's the same answer to the question: Shall we respect slavery simply because it was a part of certain societies' heritage for so long?) Some answers are too obvious to state aloud.

Any respect that is worthwhile is borne of discernment. Universal principles can be brought to bear on any given inquiry; as said principles categorically transcend the thing being evaluated: culture. Judiciously-allotted respect does not require us to abandon rectitude. Indeed, when dolled out indiscriminately, "respect" loses its currency; so loses all moral ballast. Many fail to realize that one does not need to pretend everything is estimable in order to honor the basic tenets of an open (read: liberal) society. The crucial distinction is captured by the maxim: While I respect your right to free speech, I'm not obligated to show respect for what you're saying.

Prohibiting Cul-Ap is not a matter of showing "respect" for this or that culture; it stems from (a) not understanding how respect works and (b) not understanding how culture works.

So now, at this point in the book, the question must be posed: Did I miss anything?

When taking a position on any controversial matter, it is always important to ask oneself: In what ways might I be mistaken? As with my other writing, I ardently solicit critical feedback. I sincerely strive to find out if my thinking might be flawed in some way. While I have made a concerted effort to leave no stone left unturned; I imagine that plenty of unturned stones remain.

A quick re-cap: I made a concerted effort to address the issue of power asymmetries; and to recognize the isolated cases where Cul-Ap WAS indicative of some sort of exploitative activity (the more powerful taking advantage of the less powerful). However, some may feel that I did not devote sufficient time to such scenarios. If my defense of Cul-Ap overlooked a crucial factor, I would very much like for it to be brought to my attention.

For the time being, here is what I have concluded. Cultural diffusion (which is effectively a form of memetic propagation) occurs naturally over the course of time—often, between ethnic groups that are interacting in some way. Memetic transference occurs for any number of reasons; and its occurrence does not necessarily indicate that anything untoward is happening. In other words: Incidence of cultural adoption does not necessarily mean that some sort of exploitative activity is afoot.

All reasonable people agree that cultural hegemony is a problem—specifically when imperialism / colonialism is afoot. Be that as it may, cultural **appropriation** is not the same as cultural **imposition** (Cul-Imp); as appreciation and domination are two very different things. Nor is cultural **appropriation** the same as cultural **expropriation** (Cul-Ex); as adoption and annexation are two very different things. {26} So we should not simply assume that cultural appropriation is indicative of some sort of hegemonic process, as said process is a matter of imposition, not of appropriation. It's Cul-Imp, not Cul-Ap.

It is one thing for a group in an advantageous socio-economic position to IMPOSE UPON an under-privileged / marginalized group its own customs. It is quite another thing for one group to simply make use of the customs of another group. The former is a matter of trying to control others; the latter is a matter of embracing affinities. The proper issue of concern, then, is subjugation—something that occurs with or without Cul-Ap. Ergo Cul-Ap cannot be the pivotal factor. It is a mistake to assume that meme-adoption is inherently exploitative.

Cul-Ap, it turns out, is a sign of comity; as well as an invitation thereto. By contrast, cultural imposition is a sign of hegemony (whether a matter of control or exploitation / marginalization). Cul-Ap-phobia conflates the two. When people mistake Cul-Ap for Cul-Imp, it brings to mind Dominionists who confuse religious **imposition** with religious **liberty**. In this Orwellian scheme, Christian theocracy is passed off as simply an exercise of "religious freedom". Such gross mischaracterizations are commonplace in political rhetoric—as when, say, the jingoistic foolishness of super-patriotism is considered "patriotism"; or when massive tax-breaks for the ultra-wealthy (and for large corporations) are simply called "tax cuts". (The richest 400 Americans pay a lower effective tax rate than the poorest half of Americans.) Such casuistry is also encountered when addressing the present topic. Notably, the conflation of cultural appropriation with cultural imposition / expropriation is an integral part of the legerdemain used to buttress anti-Cul-Ap ideology.

So how shall we parse legitimate grievances from the brouhaha over "cultural appropriation"? After assessing each case for power asymmetry (and any implications thereof), ulterior motives (e.g. dubious profiteering schemes), dishonesty (e.g. lack of proper attribution), and other relevant factors, we can ascertain when Cul-Ap has gone from salubrious to deleterious. This requires us to be vigilant of any ill will that may be involved.

The key to evaluating cultural diffusion, then, is to exercise discernment; and to do so without compromising our cosmopolitan ideals. In passing judgement on this or that case of Cul-Ap, we must be cognizant of the crucial distinction between antipathy and filial sentiment; and we shouldn't lose sight of the fact that there is a fundamental difference between "You need to do things the way WE want you to" (a matter of imposition) and "Nifty idea; I'd love to try it on for size" (a matter of adoption). Exploitation and participation are inimical to one another; and Cul-Ap is almost always a matter of the LATTER. More to the point: Cul-Ap is part of the natural course of all cultural metamorphosis; something it makes little sense to decry.

Partaking in different cultures enables us to grasp—in the most palpable way—that the one thing we all have in common is our humanity. This is the definition of humanism. Cultural evolution is predicated on the embrace of exogenous cultural elements. Upon surveying all the salutary effects of Cul-Ap around the world, one can't help but come away thinking: Thank heavens for the intermixture of cultures.

So is Cul-Ap a bad thing? In some situations: yes. In most cases: no. While evaluating any given case of memetic transference across cultural lines, it is important to bear in mind that cultural diffusion does not entail cultural dilution; that appropriation is neither expropriation nor imposition; and—most importantly—that appreciation and exploitation are two very different things. I pray that this book has made clear how to discern one from the other.

In spite of having devoted an entire book to the matter, I want to make clear that Cul-Ap-phobia is NOT the biggest issue facing America today. Be that as it may, it is indicative of an underlying mentality—a mentality that undergirds ersatz Progressivism, which only succeeds in sabotaging the Progressive cause. The typical corporatist Democrat declares, "Please, by all means, quibble over things like cultural appropriation. Argue about it 'til you're blue in the face. Just don't pressure us to cut the Pentagon's trillion dollar budget. And whatever you do, don't ask for universal public healthcare."

When it comes to the present topic, my diagnosis is as follows: Cul-Ap-phobes are cultural purists who refuse to admit that they are being puritanical. In their attempt to protect the marginalized, they succumb to their basest tribal instincts—devolving into a provincial mindset. In doing so, they end up betraying the most fundamental principles of cosmopolitanism. All the while, they fail to see that the adoption of exogenous cultural elements is an opportunity to forge bonds between peoples.

In reality, "cultural appropriation" is a way to deepen connections between otherwise partitioned cultural enclaves. This is something that genuine Progressives should encourage. But that's not always easy. It means recognizing that cultural differences—nay, all forms of ethnic diversity—thrive in the midst of cultural interpenetration and ethnic intermixing. To take umbrage with such things is to betray everything that cosmopolitanism represents.

It is the recognition of universal moral principles that ensures harmony is maintained…even as different ethnicities interact. As memetic cross-pollination occurs between cultures, we should remain cognizant of our shared humanity. That's why Freethinkers can enjoy (and even perform) Gospel music…just as Christians can both appreciate (and even create) secular music. And we can all appreciate Benjamin Millepied's Mexican version of Georges Bizet's opera, "Carmen"…while upholding humanist ideals.

Cultural appropriation? Indeed! We can only hope for more.

We have seen many of the salutary effects of trans-cultural fertilization; and seen many examples of memetic transference—much of which is not seen as problematic by, well, ANYONE. This process might also be thought of as a kind of weaving—whereby threads of each culture reticulate in harmonious ways, creating new patterns from old. Such eventualities involve more of a mesh than it is a clash. The result is a new tapestry; not some infelicitous corruption of "pure" cultures. For no culture is ever purely ANYTHING. There are just threads that find their way from one tapestry to the next, wending and weaving in often unexpected ways. In this sense, any culture that has ever existed is a memetic embroidery, sometimes with nifty patterns, resulting from the entwining of antecedent and adjacent cultural exigencies. That's how memes work. And that's why it makes no sense to see Cul-Ap—in any given iteration—as an iniquity visited upon the source-culture, perpetrated by the adopters.

Upon considering all this, we find that Anti-Cul-Ap crusaders are not the stalwart defenders of cultural integrity that they fashion themselves to be. For they only end up stoking acrimony—exacerbating tribalistic tendencies. It's as if human solidarity could somehow be engendered via a program of inviolable cultural demarcation.

This book should have made it clear that we can find oodles of cultural appropriation in virtually every culture on the planet. But no matter, Cul-Ap-phobes rebuke instances of ethnic convergence for fear that memes might migrate across cultural lines and intermix—forgetting that an intermixture is how any given culture formed in the first place. If not for memetic transference across cultures, Brasilians wouldn't play futbol (which originated in England) and Canadians wouldn't play hockey (which originated in Mongolia). {50}

In assessing the role of Cul-Ap in a liberal democracy, we should ask ourselves: In the grand scheme of things, what is it we REALLY want people to stop doing? And what is it we WANT people to do? The first amounts to the enabling of—and even participation in—social injustice, in all of its basic forms (domination / marginalization / exploitation). The second answer boils down to one thing: basic decency.

A final question: What is the key to fostering an open, pluralistic society—a society that champions social justice? Let's consider the Spanish term, "convivencia", which refers to inter-cultural amity. It makes sense that this is a felicitous ideation; as it literally means "living WITH one another".

Imagine.

Endnotes

1:
For more on this point, see Kwame Anthony Appiah's ***Cosmopolitanism: Ethics In A World Of Strangers***, chapters 7 and 8. I discuss the paradoxical comity-via-asperity approach of the Regressive "Left" in my previous book, ***Robin's Zugzwang***. Acrimony can never be a means to amity; so why would anyone fall for such a hoodwink? As it turns out, we find similar paradoxes in other contexts—most notably: liberation through submission in the Abrahamic religions.

2:
Nicolaus of Myra was a quasi-apocryphal holy-man from Lycia who lived in the 3rd or 4th century A.D. The first major version of the cult surrounding his personage was at Bari, in Puglia (on the Italic peninsula) in the late 11th century. It then spread to Spain in the late 15th century…and was thereafter adopted by the Dutch (whereupon he became known as "Sinter-klaas"). The legend then spread eastward, morphing into Germanic and Slavic versions…and eventually English. THAT adoption was followed by those in regions colonized by Roman Catholic (European) powers—as with the Americas and the Philippines. In the Roman Catholic world, his moniker either involved "Noel[le]" / "Natale" (birth) or some version of the name "Nikolas" (after the Anatolian saint). Germanic paganism was eventually incorporated into the Christian leitmotif—as with "Belsnickel", "Knecht Ruprecht", and "Krampus". This was a reminder that syncretism is often a part of cultural diffusion. (Virtually all Cul-Ap involves some sort of hybridization.) In Slavic folklore, "Ded Moroz" ("Grandfather Frost") was based on pagan myths, so was not influenced by Christianity. Only later—due to Byzantine influences—was this folkloric figure incorporated into a Christian motif. Again: syncretism concomitant with Cul-Ap. There's even a Turkic variation: "Ayaz Ata". So who "owns" this legend? As it happens, Santa Claus is quintessentially European. A depiction of him as anything else—be it African, Arabian, or East Asian—is not only erroneous, it shows a lack of respect for the tradition. Of course, this does not mean that non-Europeans shouldn't be allowed to dress up as Santa Claus just for the fun of it. For when people engage in so-called "cos-play", there is no pretense to ethnic

fidelity. People are just—as it were—playing around. It's "all in good fun".

3:
Hoop earrings date back to the Babylonians / Assyrians. During Classical Antiquity, they were commonplace throughout the Persian, Greco-Roman, Slavic, and Nordic world. Countless African and Amazonian tribes have worn hoop earrings over the centuries. So did the Barbary pirates. So did European pirates. The accessory has been used in countless cultures around the world at many points in history. To suggest that a particular ethnic group somehow "owns" hoop earrings is preposterous. But it is preposterous for the same reason that it is preposterous to suppose that ANY culture owns ANY meme. It makes no sense to treat cultural elements as intellectual property when there is no way to pinpoint its origins to a discrete time and place.

4:
The first to posit mermaids were the Assyrians, who associated the magical aquatic females with the goddess, Atargatis. In the Occident, the idea goes back to the ancient Greeks, who posited "sirens" (e.g. Homer's Calypso of Ogygia). The Greeks also told tales of "nereids" and "oceanids" (as with Persa, Amphitrite, and Ianeira); while "naiads" dwelled in fresh-water lakes. The Romans posited "nymphs". The Persians posited "maneli". During the Renaissance, such enchanting creatures were referred to as "undines". ("Limnaeds" dwelled in freshwater lakes—as with the Arthurian "lady of the lake", custodian of Excalibur.) In "One Thousand and One Nights", there is reference to "Djullanar the sea-girl"; and there are mermaids featured in the tale of Bulukiya. (Those last two were European embellishments of ancient Arabian folktales.) The Scots told tales of "ceasg". The French told tales of "Melusine". Medieval Slavs told tales of "rusalki". The Yakut / Sakha of Siberia told tales of "alara". The founding of the Polish capital, War-sawa, was based on the tale of a mermaid named "Sawa". Amazonian natives (spec. the "Tupi") had legends of the mysterious lady of the waters: "[u]Iara". There was the Hellenic "Tyres" (after whom the ancient Phoenician city of Sur was re-named) as well as the Turkic "Alara". Mermaids were made popular in modern times by Danish author, Hans Christian Andersen ("The Little Mermaid"). Okay. Well, then what of the Far East? Hindus and Buddhists tell tales of "apsaras". (In India, there is the legend of mermaid princess, "Suvann[a]-Maccha".) The Chinese tell of the "jiaoren" (ref. the "Classic of the Mountains and Seas"). The Japanese tell of "nin-gyo". And the Siamese tell of "pongsa wadarn". Alas, the closest that African folklore came to this ideation were androgynous water spirits known as "mami wata". There were also aquatic beings that were seen as mother-goddesses (as with the Igbo / Yoruba "Yemoja"); but they were not mermaids. "Zin" were mythical water spirits in parts of West Africa (perhaps from Malian influences); but they were not mermaids either. One of the naiads, "Achiroë", was affiliated with the Nile River; but she was Greek. There have no more been Black mermaids than there have been Latino leprechauns. (For more on this point, see Endnote 30.) We don't help marginalized ethnic communities

by pretending that they can represent mythical creatures from other ethnicities as if ethnic heritage was somehow irrelevant to folklore. It is important to be true to ALL ethnic traditions. (For more on this point, see Endnote 15.) There are some rare exceptions. Casting Lea Salonga in the Broadway production of "Les Miserables"—even though she's a Filipina rather than a French girl—worked quite well (I was a big fan). And while the casting of Haley Bailey as Ariel in the live-action "Little Mermaid" re-make was admirable (I was also a big fan), we often see a push for an inane version of "representation" in Hollywood with gender- and race-swapping in casting choices. This is done as a sop to this or that identity group; and does nothing to empower those who actually need empowering.

5:
"The Princess And The Frog" would have been linguistically Creole; and "Brave" would have been linguistically Gaelic. Meanwhile, Snow White was allegedly of German origin, while Sleeping Beauty was allegedly of French origin; though neither of those tales is necessarily specific to those ethnic traditions. (Each of them might be characterized as "generic White European".) Of the 21 films listed, 15 had a strong female protagonist (while one had a duck). Other recent animated features with female protagonists from around the world include "The Sky Princess" (African), "Sitara: Let Girls Dream" (Indian), "Ginger's Tale" (Russian), "Over The Moon" (Chinese), and "Ainbo: Spirit Of The Amazon" (Native South American) from 2020. The next year, there was "Maya And The Three Dragons" (Meso-American) and a composite of Siamese, Khmer, Vietnamese, and Malay: "Raya And The Last Dragon". (The Colombian tale of "Encanto" had a male protagonist.) In 2022, there was "Aurora's Sunrise" (Armenian), "Orkestra Lurtarra" (Basque), and "Nayola" (Angolan). (The Algerian animated feature, "Khamsa: The Well of Oblivion" had a male protagonist.) And in 2023, there was a Ukrainian animated feature, "Mavka: The Forest Song". As I write, a Pakistani animated feature, "The Glassworker", was just released.

6:
The day that the "adhan" is no longer heard bellowing in the public squares of Kabul, and, instead, one of Chopin's nocturnes can be heard emanating from an open window as a woman strolls down the street sans niqab…we will know that Cul-Ap has helped to move things forward in the Salafi sphere. Indeed, as society evolves, it secularizes—making the daily caterwauling of prayer calls and the donning of face veils things of the past. This point is not limited to (Sunni) Deobandis of the Hindu Kush. The same would go for (Shia) Khomeinism and (Sunni) Wahhabism. Rest assured, when the time comes for the Ayatollahs of Iran and the House of Saud in Arabia to meet their demise, Persians and Arabians—men and women alike—will be more at liberty to choose which customs to embrace; and do so of their own accord, without fear of persecution.

7:
The origins of barbecue are a bit hazy, yet the style seems to be from the Taino / Arawak people. Today, one of the more popular kinds of barbecue is Korean barbecue...which certainly ignores the Caribbean origins of the culinary style. Shall this be taken as an unforgivable slight toward Caribbean islanders on the part of Hanguk-in? If we apply this logic, then we would also need to proscribe "jerk" seasoning (also Caribbean) on all chicken consumed by non-Caribbean islanders. However, if we were to do so, other quandaries would soon arise. What are we to do with Cajun cuisine—a hybridization of Caribbean and Acadian cultures? Was that a matter of French Canadians exploiting Creole culture? If so, then who gets to eat a Po' Boy sandwich? Those who gripe about Cul-Ap often forget how delicious it can be.

8:
A major patroness of the arts, the (Florentine) Queen of France pioneered the use of high heels in the 16th century. She was inordinately short; and was envious of her philandering husband's tall mistresses. Meanwhile...we can thank Catherine de Medici for pioneering the ballet (de cour). Peoples from all over the world have since appropriated these two elements of European culture; yet neither the Italians nor the French seem to be up in arms about it. Latinas love wearing high heels and the Russians took ballet to new heights—both testaments to the wonders of cultural appropriation.

9:
"B-style" is a hokey emulation of American hip-hop (read: urban Afro-American) culture. So where does that leave us? According to the logic of Cul-Ap-phobes, the Japanese are guilty of exploiting African Americans. In Korea, K-pop is also based on a repurposing of American musical idioms—in often cartoonish ways—so as to bolster their own pop culture. Indeed, the propagation of the boy-band / girl-group phenomenon is a prime example of global cultural diffusion.

10:
The apocryphal tale of Pocahontas is a great one. (Not only did it yield a wonderful animated feature by Disney, but it inspired the biggest box-office smash in cinematic history. What else is Avatar but Pocahontas in space?) I mention this particular example because it turns out to be the opposite of what Cul-Ap-phobes think it is. As is often the case, when caviling about Cul-Ap, prosecutors haven't any clue what the real historical relevance of the characterization might be. The Powhatan princess named Amonute (née "Matoaka") from Tsenacommacah, in present-day Virginia (i.e. the girl on whom the folkloric figure, "Pocahontas" is based) actually eschewed her culture in favor of English culture—adopting the name, Rebecca (an English name appropriated from the Hebrew "R-V-Kah"). In one sense, the British appropriated HER PERSONALLY; yet in another sense, she willingly adopted a British identity. Therefore, for non-Native Americans to dress up as "Pocahontas"

is—in a way—an insult to Native Americans; yet for the exact opposite reason the complainants suppose. For it tacitly pays tribute to a Native American who disavowed her Native American heritage.

11:
Hindus and Jains were donning dread-locks (Sanskrit "jata") over a thousand years before it became part of Afro-American culture. Eventually, dreadlocks could be found in ancient Indian, Egyptian, and Hellenic cultures; then in Roman, Germanic, and Nordic (Viking) cultures. Hence Caribbean Islanders (spec. Rastafarians) appropriated the hair-style from Europeans. In other words: Jamaicans are the MOST RECENT culture to have adopted the hair-style as a signature stylization. To contend that this particular hairstyle is now off-limits to Anglo-Saxons is preposterous. It amounts to a historiographical conceit: "Though it has been done for thousands of years, once WE start doing it, everyone else in the world must be barred from doing it ever again." Similar things might be said about the "Mohawk", a style of side-shaving named after the Native American tribe, yet used by Celts and Vikings going back over a thousand years.

12:
Jehovah's Witnesses eschew the conventional iconography; as they consider the crucifix to be a sullied talisman. In a sense, the Watchtower Society is correct: The use of a Roman torture device as a symbol has little to do with the original movement around Jesus of Nazareth—a small community known simply as "The Way" (later derisively referred to as the "Ebionites" and "Nazarenes"), which used a fish as its insignia (as most of the apostles were Galilean fishermen). As it turns out, very few who have called themselves "Christians" have actually followed the moral teachings of a Palestinian Jew named Yeshua ben Yusuf (helping wayfarers of other tribes, turning the other cheek, loving your enemies, judging not lest you be judged, sharing your possessions with those in need, etc.) Charity and forbearance are now about as "Christian" as separation of church and state (another tenet espoused by the aforementioned Nazarene preacher). That is: Not very much at all.

13:
Examples of this symbol—be it the (Hindu) "swastik[a]", the (Greek) "tetra-skelion", or the (Nazi) "hakencreuz"—are numerous. In the Middle Ages, the [Vai-]Nakh people of the northern Caucuses used the Norse "fiël-fotr" (Germanic "vielfot"; Anglo-Saxon "fower-fot"; often rendered "fylfot") to symbolize their sun-goddess, Deela-Malkh. Norsemen used it to symbolize Thor's hammer. What's going on here? Was the Nakh's use of this symbol some slight against the Vikings? (Incidentally, during the Malkh festival, the Nakh celebrated the winter solstice on December 25, commemorating the return of the sun. And, yes, it involved decorating a tree. What are we to make of that?) The Sanskrit term for the symbol was "sauvastika". It originally represented permanence–which was construed alternately as prosperity or eternity (ref. Panini's "Ashtadhyayi" from the 4th century B.C.) It also

served as the emblem for "surya" (the sun); and was later associated with well-being and good fortune. (This is why—to the present day—the symbol is inscribed at the threshold of many Indian homes.) In Shaivism (esp. Tantric), it is associated with Kali. In Jainism, it is associated with the famed tirthankara, "Suparsh-vanatha". In Theravada Buddhism, it is associated with the footprints / heart of the Buddha. The name of the symbol was later rendered "wan" (Classical Chinese) and "manji" (medieval Japanese), roughly meaning omni-presence. It also emerged in Tibetan "Bön" as the "yung-drung". Note that the Semitic history of the swastika goes back to the Bronze Age. The Phoenicians seem to have used it as a symbol for the sun. There is also evidence in Troas (at the site of the ancient city-State, Troy) that the symbol was used by the Trojans: as the "tetra-skelion" / "tetra-ktys". In ancient Roman ruins, the symbol appears next to the caption "zotiko zotiko" [life of life]. Meanwhile, ancient Celts used a variation of the symbol–notably the "fylfot" cross of Druidism (which was later adopted by the early Gaelic tribes, as attested in the Book of Kells c. 800 A.D.) It is also used in Slavic "Rodnover" iconography as the "kolovrat": used to represent the Hands of Svarog. Most notably, there was a swastika-like symbol used in ancient Nordic / Germanic paganism (associated with the hammer of Thor)...which may have inspired its usage by the Teutonic Knights of the High Renaissance...which, as explained, accounts for the Nazi incarnation. In that latest case, Cul-Ap was objectionable not because an exogenous cultural element was appropriated; but because a sacred symbol was grossly perverted, and used as an icon for fascism (hardly in keeping with its Vedic roots). This was more about the hijacking—and thus betrayal—of a semiotic tradition than it was about memetic transference. Note: As is the case with "mandal[a]", the term, "swastik[a]" has the optional "a" appended at the end—an onomastic convention that applies to many Hindi terms, including "laksh[a]", "raj[a]", and "singh[a]". It even occurs with toponyms (as with "Bharat[a]" and the suffix, "pur[a]"), given names (as with "Siddarth[a]" and "Anik[a]"), and the names of some gods (as with "Shiv[a]" and "Ganesh[a]").

14:

Even the iconography of the star and crescent was appropriated. In Assyrian iconography, a star (representing Ishtar) was often shown alongside the crescent moon (representing Syn). Arab star-gods were prevalent at the time—as with Munim[os] and Aziz[os]. Moon-gods were also prevalent at the time—from "Aglibol" in Palmyra to "Hu-Baal" ["spirit of Baal"; alt. "Hubal"], "Almakah", and "Rudaw" (father of the Arab goddess, Allat) in Nabataea / Idumaea. Meanwhile, the Sabaeans worshipped a moon-god named "Almakah" in Yemen (ref. the ancient shrines at Barran and Awwam, near Ma'rib), who was associated with the Arabian goddess, Shamash / Shams. As it turns out, Shamash / Shams was likely based on the star-goddess, Athtar / Attar (an Arab variation on Ishtar). Recall that "Allah" was derived from the Syriac "Al-Ilah" ["the god"]. Sure enough, the star-and-crescent iconography was used by Sassanids at the time the Arabs conquered Persia (as attested by their coinage). Note the abiding reluctance of Muslims to acknowledge that virtually every element of the "Hajj" was appropriated from antecedent pagan rituals. Admitting this would bring into question the rituals' authenticity, and thereby undermine the tradition's professed Abrahamic pedigree. Most elements of the Hajj were appropriated by the early Mohammedans from pre-Islamic Hijazi culture. We rarely hear protestations from Cul-Ap-phobes about this. Such silence is mostly due to the fact that the pagan Bedouin lobby is non-existent. Meanwhile, most Muslims really, really, really don't want to concede that many of their sacred rites are a rip-off of the widely-derided "Jahiliyyah" ("ignorant people"; i.e. pre-Islamic Arabians); as such an admission would countermand the standard Islamic narrative. There are few non- Muslim Arabians remaining to mobilize a formidable awareness-generation campaign on that particular matter. This is the problem with anti-Cul-Ap crusades. For, as we have seen, grievances with Cul-Ap are–invariably–highly selective. But then again, such indictments are ALL based on an arbitrary—often self-serving—application (it applies HERE, but not THERE) and inconsistent logic (which may be suspended whenever it doesn't suit the purposes at hand). The implicit message: "It's okay for US to do it; but we shall excoriate anyone else who does it." (For more on the cultural appropriation undergirding much of Islamic lore, see my forthcoming book on the Syriac origins of Islam.) In fact, if one were to remove all the elements of Islamic ritual / lore that was appropriated from antecedent cultures, there would be almost nothing left.

15:
We do nothing to advance the cause of civil rights by abandoning fidelity to the ethnic exigencies of folklore. (Pretending Santa Claus was Siamese does Thai Christians no favors.) In her usual fashion, Oprah Winfrey was merely being flaky when she opted to cast an African American (the pop singer, Mandi) as Cinderella in the 1990's. (So much for a sincere interest in respecting cultural traditions.) Misrepresentation is not always a matter of fecklessness; it is sometimes a matter of perfidy. Ironically, precedents stemming from "identity politics" have enjoined people to indulge in rather daffy portrayals—**all in the name of** "inclusion". Imagine casting a Caucasian woman to play Harriet Tubman. It's worth asking: Why would such a thing be asinine? (Shall we also pretend that Sojourner Truth could just as well have been Slavic? How about a Chinese Phillis Wheatley?) Color-blindness only goes so far before we're just being zany.

16:
Tell that to the hundreds of millions of professional men in East Asia who now wear Western-style "business suits" (replete with ties and other impractical accoutrements), none of which makes any rational sense. When non-WASPS in foreign lands don such attire, the idea is to signal participation in a certain cultural milieu—one that happens to have originated in the Occident. In this case, the sartorial stylization is associated with professionalism—specifically in the corporate world. (Due to said stigma, in wearing such an outfit, one conveys the message: I should be taken seriously.) This is yet another reminder that political correctness

involves double standards. For we are all—every last one of us—prone to stylize our behavior according to prevailing stigmas, which come from various places for a variety of reasons. Note that, in donning (Occidental) "business suits", denizens of the corporate world in Oriental locations are not trying to assimilate into—let alone exalt—"Western" culture. They are simply partaking in a regimen of stigmatization based on certain sartorial practices that happen to have been initiated in "Western" society. In this case, a colorful cloth tied around one's neck (complementing one's collar, while veiling the buttons of one's shirt) is associated with prestige. If we were to hew to the strictures proposed by anti-Cul-Ap crusaders, though, things would have to change. Taking this logic to its extreme would entail some rather outlandish limitations. From this day forward, only male WASPs are permitted to wear polo shirts!

17:

The most ironic example of a meme has been the term "meme" ITSELF. The lexeme was originally coined by Richard Dawkins in his 1976 book, **The Selfish Gene**, when he proposed a new sociological paradigm. In the advent of the social media craze (post-2007), the "meme" meme underwent its own mutation—thereby illustrating how memes can be co-opted, and subsequently reified. Those oblivious to what the scientific term actually means started using it as slang for images with silly captions (especially those posted / disseminated on social media channels). Of course, the virality of such images was probably what first inspired someone to start referring to them as "memes" (rather than as, well, just images with silly captions). The problem is that the most aloof participants in this fad have since become convinced that THAT is all that a "meme" is. We now refer to a crypto-currency that promotes a certain brand as a "meme-coin"…which is itself a new meme. The concept of meme is a very important one; and it would be unfortunate if the actual meaning of the term continued to be vitiated in this manner. Dawkins later elaborated on the theory of memetics with his 1991 essay, **Viruses Of The Mind**. Other than Dawkins' work on the subject, see Douglas Hofstadter's **Metamagical Themas**, Aaron Lynch's **Thought Contagion**, Susan Blackmore's **The Meme Machine**, and Steve Stewart-Williams' **The Ape That Understood The Universe** (Appendix B). Most notable are the explications by Daniel C. Dennett—especially **Darwin's Dangerous Idea** (chapt. 12), **Breaking The Spell** (Appendix A), and **From Bacteria To Bach And Back** (chapt. 11). Some thinkers have attempted to explain memes in alternate ways. Notably, Merlin Donald posited "external memory storage" / "external symbol storage" to account for cultural elements and their symbiotic relationship with mental processes. W.V.O. Quine referred to (what is effectively) a memeplex (a term which had not yet been coined) as a "web of belief"; noting that we all live our daily lives within such a web. Accordingly, we are inclined to reject / accept propositions based on how well they fit into the pre-existing web of dogmas. This "web" is essentially an integrated network of memes. Beliefs at the center are most entrenched, and so are often deemed sacrosanct. Changing them would require too much retro-fitting to make it worthwhile; as it would risk a total collapse of the memetic structure; so it is only beliefs on the periphery that are up for discussion (see Endnote 21). At the end of the day, no other paradigm of cultural transmission has the explanatory power of memetics.

18:
Naturally, the socio-economic elite take measures to maintain the conditions on which their vaunted status depends. They do this, in part, by dividing the masses into squabbling factions. This is done by touting the "every man for himself, devil take the hindmost" approach for the American Dream. The public discourse subsequently degenerates into a clusterfuck of petty squabbles—the majority of which have nothing to do with challenging incumbent power structures. For identitarians, identity-group is pitted against identity-group. Consequently, the polis is fragmented along demographic lines. For p.c.-mongers, the concern is entirely diverted from the institutional to the personal. Consequently, the focus is on the sentiments of this or that party rather than the architecture of power structures. In the end, the working class stops working in solidarity (to challenge those at the top of the socio-economic hierarchy); and squanders their time and energy on petty squabbles. Here, one feels obliged to compete with one's fellow laborers—jockeying for position in frantic pursuit of a mirage (see "American Dream"). This mad scramble seems worth it—at least insofar as the myth of meritocracy can be sustained (see Endnote 54). In this perfidious scheme, wealth EXTRACTION (from the masses) is passed off as a special kind of wealth CREATION (for the well-positioned few); so is lauded as the engine of the economy. The idea is that the outsized benefits to the socio-economic elite will eventually somehow "trickle down" to the common-man (see Endnote 57). In America, this ruse is tragically effective (see the Appendix), leading to ruthlessly plutocratic regime. The result is effectively kakistocracy. Contrary to the myth of meritocracy, many of those at the pinnacle of the socio-economic hierarchy are from the bottom of the barrel of humanity. This is illustrated not only by blithering morons like Donald Trump and Elon Musk, but by the towering fatuity of dimwitted Silicon valley tycoons like Mark Zuckerberg and Marc Andreessen. Behold the gaggle of tech billionaires with room-temperature IQs who are heralded as geniuses by legions of right-wing "libertarian" rubes. If we look into it, we find that many oligarchs have never done an honest day's work in their lives; yet they feel obliged to lecture the world about the merits of hard work (see Davos; World Economic Forum). In reality, it is savvy maneuvering (making strategic connections; gaming the system), not contributions to the betterment of society, that determines who rises to the top. For those who enjoy a privileged existence, this is all as it should be. The plan is simple: When everyone fashions themselves as mini-entrepreneurs (jockeying for primacy in a dog-eat-dog marketplace), communities are atomized. Civic-mindedness quickly dissipates; and organized resistance becomes a distant dream. (Without collective bargaining, the working class has no leverage, so is at the mercy of the power elite.) Under such circumstances, avarice is the primary driver of socio-economic advancement; and moral principles are promptly defenestrated (see United Healthcare, General

Dynamics, Monsanto, KBR, Bridgewater, Blackrock/stone, and McKinsey). In the midst of hyper-privatization, public resources—including physical spaces—have gone the way of the dodo. A fragmented polis ensures that the average Joe will have no say in the governance of the society of which he is a part. Identity politics brings about such fragmentation on the group level; as it divides the general populace into competing identity groups. Imbroglios based on group affiliations end up being elaborate distractions. A working class that has been broken into squabbling factions ensures that the incumbent power structures will remain fully intact into the foreseeable future. As the socio-economic elite feast at their hedonic banquet, the rest of us fight each other over the table scraps…and then blame each other when things don't work out well.

19:
Incidentally, the "Rama-yana" was appropriated by myriad cultures in the Far East, each of which rendered their own version of the classic Indian tale. (I list dozens of incarnations in part 1 of my essay on "Mythemes".) This makes perfect sense, of course, as Buddhism's roots are in Hindu lore. Yet how often do Indians grouse about the adaptations of their ancient motifs in, say, Thailand? Never. Why not? Because it would make no sense. After all, that there have been myriad incarnations of the Rama-yana isn't a bad thing. It is a reminder that even the most classic work of the Far East has been adapted over and over and over again…without any fuss.

20:
The key difference between items like tortillas and burritos (on the one hand) and items like caesar salad and popcorn (on the other) is that the former have become an integral part of Mexican culture; whereas the latter have not. But is THAT to be the clinching factor for determining the legitimacy of Cul-Ap? If so, then it does not matter who established the meme after all. (!) Where it originated becomes a moot point. Instead, we are to proceed according to the following protocol: In the event that a meme becomes an integral part of a particular culture, nobody else on the planet shall be permitted to use it evermore. The reductio ad absurdum of such a maxim should be obvious. For who, then, shall lay claim to, say, wine? And what of things that are the result of cultural hybridization—as with fajitas, quesadillas, and chimichangas? Even with something as hokey as Tex-Mex, it's hard to tell where one culture ends and the other culture begins. This is a reminder that no culture has a distinct—or even a static—boundary. So it is unreasonable to plant a flag and demand that nobody cross it.

21:
Many of society's most affluent people are morally depraved (see Paul Singer and Bill Ackman); and some are just dumb (see Endnote 18). As a result of severely misjudging those who are—and those who are NOT—founts of wisdom, the American polity isn't merely ill-informed; it is HORRIBLY informed (see Endnotes

43 and 54). The thing about know-it-alls is that they think they know something about everything, yet often don't know much about anything. These modern-day Euthyphros fail to see how dogmatic they actually are. Such people are bereft of intellectual curiosity; yet have an outsized estimation of their own sapience. As far as they're concerned, they already have all the answers; hence they tend to only acknowledge those who agree with them. Nobody else is worth listening to—least of all actual scholars. As a matter of course, those afflicted with epistemic narcissism have nothing but contempt for those who have more knowledge about a topic than they do. Such interlocutors are held in abeyance; as they jeopardize the ramshackle dogmatic edifice on which the epistemic narcissist has precariously erected his (delusive) self-esteem. This rickety scaffolding is unable to withstand even the slightest perturbation…lest it all collapse in a whirlwind of abject humiliation. Exuding over-the-top confidence is such a person's only defense against that terrifying eventuality. (Hence the personality profile of virtually every demagogue and cult leader.) So it goes: Those with superior knowledge pose a threat to the narcissist's frangible constitution. Anyone who has the gall to profess erudition in his midst is promptly disparaged…and, if possible, silenced. Mental lethargy undergirds such hubris; as intellectual integrity requires lots of cognitive exertion. Therein lies the appeal: One can feeling as though one knows better without having to go to the trouble of actually learning anything. (It's an enticing proposition: One can be lazy and feel superior at the same time!) Epistemic narcissists are especially insecure when it comes to illusions about their own erudition; as they would be quickly thrown into psychical upheaval should they concede that they don't already have all the answers. This malfunction stands in stark contrast to the mind of those who genuinely seek Truth (rather than self-aggrandizement and constant validation). Generally, people who are intellectually curious are looking for where their thinking may have gone awry. Aspiring to perspicacity, they search in earnest for anything important that they may not yet know. As such, they do not seek out those who agree with them; they seek out the most knowledgeable people they can find (preferably world-renowned scholars in the relevant field; taking care to factor for intellectual / ideological capture, corporate capture, and other conflicts of interest). Such people tend to not settle on a conclusion unless there is a clear and overwhelming scholarly consensus on the matter. This approach requires a prodigious amount of mental discipline—something that many people lack. Intellectual integrity asks that one leave one's ego at the door; and to have the courage to recognize what one does not yet know. In the end, we must always be cognizant of the Dunning-Kruger effect—whereby confidence is inversely proportional to sapience. This effect is especially pronounced in the midst of staunch ideological commitments. To paraphrase William Butler Yeats: While the best of us often lack conviction, the worst of us propound their ideals with passionate intensity.

22:

"Beauty And The Beast" was actually adapted from a 17th-century tale by French author, Gabrielle-Suzanne Barbot de Villeneuve. And HIS rendition was based on an ancient Roman tale—most famously rendered by Lucius Apuleius Madaurensis in his tale of "Cupid and Psyche". The theme is timeless and universal: True love goes beyond mere appearances. This is a reminder that certain things transcend cultural differences.

23:

Demands that we all "know our place" are inimical to cosmopolitanism. The implicit request seems to be: "Celebrate cultural diversity, but do it from a safe distance!" How quickly the misguided instinct to proscribe Cul-Ap turns into a mandate to engage memetic hoarding along ethnic lines. Accordingly, mankind is divvied up; then assigned to cordons based on group affiliation. Ethno-centricity is often so treacherous because we often don't notice when we've succumbed to it. Consequently, we often slip into tribalistic thinking without even realizing it. The proclivity can soon become a pathology. The moment we hear someone insist that we "stay in our own lane", hints of fascistic thinking are afoot. This admonition should sound eerily familiar. It takes us down a dark road.

24:

Zhao's novel was a well-crafted narrative about the horrors of marginalized groups being exploited. It addressed such issues as discrimination against subaltern communities by a socio-economic elite, human trafficking, and that—even in the midst of our most fraught ethnic divides—our humanity can shine through. (Apparently, only African Americans are allowed to pen such novels!) This shameful episode is a striking illustration of how Cul-Ap-phobia can devolve into absurdity. For anti-Cul-Ap crusaders, our shared humanity is something to shun, not to celebrate. The castigation of Zhao reminds us that said crusade is a RIGHT-wing phenomenon: puritanical and authoritarian. Regarding the authoritarian aspect of the anti-Cul-Ap crusade, we should be especially wary of the penchant to PERSECUTE in the name of social justice. (The m.o. of identitarians is retributive rather than distributive justice.) The more ornery commissioners of these strictures are prepared to conduct an auto-de-fé whenever even a minor infraction is encountered. This does nothing to help bring about civil society.

25:

For more on this topic, see K. Van der Toorn's *The Iconic Book: Analogies Between The Babylonian Cult Of Images And The Veneration Of The Torah*; as well as Z. Zevit's *The Religions Of Israel*. Of course, no Faith community likes to admit that its creed is derivative; as such an admission would undermine the supposition that it is sui generis—that is: written in the stars and/or sent down from god. To concede that any given religion is derivative BY NATURE would be to concede that it is merely an accident of history—nay, a social construct like any other institution. Its sacrosanctity would thereby be brought into question: an eventuality that True Believers cannot abide. The only alternative is to confabulate a sacred history—that is: a "just so" story to explain why the religion is now the way that it is. The universality of the hexagram is attested to in Assyrian, Babylonian, Mycenaean, Illyrian, Roman, Armenian, Byzantine, Persian, Bactrian, Indian, Tibetan, Japanese, Malay, and Balinese iconography. The shape also has mathematical significance: the fractal hexagram (a pair of superimposed triangles, one inverted) is referred to as the Koch snowflake. There is nothing inherently Judaic about this familiar star. It is as much the star of Kartikeya as it is the star of David.

26:
The term "appropriation" did not originally mean to seize or confiscate something; it simply meant to use something for a specified purpose (as when the government "appropriates" funds for certain purposes; i.e. the allocation of federal outlays). Hence the distinction that was traditionally made between ***appropriation*** and ***expropriation***. (Note Karl Marx's use of the latter when he referred to seizure / confiscation. He referred to the capitalist class as "expropriators" because they dominated and exploited everyone else.) Even as "appropriation" is now used interchangeably with "expropriation", it is only the latter that I take to mean: Using—or taking control of—something for which one did not receive permission from its rightful owner / custodian. Until recently, "appropriation" was a term used in sociology to mean adoption (that is: the incorporation of an exogenous meme into an indigenous memetic repertoire). The notion of SEIZING / CONFISCATING a meme is, of course, nonsensical; so it makes no sense to say that a cultural element has been "expropriated"—that is: annexed. (The only way in which a meme can be "expropriated" is in a scenario where it has been legally designated as intellectual property, and the rightful owner of the copyright / trademark / patent opts to redeem it from parties that have used it illicitly.) Consequently, I use "appropriation" in its original sense rather than as a synonym for "expropriation". This distinction is crucial if we are to appraise the notion of "cultural appropriation".

27:
The alternate term used for salutation is "namaskar[a]". Amongst those enraptured by "New Age" mumbo-jumbo, we also encounter vapidity with the use of the "anjali mudra" ("wai" in Siamese / Lao). The over-use of this physical gesture is rather grating for those of us who are familiar with Hindu and Buddhist cultures. The comical irony of all this is that many Cul-Ap-phobes are also "New Age" enthusiasts. As they sip mojitos after yoga class, LuluLemon-clad housewives deliberate about how to best align their chakras. While they are reading each other's auras and choosing their spirit animals, they debate who does and doesn't get to wear hoop earrings (see Endnote 3). Their contribution to civil rights activism is limited to daft comments on each other's social media accounts.

28:
References to Saturnalia, used to mark the winter solstice, preceded the establishment of the Roman Empire—as attested in the writings of Catullus. The writer, Macrobius was still talking about the tradition c. 500 A.D. It (ostensibly) com-

memorated a halcyon era, during the fabled reign of Saturn, when there was no slavery and no private property. Nobody was above anyone else; which is to say that nobody was driven by avarice. It was a vision of an idyllic society, which involved no exploitation, no material accumulation, and no privation. This was eventually used as an occasion to pay tribute to Sol Invictus—who's birthday was considered December 25th (marking the re-birth of the sun). This "Natalis Invicti" was recognized through the 4th century—as documented on a Roman chronograph from c. 354. Through Late Antiquity, the birth of Jesus of Nazareth was presumed to have occurred in a cave on the outskirts of Bethlehem (as attested by Justin Martyr as well as in the proto-Evangelium of James). Not until the 12th century did there appear any reference to this auspicious time as, well, CHRIST-mas. And that came from the Syriac writer, Dionysius bar Salibi of Melitene (in Cappadocia). Only later did Roman Catholics decide to adapt the date for a celebration of the birth of their god-child; then create a romanticized "nativity" tale involving Polaris, three wise men, angels, a manger, and—eventually—even a little drummer boy.

29:
To evaluate any given instance of "cultural appropriation", we must consider all the historical contingencies that led to it. This includes taking into account insights gleaned from evolutionary psychology and all related fields—from geo-politics and sociology to ethnic studies and epidemiology. When exploring group identity, a good place to start is Kwame Anthony Appiah's **The Ethics Of Identity**. Benedict Anderson's **Imagined Communities** is a classic in this field. When it comes to moral judgement, also insightful is Appiah's **Cosmopolitanism: Ethics In A World Of Strangers**.

30:
We can applaud the casting of an African American actress (Halle Bailey) in the leading role of Disney's live-action rendering of "The Little Mermaid"; while keeping in mind that—even when it comes to fictional characters—there is nothing wrong with acknowledging ethnicity. Santa Clause, for example, is a fictional character based on an Anatolian saint (Nikolas of Myra); meaning the historical figure wasn't Anglo-Saxon, even as the fictional character was. That said, Kris Kringle was certainly not Native American or Latino. Nor was he African or Arab. Nor was he Persian or Indian. And he certainly wasn't Chinese, Japanese, or Siamese. I digress. Black mermaids—like, say, Mongolian or Pashtun mermaids—were never a thing…until, that is, 2023. The only instance of a mermaid-of-color seems to have been the Turkic "[su]Sulu" / "[su]Suna" / "[su]Sona". The Yoruba river goddess, Yemoja [alt. "Yemanja"] was sometimes thought of in vaguely mermaid-like terms; however she was not a mermaid. Suffice to say, Hans Christian Andersen did not have Yemoja in mind. Rather, he would have been inspired by the Greek myth of the Sirens made famous by Homer (daughters of Calliope who hailed from the Cretan islands known as "Leukai"). That's probably where the Poles got the idea for "Syrenka". These mysterious aquatic maidens were preternatural denizens of

the Mediterranean; so probably were assumed to have olive skin. Andersen, meanwhile, likely had ancient English / Scandinavian folklore in mind, so was influenced by the depiction of alluring maritime creatures found in, say, the Anglo-Latin work, "Liber Monstrorum" from the 8th century. Being in the North Sea, they were likely fair-skinned. (For more on mermaids, see Endnote 4.) As for the matter of dark-skinned elves; that was eventually addressed in the Netflix series about Middle Earth in an era preceding the Lord Of The Rings: The Rings Of Power. For more on this topic, see Endnote 15.

31:
In Exodus 22:18, when we are told that we mustn't "suffer a witch to live", the Semitic term for the person of opprobrium ("me-khashepha") is best translated as "poisoner"; as "khasheph" referred to potentially harmful herbs. (The pejorative is also used in Deuteronomy 18:9-10. It was rendered "pharmakeia" in Koine Greek; and "maleficius" in Vulgar Latin.) When we say that someone is a "snake", we mean that they are seeking to do harm in devious ways; and hocking some kind of poison. Recall that in Genesis, Satan (the Semitic term "na[c]hash" actually meant "shining one") is represented as a serpent, and is associated with temptation / deception. Just as a staff was used by Moses to channel god's power in order to part an entire sea, a staff might be used to employ god's power to protect people from harm. It is no coincidence that wizards are often depicted with a staff / scepter; as the object is typically associated with supernatural powers—as in, say, the Book Of Genesis (49:10). This semiotic is common across most cultures. The ancient Egyptians had the "was". The Sumerians had the "gidru". The Assyrians had the "hattum". The ancient Greeks had the "skeptron"; which the Romans later referred to as the "sceptrum". Throughout history, around the world, this idiom has been ubiquitous. The Chinese used it. The Persians used it. The Norse used it. In yet another twist of irony: Later in the Hebrew Bible, this well-known icon was scornfully referenced by the reformist king, Hezekiah as the "Nehushtan"—that is: as something to be rebuked. Good grief.

32:
Judaism as a creed was codified during the Exilic Period (6th century B.C.) in Babylon by a handful of scribes…who were working from exigent lore. This yielded what are now known as the Deuteronomic—plus the Elohist and Yahweh-ist—sources (typically denoted D, E, and J). The origins of said lore would have primarily been the preceding century—that is: the 7th century B.C.; much of which was simply a revamping of antecedent Assyrian lore. (The tale of Moses' provenance was inspired by tales of Sargon of Akkad; and the tale of the Exodus was likely based on the Hyksos.) By the time Persian king, Cyrus repatriated / re-enfranchised the Judah-ites, much of the scripture (the Torah and the Nevi-im) would have been compiled in Babylonian Aramaic. It was not until Classical Antiquity (spec. the Hasmonean period) that the Ketuv-im were composed. Here's the thing. The pivotal period for the formation of (what came to be) Judaism was primarily HEL-

LENIC. To understand the timeline, note that the Greco-Persian wars took place during the first half of the 5th century B.C.; while the Peloponnesian War occurred during the last three decades of the 5th century B.C. Alexander's conquests in the latter half of the 4th century B.C. ensured the Hellenization of the Levant, which continued through the Seleucid era. The Seleucids had become hostile to Levantine Jews—not to mention those still living in Mesopotamia—under the despotic regime of Antiochus IV in the early 2nd century B.C. The hero of the revolutionary Jewish movement was a man from the House of Hasmona, Judah ben Mattathias of Modi'in…who was known by his Aramaic sobriquet, "Makkaba": the "Hammer" (Hellenized to "Maccabeus"). Hence the moniker for his following: the Maccabees. The triumph of the Maccabean revolt is commemorated by the candelabrum that was (purportedly) used to illuminate the re-acquired temple. (The miracle was that the candles burned for over a week on only a small amount of oil.) This apocryphal tale was likely a riff on the re-lighting of the fire (on the altar to Yahweh) by Nehem-i-[Y]ah (alt. Zerub-Bab-El ben She'alt-i-El ben Yecon-i-Yah) which was purported to have occurred almost three centuries earlier. That led to the "menorah" becoming the new emblem of Judaism; thereby shifting the iconography from the "aryah" of Judah and the owl of Minerva. (The original occasion for commemorating said lighting was the "Chag ha-Sukkot" ["Festival of Booths"].) The hexagram would not be adopted as an emblem for Judaism until the Late Middle Ages, whereupon it came to be known as the "Magen David".

33:

In an ironic confluence of iconography, ancient manuscripts of the "Bardo Thodol" (a.k.a. the "Tibetan Book of the Dead") feature a mandala wherein a hexagram circumscribes a swastika. This was often done in the Vajra-yana tradition. Such a seemingly discordant concurrence is an illustration that those two symbols have a history that is vastly different from the semiotic precedents with which people in the Occident have come to be familiar. This is where the relevance of INTENTION comes into play. When we look at ancient Buddhist iconography and see swastikas inside hexagrams, we know that it has nothing to do with Nazis and Jews. However, when Kanye West Tweeted an image of a hakenkreuz embedded within a Star of David (on December 1, 2022), we know that it was yet another expression of his anti-Semitism…and his bizarre fascination with the Third Reich. How are we to handle such disparate occurrences? Well, the same way we should handle ANY expression: Ascertain what's behind each gesture. In this case, while there may be visual parity, there is not necessarily semiotic parity. Passing judgement on mere appearances (e.g. superficial resemblances) sets us up for mis-impressions. In Tibetan iconography, this seemingly odd combination of symbols is a reminder that things have significance beyond that which WE may be inclined to assign. This is further confirmation that pan-cultural integration is nothing new; and nothing to fear.

34:
There is no single reason that someone would adopt the puritanical, authoritarian mindset of the Regressive "Left". The explanation is multifarious because people are often complicated; and everyone is wrestling with their own inner demons. Those who peddle a counterfeit "Progressivism" can be driven by anything from avarice (the assiduous pursuit of financial gain and/or notoriety) to vindictiveness (seeking retribution for the tribulations they claim to have personally endured). Let's consider these two sorts of cases. The former are grifters and clout-chasers; the latter are popinjays who yearn to lord it over others. The former hoodwink their target-audience—effectively saying, "Trust me; I know the way to the Promised Land." The latter indict others—effectively saying, "I've been shunted aside my whole life, so now I'm going to stick it to someone else." The former peddle salvation; the latter are bullies pretending to be victims (engaging in "reverse victimization"). The former is impelled by hubris; the latter by vindictiveness. Both are self-righteous. Both are excruciatingly petty. Both seek to control everyone around them. Both exploit the frustrations / resentments / insecurities of others. And—above all—both are narcissistic. The pivotal difference: The former's narcissism translates to self-aggrandizement, whereas the other takes the "woe is me" route.

35:
Note that ***projection*** mustn't be confused with ***deflection*** (a.k.a. "what-about-ism"), whereby one simply diverts attention from one's own iniquity / dysfunction to the purported iniquity / dysfunction of others. The implication is: "Why criticize ME if others are doing it too?" With projection, though, one imputes one's own iniquities / dysfunctions to others—that is: accusing others of what one is guilty of oneself. We often encounter this with those who are hoodwinked by the propaganda in North Korea, China, or Israel; as such people are led to believe that *everyone else* is brainwashed, and THEY are the only ones who truly see the light. Hence the Revisionist Zionist who thinks that anyone who pushes back against his/her virulent racism are THEMSELVES racist (i.e. anti-Semitic). There are ironies galore here. With respect to the current genocide in Palestine, there have now emerged a new breed of holocaust deniers…who, while rightly inveighing against the old Holocaust deniers, turn around and deny the holocaust that is occurring right under their noses. (These new holocaust deniers are arguably even worse than the old, as many are ACTIVELY SUPPORTING a genocide.) So it goes with selective anti-racism: "I am against racism with regard to these people over here, but not when it comes to those people over there." (See Endnote 51.) The perverse irony is that virtually anything and everything Revisionist Zionists accuse Hamas of doing, the Israeli government (along with the Judean settler movement) does *a hundred times over*. This seems to work, as they do not have a principled stance against the iniquities they claim to be against. They are perfectly fine engaging in such heinous acts themselves; it's only when OTHERS do it—even a tiny fraction of how much they themselves do it—that it is suddenly a problem. Projection isn't limited to Revisionist Zionists and deluded conspiracy theorists. This is how things work when

it comes to ALL forms of reverse victimization. For example, many who gas-light others accuse THEM of being the ones who are doing the gas-lighting. (After all, the ACCUSATION OF gas-lighting is often part and parcel of the gas-lighting.) This tends to occur when the target accurately calls out the ACTUAL gas-lighter for gas-lighting. When the gas-lighter resorts to the "I know you are, but what am I?" defense, the victim must then devote his time and energy to explaining why he isn't the culprit (see also Endnote 57).

36:
Cultural exportation is often a felicitous affair. (To everyone's delight, Iberian Galicia introduced the empanada to all of Latin America.) However, cultural exportation isn't always salubrious. After all, Europeans brought Roman Catholicism—replete with all its horrific depredations—to North and South America, to Africa, and as far away as Papua New Guinea and the Philippines. In the modern era, negative influences aren't only from the U.S.; they can come from all over. While the U.S. exported the Watchtower Society to the rest of the planet, India exported the International Society For Krishna Consciousness. And while the U.S. exported the Church Of Latter-Day Saints to the rest of the planet, Korea exported the Church Of Unification. So now we encounter Jehovah's Witnesses, Hare Krishnas, Mormons, and Moonies all over the world—a reminder that some cultural diffusion can be nocuous; and that there is no single culprit. (Luckily, cult activity usually has limited reach.) Meanwhile, there are cases in which we might wish there HAD been memetic transference when there wasn't. Most countries never adopted the table call-buttons at restaurants used in Japan; and there's no ranch dressing in Britain. (Even more regrettable: The latter never got the memo that monarchies are asinine.) In the midst of all this memetic propagation, gringos making tortillas hurts nobody.

37:
Much of the nescience in contemporary society can be attributed to the online ecosystem in which most of us operate: a disturbingly hospitable place for mountebanks (that is: those who have figured out ways to generate a profusion of engagement). There is, of course, a difference between a judicious use of social media (pro-social) and an obsessive use of social media (dysfunctional). The problem is that—like crack cocaine—such tools are DESIGNED to be used obsessively. How conducive technology is to the commonweal is contingent on how it is used. For example, A.I. can serve as a (bionic) prosthetic for various cognitive functions. Be that as it may, its upside only exists insofar as its prodigious power is harnessed—and applied—with discernment. The same goes for social media. Used judiciously, social media channels enhance our capabilities for communication—thereby offering a plethora of avenues for remote interactions. However, used IN-judiciously, social media transplants genuine human connection with a plethora of superficial social "connectivity". Unfortunately, many tend toward the latter of these two scenarios. Why worry? The indiscriminate use of online tech has led to a precipitous

deterioration of the social fabric. When it isn't just an endless churn of vacuous verbiage, much of social media is overwhelmed with a fusillade of sniping and trolling. As we are inundated with pithy comments and perfunctory "likes", we find ourselves isolated and riven with anxiety. So we try—often in vain—to conduct serious conversations as we trudge through the toxic muck of social media postings, seeking out the rare gem.

38:
The right wing's assault on Progressivism is illustrated by their ham-fisted effort to associate post-modernism with Marxian thought (and vice versa). They also try to associate secularism / humanism with relativism (Marx was a secularist / humanist, but not a relativist). They then characterize identity politics as a kind of "neo-Marxism"; and political correctness as "cultural Marxism". As I discussed in **Robin's Zugzwang**, one embracing Marxian ideals means rejecting relativism and cultural engineering. I also point out that the only way to embrace Marxian ideals is a wholesale rejection of tribalism (read: identity politics); as he touted "species-being" in lieu of tribal division. Alas, other than perhaps Nietzsche, Marx is probably the most mis-understood—and misrepresented—thinker in human history. Contrary to the asseverations of right-wing polemicists, Marx did NOT believe that everyone should have the same amount of wealth. (His compunction with "private property" was only with capital—that is: property used to exploit others.) While he addressed proper contribution as function of ability and proper distribution as function of need, Marx was not advocating for equal outcome for all. His indictment was of highly-concentrated wealth / power…and the exploitation of the common-man that invariably ensued from such severely skewed distribution. In other words: His primary concern was with a society in which a well-positioned few game the system for their own aggrandizement…while lording it over everyone else. In the U.S., wealth / power is becoming ever-more highly concentrated. Today, 80% of Americans account for only 7% of the nation's wealth. (Fully half of the American population—taken all together—account for only 2.6% of the nation's wealth.) To be clear, wealth aggregation via wealth extraction is a global phenomenon: In 2024, the world's 500 wealthiest people surpassed $10 trillion in collective assets; and $1.5 trillion of that were gains from just that year. (Eight tech billionaires alone posted a collective increase of $600 billion during the year…even as destitution is on the rise for virtually everyone else.) As was shown in Wilkinson and Pickett's **The Spirit Level**, drastic socio-economic inequality leads to severe societal dysfunction. Marx recognized that, in a world of unbridled capitalism, wealth / power accumulation is inevitable. While the well-positioned few enjoy the spoils of economic activity, the rest of us scramble frantically to survive. His clarion call was for emancipation, not for homogeneity; for equitable distribution instead of inexorable concentration; for bottom-up instead of top-down control. (See also Endnote 54.) In a sane world, it would be inconceivable that any one person would accumulate over a billion dollars in wealth, or that large corporations would control public policy. Companies like Meta, Coinbase, and Nvidia would not exist; nor would any health insurance

companies, hedge funds, or financial investment firms. In other words, society would be truly democratic…just as Marx envisioned.

<u>39</u>:
There are various ways to address feelings of inadequacy—from religionism (predicated on false hope and false certainty) and tribal chauvinism (predicated on false pride) to machismo (predicated on a false conception of masculinity) and sanctimony (predicated on false confidence). Dogmatism and tribalism are the refuges of those who are addled with insecurity; hence the allure of cult activity. Insecure self-esteem—in all of its manifestations—tends to lead to one or another kind of over-compensation. In American males, this often takes the form of gun-toting braggadocio, whereby firearms serve as a prosthetic for masculinity. Oftentimes, adult males who feel alienated want desperately to prove their manliness to the world…without having to actually cultivate strong character. Behold a cadre of overtly-hostile, cognitively-docile men who aspire to cartoonish versions of swagger—from militiamen to edge-lords. Such wayward souls end up seeing pompous buffoons like Elon Musk as an avatar of manly prowess. (In spite of his imbecility, Musk is an unintelligent person's idea of an intelligent person.) Tragically, such right-wing sycophants are now commonplace across America's heartland. Question their worldview, and they quickly become apoplectic. Such psychical friability leads to all sorts of daffy behavior. When insecure masculinity manifests as TOXIC masculinity, it leads to aggression. Indeed, insecurity often translates to hostility; and prompts one or another kind of over-compensation. As Chris Hedges has pointed out, toxic masculinity is the bedrock of ethno-nationalism, and fascism in general. But the problem with toxic masculinity isn't the masculinity; it's the toxicity. In the United States, insecure masculinity is epitomized by the cult of MAGA. (MAGA is, in large part, an ethno-nationalist cult that appeals to ill-informed, insecure, White Christian men.) Negative social conditions—not only social / economic insecurity, but protracted despondency and frustration—can augment the tendency to seek a simulacrum of self-esteem in dysfunctional ways. Behold millions of disaffected American males floundering as they feverishly pursue a tough-guy image. In the midst of this dejection, people seek a meaningful role to play—something that offers a sense of hope (and of certainty) in an oft-beguiling world. We adopt the most readily-available option, even if it means embracing false hope and false certainty. People who are in dire straits are often searching for something to hold onto. Many find themselves fumbling around in the dark—frantically grasping for anything that is within reach; and are willing to go along with whatever offers reprieve from their state of existential vertigo. Disoriented and desperate, when they find something that seems solid, they will tend to hold onto it…and cling to it 'til Kingdom Come. Once they seize onto that solid-seeming THING (like a drowning man who, in the midst of flailing, finds himself clinging in desperation to a life-raft), they will be reluctant to ever let go. This explains why those who are lost at sea (read: insecure) tend to gravitate toward cult activity of one sort or another. (Note that MAGA is largely the result of people trying to make sense of

inchoate frustrations, and finding a way to channel their angst.) Cult activity of all kinds demonstrates that when people are craving hope, they will go with even false hope in the event that it is the most readily available panacea presenting itself. (To reiterate: America's gun-fetishism is a textbook case of insecure masculinity.) Insecurity manifests in myriad different ways; but in every case, the question is: How do people address it? More pressing: How is it exploited? MAGA has been so successful, in part, because it speaks to all sorts of insecurities—offering a marvelously simple means of compensation. In due course, the movement has become a haven for insecure men—the poster-boy for whom is currently Donald Trump (along with Elon Musk). By waving a flag and kissing Trump's golden ring, participants in this daft charade imagine a magical infusion of testosterone. As they hold a bible in one hand and a gun in the other, they presume that a mawkish pantomime of swagger is a surrogate for manhood. After renewing their NRA membership, chugging some raw milk, and buying another bottle of "tough guy" pills from Alex Jones, they can bask in the illusion that they have the faintest clue what "manliness" might look like.

40:

Some fictional characters **really are** race-neutral—as with, say, the Na'vi in the Avatar films. And some fictional characters **really are** gender-neutral—as with, say, Puck in Shakespeares' "A Midsummer Night's Dream". Want a strong female protagonist? No need to upend legacy I.P. A great way to portray heroic women is to create compelling characters. (My personal favorite: Morn Hyland in Stephen R. Donaldson's Gap Cycle.) This has been demonstrated numerous times in film—from Ellen Ripley to Sarah Connor; from Laura Croft to Beatrix Kiddo; from Salt to Peppermint. (Anime has always managed to offer great heroines—be it Aeon Flux, Ghost In The Shell, or Fate / Zero.) This is done not by upstaging a male protagonist (e.g. a decrepit Indiana Jones) with a female protagonist (e.g. a saucy god-daughter with a chip on her shoulder); it is done by creating novel characters. Strong heroes and strong heroines are not mutually exclusive; they can operate in unison. Think of Gina Davis in ***A Long Kiss Goodnight***, Carrie-Ann Moss in ***The Matrix***, and Emily Blunt in ***Edge Of Tomorrow***. Such productions empowered females without denigrating males. No Mary-Sues required. What those who are preoccupied with superficial notions of "representation" fail to grasp is that empowerment is about far more than snazzy optics and token gestures. They also don't seem to recognize that uplifting one demographic does not require us to diminish another. (It isn't necessary to debase Luke Skywalker in order to put an inspiring female Jedi center-stage.) Misandry is no more the answer to misogyny than racism in one direction is the answer to racism in the other direction. New counter-bigotries do not attenuate extant bigotries; the former exacerbate the latter. The bottom line is this: When it comes to Progressive entertainment, no gender- or race-swapping is necessary. There is no need to jettison established lore to uplift a formerly-marginalized group. (Why create a female Silver Surfer when we could just as well do a film about Firestar or Spiderwoman?) Whether or not we are dealing with celebrated fiction or sacred history, we do ethnic heritage a disservice by distorting it for ideological purposes. Want to tout female empowerment? Great. We can create new heroic figures—as was done in films like Colombiana, Wanted, Haywire, Hanna, Ava, Anna, Lucy, Kate, and Red Sparrow (as well as in series like Charlie's Angels, Buffy The Vampire Slayer, Alias, Dollhouse, and Quantico). In sum: We don't make the future better by pretending the past—whether in the real world or in fictional tales—was different from what it actually was. Nor do we need to engage in some race- / gender-swapping frenzy when harkening back to cherished lore. The world doesn't need a Jamie Bond; it needs more Atomic Blondes.

41:
This can be juxtaposed with arguably the greatest pop vocalist on the planet, Morissette Amon, who enunciates every syllable with astonishing clarity. Morissette's preternatural breath-control enables her to achieve jaw-dropping feats when she sings. Each phoneme is taken seriously…even as she employs masterful phrasing in every key, in every register. (I regret that my father—a vocal adjudicator—was not alive to hear this Filipina phenom.) When there is actual merit, there is no need for fudging. Alas, at a time when the use of auto-tune has become routine, the respect for authenticity—and reverence for actual talent—has vanished.

42:
The corporatization of pop culture has gone so far as to include the commercialization of "COUNTER-culture", whereby ostensive **novelty** comes off of an assembly-line—designed by corporate execs who care little for artistic expression. We wind up with a memetic ecosystem in which even counter-culture is reduced to banality. So even that which is purportedly "edgy" is glamorized; then leveraged for commercial gimmickry. This is a phenomenon that we've seen a thousand times—from The Ramones to Billie Eilish. Adolescent "rebellious-ness" is invariably just a mawkish spectacle of sophomoric antics—from goth to emo subculture. (The prime case-study of such Kafka-esque commercialism is 90's "grunge"—which petered out the moment it became the very thing it was supposed to be railing against: the mainstream.) These ersatz rebels see their petulance as defiance; so treat rebellion as a performative act. They seek to nettle and peacock rather than to spur revolutionary change. Their rebelliousness is a posture, not a principled stand. They thus reduce dissent to mere gimmickry, then pretend that it is a bold act. Hence they goad others, yet rarely evolve themselves. For them, agitation is an emotive state, not a social strategy. An ersatz rebelliousness slakes our abiding hunger to channel our rage against the Machine. The "catch" is that it channels our anger in ways that don't **actually challenge** the Machine. This gambit affords the rabble a chance to vent in a way that may have otherwise posed a problem for the power elite (and that would have challenged incumbent power structures). The impresarios of the culture industry know: The best way to ensure people remain subservient is to keep them distracted / amused; and thus placated. This can be done by incessantly feeding them enthralling fatuity. Here, rebellion is reduced to mere

shtick—an enticing gimmick to be marketed and sold to the rank and file. This works insofar as the masses are consumed by their own insatiable consumerism… even as they want to think that they are doing the latest COOL THING. In due course, many find themselves clamoring to keep up with the current trends in order to maintain some sort of social cachet. In a world where it's all about optics, the mere APPEARANCE OF defiance suffices to make one feel like some sort of firebrand. Even obsequiousness can be passed off as valor. Naturally, the power elite REVEL in this arrangement; as the commodification of illusory radicalism leads to the extinction of SUBSTANTIVE radicalism. Rather than ACTUAL defiance, we get performative recalcitrance…along with oodles of confectionary authenticity. In place of a revolutionary spirit, there is only a pantomime thereof. This way, even sycophants can feel valiant. (Note how "brave" religious fundamentalists fashion themselves when deciding to go "all in" with their Faith—construing their subservience as a courageous act.) Pop culture is at the mercy of a (corporate-run) culture machine. In this scheme, tacky knock-offs of "counter-culture" are mass-produced by giant, trans-national conglomerates who couldn't care less about the underpinnings of civil society; and ***most certainly*** want nothing to do with genuine revolution. After all, their continued primacy is predicated on keeping the institutional underpinnings fully intact. (Tech billionaires are the most blatant examples of this—railing against "the Establishment" while doing everything in their power to maintain incumbent power structures.) The ruse works because many of us never outgrow the ersatz rebellious-ness of our teenage years. This puerile sense of **taking a bold stand** and **stickin' it to the man** (without actually doing anything substantive) is what drives both the Regressive "Left" and MAGA. While guzzling the Kool-Aid, they fail to notice that they are actually SERVING the impresarios of the established order. For millions of Americans, "anti-establishment" is little more than a branding exercise: a way for rubes to pretend that they are bold revolutionaries…even as they do nothing but give tacit support the power elite. Those on the political right vociferously inveigh against the cultural and intellectual elite…and pretend that it is the same as taking a bold stand against the socio-economic elite. (So they resent artists and scholars, exalt rent-seekers and robber barons.) Such misdirected ire is music to the ears of the oligarchs. MAGA—like its precursor, the Tea Party—fashions itself as "anti-establishment"; but this is, of course, little more than hot air. One can proclaim that one is "anti-establishment" at the top of one's lungs 'til the end of time; but if one mis-diagnoses what, exactly, the incumbent power structures are (as well as how they operate and who supports them), then one will only end up (unwittingly) abetting the very thing one purports to be taking a stand against. Howling at the moon does not alter the course of the celestial spheres.

43:

Narcissism is not to be confused with vanity. Though they often go hand-in-hand, being full of oneself and being self-absorbed are two different things. (Contrary to the etymology, Narcissus' problem was vanity, not narcissism.) While there is false pride involved in both cases, vain people aren't necessarily narcissistic; and narcissistic people aren't necessarily vain. Even as both involve hubris (artificially-inflated self-esteem), a preoccupation with how one is perceived by others (a matter of appearances) is not the same as a myopic way of viewing the world (a matter of epistemology). The former conceit is based on IMAGE; the latter conceit is based on ENTITLEMENT. Vanity does not necessarily preclude empathy; but narcissism ALWAYS does. Narcissism is, of course, often accompanied by every strain of vanity—from Hillary Clinton (phony) and Oprah Winfrey (fatuous) to Elon Musk (delusional) and Donald Trump (bombastic). Even when vanity is not involved, avarice always is. When we subject those with wealth / power who are narcissistic to critical analysis, we find that—in virtually every instance—there is a complete obliviousness to the lives of regular people. Meanwhile, such figures tend to have an outsized view of themselves—their astounding capabilities, formidable accomplishments, and winning personality. Trump often avers about those who do/don't contribute to the nation…when he himself has not once contributed anything to the betterment of society. He pontificates about hard-working Americans…when he has personally never done an honest day's work in his life. He inveighs against corruption…when he is almost certainly, by far, the most corrupt POTUS in the nation's history. He routinely boasts about his prodigious intelligence…when his IQ is almost certainly not much more than 80. (The threshold for mental retardation is 70. Elon Musk isn't much smarter—effectively an imbecile masquerading as a genius. Such is the case with many Silicon Valley tycoons. Of course, mentally handicapped politicians aren't limited to one party. As I write, the mayor of New York City is Eric Adams. Idiocy has no party affiliation.) Trump rails against the cultural "elite" when he is the epitome of a socio-economic elitist. He's a convicted felon who complains about crime; a serial liar who chastises dishonest politicians; a self-proclaimed Christian who is utterly clueless about the Abrahamic religions; and a habitually bankrupt, chronically delinquent businessman who croons about good business sense. Delusions of grandeur are typical of those who are pathologically narcissistic. Had a person as flagrantly reprobate as Trump been a woman of color, it is inconceivable that so many would be willing to accord her so much esteem. Given such a horrifying track-record, no one other than a White male would have been given the benefit of the doubt. (For more on the programmatic exaltation of idiocy, see Endnote 54.)

44:

Also of note is Gwen Stefani's incorporation of Harajuku leitmotifs into her musical performances. Growing up, she spent many of her formative years in Tokyo, becoming intimately familiar with the culture. One would think this to be relevant. But sure enough, she was castigated by anti-Cul-Ap crusaders. For them, that her ingenuitive artistic choice was made to PAY TRIBUTE to Harajuku culture was entirely beside the point. So far as they were concerned, **_intentions don't matter_**. Consequently all the Japanese influences in Stefani's life were immaterial to their assessment. The only factor was her RACE. Ironically, the very people who harangued Stefani for this purported travesty understood nothing about Harajuku. And none of them stopped to consider how big of a hit Stefani's performance was IN JAPAN.

45:
What's the deal with twelve? This leitmotif crops up in Ancient Greece (gods on Olympus), Hinduism (manifestations of Shiva), Norse mythology (sons of Odin), Judaism (tribes of Israel), Christianity (apostles), Shia Islam (imams), and astrology (signs in the zodiac). Notably, twelve was the most significant number for the Etruscans; which may have inspired its role in Mithra-ism. Other numbers have been ascribed cosmic significance. (I discuss the significance of three—i.e. trinities—in part 2 of my essay on "Mythemes".) There seem to be certain leitmotifs that hold appeal for all humans—irrespective of ethnicity. Indeed, certain things transcend culture, so have universal resonance—a matter addressed by Pascal Boyer in his landmark work, **Religion Explained**.

46:
Can subalterns be bigoted? Of course. Those who claim that racial minorities cannot be racist against racial majorities are broadcasting their own racial bias. Making such a suggestion is perfidious (see Endnote 51 below). By the same token, misogyny exists; but so can misandry, even in a patriarchal society. As Palestinians have every right to protest the Israeli government and its heinous policies, there's no excuse for any of them to be anti-Semitic. No human is exempt from moral responsibility. Power asymmetry and bigotry are sometimes related, but they are independent variables. They are not inextricably correlated. Socio-economic status does not create the bigotry; it merely affords the bigot the requisite resources to have sway over others. Put another way: Bigotry does not necessarily come from a place of privilege; it comes from a place of conceit.

47:
This is not the same as, say, "ni-ga" in Chinese (which is the equivalent of "…um…" or "…uh…") Rather, it is as if one were saying, "let me figure out what word I'm going to blurt out next" during a stream-of-consciousness. A similar filler is "ah-no" in Tagalog—which is literally asking oneself WHAT one is going to say next. Such verbal hiccups are an indication that one has not thought through what is coming out of one's mouth from one moment to the next. This is not to say that being extemporaneous is a bad thing. It's good to "wing it" from time to time. The problem is when ALL discourse is perfunctory and disjointed. (In addition, it is common for utterances to be strewn with verbal hiccups. In America, verbiage is often festooned with "…like…") While this critique may seem like nit-picking; these subtle quirks in daily speech are indicative of a much wider pathology. It is worth pointing out that *even something as jejune as demotic language exhibits signs of this new epidemic of hyper-mercurial thinking*. Within such a climate, it is no wonder that perspicacity is on the verge of extinction. (Currently, prominent examples are

Donald Trump and Elon Musk—dimwitted men who are incapable of articulating a coherent thought—clumsily stumbling from one sentence fragment to the next. Their mindless rambling is punctuated by an endless supply of verbal hiccups.) Much of the degradation in elocution is due to the diminution of standards in basic communication. Rather than being fastidious in our thinking, social media has trained us to be increasingly impetuous. At any given instant, our attention flits from one tantalizing thing to the next, precluding any chance for sustained concentration. Rather than an expression of well-thought-out ideas, demotic language has become an oral enactment of what can only be described as a stream-of-consciousness. We live our lives from one-attention-grabbing moment to the next…which is what is bound to happen when self-absorption becomes the norm. Mental processes are reduced to a series of disjointed impulse-reactions—making sustained concentration all-but-impossible; and critical reflection unfathomable. Notable is the diminution of willingness to make eye contact with other human beings while interacting with them. This goes hand-in-hand with an increasingly widespread inability to maintain focus during in-person conversations (that is: without being distracted by activity on one's mobile device). In the online ecosystem, we fetishize connectivity, yet rarely forge genuine connections; so superficial encounters suffice. With severely stunted attention spans coupled with an incessant craving for instant gratification, serious discourse becomes a Sisyphean task.

48:
With regards to commercializing the sacred: I once saw a crèche sponsored by McDonalds…but not AT a McDonalds. (What's next? A Buddhist shrine brought to us by Verizon?) Surely, it's only a matter of time until the curia opens a Starbucks in the Vatican. Perhaps Nike could sponsor the next Passover; or Google could sponsor the next Hajj. When it comes to the profit motive, nothing is off-limits; and only cash is deemed sacred. Alas. Corporate sponsors have taken over pop culture—from the naming of sports stadiums / arenas to the themes found in network programming (both on television and streaming platforms). First, there was conspicuous product placement WITHIN the content; now the content itself has become little more than a product (or, worse, a vehicle for propaganda). Reducing culture to a marketing gimmick makes cherished social norms for some people into a mere accessory for others. For early insights on the commodification of culture, see the critiques done by the Frankfurt School—specifically their discussion of the "culture industry".

49:
Many are inclined to treat morality as performance art. I submit the following maxim: For any given X, performative X is not genuine X; it is a pantomime thereof. Since the introduction of auto-tune and photo-shop, we have lost touch not only with the importance of authenticity; but with the MEANING OF authenticity. Both hyper-commercialism (superficiality run amok) and post-modernism (subjectivism run amok) are responsible for the normalization of fatuity. In the

autumn of 2024, the marketing department at Jaguar thought there was something avant-garde about brightly-colored androgyny. This prompted an odd television commercial that confounded virtually everyone. Such thinking leads us to do silly things—in this case: making automotive design more about demographic profiles than mechanical engineering. (For the past decade, identity politics have infiltrated advertisements.) So vendors found themselves touting the putative audacity of androgeneity rather than the importance of technological innovation. (Memo to Jaguar: There is nothing bold or creative about being garishly androgynous.) Artists resist any and all pressure to conform to a manufactured orthodoxy, which is often defined by social norms that have been engineered by large corporations. Lost in all this mawkish posturing is a simple fact: Meaningful heterodoxy proceeds from autonomy. Rather than mere contrarianism, it is born of courage and creativity. When it comes to artistic expression, we should remind ourselves that truly innovative thinkers aren't trying to be gratuitously provocative. The cloying theatrics espoused by identitarians and p.c.-mongers is not a mark of intrepidity; it is a mark of insipidity. Jaguar's daffy marketing campaign was a reminder that the world needs pioneers, not popinjays.

50:
Hockey began during the Middle Ages in Mongolia—as "bei-koo" amongst the Khitan people—probably during the Liao period. This does not necessarily entail a direct link between their version (played on the tundra; and possibly on frozen ponds in the steppes) and the modern sport (played on a rink using ice-skates). This is yet another illustration of why the ***"We were the first to do it; so now we own it for the rest of eternity"*** approach to culture is asinine. If we were to honor this precedent, only the Daghur would be allowed into the NHL.

51:
Part of selective anti-racism is being out of touch with the common-man. Behold an armada of voracious moralizers for whom the universal application of moral principles is too much to ask. And so it goes: Many of those who propound ersatz Progressivism are fine with endorsing a genocide in Palestine as they cavil about micro-aggressions in between sips of chardonnay. ("The Israeli government may be slaughtering tens of thousands of innocent civilians, but let's focus on the fact that Bob said something racially insensitive to Betty in the break-room at work yesterday.") Such posturing is nothing more than rank duplicity. Wonder whether or not people of color can be virulently racist? Consider Ritchie Torres, Hakeem Jeffries, and Bakari Sellers: each an illustration of how selective anti-racism translates to selective racism. The attitude of such men amounts to: Prejudice against African Americans may be wrong, ladies and gentlemen; yet genocide against Palestinians is perfectly justified. (It's worth recalling the words of Voltaire: "Those who can make you believe absurdities can persuade you to commit atrocities." Moral bankruptcy paves the way for immoral conduct. Errant beliefs often lead to iniquitous actions.) The double standard here is glaring. That ten thousand Ukrainian civil-

ians have perished (largely as collateral damage) since Russia's incursion into their country is seen as cataclysmic. Meanwhile, Israel has deliberately slaughtered at least TEN TIMES that number of Palestinians in the past year, but that is met with a dismissive shrug: "Hey, that's war. Whaddaya gonna do?" Therein lies the hypocrisy undergirding selective anti-racism: It amounts to being selectively racist. When one is against racism for only certain kinds of people, it follows that one is racist when it comes to everyone else. (This derangement goes back to the Torah—effectively a book based on the maxim: It's fine when WE do it; but not when anyone else does it.) To make matters worse, the more delusive proponents of identity politics are determined to see bigotry everywhere…even where it clearly does not exist. They could look at a kitchen sink and see a scourge of racism (a phenomenon I discuss in **Robin's Zugzwang**). Let's look at two examples. ONE: When someone complains about the acrid stench emanating from a bystander with intense body odor, and said bystander happens to be a person of color, fanatical identitarians will insist that the complaint must be born of covert racism. (It couldn't possibly be that it is the malodor—regardless of from whom it was emanating—that was at issue.) TWO: If a person of color is reproved for being routinely tardy at their place of employment, fanatical identitarians will insist that the complaint must be born of covert racism. (It couldn't possibly stem from expectations that people be on time for work.) What's going on here? Gossamer bigotry (see Endnote 58). There is real racism out there; and mis-using the term in such ridiculous ways does a grave disservice to ACTUAL victims of racism; it only dilutes the semiotic ballast of the term. Such perfidy reminds us that some people do not come to the conversation in good faith; but are instead determined to cast things in whatever terms validate their predetermined conclusions. This perfidy—masquerading, as it often does, as "anti-racism"—has severely debilitating effects on the public discourse; as such absurd accusations make it that much more difficult for the rest of us to point out ACTUAL instances of racial injustice.

52:

In the event that someone makes a statement that happens to correlate with a stereotype, are we to automatically accuse them of stereotyping? If so, one ends up VALIDATING the stereotype…even as one haughtily denounces it. Consider the pernicious trope of the money-grubbing Jew—which persists no thanks to the likes of Lloyd Blankfein and Sheldon Adelson (who serve to perpetrate this vulgar stigma). (Newsflash: The vast majority of money-grubbers in the world are not Jewish.) When someone uses the term, "shyster" (a race-neutral descriptor), some interlocutors accuse the person of invoking an anti-Semitic trope. This accusation is ITSELF anti-Semitic, as it implies that to be a shyster is to be Jewish. The same goes for those who tie the term, "thug" (another race-neutral descriptor) to people of color. The accusation insinuates that to be a thug is to be a p.o.c., thereby **playing into** another vulgar stigma. These terms are only racially-charged when they are said / heard by racists. Such grave misapprehension has nothing to do with the rest of us. (Friendly neighborhood reminder: WASPs can be shysters and thugs too.)

We should bear in mind that not all stereotypes are based in statistical reality. Pop quiz: Which racial group eats the most watermelon? (Answer: East Asians.) And who are—by far—the biggest tea drinkers? The Turks. (The Chinese don't even break the top ten.) Alas, in the midst of the tsunami of poppycock circulating online, risible misconceptions abound. While there are clear social norms from one place to the next (yes, most Chinese regularly drink tea; and most also chew—very loudly—with their mouths open), not everyone from China embodies those norms. It is important to judge people on an individual-by-individual basis (see Endnote 59).

53:
The primary Stoic thinkers were Epictetus and Seneca the Younger. Also note the "Enchiridion " by the philosopher, Arrian of Nikomedeia and the "Meditations" by Roman Emperor, Marcus Aurelius. The equanimity they championed stands in stark juxtaposition to the histrionics of the Regressive "Left"—a programatic tetchy-ness that helps nobody. Stoicism is about having control over one's emotions; and maintaining a cool head when encountering the slings and arrows of life. That said, the ancient philosophy of Stoicism is about more than simply maintaining composure in the face of adversity; it is about resisting all the trappings of narcissism. After all, emotional resilience is a precondition for mental lucidity; and thus for broader thinking. In addition to chronic self-absorption and a complete lack of empathy, emotional instability is a hallmark feature of narcissism. As such, the narcissist becomes incapable of critical reflection…and thus of critical deliberation. The primary tenet of Stoicism is mental discipline; as mental discipline is a pre-requisite for three crucial things: prudence, integrity, and empathy. The frangible disposition that has become so commonplace in modern society stands in stark contrast to the Stoic ideal. Such frangibility—the antithesis of equanimity—explains why p.c.-mongers have posited a "right not to be offended". Not only does political correctness sabotage the public discourse, it precludes our ability to forge deep bonds with fellow human beings—thereby undermining social cohesion. The mark of the true Stoic is to be everything the narcissist is not. This includes level-headed decision-making (enkrateia), an unwavering adherence to moral principles (arete), and giving a shit about other people (agape). In a nutshell: mental discipline. Stoicism does not discourage compassion for others when they are enduring (real) tribulation. Equanimity is not apathy. Stoicism does not adjure us to accept injustices; it shows us how to address them in the most efficient and effective way. Nor is equanimity the same as complacency. Stoicism is not antithetical to aspiration; or even well-directed passion. Rather than mandate unconditional satisfaction with our circumstances; it simply shows us how to stop getting in our own way as we pursue our endeavors. The point is to recognize how we often self-sabotage, and thereby fail to achieve eudaimonia. Lastly, Stoicism is not a license to gaslight others (telling those who've been mistreated, "It's just in your head"). Avoiding needless psychical turmoil does not entail denying the existence of actual turmoil.

54:

As the socio-economic elite remain comfortably perched atop their gilded rostrum, chortling about the wisdom of Ayn Rand, they insist that YOU TOO might join their vaunted ranks if only you had what it takes. The message we receive is not that the system is rigged; it's that, if only we keep our nose to the grindstone, we may soon have the yacht, the private jet, the calendar cars, and an opulently-furnished solarium—plus a hot spouse and an unlimited supply of Kobe steaks. In America, tens of millions remain forever mesmerized by this fever-dream. The narrative is compelling because it depicts a society that is ostensibly meritocratic, not because it describes a society that is actually meritocratic. Here, "meritocratic" is heard as "fair": everyone gets what they deserve, so the world is as it should be. The thinking proceeds thus: "Those with money and power have it for good reason. So respect your betters; and accept your lot in life." Consequently, any major reform should be seen as an unwarranted disruption to the established order. The myth of meritocracy (a.k.a. the Horatio Alger myth) boils down to a simple proposition: In the end, everyone gets what they deserve. This is, of course, laughably erroneous (see Endnotes 18, 43, and 57). Mao Tse-Tung proved that a person can be a complete moron and seize control of an entire country. Many other world leaders have clearly had mental handicaps. I submit that the average IQ at Davos during the World Economic Forum is not an iota above that found amongst the commonfolk dwelling in any of the world's most squalid slums. To illustrate this point, consider two of the most opprobrious American tycoons: Elon Musk and Donald Trump. Behold a pair of imbeciles who enjoy obscene amounts of unearned privilege—and wield a disconcerting amount of power—after having personally contributed nothing to society. Each exposes the lie of some pristine American meritocracy…in which we all get ahead based sheerly on grit, talent, and achievement. Had the former man not been born into such privileged circumstances, and not found himself in the charmed socio-economic position in which he ended up finding himself, he would now likely be some weirdo bagging groceries at the local food-mart. And had this been the case for the latter man, he would now likely be an obnoxious geezer rambling incoherently at the end of the bar at some backwater hole-in-the-wall (drinking spritzer out of a straw while ogling the female patrons). Instead, Musk and Trump are now—arguably—the two most powerful men on the planet. Something is horribly amiss. The short explanation: The system is rigged. While this sounds oddly conspiratorial, it requires no cabal of diabolical puppet-masters, smoking cigars as they pull the strings from some secret, underground lair. Rather, it is due to the architecture of society's major power structures; which evolve according to various social and economic factors. This process does not play out according to some blueprint; nor does it happen according to the guidance of any particular party. There is no "intelligent design" involved. Power tends to aggregate in a few hands, so tends to become ever-more-highly-concentrated. This aggregation occurs as a matter of course. Consequently, those who most benefit from incumbent power structures find themselves at an advantage. As such, socio-economic privilege is due to a combination of five things: accident of birth, personal connections, ambition, savvy maneuvering, and dumb luck. Add to this a complete lack of ethical scruples; and the recipe for affluence is complete. (Intelligence and hard work are what help people thrive in the MIDDLE class. Most speculators and rent-seekers have not made their outsized fortunes because they are smarter than the barista who brewed my coffee this morning, or more industrious than the ER nurse who helped my cousin this afternoon.) When we listen to, say, Peter Thiel, we realize we're listening to the ramblings of an imbecile who's managed to amass billions by placing the right bets in the right places at the right time. Shrewd? Perhaps. A genius? Not by a long-shot. The evidence that modern society is ameritocratic—oftentimes ANTI-meritocratic—is overwhelming. Consider this: A competent public school teacher does more for society in the average week than many hedge fund managers will do over the course of their entire careers. In the upper echelons of America's socio-economic strata, we find prima donnas with empty minds and full bank accounts—many of whom do virtually nothing to contribute to the commonweal. This phenomenon is not unique to the U.S. When it comes to ameritocratic outcomes, case-studies include many of the world's most notorious oligarchs—the majority of whom would (but for their inherited socio-economic status and stellar fortune) have qualifications roughly on par with the guy stocking shelves at the corner store. Yet the ultra-rich encourage the notion that they have so much wealth because they are superior; and that they are superior because they have so much wealth. Au contraire, the socio-economic elite is populated not by society's best, but by those who—by hook or by crook—have managed to secure a lofty position in the machinery of power. The result of all this finagling is an esteemed cadre of savvy operators with far more money than brain-cells; yet who proudly fashion themselves as stalwarts of "success". (If only we could all be so charmed.) This disjuncture between perception (the best and the brightest) and Reality (a gaggle of tremendously fortunate dregs) has to do with the fact that the U.S. has a disconcertingly gormless population—many of whom are perfectly willing to participate in this odious charade. After all, in their minds, THEY TOO might someday be blessed enough to join the vaunted ranks of "the elect"…if only they play along. They are victims of their own false hope. So now here we are. Due this widespread misapprehension, tens of millions of Americans have been snookered into supporting a con man who fashions himself a maestro of deal-making (see the Appendix). The fact that such a buffoon is so exalted by so many is flabbergasting to anyone with a functioning moral compass (and with even a rudimentary grasp of the facts). Yet it is testament to how potent the myth of meritocracy has become. To keep up this dazzling facade, the socio-economic elite require what Noam Chomsky dubbed "necessary illusions"; as, so long as the rabble remain blissfully entranced by these hallucinations of limitless "freedom" and "opportunity", they will acquiesce to the established order. Those at the top understand that false hope will keep the masses from revolting; so they ensure the myth of meritocracy is propounded; and that—even as they bilk the working class—they continue to promise better days ahead (see Ronald Reagan; "It's morning in America"). As they hoard the fruits of America's economic activity with reckless abandon, the rest of us are urged to read "Atlas Shrugged"—daydreaming that all those spoils may someday magically trickle down to the working class. The well-positioned few continue to game the system—amassing ever-more wealth without having to actually contribute anything to society; and they are revered for the gesture. The American dream is as intoxicating and addictive as a chemical narcotic; and it is every bit as detrimental to our health. (For other perspectives on this, see Daniel Markovits' *The Meritocracy Trap* and Michael Sandel's *The Tyranny of Merit*.) In the 18th century, Voltaire strove to divorce conceptions of merit from socio-economic status. While he made substantial headway, his legacy was tragically short-lived. The veneration of (what is essentially) gilded depravity has become de rigueur in modern American life. Wealthy knaves are revered as stalwarts of the entrepreneurial spirit. Today, all-too-many are willing to lionize even the most morally degenerate actors…so long as those actors are swathed in the ornate vestments of "success". All-too-often, socio-economic status is seen as a proxy for excellence; wealth as a barometer for virtue. One can tell a lot about how intelligent someone is by who he/she believes is intelligent. When people start viewing imbeciles as intellectual giants, it's time to be concerned. For not only are such people sanguine when it comes to idiocy (which is bad enough); they don't even know idiocy when they see it (which can be quite dangerous; see Endnote 43). I have never met an intelligent person who's seen Elon Musk as anything other than a blithering moron; yet…he is seen as a virtuoso by tens of millions of gormless Americans. As Voltaire rolls in his grave, legions of rubes will continue to extol unscrupulous robber barons… while chiding serious scholars.

<u>55:</u>

People in most cultures tend to be serious not only about honesty, but about the conceptualization of Truth. Tellingly, in some languages, the word for "true" and the word for "real" are the same—as with Japanese ("shinko"), Siamese ("tsing"), and Tagalog ("talaga"). What is true is only what is REAL, which is distinguished from personal impressions (what any given person my happen to have in their own minds). The notion that someone might have a personal claim on what is "shinko" / "tsing" / "talaga" is seen as preposterous; even incoherent. (In such languages, qualifying the aforementioned term with a possessive affix / article would be nonsensical.) Why? Because all sane people recognize that something is either (objectively) real or it isn't; and that this has nothing to do with the subjective state of any given bystander. The alternative to "shinko" / "tsing" / "talaga" is for something to be erroneous (alt. a figment of one's own imagination; whether wishful thinking or a deliberate falsehood). Noting a correlation with Reality—or a lack thereof—is the entire point of these terms. Anything less, and they become meaningless (not to mention, practically useless). Alas, in English, we are perfectly fine modifying "true" / "truth" and "real" / "reality" with a possessive pronoun. Thankfully, in English, there is a descriptor for someone who unwittingly passes off fictions as statements of fact: **ignoramus**. There is also a descriptor for someone who knowingly passes off fictions as statements of fact: **liar**. And—per Harry Frankfurt—there is a descriptor for someone who doesn't even care that a difference between the two EVEN EXISTS: *bullshitter*. A simple experiment should suffice to make the point. in Japan, try asserting that something is "shinko" JUST FOR ME. Then, in Thailand, try asserting that something is "tsing" JUST FOR ME. Then, in the Philippines, try asserting that something is "talaga" JUST FOR ME. One will be met with incredulous laughter in all three countries. For any level-headed person understands that it is not about what one happens to THINK is true / real; it is about what ACTUALLY IS true / real. This nifty lexical feature does not preclude people in Japan, the Philippines, and Thailand from being mistaken (every country has ignorant people; and every country has those who are completely full of shit); but it behooves speakers to acknowledge that there is a distinction to be made.

56:
A deliberately ironic use of Beethoven's Ninth was offered by Stanley Kubrick in his film, "A Clockwork Orange", wherein he juxtaposed audio sublimity with human depravity. There have been many profound interpretations of this famous symphony—notably by Friedrich Nietzsche in "The Birth Of Tragedy". Nietzsche believed that this particular piece of music captured the Dionysian (aesthetic) aspect of life; as—over the course of its movements—it brings dissonance (representing the vicissitudes of the human condition) into perfect harmony (representing transcendence). He was certainly on to something profound. One thing is for certain: This masterpiece (the original lyrics for which were patently secular) has no place in a Catholic Church.

57:
A prime example of projection is the characterization of America's cadre of rent-seekers and investment bankers (vis a vis everyone else). Behold society's most flagrant parasites…who often accuse many of those in the working class of being moochers (spec. insofar as vital social services are needed to keep them afloat). In this deranged schema, wealth *extraction* (hoarding) is passed off as a kind of wealth *creation*. Accordingly, venture capitalists (who's sole gambit is speculation) operate under the aegis of "innovators" or "creators". (In reality, private equity and hedge fund behemoths are parasitic in nature. They can only thrive in an economy that has been hyper-financialized; and depend on the productive efforts of OTHERS to amass their wealth.) In the American psyche, venture capitalists and other financial tycoons are seen as "innovators" / "creators", when—in fact—they personally produce virtually nothing. The irony here is mind-bending; as it is THEY who mooch off of the productive activity of society's most productive thinkers and workers. Such figures—the pompous sinecures of the rentier class—operate under Orwellian rubrics like "entrepreneurs" and "job creators" and "titans of industry"…when they are little more than speculative investors, playing with other people's money…as everyone else does the real work. (So-called "venture capitalists" are, in reality, simply VULTURE capitalists.) The confusion on this matter is significant: We rightfully inveigh against hooligans looting retail stores;

yet we seem to have few qualms with large corporations looting the treasury. (Petty theft rankles us even as corporate socialism is seen as a splendid way to bolster the nation's economy.) And so it goes: Those who are gaming the system the most are the first to scold the rabble for trying to game the system. In other words: The socio-economic elite avert culpability in society's glaring inequities by placing the blame on those who are struggling in a cut-throat marketplace. (This is not a difficult ruse to maintain. The key is simply to be as petty and acrimonious as possible when regurgitating right-wing "libertarian" talking points; see Endnote 54.) As a result of these wearying conditions, those who most need to do work on themselves are most apt to cast aspersions at others. Ergo projection: The sins I accuse you of committing are really my own sins.

58:
Due to its diaphanous qualities, I refer to inverted bigotry as "gossamer bigotry". This amounts to **internalized racism** (which is to say: racism that is subconscious and inwardly directed). As such, gossamer bigotry tends to have ANTI-racist pretenses even as it is predicated entirely on racist presuppositions. (In this sense, it could just as well be called "alabaster bigotry".) Such a condition often takes the form of passive bigotry—in that it translates to a demographically-targeted diminishment in standards. (Note, for example, the knuckleheads who insist that literacy and/or punctuality is a White people thing.) Imagine saying of an African American who is chronically tardy or has shoddy grammar: "Oh, well he's Black; so that's to be expected. Let's just overlook it." Instead of empowering Black people, this demeans them. It is passive derogation. When reasonable standards are deemed WHITE standards, we've gone through the Looking Glass. Rather than create avenues for career advancement, such thinking serves to perpetuate negative stigmas…while exacerbating alterity. Once only ends up short-changing people when opting for a targeted diminishment in standards. In a ham-fisted attempt to give a leg up to marginalized communities, identitarians don't give themselves—or others—enough credit. A targeted diminution of standards is, at best, condescending; and oftentimes debilitating. The response to such gossamer bigotry, then, is quite simple: Give people more credit. I explore the implications of gossamer bigotry in **Robin's Zugzwang**. The point of promoting social justice is to ensure that everyone has the same starting line. The point is NOT to adjust the finish-line—in an ad hoc manner—so as to create the illusion of equal achievement. Doing so does not empower the disadvantaged; it short-changes them. One does a marginalized group no favors by patronizing them.

59:
Enculturation is an integral part of group identity—especially when it comes to how people define themselves in ethnic terms. We intuitively understand that this is how ethnicity works. So when watching the winter olympics, do we get bent out of shape upon seeing that there aren't many Black people participating in the curling competition? No. How about not participating in ping-pong at the sum-

mer olympics? No. Why not? Simply put: the conditions in which the majority of Black people live. The lack of Punjabis in the NBA, lack of Jamaicans in the NHL, and lack of Indonesians in the NFL says nothing about exogenous (racial) biases. Such trends primarily reflect **acquired affinities** (endogenous biases); which often emerge along cultural lines. Those affinities are, in part, attributable to prevailing social norms (spec. inculcated sensibilities). They are also attributable to the anatomical / physiological characteristics of certain haplo-groups. (Most Chinese and Koreans don't need to wear deodorant; and the majority of females don't need to shave their legs. Also, many are lactose intolerant and allergic to cats. Unlike Latinos, they tend to love the taste of root beer. And many East Asians are unable to wink with both eyes. Meanwhile, they have much smaller frames than, say, Anglo-Saxon, Nordic, and Slavic peoples; which explains why so few of them are rugby players.) Our focus here, instead, is on **socialization**, which has to do with conditioned responses rather than with congenital attributes. This is simply to say that ethnic markers are learned, not innate. Even as we'd all like to believe that ethnicity were somehow written in the stars, it is not. Indeed, it has been shown that a person of a given race raised in different environment will acquire social habits—including affinities—germane to that environment (spec. as a result of the experiences had during the formative years). Only racists misconstrue enculturation as an indication of traits that inhere in one's race. Such race essentialization is often given the green light by identitarians.

60:
The mantra of the aristocracy has always been some form of: "We may not be principled, but at least we maintain a high degree of decorum; and that's something that everyone should admire." Throughout modernity, the rank and file were not referred to as the "unwashed masses" for lack of soap; it was for lack of **propriety**. Finishing schools didn't exist to foster moral virtue; they were there to ensure decorum was maintained—specifically: amongst the ruling class—so as to demarcate the terms of PRIVILEGE (read: who matters vs. who doesn't). In considering what role propriety might play in effecting civil society, we should note the incidence of tyrants with impeccable manners. The conclusion soon becomes crystal clear: How polished someone happens to be has no correlation whatsoever to their moral integrity. In fact, it is oftentimes INVERSELY proportional.

61:
The interplay between culture and technology is highly complex. Certain cultural elements abet technological advances; others impede those advances. Which cultures are more conducive to progress OVERALL? This is no mystery. The answer is incontrovertible: Those that best emulate liberal democracy—replete with civil rights (race and gender equality; separation of church and state; free speech; etc.) This means a SECULAR society in which there is a strong emphasis on universal suffrage / education / literacy; and where power / wealth is distributed. There are, of course, reciprocal effects between culture and technology; as each impinges

upon—and so affects—the other. (This reciprocity was demonstrated by the introduction of print, then telecommunications, then radio, then television, then the internet, then social media.) Be that as it may, technology is not ITSELF a cultural element. While the adoption of technology is not a matter of cultural appropriation, it certainly affects the gradients of cultural diffusion.

62:

It is worth quoting Ernest Becker's **The Birth And Death Of Meaning** at length: "The self exists in a world of social performance. People have to be able to play in their social ceremonies predictably and well…because the social encounter is where we expose our vital self-esteem to the possible undermining by others." He continues: "A hopeful enjoinder that animates social life is a whispered, 'Let us all protect our fragile selves so that we can carry on the business of living.' If the plot does not have competent stage personalities, it cannot go on." This is the predicament of facticity with which Sartre was concerned. The question arises: Given such dire circumstances, what is one to do? Autonomy, Becker noted, is the answer. "The person has to learn to derive his self-esteem more from within himself and less from the opinions of others. He has to try to base it on real qualities and capacities, things he can make or do, as Goethe argued; and not on the mere appearances that others like to judge by." (Both passages are from the chapter, "What Is Normal?") Constructing—and acting out—said "stage personalities" has to do with keeping up appearances in order to, as it were, maintain street-cred. Doing so helps us find a way to be part of something (ostensibly) important—that is: feel as though one **matters**; that there is **a point to it all**. But an existential narrative does more than simply cast one in such a role. It provides answers to pressing questions like: "What gives my life meaning?" and "What makes life worth living?" How so? Such a narrative provides our lives with purpose. The **communal** aspect here is key; as we all need to feel as though we are a part of something important. (Translation: We all need to feel as though we **belong**. We need to feel **accepted**.) Participating in this scheme gives us a reason to get out of bed each morning (as well as motivation to get through the next day). Put another way: It gives us something to shoot for (enabling one to confidently say, "My life has a point!") The most common delivery mechanism for such a narrative is some sort of cult activity (a.k.a. religion). The "catch", of course, is that there is an alternative way to satisfy these existential needs—one based in autonomy rather than heteronomy. In sum: One does not need to indulge in "facticity" (on the individual level) or engage in religionism (on the group level) to give one's life a sense of purpose / direction.

63:

The coining of loony locutions is indicative of how out-of-touch the Regressive "Left" has become. "LatinX" is but one of the many ridiculous examples of gratuitous linguistic modification—which, to be clear, is used for the sole purpose of virtue-signaling. (Only about 3% of Latinos find the term, "LatinX" copacetic.) To recognize the fatuity of such nomenclature, we need only universalize it. One would wind up with Latin-based ethnonyms like "MexicanX" and "ColombianX" and "DominicanX" and "BrasilerX" and "FilipinX" to label the respective peoples… as well as Slavic ethnonyms like "PolskX" and "RuskX". (If one is good-looking, one would be called "guapX"!) Ardent virtue-signalers insist on a slew of asinine modifications—as with, say, "people-kind" in lieu of "mankind". Shall we henceforth refer to fair play as good "sports-people-ship"? How about calligraphy as fancy "pen-people-ship"? Where does it end? Do we need to say "hu-people" instead of "humans" now? (Other zany modifications include "womyn" in lieu of "women", "her-story" in lieu of "history", and don't forget "un-housed" in lieu of "homeless".) Such absurdity goes hand-in-hand with "birthing / menstruating people" (the p.c.-mongers' preferred way to describe biological females). Many Potemkin Progressives fail to see that, far from being part of the solution, they are part of the problem. For the use of such wacky vernacular repels the very people to whom we most need to get through. In other words: It creates unnecessary brink-people-ship.

64:
The kind of dough known as short-crust pastry was developed by a Norman (Guillaume Tirel) in the 14th century, during the Capetian epoch in France. THAT was adopted by a Lombard (Bartolomeo Scappi) in the 16th century This all makes sense, as it had been a part of Frankish cuisine going into the Renaissance.

Appendix: A Tale Of Two Debacles

In the United States, much societal dysfunction is clothed in pseudo-Progressive garb. Alas, such "woke" Neoliberalism has served as an elaborate distraction from class consciousness. The party duopoly in the U.S. entails an either/or contest between two entrenched political juggernauts: the Republicans and the Democrats. For many voters, this is a Sophie's choice: In each electoral cycle, people are obliged to go with the less repulsive alternative. Which of those two parties advocates for universal public healthcare? Neither. Which is willing to flout corporate interests? Neither. Which is willing to get money out of politics altogether? Neither. It's no wonder the 2016 and 2024 presidential elections turned out as they did.

Since 2016, America's corporatists have been happy to see the Democratic party establishment go to war with MAGA (or, at least, allow the feud to be couched in these terms). For they know that, however each election turned out, they would ultimately prevail. Translation: So long as the choice is between the corporatist Democrats and the G.O.P., plutocracy wins.

With regard to the Democratic party, there remains the nagging question: What does it say about a political party that was defeated by a buffoon—and such an obvious con-man—twice? That such a party is feckless would be an understatement. In performing a post-mortem on Kamala Harris' doomed presidential run, we find that it was a variation on the same mistakes made by Hillary Clinton eight years earlier; and, to a lesser extent, by Joe Biden four years earlier.

The 2024 presidential election was a deafening wake-up call. More to the point, it served as corroboration of an incontrovertible yet oft-overlooked fact: Faux populism isn't vanquished by anti-populism; it can only be vanquished by real populism. Put another way: MAGA will thrive so long as the Democratic party only offers an alternate flavor of corporatism…while renouncing actual populism.

As it happens, it is a shrill minority on the so-called "Left" that gives the Progressive movement a bad name. Consequently, we genuine Progressives find ourselves in somewhat of a pickle. Those of us who criticize the Democratic party from the LEFT are effectively told: "Quit your bitchin'. It could be worse. So fall in line, take what you're being offered, and be thankful that it's less odious than the G.O.P." The DNC proffers a flattering version of Neoliberalism in lieu of a genuinely populist economic vision; so, in each election cycle, we are expected to bite the bullet and capitulate to their agenda.

The "at least we're not as bad as the Republicans" line is hardly inspiring. Far from galvanizing nascent activists, the insistence that we pick the lesser bad of two bad options soon becomes exasperating. No matter. Just as sure as the sun rises and sets, we are subjected to an un-ending barrage of messaging that is more off-putting than motivating. As if that weren't bad enough, much of the material only provides cover for the Democrats' sugar-coated corporatism.

In the wake of November 5, 2024, we can see one thing clearly: The cadre of Potemkin Progressives walking the halls of power have once again proven how truly out of touch they are with the common-man. Once the party of the working bloke, the Democratic party is now led by a gaggle of self-important operatives who issue edicts from the cozy sanctum of their lavishly-appointed parlors. With an ample amount of hand-waving, they deign to give their fatuous pontifications a shimmering, pseudo-Progressive gloss…even as they remain resolute in their service to their corporate paymasters.

The U.S. government is a veritable orgy of quid pro quos; and the Democratic party—infested with corporatists—is almost as guilty as the G.O.P. when it comes to legalized graft. After all, both parties are largely captured by corporate interests. (When it comes to legislation, Capitol Hill is essentially a giant auction block.) The problem, then, is not that the working class let the politicians down; the problem is that the politicians let the working class down.

Taking a wider view of the Washington Beltway, we stand witness to political catastrophe. (Washington D.C. has always been a venue for back-room deals made between unscrupulous power-brokers. Now, oligarchs are swapping favors in between tee-offs at Mar-A-Lago; no back-rooms required.) Public officials no longer serve the public; they serve their big-money donors; so seek mutually-beneficial arrangements…even if it means screwing over everyone else. With skyrocketing socio-economic inequality, it has become abundantly clear that the Washington Consensus is no longer viable. Yet mainline Democrats offer no credible alternative to MAGA.

It is worth recognizing that, in both the 2016 and 2020 presidential elections, the Democratic party had someone who could have handily prevailed over Trump. But instead of embracing Bernie Sanders, the party leadership castigated him; and—for good measure—ostracized his followers (dismissing them as "Bernie Bros" and secret misogynists). In doing so, they rebuffed the most vital segment of the electorate: the working class. (But, hey, it made Lloyd Blankfein happy. So what's the problem?)

How are we to make sense of this? As it turns out, establishmentarian Democrats despise Progressives even more than they despise MAGA. (One need only watch five minutes of MSNBC or CNN for this to be clear.) Their dirty little trick is to paint left-wing populists (actual populists) as right-wing populists (faux populists; the most extreme manifestation of whom are fascists); and then malign them both. This perfidious approach to politics is tremendously beneficial to the Democratic party establishment, as they hit two birds with one stone. Anyone who fails to support them is the enemy, so such people can all be thrown into the same vortex of derision.

Lost in this is a fundamental distinction—an obfuscation that creates misconceptions that further embroil us in pointless feuds. Faux populism is about appealing to the common man, even as it serves centers of power; genuine populism is about supporting what is actually good for the common man, even as it undermines centers of power. The difference is between placating the masses vs. empowering them. Right-wing populism (a.k.a. fascism) is about pretending to look out for the regular Joe, yet ultimately screwing him over. By stark contrast, "Left" populism (a.k.a. Progressivism) is about actually looking out for the regular Joe. (Note: All demagogues—especially fascists—profess to be a "man of the people".) This brings to mind a famous line from the film, The American President. I paraphrase: "The people are so thirsty for leadership that they'll crawl through the desert toward a mirage. And even though there's no water there, they'll drink the sand—not because they're thirsty, but because they don't know the difference."

Corporatists in the Democratic party are happy to paint ALL populism as right-wing populism (in order to scare people away from genuine populism); while the MAGA movement is happy to paint themselves as populist (in order to earn the support of those seeking bold solutions). {A} Labeling the Regressive "Left" as the "far Left" is tremendously misleading, as it leaves the impression that what we need to do is ease up on demands for universal public healthcare (imperative).... rather than curtail demands to be politically correct (foolhardy). By mis-characterizing genuine Progressivism as "too far to the Left", we end up acquiescing to corporatism. Instead of rejecting identity politics, we abandon efforts to get money completely out of politics. In other words, we misdiagnose the debilitating dysfunctions of the Democratic party, and—in doing so—play right into the hands of the right wing.

So what happened in 2016 and 2024? In assaying these two electoral debacles, let's start with a basic truth. There are only two possible reasons anyone would consider—for even a moment—supporting Donald Trump: severe ignorance or severe iniquity. In other words: such a person is either egregiously misinformed or egregiously immoral. (If he/she is not one, he/she is—ipso facto—the other.) There is no other plausible explanation for throwing in one's lot with MAGA. This means that when decent people supported Trump (of which there were plenty), they did so because they were nescient. When those who should have known better did so, it was because they were venal. {B} Alas, all we can do is address the former problem; as any attempt to "fix" the broken moral compass of others (plutocrats, bigots, Christian theocrats) is a quixotic venture. There's just no getting through to such people. (Addressing the rampant moral bankruptcy—and protracted intellectual stagnation—of modern society is another task for another day.) Fortunately, it is the former group that is far larger. So it is to this task, the attenuation of ignorance, that we turn here.

Such an endeavor can be accomplished primarily by generating awareness—something that requires a compelling narrative (spec. one that effectively counteracts right-wing agit-prop). Said narrative cannot presume that the audience is well-informed. Pursuant to the presidential election of 2024, we've once again learned that we should never underestimate how incredibly low-information America's low-information voters actually are. {C} Pace iniquitous actors (the incidence of which was significant yet not determinative), how well- / ill-informed someone happened to be was—by far—the best predictor of MAGA support. Consider three befuddling disconnects:

ONE: Even as pro-choice sentiment increased across the general population, support for the anti-choice presidential candidate actually gained support amongst women—including self-professed pro-choice voters.

TWO: Even as people are more fed-up than ever with rampant corruption, support for a man who is—by far—the most flagrantly corrupt politician in the nation's history went UP.

THREE: Even as most people are sick and tired of "elites" not looking out for the interests of the working class, they opted to back a man who off-shored hundreds of thousands of jobs (think of the UAW workers who supported Trump even as he sent many of their jobs to Mexico)…and then passed tax-cuts that almost-exclusively benefited the ultra-wealthy.

What in heaven's name is going on here? Well, as it turns out, due to a confluence of heightened emotion (primarily: frustration) and mental lethargy, many Americans have been swept up in MAGA fervor. It is their lizard brains, not their critical faculties, that have guided them. {J} Moreover, many of those who are ignorant are not interested in learning. Such people will tend to not be receptive when inconvenient truths—no matter how incontrovertible—are brought to their attention. (This goes especially for facts that do not accord with the conclusions on which they have already settled.) Rather than set their ego aside and modify their views, the Dunning-Kruger effect takes hold. Consequently, they will plant their flag and dig in their heels. Such obstinacy is chilling to contemplate; yet we must deal with the world we have, not with the world we wish he had. Unfortunately, this is how most people operate. Why? In the advent of social media's domination of our daily lives, intellectual curiosity is becoming increasingly rare; attention spans increasingly short; and intellectual courage more a liability than an asset. Worst of all, social media usage turbo-charges narcissism; as self-absorption is encouraged at every turn. In this debauched scheme, performance trumps erudition. Consequently, being intellectually curious is more an encumbrance than anything else.

So the question is: Given this set of exigencies, what are we to do?

Amongst those of us who (ostensibly) espouse Progressive ideals, there was a monumental miscalculation regarding the degree to which resentment—unmediated by critical reflection—often translates to irrationality. This miscalculation also failed to factor in the degree to which tantalizing optics take precedence over substance. Many (including the present author) underestimated how capriciously many will throw in their lot with a bumbling fool…sheerly out of spite.

It is no coincidence that, when it came to a demographic breakdown of voter choice, the Democrats bled support from people of color (especially with Latino men). How does this make sense? The most salient disparity in the 2024 election was not race; it was college educated vs. uneducated. I point this out not to disparage those without higher education, but to make sense of those who fell for the MAGA sales-pitch. People without a solid education often lack the exposure to (even basic) knowledge about the wider world; and tend to be deficient in (even basic) critical thinking skills. This is not to say that graduate degrees are requisite for erudition. (Plenty of morons have an expensive sheepskin—framed in mahogany—hanging on their wall.) It is simply to say that those who are more provincial-minded are far more susceptible to being swindled by Trump's pseudo-populist ramblings.

The solution: Don't shame such voters for being uneducated; educate them. That is: Proactively take measures to ensure they are better informed. Awareness-generation is an integral part of activism; so there is nothing earth-shattering in this recommendation. The key point is that many working-class Americans are drawn to faux populism—and thus MAGA—under the mistaken impression that Trump is looking out for them.

It is imperative that such people be disabused of this grave misimpression. In 2024, Kamala Harris lost the presidential election largely because she left the average Joe with little confidence that she sincerely cared about his travails. In effect, she did / said virtually nothing to allay his concerns about the elevated prices of groceries, gas, housing, medical care, or anything else. Instead of promising to stop sending truckloads of taxpayer money to Ukraine and Israel (which most Americans were adamantly against), she trotted out celebrities, CEO endorsements, and even Liz Cheney. This was not only a grave misreading of the electorate, it was a strategic blunder of epic proportions.

MAGA gimmickry may be a shell game; yet it involves an easily-digestible, compelling narrative. This explains why it has captivated many of those who were frantically looking for clarity during trying times. Throw in a scapegoat, and presto! A convenient way to channel pent-up angst. "Never mind Blackstone; it's those pesky Brown people receiving medical assistance who are driving up housing prices!" The Harris campaign did nothing to dispel such misapprehensions; and did very little to address the underlying problem. "Dog-gone it! Those undocumented immigrants are putting undue strain on an already-strained healthcare system." Pay no heed to the fact that it is strained because it is over-privatized; and could handle the demand were it to be rendered a public service. "And we're fed up with all the petty crime!" Pay no heed to the fact that undocumented immigrants commit crime at a lower rate than native born citizens. Instead, just read "The Camp Of The Saints" and you'll see that our ire should be directed not toward corporate power, but toward those who are seen as outsiders. (And while you're at it, don't forget to check out some Ayn Rand and Curtis Yarvin.)

One might say that the implied message of the Democratic party boiled down to the following: As you struggle to pay the bills, we're going to send taxpayer money overseas to fund pointless wars…which only serves to divert federal outlays into the coffers of private military contractors. (Oh, and by the way, you're a bigot if you think biological males with gender dysphoria should be allowed to compete against biological females in sports.) Say Democratic operatives: We'll serve our corporate paymasters; but just not the same ones as the G.O.P. Plus, haven't you heard that we don't like racism?

We should not be entirely surprised that all the stage-managed pomp—and endless virtue-signaling—by the Regressive "Left" did nothing to stanch the attrition of support amongst p.o.c. In fact, such antics likely CONTRIBUTED to that attrition. When we assess Trump's 2024 triumph vis-a-vis the two previous elections, we find that it was not so much that he gained support amongst non-p.o.c.; it's that legions of rankled p.o.c. migrated to the MAGA movement…by default. (We encounter a similar problem with the working class IN GENERAL: a precipitous erosion of support for the Democrats since Obama.) Translation: A regiment of political correctness and identity politics did far more harm than good. This is not simply about losing elections; it's about losing THE ELECTORATE.

But wait. What of the beguiling appeal of a man who is not only a demagogue, but a known con-man; and—to be frank—a buffoon? From the extensive testimonials of his fawning supporters, the thinking was roughly as follows: "He hates 'the system' just like I do. And—like me—he is derided for it by all those polished Washington insiders (in concert with a phalanx of pompous media elites). There's gotta be something to it."

In other words: The average Joe could relate to him. For many, Trump's bombastic style worked in his favor, as it made him seem more like an outsider…instead of just another over-rehearsed politician, reciting talking-points from an assigned script. Here was a man who's willing to break the rules in order to get things done. His brashness was taken as an indication that he was a no-nonsense, shoot-from-the-hip kinda guy. A man of action, willing to take the bull by the horns…and not take any guff from those weaselly Washington insiders. Trump's swooning fan-base doesn't see him as just another regular politician. After all, HE was the guy from "The Apprentice" who knew how to get stuff done. Wasn't he?

The key, then, was that Trump was UNSCRIPTED, so seemed to mean what he said. Rather than the twaddle of a bumbling fool, Trump's semi-coherent asseverations were seen by some as the bold statements of a fearless leader. Trump's ardent fans mused, "Gosh-golly. Nobody can tell THIS guy what to do!" They failed to realize that anyone who buys him off tells him what to do.

But why the preponderance of such shoddy judgement throughout the polity?

The Trump-ification of our culture has amounted to a program of glamorized derangement—whereby charismatic speakers are able to capitalize on the ever-present proclivity for mass hysteria. {D} As a consequence, the veneration for gilded depravity is rampant. In Washington D.C.'s pay-to-play system, even the most reprobate politics is seen as "politics as usual", and thus allowed to persist…so long as it is given a dazzling gloss.

Like any other corrupt politician, Trump's motivation is self-aggrandizement, not civic duty. This poses little problem; as today's politicians rise and fall due to OPTICS rather than the credence of their claims. It was his remarkable ability to MAKE IT SEEM as though he was looking out for the average Joe that enabled Trump to earn the good graces of so many.

And so it went: Even as everything he does serves only the socio-economic elite, Trump made himself seem RELATABLE.

Pointing out this hoodwink is no easy task; as entrancing people is one thing; breaking the trance is another. (As Mark Twain noted, it is easier to fool a man than to tell him that he's being fooled.) Amongst the rank and file, many are inveigled into construing their subjugation as a kind of emancipation. It was only a matter of time before many disaffected Americans were persuaded that throwing their lot in with MAGA was the best way to stick it to "the Establishment". Little did they realize that Trump and his ilk were only interested in enriching their cronies… while robbing the country blind.

The tendency for so many to succumb to—what is effectively—political Stockholm Syndrome is as profound as it is baffling. This peculiar yet oddly-common susceptibility can be attributed—in large part—to the fact that most voters do not base their choices on a fastidious evaluation of policy. Rather, they base their choices on overall vibes—which is to say: BRANDING (and the emotive response it elicits). Here's the catch: Emotion is not evoked based on an accurate picture of the world. Rather, it is guided solely by personal impressions…brought to bear on all the hopes and fears people harbor. This paves the way for folly. For in America's dyspeptic heartland, the rank and file is still grappling with the fallout from a half-century of candy-coated Neoliberalism. In the midst of their bewilderment, many have been duped into believing that the salve for their woes is…..MORE corporatism. For clearly all that "Left-ist" clap-trap isn't working.

Since Machiavelli, it has been understood that politics is about taking control of the narrative—which means managing the impressions people have of things (see Joseph Stalin, Mao Tse-Tung, and Kim Il-Sung). Leo Strauss understood this and encouraged it. So did Henry Kissinger. Hence their brand of "Realpolitik". (Noam Chomsky understood this too. The difference is that he rang the alarm bells; as he did in Manufacturing Consent and Necessary Illusions.) Emotional manipulation is a matter of knowing what triggers people to react to their circumstances in certain ways. The idea is to then ensure they are presented with whatever stimuli will elicit the desired response. In other words: It's knowing how to "push people's buttons".

How can this be done? In a word: conditioning. Conditioned responses are about creating associations (by dictating what impressions people have when they encounter certain things—be it high inflation or the scent of lavender). So, in politics, presentation trumps substance. For, at the end of the day, it is personal impressions—not sound judgement—that determines most voters' decisions. Consequently, political success is more about savvy branding (which is largely about instantiating certain associations, no matter how illusory) than it is about objective merit.

In this sense, politicians find themselves operating in a marketplace rather than in an agora; and voters are more consumers than they are participants in deliberative democracy. They're shopping around for whichever product most tantalizes their fancy…while avoiding brands that carry any negative stigmas. Choices are made not rationally, but based on how enticing an image happens to be. Objective reality is beside the point. Create the right FEELING, and even the most toxic stake-oil will fly off the shelves.

The best way to manipulate people is to keep them from noticing that they are being manipulated. (The best way to control people is to convince them that they're not being controlled.) That's why the illusion of empowerment is far more effective than (overt) disempowerment. This is how religion works; and it is how agit-prop works. The results of both the 2016 and 2024 presidential elections were jolting reminders of how powerful propaganda can truly be (see hasbara in Israel; Juche in North Korea; xuanchuan in China). {C} Both elections were political catastrophes; and we court continued disaster if we allow those in the Democratic party who were responsible for both outcomes to offer an errant diagnosis of the problem; and thereby dictate the plan going forward.

Who are the easiest people to manipulate? Those who are frustrated and/or insecure. Mental lethargy makes this all the more easy; which means a gormless population is an ideal mark for aspiring demagogues. (Since time immemorial, tyrants have seized upon a simple truth: One is best able to manipulate people through anger and fear.) The moral of the story: Only when there is a yawning vacuum of critical thinking—and mechanisms are in place to ensure widespread mis-information—is something like MAGA possible.

And so it went: In 2024, rather than simply Googling "what causes inflation?" or "what effect do higher tariffs have on prices?" or "who benefited most from Trump's 2017 tax-cuts?", many Americans simply went with a functionally-illiterate nincompoop who seemed to give a shit about their financial woes; and proposed audacious solutions. He talked tough; and seemed unafraid to speak his mind. In the minds of many, that was enough to pass muster.

Aside from overactive limbic systems and inert pre-frontal cortexes, many people are simply suckers for a good story. So it is a compelling narrative (rather than a firm grasp of policy implications) that ultimately swayed them. With this in mind, the Democratic party now needs to ask: What led us to this moment? The problem, though, is that introspection is not, exactly, the DNC's strong suit. People are looking for bold solutions; and the party's feckless leaders have no idea how to deliver.

In the midst of these circumstances, Progressives should be careful not to be consumed with resentment and bitterness. We must maintain level heads; and work diligently to get to the bottom of things. Despondency gets us nowhere. Even as we may be confounded by recent events, any Progressive worth his/her salt needs to stand by the foundational principles of civil society. Capitulation makes one LESS appealing, not more appealing.

    Step one is to reject identity politics wholesale. Why? Well, for starters, the cosmopolitan ideal offers the most promising vision for the United States. Don't forget that purportedly "anti-racist" identitarians obdurately claim that all White men are inherently—and irredeemably—racist / sexist. They rant about "White privilege" and "cultural appropriation"; and insist that we all use daffy terminology (like "menstruating / birthing person" when referring to women). They then proceed to castigate anyone who neglects to use plural pronouns for gender non-binary individuals. (Wonder how off-putting all this is? Consider the tagline for the most-run—and most successful—Trump ad of 2024: **"She's for they/them; he's with you."**) It's almost as if Potemkin Progressive were looking for the most surefire way to get as many people in America's rank and file as possible to say, "Go fuck yourself."

    Never mind any of that, though. Potemkin Progressives have an ideological agenda to pursue, as well as big-money donors to appease; so they won't be deterred.

    Putting oneself in the shoes of the average, working-class bloke, we are obliged to wonder: If one is racking one's brain about how to cover exorbitant medical bills, it's hard to take someone seriously who is obsessing over pronoun usage. The economic tribulations of most Americans must be front and center. So those who prioritize identity politics will be sure to never resonate with voters. "You may be struggling to keep up with the rent, to make car payments, and to feed your family, but we'll ensure you're castigated for cultural appropriation."

    Identity politics ends up becoming an elaborate distraction, diverting our attention away from the actual explanation for social injustices—to wit: the increasingly high concentration of wealth / power in so few hands. (It doesn't matter what color those hands happen to be; it is the aggregation that is the problem.) While the well-positioned few hoard the fruits of the nation's economic activity, the rabble devolves into a cacophony of quibbling between identity groups.

    The identitarian mindset tells us nothing about the cartels that bilk us each and every day—from big Pharma to big Oil. As the socio-economic elite feast at their sumptuous banquet, the rest of us fight each other over the table scraps; then blame each other when things don't work out well (see Endnotes 18 and 57). For, you see, OUR financial woes are the fault of THE OTHER (i.e. a scapegoat, strategically defined in terms of a convenient demographic category). This stratagem is straight out of the oligarch's playbook. "Pay no attention to the financiers gaming the system; it's those dastardly foreigners who are responsible for all our woes."

    We are led to believe that our plight has nothing to do with the architecture of society's major power structures: the depredations of the for-profit sickness-treatment industry, the racket that is the prison-industrial complex, the malefaction of the gun lobby, the control over our food by gargantuan agricultural conglomerates, the stranglehold that private military contractors have over Capitol Hill, and the outsized influence of the financial services industry on the world's economic machinery. No. Instead, we must focus our ire instead on those who are different from us. Never mind the rent-seekers who've rigged the system for their own benefit...at everyone else's expense. That dark-skinned fellow trimming the hedges is receiving medical support? Let's blame him! Inflation is at unacceptable levels? It's because too many people of color are receiving food stamps!

Racial animus—coupled with outdated stigmas about poverty—keeps us all divided. This goes both ways. While some WASPs don't always want to listen to p.o.c., there are some p.o.c. who refuse to listen to Progressives if they happen to be WASPs. It is remarkable the degree to which people cannot see how alterity is a two-way street. (Bigotry in one direction is not cancelled out by pointing it in the other direction.) With their endless supply of supercilious discourse, Potemkin Progressives have become extremely proficient in alienating large swaths of the electorate...in a bumbling attempt to attract large swaths of the electorate.

So here we are. While weighing in on the issue of social (spec. racial) injustice, the Regressive "Left" touts a divisive program that would have many p.o.c. say things like, "Well, if it's coming from a White person, then I don't want to hear it." This obstreperous declaration has several variants—including:

• "You being White automatically makes you part of the problem." (The implication: "You are therefore disqualified from contributing to the discussion; and should accept the charge of guilt-by-association.")
• "If you're White, we'll insist that you have unfair 'privilege', no matter what your circumstances might be." (The implication: "Even if you are destitute, you are complicit in all racial injustice by dint of your racial identity; so you forfeit your right to weigh in on the matter.")

As I argued in my previous book, Robin's Zugzwang, this attitude is worse than unproductive; it is profoundly counter-productive. Not only is it detrimental to the Progressive cause; this tendentious posturing repels many of those who might otherwise be on board with Progressive policies.

Such a misguided approach is based on a grave misapprehension of racial injustice: what it is, how it works, and what causes it. In reality, the crux of the problem is structural, not personal; as we live in a society that is anti-meritocratic; and—more to the point—anti-meritocratic in favor of certain demographics (wealthy, White, Judeo-Christian men). Because of the skewed nature of America's institutions, belonging to this demographic intersection makes it far more probable that one will be in a position to benefit from unearned socio-economic status (a.k.a. "privilege"). But it does not follow from this that White-ness in and of itself is a privilege. For some it is; for many it's not. Holding everyone in the more statistically "privileged" demographic culpable for this inequitable state of affairs is tantamount to collective punishment. There is no more something wrong with being White than there is with being Brown or Black. Whiteness PER SE is not the problem; it's the system that favors it that's the problem.

I submit that with every diagnosis of social injustice, one must stipulate: "And although these structural defects adversely impact a disproportionate number of p.o.c., it is not ONLY p.o.c. who end up with a raw deal. Structural inequalities impact a lot of struggling White people as well." Until the Regressive "Left" learns this crucial lesson, it will continue to drive tens of millions of working-class WASPs into the arms of MAGA.

How, then, are we to make sense of structural inequalities that exist along racial lines? The point is not to blame White-ness per se; it is to recognize that not being a person of color makes the chances much higher that one will be granted opportunities that many p.o.c. don't have. Be that as it may, it is imperative that we recognize that this is not because of some nebulous thing called "Whiteness"… permeating society like a noxious aether. Rather, it is due to the grotesquely defective architecture of America's power structures, which determine who is granted avenues for success (access to affordable housing in safe neighborhoods, to quality education, to gainful employment, and to good healthcare). The unfairness is due to a SYSTEM (which has been set up to favor one demographic profile over another—from jurisprudence to career opportunities); not due to the level of melanin in any given person's epidermis.

So what are we to make of the faux populism that is MAGA? Recognizing the ominous parallels with fascism is important; but it only gets us so far.

If we are to ascertain the (actual) agenda espoused by Trump, we might consider a handy rule of thumb: Don't listen to what he says; heed a slightly different version of the old adage: Follow the money (which reveals ulterior motives and clandestine influences). So I recommend an alternative adage: Follow the glee. In other words: Amongst those with power, see who is happy that Trump won.

Question: On November 6, 2024, which big money donors were high five-ing? One will soon find the answer is as clear as day: a motley array of fascists—from unabashed ethno-nationalists to rapacious plutocrats. (Consider Trump's cabinet appointments. We find ourselves beholding a rogue's gallery of degenerates and lunatics—from Wall Street goons to "libertarian" tech bros.) Another question is worth posing: Which ideologues were offered cushy appointments in the administration? (Answer: Christian theocrats, Revisionist Zionists, anti-choice zealots, gun-nuts, and free-market fundamentalists.) During the fortnight following the election, Elon Musk's net worth increased by about $60 billion. This tells us much of what we need to know about what lay behind Trump's policy positions—to wit: who's interests those positions serve. (Hint: Not the 99%.)

On Capitol Hill, legislation has always been sold to the highest bidder; but, under Trump, the entire government is now up for sale. Consequently, as is the case with most plutocracies, the U.S. is steadily becoming a kakistocracy. (Note that "follow the glee" is a variation on the litmus test, "Cui bono?" In the case of Trump's re-election, the answer is: Evangelicals, Neocons, and Oligarchs.) Make no mistake, as every devastated Progressive was reeling in dismay in the weeks following the election, virtually every other client of Kamala's corporate consultation firms were popping champagne. (Thanks, West Exec Advisors, Bully Pulpit Interactive, Canal Partners, and Gambit Strategies.) But make no mistake: Whether or not [insert corporate Democrat here] or Trump prevailed, crypto-currency tycoons, private military contractors, rent-seekers, and foreign oligarchs would be laughing all the way to the bank.

Meanwhile, many on the putative "Left" still find themselves embroiled in petty squabbles—fussing over "micro-aggressions", "trigger warnings", and "safe spaces". When they see such Tomfoolery, corporatist Democrats are eager to play along. Their reaction is essentially: "Go ahead. By all means, tie yourselves in knots over political correctness and identity politics. Just don't demand universal public healthcare. And, by the way, you know that we're one of the good guys, because we've convened yet another D.E.I. workshop. The result may still be a plutocracy; but—hey—at least the plutocrats are more ethnically diverse." Suffice to say, this was somewhat less than electrifying.

Though unintended, the Harris campaign's pleas to the electorate amounted to the following: "Even though we are not delivering for you nearly enough, we expect you to deliver for us in the voting booth…because, well, look at the bright side: We're slightly less corrupt than the horrifically corrupt alternative." This is not an especially enticing proposition. One may as well announce: "What we'll do is… we'll ease up a bit on the corporatism; but we'll then throw in some identity politics; and insist that everyone be politically correct. So that should keep everyone placated."

It's a wonder that anyone still finds the Democratic party appealing.

Those who normally vote Democrat have to start asking: Who serves who when party bosses expect constituents to fall in line rather than vice versa? In light of its manifold depredations, it is not entirely surprising how much credibility the Democrats have lost with America's working class.

The most pressing question NOW is: How did this faltering party alienate so many otherwise gettable voters? Rather than a party of (real) populists, it has become a party of Wall Street bankers, toadies for the military-industrial complex, and shills for the grossly-inefficient for-profit sickness-treatment industry (PhRMA, AHIP, the AHA, etc.) As if that weren't disgraceful enough, terrified of being accused of "anti-Semitism", many with a (D) next to their name have cozied up to Revisionist Zionists just to stay in the good graces of AIPAC (and the foot-soldiers at DMFI)…even though doing so means endorsing genocide. So many mainline Democrats have been willing to endorse crimes against humanity in faraway lands in order to avoid censure by the Israel lobby.

This makes them look obsequious, not intrepid. {E}

Will the devastating election result in 2024 be a wake-up call to the Democratic establishment? Sadly, probably not. After all, the Democratic party is now primarily a corporatist party—a lamentable fact that has been demonstrated time and time again. The DLC and its well-coiffed sycophants have made crystal clear that they have nothing but contempt for genuine Progressives. Why? Because genuine populism would undercut the corporate interests they so loyally serve. It's no wonder that "populism" has become a bad word in the argot of Democratic apparatchiks.

Most Americans have forgotten what it's like to have (sincerely) civic-minded public officials. Barring an inadequate bid by Bernie Sanders in 2016 and 2020, there has been a yawning, agonizing vacuum of principled leadership in the Democratic party. So…as with 2016, in the wake of the 2024 results, the Democratic party's top brass will bend over backwards to ensure that they learn absolutely nothing from their missteps. It comes as little surprise, then, that since the election, we have heard questions like: "The socio-economic elite adored her. What, then, could the explanation for Kamala's loss possibly be?!?"

Harris actually sent out a letter boasting about the slew of endorsements she'd received from corporate CEOs—a gesture that was almost as boneheaded as touring with Liz Cheney in the Rust Belt. We also heard comments like, "Kamala had all those celebrity endorsements, so how could she have lost?" Lost, indeed. Lost on the high-priced political consultants is the fact that those highfalutin endorsements not only didn't help; they reminded a restive electorate how astonishingly out-of-touch mainline Democrats were (and still are). While many of us love Beyoncé, it would be foolish to suppose she GETS the average bloke working 9 to 5 in small-town America. For many, celebrity endorsements often served more as a handicap than an asset.

One might say that while the Democratic establishment is utterly tone-def, Trump plays his audience like a fiddle. Either way, the rank and file gets the shaft. Big money is the problem with the Democratic party, not the solution. Unless Democrats first have a major reckoning, they cannot have a revival.

What else proved fatal? Against all sense, Kamala hitched her cart to Joe Biden's pallid horse. Barring a brief nod to the working class via the selection of Tim Walz for the bottom of the ticket, her foundering campaign eschewed full-bore Progressivism. She thereby retained the repellant stigma of the establishmentarian candidate. Calls for pruning the obscenely-bloated military-industrial complex? Crickets. Calls for universal public healthcare? Crickets. Reigning in Wall Street? Crickets. Suggestions to stimulate the economy by robust investment in public infrastructure? Mealy-mouthed lip-service. In light of this, every corporatist associated with the Democratic party was elated. (Here's looking at you, Jamie Dimon.)

Alas. In spite of the mountain of evidence pointing to why MAGA once again prevailed, we are now treated to a panoply of birdbrained analyses like: "Kamala had the backing of the Swifties and the BeyHive, and even campaigned with Liz Cheney! So the explanation for her loss must be that most Americans don't want a woman of color in the Oval Office!" (Point of contrast: Mexico is both more Christian and more riven with misogyny than the U.S., yet…overwhelmingly voted in a Jewish woman for president. Wherefore? She had a powerful—and sincere—Progressive message.) Phyllis Schlafly, trailblazer of Christian Nationalism, was a woman. Susie Wiles, the mind behind the MAGA movement, is a woman. Half the talking-heads on FoxNews? Women. This is simply to say that there are despicable people of all demographics.

The moral of the story: Judging people by their genitalia and/or skin-tone is—at best—an exercise in fatuity. Yet the DLC refuses to recognize any of this. Taking a broader view: Since 2016, Democrats have failed to see that they are dealing with an intellectually-benighted, chronically fickle electorate that was fed up with the same ol' song and dance.

Low-information voters don't want to feel preached to, they want to feel HEARD. The Democratic leadership wasn't listening.

In between her melodramatic paeans to "democracy", Kamala failed to persuade cynical voters that she was willing to take a bold stand against "the Establishment" that they so despised. The Establishment? To most people, everything that was wrong with the country could be pinned on this vague, menacing abstraction. And—for reasons that should be clear to anyone with open eyes—since Obama left office, the Democratic Party has become SYNONYMOUS with this omni-present hobgoblin.

During the course of its three months of existence, the Harris campaign failed to see how important it was to explain the reasons behind the working class' plight; which would have meant providing a cogent explanation for why a transition to a Green New Deal wouldn't endanger employment opportunities, but BROADEN them. Many of those in dire economic straits did not—and still don't—understand that investment in basic public infrastructure stimulates the economy and CREATES jobs—to wit: that it redounds to appreciable benefits for the working class. Had the full version of "Build Back Better" been allowed to pass in 2021 (and the Green New Deal been allowed to materialize), the American economy would have soared. Instead, we got a severely emaciated "Inflation Reduction Act"—a pathetic half-measure, the limited benefits of which were set to be delayed for many years.

All the while, the rank stench of the status quo lingered. It was Kamala's unwillingness to distance herself from the despised Democratic machine (read: Biden, Pelosi, Schumer, et. al.) that accounted for her inability to cultivate support in America's heartland. Instead of "turning the page", as she often put it, she opted to tout continuity with an administration that represented the very "Establishment" for which most of the working class—of all demographic profiles—had nothing but scorn. (!) From all this, Kamala's grossly over-paid advisers (most of whom had no idea what they were talking about) concluded: "We need more Cheney fans!" (Those same consultation firms all serve corporate power.) So the Harris campaign proceeded to parade around with a woman who's father was the high priest of Neocon ideology…and who voted with Trump 95% of the time. Kamala did this even as her campaign managers told Palestinian rights activists to fuck off.

It should now be crystal clear to anyone paying attention: Such operatives are paid obscene amounts of money to doll out horrible advice. After all, for the consultant class, the idea is never to recommend the moral course; it is always to recommend that which is most beneficial to those in power. What matters is not the common good; it's only the good of those who are in the privileged echelons of the American "greatness" who truly matter.

Since Trump's first administration, many Neocons have come to call the Democratic Party home. As for upsetting the Pentagon's gold-plated applecart? Well, that's completely out of the question. (Kamala Harris' position could be distilled as follows: "I'm kinda sorta against war. By the way, let me introduce you to my new pal, Liz Cheney.") Making the case for human rights while tacitly supporting genocide sends rather mixed messages.

Also notable was Kamala's failure to explain what had caused inflation…AFTER the pandemic-induced supply-chain disruptions had been rectified. (Answer: rampant corporate malfeasance coupled with a lack of basic restraints on the financial services industry.) As might be expected, inflation was the source of many people's ire. Taken with a slew of outrageous misapprehensions, they were certain to channel that ire in the wrong direction (not toward corporate power, but instead toward policies that would have alleviated the inflation). Kamala's delinquent messaging caused her to hemorrhage supporters amongst crucial parts of a dispossessed electorate…who, it cannot be emphasized enough, were irate about price increases; and were frantically looking for explanations.

Few people were aware: It was private equity firms that drove up real estate prices, thereby eradicating affordable housing. Meanwhile, giant corporations—with quasi-monopolistic control—engaged in price-gouging with impunity, affecting everything from poultry and eggs to car insurance and gas. It was unfettered corporate power—and insufficient investment in vital social services—that led to all the jarring inflation. And so it went: The Harris campaign's abject failure to dispel the absurd contention that inflation was somehow due to TOO MUCH public investment probably is what may have cost her the election. Such a ruinous misimpression entailed that the blame for economic hardship would be entirely misplaced. {F}

To be clear: Said misimpression led to the (erroneous) supposition that perhaps EVEN MORE right-wing economic policy (read: austerity measures, accession to corporate interests, and massive hand-outs to the super-rich) might be the magical solution to their financial straits. In the meantime, low-information voters were inclined to blame stratospheric real estate prices not on plutocrats, but on impoverished immigrants. ("High rent? It's because of those darned Mexicans!") Little did many in the working class realize: Socio-economically, they have more in common with said immigrants than they do with Donald Trump and his cronies.

All this misdirected angst virtually guaranteed that people would not understand why society has the problems it has. They failed to grasp that it was because economic policy wasn't Progressive ENOUGH that inflation occurred. The answer to their woes was MORE investment in vital social services, and FEWER tax-breaks for financial behemoths. Yet, in the throes of their resentments, biddable voters were more willing to believe that Haitian migrants were eating their pets than that Trump's policies only benefited America's most affluent…while screwing over everyone else.

The working class abandoned the Democratic party because the Democratic party abandoned them. Saddled with images of Biden's senility, Kamala soon became the new face of an out-of-touch "Establishment". ("Crime is low in wealthy neighborhoods; and the stock market is doing fabulous! So why's everyone complaining?") To this day, corporatist Democrats are more smitten with Neoliberalism—replete with its full array of depredations—than they are sympathetic to the plight of the working class.

So what happened? The Harris campaign burned through TWO BILLION DOLLARS in just three months. On what? On disastrous messaging (thanks to the aforementioned brigade of corporate consultants). As a result, Kamala was seen as merely the latest proxy for "the Establishment", interminably aloof and always foreboding. (Speaking to her audiences like she was speaking to a room-full of kindergarten children—replete with stilted affectation and vocal fry—only affirmed this image.) While there is certainly no love lost between most Americans and country-club Republicans, there is a comparable sentiment regarding "limousine liberals"…for whom the DLC is ground zero. In the (admittedly provincial) minds of Trump enthusiasts, support for MAGA was a searing repudiation of the same ol' tired bullshit.

More to the point, the groundswell for MAGA was a stern rebuke of corporatist hacks who didn't even pretend to understand the concerns of the average working-class voter. (Although Trump lies through his teeth with every breath, at least he PRETENDS to care about the typical working-class bloke…even the WHITE ones.) When people wracked with frustration do not have a productive way to vent, they will often channel their ire in extremely dysfunctional ways. In 2024, endorsing a blow-hard who pretends to care about them, and who—like them—scorns politics-as-usual, seemed to be a good idea. It seems like a good idea to have a bull in a China shop when everyone despises the China shop.

Eliminate government waste? Sounds good. Yet the lie was exposed the moment the new administration—in all of its cost-cutting fervor—announced that it would seek to obliterate the Consumer Financial Protection Bureau rather than trim the Pentagon budget. Why? Oligarchs need to remove all oversight as cash in on private military contracts. Curtail the ridiculous tax-breaks to Wall Street, you say? Nope. Instead, it's going to gut the National Labor Relations Board. Mitigate the ability of private hospitals, pharmaceutical conglomerates, and insurance companies to charge extortionate prices for medical services? Fat chance. Instead, the Trump administration is going to defund the National Institute Of Health…while preventing poor people from accessing basic healthcare. D.O.G.E. may just as well stand for the "Department Of Government Evisceration".

Yet the appeal of MAGA abides. After all, something is clearly amiss; and, at the end of the day, people need an outlet for their angst…so will opt for whichever outlet best presents itself. It's worth reiterating: We humans tend to be suckers for a good story, so will gravitate to whoever is proffering the most compelling narrative. Many Americans understandably felt betrayed by the Democratic party; as—since FDR—it had always upheld a somewhat plausible facade of populism. By contrast, when it came to MAGA, there was no sense of betrayal. After all, until recently, the G.O.P. never really even pretended to be the party of the working class. (The sole achievement of Trump's first term in office was to give enormous tax-breaks to the country's most affluent.) Now it is seen as the fresh new alternative to a party that—for the past half century—has done nothing but dash the hopes of everyone who put their faith in it. Trump and Elon are gonna shake things up? They're going to CLEAN HOUSE? Please, by all means!

(But Trump only offers copious amounts of bullshit and hot air, you say? Sure. But the Democrats looked no more sincere.)

Many swing-voters couldn't be blamed for thinking: If Democratic party leaders were willing to be dishonest about something as blatantly obvious as Biden's drastic cognitive deterioration, then what else were they willing to be dishonest about? "His glaring dementia? His severely slurred speech? Don't worry; he's sharp as a tack! The embodiment of lucidity and vitality!" Predictably, NOBODY bought this obvious fib. {G}

With regard to the issue of political correctness and identity politics, a few thoughts are in order. Though Kamala opted not to go out of her way to engage in such "woke" shenanigans; she did little to dissociate herself from them. Simply refraining from prioritizing her identity on the hustings was inadequate for disabusing most Americans of the impression that the Democrats were still wed to said ideology. She did not place identity politics front and center—a prudent choice. However, like it or not, short of explicitly disavowing all the "woke" nonsense (as most people saw it; and still see it), Kamala would continue to be tied to it. For it had (regrettably) become an almost indelible part of the Democrats' brand…along with myriad other revolting feature: the party of "open borders" (even though it was no such thing) and of "inflation" (even though it was RIGHT-wing policy that was responsible for Middle America's financial travails). {F}

That proved to be fatal. For it was extremely difficult for the average Joe to relate to those who lectured him about implicit racial biases, cultural appropriation, and all the rest. The majority of America's rank and file effectively said to itself: "If you think it's fine to give puberty blockers to children who are confused about gender, then how in heaven's name are we supposed to trust you on anything else? And if you think that all White men are inherently racist and misogynist, then how am I to believe that you sincerely care about my well-being?"

To this day, such an out-of-touch perspective can still be found in elitist circles.

Republican or Democrat, we are still sold the idea that proper etiquette are—somehow—a surrogate for moral principles. While there is a mixture of Democrats and Republicans amongst America's socio-economic elites, most of them share the same country-club memberships. Looking down their noses at the proletariat is, for them, par for the course. Why? Because the myth of meritocracy persists: If people are affluent, it must be because they've done something admirable to deserve it; and if people are poor, they have nobody to blame but themselves.

"But Kamala rarely mentioned her gender or her skin-color." Granted. But too little too late.

While she did not emphasize identity politics, Kamala stopped short of rejecting it outright; so failed to distance herself from its debilitating stigma. Touting a so-called "opportunity economy" did little to ingratiate the electorate; for, at the end of the day, that was little more than a slogan. People are not moved by abstractions; they often need specifics. Anything less than explicitly repudiating the scurrilous accusation of "White privilege" was going to be insufficient for shedding the tainted brand.

After Kamala was effectively coronated at the Democratic National Convention (as heir-apparent to Biden), there was very little that seemed organic about her. Even as she paid lip service to a few quasi-populist initiatives (e.g. the child tax credit; paid family leave; new anti-trust measures; tempered support for organized labor; a robust CFPB, and a rejuvenated NLRB), she ultimately remained a standard corporatist Democrat—eschewing full-bore economic populism in favor of Neoliberal (and Neocon) framing.

Her handlers failed to realize that politics is about perception, which makes mass-appeal a matter of image-engineering. Couple this careless oversight with a slew of glaring inconsistencies (the hypocrisy of denouncing the fascistic elements of MAGA while supporting Judeo-fascism in Palestine; crooning about democracy while sidelining primary challengers), and the party platform degenerated into a risible farce.

In response to Trump's "blame all your problems on the Left" schtick, the DNC insists on running figures that are the opposite of what the Average Joe is looking for: someone who is relatable and down-to-earth, and is unscripted. Instead, they opt for oleaginous establishmentarians who offer only canned statements and empty rhetoric; and simply do whatever their corporate consultants tell them to do.

It can't be repeated enough: The difference between run-of-the-mill Democratic and run-of-the-mill Republican corporatists is largely one of branding. The former engage in ersatz Progressivism; the latter tend to be a bit more brazen about their sympathies for ethno-nationalism. Reactionaries of ALL stripes are often fine with colossal social injustices…so long as they're attending the right galas, commiserating with the right people, and using the appropriate fork at dinner. This is all a reminder of skewed priorities. (Many Americans are more focused on stockpiling guns in their homes than building public infrastructure. They'd rather be stuck in traffic in SUVs than invest in expedient high-speed rail systems. We may not have universal public healthcare, but at least we sing the Star Spangled Banner before every sporting event.)

When it comes to speaking to the masses, the well-groomed popinjays of the commentariat—from CNN to OAN—see fit to hold forth from the safe remove of their in gated communities. It turns out, though, that it's rather difficult to see the consequences of their avarice from behind the castle walls. So it is no revelation when we find that, on the cocktail circuit, Washington's movers and shakers don't hear much about the tribulations of America's abiding socio-economic injustice (let alone about the dire consequences of extreme wealth inequality). For they are only made privy to policies tailored to the corporate interests they serve—interests, that is, which ensure THEIR OWN continued position at the highest tiers of the socio-economic hierarchy.

Again: This goes for corporatists in both parties. Sure, the country-club Republicans AND "limousine liberals" pretend to lament the plight of the everyman. But they ALL do so even as they are drenched in sanctimony. The former reminisce about the good ol' days, when everybody knew their god-given place; the latter telegraph their "woke" bona fides in between ships of chianti. Both decry the arrogance of "radicals".

It rarely dawns upon most swing-voters that the U.S. already has a right-wing party: the Democratic party. The only viable alternative is a proto-fascist cult that used to be the G.O.P. Any attempt to go elsewhere is considered a "wasted vote"—a stubborn refusal to come to terms with the inevitable. Such is the nature of the current party duopoly.

It beggars the imagination that the world's most famous representative democracy does not have a viable Progressive party. This presents somewhat of a predicament for many of those who are NOT prone to fascism. If the wayward voter is fed up with the Democrats, then he feels obliged to go elsewhere. Where might that be? Well, the only other place available. (Welcome to MAGA! Please pull up a seat, kick back and have a beer.) Sure enough, that's how things played out in BOTH 2016 and 2024.

CONCLUSION:

In 2024, Progressives were once again reminded that they must never underestimate the degree to which much of the American electorate is abysmally ill-informed; and—as a consequence—apt to (unwittingly) vote against their own best interests. From the Atlantic to the Pacific, political Stockholm Syndrome is now rampant…just as it is in so many other countries (which have themselves fallen victim to the trappings of faux populism).

In a nutshell, the modus operandi of those who join faux populist movements is: "We're fed up with those serving the 'elites'; and who care nothing about the common man; so we will vote for someone who serves corporate interests more than anyone else…and couldn't care less about the general welfare." Of course, this is not how THEY think of it. They simply want someone who promises to SHAKE THINGS UP. A man who GETS them. A man who—gosh-darn it—will finally secure the damn borders. And a man who is audacious and strident and willing to join them in saying "FUCK YOU" to the despised "Establishment".

The solution to this is not hemming and hawing; it is generating awareness. For it is crucial to recognize the degree to which many Americans were so utterly confused when it came to policy. Note, for example, those who toggled between Bernie Sanders and Donald Trump over the course of the past decade. It should not be entirely shocking, then, that—in 2024—many checked the box for pro-choice initiatives and for Trump on the same ballot. Take away the plutocrats, bigots, and Christian Dominionists, and we find that many of those who joined MAGA in 2024 had been partial to Bernie Sanders in the previous two presidential elections. (!)

That a person who is NOT suffering from multiple personality disorder could go from supporting Sanders for almost a decade to supporting Trump attests to the staggering degree of confusion involved. (One imagines flipping a coin between the ACLU and the Klan.) Clearly, such a bizarre shift could not possibly have been due to a firm grasp of policy implications; as the policies of the two figures were diametrically opposed. We can only conclude that other factors determine voter choices (frustration, resentment, nescience, insecurity, desperation, etc.)

Even more heartbreaking than all the cognitive dissonance: Countless voters of color were adamantly against the Democrats' support for the genocide in Palestine, so opted instead for Trump…who, it turns out, supports the Israeli government EVEN MORE. (Consequently, there were many disillusioned voters who voted for, say, Alexandria Ocasio-Cortez down-ballot, yet Trump at the top!) Yes, most people want law and order. YET, they will then pull the lever for a known fraudster with 6 bankruptcies and 34 felony convictions. (It's like encountering a habitual arsonist and pretending he's the fire marshal.) While this stultifying discordance represents a kind of political schizophrenia, it reveals how many swing voters actually operate. People are dazed and confused; disoriented and irate.

It bears worth repeating: The impulses of such voters are not governed by a meticulous critical analysis of all available evidence. Instead, they base their decisions on vibes. Rather than participants in deliberative democracy, many Americans are like impulse buyers—easily snookered into making rash decisions. (For more on this point, see Thomas Frank's What's The Matter With Kansas.) While the proliferation of such self-sabotage boggles the mind, it is important to understand HOW and WHY it occurs. America's Political Stockholm Syndrome serves as a reminder that cultic thinking is like Novocaine for cognitive dissonance. {J}

Frustration short-circuits our rational facilities; and hampers our ability to engage in critical deliberation. Bogus as it is, Trump's anti-establishment schtick was astoundingly effective amongst those who were fed up with the usual rigamarole (read: the annoyingly "woke" Neoliberalism of the Democratic party). For many, a vote for Trump was a giant middle finger to what they see as "the Establishment": a cabal of feckless political operatives who are—day in and day out—so obviously completely full of shit.

When ill-informed Americans hear Donald Trump, they feel as though he speaks for them. When those same people hear Democratic establishmentarians (most infamously, Hillary Clinton), they are confident of one thing: "He/she does not speak for me." With their perorations about protecting "democracy", Kamala and co. didn't exactly instill confidence in the electorate. With their dereliction on "kitchen table" / "bread and butter" issues, they failed to "read the room", as the saying goes. By stark contrast, Trump knows how to play to the crowd—hitting just the right buttons with his brazen proclamations. He tells his target audience what they want to hear—often in vagueries and platitudes. For most con-men playing the long game, the sales-pitch is a familiar one: "I'll make your problems go away. Just give me the power (and your money if you're willing); and let me take care of things." (In 2016, Trump only had to DECLARE that he was "draining the swamp"; he didn't have to actually DO it. Sure enough, his policies actually made the swamp far more noxious. Yet this catchy slogan continued to ring in the minds of his supporters, who were convinced, against all evidence, that he was rooting out corruption rather than putting it into overdrive.) In the eyes of many, Trump's bloviation was seen as a sign of bravery—an indication that he MEANT BUSINESS. They confused confidence with credibility.

Instead of a genuine movement championing civil society, the Democratic party was reduced to little more than a quavering "anti-Trump" party. In the absence of REAL populism, the country's rank and file will opt for a cheap knock-off if it is hawked to them with enough pizzaz. Ergo Trump.

My contention is this: Faux populism can only be defeated by genuine populism. Since Bill Clinton, though, the Democratic party has offered only anti-populism. The Harris campaign had all the money in the world, yet had no bold positions. As if to make matters worse, it turns out that all its celebrity endorsements were paid for. The grand vizier of narcissism herself, Oprah Winfrey, insisted that the campaign PAY HER a million dollars to make a couple appearances. This one fact is quite revealing. (The Black woman who welcomes me at the local Walmart—likely for minimum wage—gave more money to the Harris campaign than this self-absorbed billionaire.)

Again, there was no answer when it came to standing up to corporate interests; or to ensuring affordable healthcare; or to curbing the price of gas, groceries, medical care, and housing. While serving America's most affluent (and hewing to corporate interests at every turn), it SHOULD be apparent that Trump and his cronies do not care about the well-being of the everyman; but it is NOT apparent to millions of low-information voters. Why not? Well, because Trump and co. ACT like they care. So many Americans feel seen by them. When people are frustrated, they are looking for clear-cut answers…even if those answers are largely baloney.

So the question is not why so many Americans are unable to see through the sham that is MAGA; the question, rather, is why the Democratic party is unable to see THEM.

It is not the working class' job to support the Democratic candidate; it's the Democratic candidate's job to support the working class. Instead, corporatists located at key positions within the Democratic party do little more than serve the powerful lobbies that write them hefty checks. As they dance to the beat of their big-money donors, they pay lip service to lofty ideals like "freedom" and "family values". They then turn around and castigate anyone who has the gall to request that they serve the common-man rather than the power elite. The Democrats' message to the electorate is effectively: "We engage in tons of corruption, but just not quite as much as the other party. Therefore you should go with us."

This is not a good sales pitch.

We mustn't let a cadre of loud, cantankerous pseudo-activists ruin things for the rest of us. The Regressive "Left" makes the REAL Left look ridiculous; and provides right-wing polemicists with bountiful ammunition to paint genuine Progressives as nutty ideologues. (The Democrats' rampant corporatism didn't help.) To most of those in Middle America, the Democratic party simply reeks of the status quo.

On all the corporate networks, those of us who care very deeply for the Progressive cause are painted with the same brush as those who offer only specious claims, frivolous indictments, and harebrained ideas. For those who are bamboozled by right-wing propaganda, the thinking is effectively: Why go with Republican lite when you can get the real thing?

Trump disguised himself as a man of the people. For low-information voters, this worked like a charm. The reality is, of course, strikingly different from such (mis)impressions. All Trump ACTUALLY does is eliminate funds to vital social services and to important infrastructure projects…while dolling out a slew of enormous corporate tax-breaks. He happily pushes draconian austerity measures of the sort that have wreaked havoc in countries around the world (whenever those countries have become overtaken by right-wing economic policy). It makes sense, then, that right-wing libertarians have been appointed to bogus positions of "government efficiency".

Entirely lost on his mesmerized audiences was the fact that—during his first term—almost none of the much-touted tax cuts went to the working class (the cuts predominantly benefited the ultra-wealthy); childhood poverty skyrocketed; over 200,000 jobs were outsourced; millions of people lost healthcare; and—to add insult to injury—the G.O.P. blocked overtime pay for about 8 million workers. (Stiffing workers is, after all, Trump's stock in trade.) Alas, these devastating facts were irrelevant; because Trump managed to brand himself as the outsider who was audacious enough to take a stand against "the Establishment". Meanwhile, virtually every Democratic figure had become a MASCOT FOR said "Establishment".

The thesis here is worth re-stating: Given America's party duopoly, when presented with turbo-charged Reaganomics, the only other choice was a more collegial version of corporatism. It didn't always used to be this way. Until the turn of the millennium, the Democrats' Neoliberalism left room for some paeans to civil rights…even as it has been doing the bidding of its corporate paymasters. But by the opening years of the 21st century, Democrats offered artificially-flavored hogwash as the only alternative to the Republicans' bald-faced corruption. And for the past generation, the preponderance of ersatz Progressivism on the so-called "Left" have only made the Democratic brand look worse.

Considering its refusal to be genuinely populist, it's no wonder that—ever since the waning years of the Obama administration—the Democratic party has lost support from almost every demographic. {H}

Recall an ironclad law of politics: When not challenged by genuine populism, faux populism (a.k.a. fascism) wins every time. This has been demonstrated over and over and over again, in country after country after country—in virtually every instance that a demagogue has risen to power. Fascists succeed when their message finds purchase in the minds of an exasperated population that feels that it's been left with no other good options. Therein lies the rub: This occurs whenever the alternative party fails to deliver. (To reiterate: Rather than a genuinely populist movement, the Democratic party has been reduced to the party of "not Trump"—not exactly an invigorating rallying-call.)

When people are fed up with the status quo, they go elsewhere…anywhere…looking for solutions. In both 2016 and 2024, we saw that faux populism was oddly effective insofar as there is a vacuum left by an absence of genuine populism. The DLC would much prefer to see the G.O.P. prevail than give Progressives any birth (ref. Obama's panicked call to James Clyburn in the spring of 2020). As it turns out, corporatists associated with the Democratic party would prefer to see proto-fascists win than stand up to Wall Street, Big Pharma, AHIP, private military contractors, and AIPAC. Election cycle after election cycle, they have dependably chosen to cozy up to Blackrock, Goldman Sachs, and Raytheon…instead of fighting for social democracy.

And—most reprehensibly of all—the Democratic leadership would rather lose an election than defy their beloved AIPAC. (Wondering if racism / fascism has also infected the Democratic party? There's your answer.) As it turns out, for mainline Democrats, ethno-nationalism is fine overseas…as long as we quash it here in the U.S. So even as they stridently denounce racial prejudice in corporate boardrooms, Democratic party operatives are content to look the other way when geo-political allies perpetrate atrocities in faraway lands (see Israel; Saudi Arabia). Many Democrats fail to recognize that it is extremely difficult to take a credible stand against ethno-nationalism at home when one is supporting it abroad.

Kamala Harris was completely on board when the Biden administration insisted that yet more public funds be diverted to support not one, but TWO genocides: one perpetrated by the Saudi regime in Yemen (fascism based on Wahhabism), one perpetrated by the Israeli regime in Palestine (fascism based on Revisionist Zionism). Salafi fascism or Judeo-fascism: pick your poison. Along with the G.O.P., the Democratic party picked both.

The Washington Beltway has always been a Bacchanal of influence-peddling and horse-trading. With Trump back at the helm, it is now open season for self-dealing and favors-swapping. Trump has already been bought off so as to ensure his AUGMENTED support for a pair of heinous regimes: two billion dollars to Jared Kushner from the House of Saud; and hundreds of millions of dollars to Trump from the Adelsons. (This is not to mention the Kochs and Mercers; as well as Tim Mellon, Paul Singer, and all the other usual suspects.) Considering all this, it is an earth-shattering irony that many of those who were persuaded to back Trump did so because they were fed up with all of the DEMOCRATS' corruption.

Nobody in the history of American politics has ever been so eager as Donald Trump to sell policy to the highest bidder. This is his own "art of the deal". As crazy as it sounds to those of us who know better, the fact that Trump is more engorged with corruption than virtually anyone else in American history does not matter to many of America's woefully un-informed voters…who only see him as the guy brave enough to buck "the Establishment." (To repeat: The only alternative seems to be corporatist Democrats who seem to always be engaged in cloying theatrics.)

In terms of presentation, the contrast between Trump and Harris couldn't have been more stark. Like any demagogue, Trump continued to be the consummate crowd-pleaser…playing to his audience like a savvy performer on a Vegas stage.

For those who pay no attention to policy, this seemed to be a breath of fresh air. Meanwhile…during her tub-thumping, whenever Kamala managed to NOT sound overly-scripted, she devolved into a kind of sanctimonious blather. At almost every turn, she only succeeded in reminding swing voters (i.e. the people who decide elections) that she was beholden to her donors; not to the everyman. Amidst all the mawkish fanfare and overwrought choreography, she failed to sound like anyone other than an emissary of Washington's political machine—recycling pre-packaged talking-points and spouting market-tested bromides in between nervous laughs. (That her riffing on the stump often turned into word-salad didn't help either.) Rather than take bold stands (e.g. speaking out against the effort to privatize everything under the sun), she opted instead for sloganeering…which elicited more eye-rolls than inspiration.

I ask the reader to consider the following message to America's White working class:

While you are struggling to pay extortionate medical bills and scrambling to meet next month's increasingly-high rent (with the meager wages you receive from a stressful job), we insist that inflation isn't all that bad; and that crime isn't still a problem. And we will scold you for "implicit racial bias"…while begrudging you for not being a person of color. You're overworked and underpaid, yet shall be chastised for some sort of "privilege" you have never noticed you had…which, so far as you can see, has yielded diddly squat since the day you were born.

One may as well presage such an ornery pronouncement with, "I do declare…" in a cut-glass British accent. (All the better if said when sipping cognac whilst lounging on ornately-upholstered divans. Eye monocle is optional.) Or consider this:

Inflation is a bit of a problem, but White-splaining / man-splaining is even worse! And sure, rampant graft may be undermining the democratic process, but make sure you specify your pronouns in your online profile.

This is the message that much of the rank and file hears from the Regressive "Left"; and it explains why tens of millions of Progressively-inclined Americans THRICE cast a ballot for Trump. Begrudging people for their ethnicity is never a good idea. Shunning them for imagined transgressions instead of hearing about their very real problems is a surefire way to not get their vote.

Instead of being recognized as a movement that's looking out for the common-man, Progressivism is stigmatized as a brigade of ornery schoolmarms—sanctimonious and persnickety—who tacitly endorse genocide in Palestine while insisting that children should have access to on-demand puberty-blockers. This is a recipe for abject electoral failure. While some of Kamala's lack of support amongst the far-right can be attributed to gender and/or racial biases, such prejudice does nothing to explain, well, EVERYONE ELSE who opted not to support her on election day. {H}

Looking back: A successful campaign against the MAGA movement would have conveyed the following sentiment: "I understand why some of you might be tempted to join the MAGA bandwagon. You're frustrated; and you want to tear down the system, which REALLY IS rigged against you. Trump seems to be the only one who is brazen enough to do it." Translation: I hear you. And I understand your concerns." {I}

Want to get the working class vote? Don't scold them; understand them. Only then can one help THEM understand which policies will best serve the common good. The average, working-class American simply wants a fair shake; and public servants who are willing to stand up to a system that EVERYONE knows is rigged. Put another way: Don't tell people what they are supposed to believe; instead, give them the unvarnished facts (providing evidence, as needed), then articulate the basic principles on which the proposed position is based.

Don't make it about joining the right team; make it about alleviating their travails. This can be done without compromising Progressive principles. It would be a misreading of this essay to suppose it is—in any way—calling for a movement rightward; or for making "strategic" concessions to the right wing. Getting through to people and capitulating to them are two entirely different things. (Extending an olive branch to voters is not bending the knee to politicians.) The proposed course is a matter of edification, not of "compromise". Reaching out to those who are sympathetic to MAGA is in no way conceding that the opprobrious movement ITSELF has credence; it is merely recognizing that some of the concerns that some Trump voters have actually makes sense.

It is possible that such a revolutionary endeavor might spur major transformation within the Democratic party. Perhaps it will even give birth to a new political party. This depends on how entrenched corporate interests are in the party's infrastructure. I like to believe that the Democratic party is not irredeemably corrupt. After the old guard passes away, we'll find out.

FINAL THOUGHTS:

MAGA cannot be defeated by a campaign; it can only be defeated by a sustained movement—a movement that actually addresses all the things the Trump PRETENDS to address. The Democratic party—in its current incarnation—is ill-equipped to mobilize such a movement. How so? Because only genuine populism can defeat faux populism. This is why—had he been permitted to be the Democratic nominee—Bernie Sanders would have clobbered Trump in 2016, as well as in the two subsequent elections. (Note: Had they been run on the level, Sanders would have prevailed in BOTH Democratic primaries in which he ran.) So what is to be done about Trump's proto-fascist (cult) movement? An actual Progressive would offer a compelling and meaningful counter-vision. This would entail offering a stark alternative ON POLICY; which would itself entail bucking the demands of virtually all big-money donors. Identity politics would not play a role in this vision. Nor would corporate lobbies.

The panoply of distractions decried here includes gripes about "cultural appropriation", which sows needless discord. While it is important to tout lofty ideals, specific policy proposals are where the rubber meets the road. So it is on policy that we must focus. A worthwhile Progressive movement requires both integrity and tenacity—two things notably lacking in the current Democratic party. (While the G.O.P. has none of the former, it's got the latter in spades.)

As the American Republic verges on self-immolation, we must stay firm in our commitment to civil society. Deliberative democracy takes work; and quickly disintegrates when neglected.

Never mind that Kamala refused to take a stand against the ethnic cleansing in Palestine (undertaken with her own administration's support)…while actively marginalizing Muslim Americans (or anyone speaking up for Palestinian rights, for that matter) during the course of her campaign. Never mind that she remained a lapdog for the military-industrial complex (including a rube for the boondoggle in Ukraine, which proved to be a bonanza for private military contractors…with almost nothing else to show for the massive infusion of tax-payer money). Never mind that she failed to explain the reasons for inflation. And never mind she stubbornly refused to fight for universal public healthcare. According to identitarians on the Regressive "Left", Kamala's failure to win over hearts and minds in the Rust Belt was largely due to the fact that she has brown skin and a vagina. They are wrong.

Working-class Americans want good policy. The "catch" is that they need its merits explained in a cogent way—preferably via a simple, compelling narrative—by someone who really means it (see Ilhan Omar). Given the right policies and savvy messaging, a green-skinned hermaphrodite would prevail in every election… even in a country where racism and misogyny are still a problem. {J}

Few genuine Progressives have the courage to tell the denizens of the Regressive "Left" (or the Democratic party's astonishingly feckless leadership) that THEY are part of the problem. Put bluntly: Corporatism in both major political parties helped to get Trump elected. Twice. So did ersatz Progressivism, which has sabotaged the Democratic party for decades. In recognizing this, it is worth recalling a statement made by Abraham Lincoln in his Lyceum speech of 1838: "If destruction be our lot, we ourselves will be the authors."

Footnotes:

A: The same stunt was pulled with "socialism", which both Neoliberals in the West AND Stalinists in Russia—as well as Maoists in China—were more than happy to associate with Soviet-style "communism". This was done whether the aim was to frighten people away from GENUINE "socialism" (in the first case) or to garner support for what was, in actuality, a fascist regime (in the case of Russia and China) by employing populist rhetoric. If we look at North Korea, which (preposterously) characterizes itself as "communist", we see a textbook case of fascism (to wit: totalitarianism based on theocratic ethno-nationalism); not a liberal democracy in keeping with Marxian ideals. (Also see right-wing Cubans / Venezuelans in Florida, who—in a classic case of political Stockholm Syndrome—end up endorsing in the U.S. a different version of the very thing they denounce in their country of origin.) It should go without saying that a system of high-concentrated wealth / power and top-down control over the population is the polar opposite of a vision based on distributed wealth / power and bottom-up control (whereby people maintain sovereignty over their own lives). Some of the best exposition on genuine populism—and the current lack thereof in U.S. politics—has been done by Thomas Frank in his books Listen, Liberal and The People, No. If only more people understood what "Left" politics actually entailed. However, generating awareness in today's political climate is easier said than done. The problem is a perennial one: Staunch ideologues often hear only what they want to hear; and often see only what they want to see. In the advent of social media, this dysfunction has been supercharged. The algorithms that govern such platforms ensure that people are only exposed to the content they prefer; as they are only interested in having their presuppositions re-affirmed in perpetuity. Rather than a flaw, information silos are a design feature; as they are seen as a PERK. So the question arises: How can we breach these seemingly-impenetrable memetic enclosures?

B: This is a frank diagnosis, not an aspersion. It is simply stating an incontrovertible fact: Solid moral principles married to a thorough understanding of policy would preclude someone from supporting such a horrific political figure. To make such a bad choice, there needs to be either a case of severe moral depravity, or, if not, then a colossal ignorance of the implications of Trump's policy positions. (Case in point: Most Americans don't even understand that the economy is stimulated from the demand side.) This essay attempts to show how those with the latter problem might be understood; as most of those who pulled the lever for Trump arguably meant well, yet were extremely misguided. Such people are, in theory, open to persuasion. As for those who are morally depraved (that is: motivated by greed and/or bigotry), the problem goes far beyond the purview of sociology and political theory. More often than not, trying to get through to such people is a fool's errand. Those driven by avarice don't care who is harmed, so long as obstacles are removed to further concentrate wealth / power in their hands. And those who are driven by racism / sexism are not going to be swayed by sound argumentation. So it is to those who are well-meaning yet stupendously ignorant that we turn here (see Footnote J below). Due to their nescience, such people are useful idiots. Corrupt politicians ingratiate themselves with said audience in order to be elected; but once in office, their primary mission is to serve the power elite. (Many of those useful idiots are American Evangelicals. Starting in the 1970's, Republican politicians made a Faustian bargain with Christian nationalists that was roughly as follows: "I have something you want: political power. You have something I want: voters who can help give me that power." For more on this, see Chris Hedges' American Fascists.) It is only those who are NOT morally depraved with whom Progressives should be concerned; as, given the right messaging, they are reach-able. How? By offering a compelling narrative—namely one that helps voters see which policies will ACTUALLY benefit them. While it is tempting to dismiss all MAGA voters as a mob of blundering idiots, doing so would be a mistake. Granted, idiocy may explain some of their political choices (they are, after all, dupes). However, a yawning paucity of sapience does not necessarily entail a complete lack of intelligence. (In any case, plenty of registered Democrats are idiots as well.) To understand how and why this sort of thing occurs, it is worth considering how many (otherwise) intelligent people have been hoodwinked in other contexts—as with, say, those who succumb to cult activity in its myriad forms. The question becomes: How stunted do one's critical faculties have to be for one to not figure out that Trump is a complete fraud? Granted, we cannot all always recognize con-men when we encounter them; but when it is this obvious, there must be some sort of mental deficiency (see Footnote J). So questions arise: How did such a deficiency emerge? And what can we do about it?

C: Soon after the election, analytics revealed that the less-informed voters were, the more likely they were to throw in their lot with MAGA. Level of education (along with frustration with economic issues) was the most salient factor for those in the working class who were persuaded to support Trump. This is a reminder that deliberative democracy cannot abide in the midst of extreme nescience. How serious is this problem in the U.S.? There are three countries in the world wherein the vast majority of the population is completely brainwashed: North Korea, China, and Israel. I submit that, though not nearly as extreme, the U.S. would be next on that list (though it has some stiff competition from the likes of Turkmenistan, Saudi Arabia, and Mauritania). The only way to remedy this is by persistent, effective messaging—messaging that conveys the merits of (genuinely) Progressive policies; and shows who, exactly, promotes said policies.

D: Harris needed to do three things. ONE: Disassociate herself from the dreaded "Establishment" (which entailed distancing herself from the incumbent administration, replete with its depredations). TWO: Disavow all the "woke" nonsense that annoyed so many working-class people. Simply refraining from identitarian framing was insufficient; a loud and clear repudiation of identity politics was required. THREE: Explain how Progressive economic policy would help the working class (which entailed explaining how Trump's agenda would not). Three was, of course, the most important. (It's lodestar would be a call for universal public healthcare.) Not only did Harris do none of these things; it would have been difficult for her to do any of them with sincerity. For she was part of the said "Establishment"; and she routinely flouted Progressive policy—both economic and foreign—in favor of the usual lip service. This led to her electoral downfall.

E: Edward Snowdon put it aptly: "When exposing a crime is treated as committing a crime, you are being ruled by criminals." Those who characterize the indictment of Revisionist Zionism (i.e. Judeo-fascism) as "anti-Semitic" only succeed in providing the world with proof of their own moral debasement. This is classic projection—every bit as risible as a rapist accusing his victim of an abomination for having the gall to resist his assault. Fascist regimes thrive insofar as people develop an allergy to—nay, hostility toward—veracity. So goes the adage: Truth sounds like hate to those who hate Truth. We might say that Capitol Hill's dirty little secret is that the Federal government runs almost entirely on legalized graft (if by "little secret" we mean "commonly-known fact").

F: In 2020, inflation occurred due to drastically-limited supply, which was caused by pandemic-induced global supply-chain disruptions. In the wake of this, corporations gamed the system to no end. Once the supply chains were mostly restored, the fix was already in. Subsequent inflation was not driven by an increase in purchasing power (not by an increase in demand); it was largely induced by corporate malfeasance (greed). Purchasing power actually DE-creased. Per the conventional supply-demand dynamic, prices increase when people have the ability to pay higher prices (that is: because they have more money in their pockets)… even as the supply of goods does not increase to meet the augmented demand. The theory here is simple: If you put more money into circulation while holding supply constant, then prices will increase. Businesses charge as much as they can get away with. So an increase in purchasing power is ONE reason prices would go up in the event that supply remains the same…or even decreases. But in THIS instance (2021, 2022, and 2023), prices increased even though most people were struggling to pay. In other words: There was an over-riding factor. That factor was unbridled corporate power. It turns out that the supply-demand curve does not take into account enormous power / information asymmetries, whereby pricing can go up due to things other than an augmented purchasing power of (most) consumers. Corporations found that they could exploit latent exigencies, and get away with bilking consumers; so that's exactly what they did. (Proof that most corporations weren't "forced" by dire circumstances to boost prices: virtually all of them posted record profits for these same years.) Even as many parties gamed the system (due to the sloppy implementation and poor oversight of the CoViD stimulus program), the contention that overall inflation could be attributed to TOO MUCH STIMULUS is not only false; it is exactly backwards. (Contrary to the myth of supply-side economics, still prevalent in right-wing circles, economies are stimulated from the demand side.) So what would have prevented inflation? Less catering to corporate interests and more investment in basic public infrastructure. Comprehension of this simple fact would have made support for Trump utterly inconceivable (for anyone with a moral compass, that is). So what needs to be done? Step one is tying inflation to corporate greed. But step two is even more crucial: Recognizing the simple fact that--regarding economic policy—the further to the right we go, the more severe corporatism becomes; and the more consumers get screwed. Trying to mitigate inflation by supporting the G.O.P. is like trying to make ice by boiling water.

G: Stammering and mumbling, a somnambulate Biden stumbled through each teleprompter reading as his handlers pretended not to be embarrassed. (Early signs of dementia were evident as far back as 2020, during his initial presidential run; and only increased thereafter.) Biden's staff then castigated anyone who pointed out the obvious: his deafening obliviousness and slurred speech were indications of precipitous cognitive decline. For most people, witnessing this was unbearable. As if playing "Weekend At Bernie's" with POTUS wasn't bad enough, the administration opted to give Hillary Clinton the Medal of Freedom even as she—and the entire Democratic leadership—continued to endorse genocide. The world stood by as Uncle Joe struggled to remember where he was standing at any given moment of each day.

H: In Michigan, had she gotten the entire Muslim vote, Kamala would have handily won the state. In Pennsylvania, had she gotten the Green Party vote tally, and 43,000 people who'd swung for Trump had remained steadfast in their support for the Democratic candidate, Kamala would have prevailed there. And in Wisconsin, just 15,000 people voting differently would have done it. (!) Never mind the tens of thousands of un-inspired voters in those three crucial swing-states who decided to just stay home. (Nationwide, 6.3 million fewer people pulled the lever for the Democratic candidate than in the previous election.) Even as Trump received about 3 million more votes than he did in the last cycle, the majority of those gains were not in swing-states. The increase was predominantly flocks of disenchanted, working-class voters in solid Blue and solid Red states. (In California alone, more than 1.8 million people who'd voted for Biden four years earlier either switched parties or stayed home.) There was also a smattering of Muslim voters who were so disgusted by the Democrats' support for the genocidal regime in Israel that they pulled the lever for Trump sheerly out of spite (or, rather, out of desperation). For them, a vote for Trump was like a Hail Mary, thrown in a fit of vexation. According to a survey done by YouGov, of the 19+ million voters who voted for Biden in 2020 yet opted to stay home in 2024, almost 6 million cited the administration's support for the genocide in Palestine as the top reason for not going to the polls the second time around. (This includes the present author.) In fact, that single issue may have been the decisive factor in Michigan, Wisconsin, and Arizona. (!) It turns out that most sane people are against ethnic cleansing; and don't support the pointless slaughter of over a hundred thousand innocent civilians. Go figure.

I: Helpful tip to Democratic party leaders: Try listening to Briahna Joy Gray instead of Joy Reid. Want guidance from Progressive Black scholars? Rather than seeking counsel from (corporatist) consultation firms, heed the wisdom of Cornell West, Adolph Reed Jr., Waleed Shahid, and Butch Ware. And—most importantly—support Progressive firebrands like Barbara Lee, Ro Khanna, Nina Turner, Cori

Bush, and Greg Casar rather than establishment apparatchiks like Chuck Schumer, James Clyburn, Kirsten Gillibrand, Debbie Wasserman-Schultz, Josh Gottheimer, and Nancy Pelosi. In the long run, the party must divorce itself from all big-money donors. Every last one. If, on the other hand, the party wants to ensure more losses in the future, it should appoint a corporate stooge like Rahm Emanuel as chair of the DNC.

J: In studying fascist movements around the world, I have come to the following conclusion: If a person is highly intelligent AND has a solid moral compass, it is unfathomable that he/she would succumb to right-wing thinking. Why? Because such a person's intelligence makes it very unlikely that they will be stupendously ignorant; and—barring any mitigating psychological factors—their moral intuitions would preclude any chance that they would be inclined to support opprobrious regimes. How crippled one's moral intuitions have to be for one to not to notice Trump's flagrant depravity is an open question; as myriad psychical problems could be at play. While some sociopaths have relatively high IQs, I suspect that there is an intelligence ceiling for Trump supporters. (Conjecture: A highly-intelligent MAGA sympathizer does not exist. If a person was sufficiently ignorant and/or sufficiently immoral to make such a poor choice, their cognitive capabilities could not possibly be stratospheric.) The problem is that most people are not anywhere close to geniuses; so, when it comes to MAGA, we are dealing with tens of millions of voters with less-than-stellar cognitive functioning. Be that as it may, such people usually have adequate intellectual capacity to figure out which policies are estimable…if given a nudge. The role of Progressive activists, then, is to give those people this nudge. I have spoken with many well-meaning yet astoundingly ill-informed people who were snookered into supporting Trump. This means that they WOULD have voted more prudently had they had a better understanding of policy implications. The solution to America's political malady, then, is improving awareness-generation—an endeavor that is about far more than disseminating information. There must be didactic HEFT to the dissemination, which means constructing a compelling narrative. Pedagogy is as much about persuasion as it is about edification..

Postscript

As we've seen, there have been many felicitous instances of cultural appropriation. Myriad examples come to mind. Rewind to the 1970's and 80's, and note that punk rock (out of America and Britain) influenced the development of "Ostrock" in the G.D.R. (as with Feeling B and The Puhdys). Meanwhile, folk rock influenced the formation of bands like Mashina Vremeni and Aquarium in Soviet Russia. In both cases, a closed society was given a refreshing taste of free expression. As modern music went East; literature went West. Germany gave America Goethe, Mann, and Hesse; while Russia gave us Dostoyevsky, Pushkin, and Lermontov. * Today, we are blessed to have an amazing Russian pianist (online handle "Gamazda") doing covers of American pop music—including hard rock—better than anyone else on the planet. This is trans-cultural fertilization at its finest. To all such artists, we should say: "Please, by all means, engage in Cul-Ap to your hearts' content!"

When did this cosmopolitan outlook emerge? It took a while; as homo sapiens are tribal by nature. The Enlightenment brought with it key insights into what constitutes a just world. With Kant in Prussia, Voltaire in France, Mill in England, and Paine in America, the stage was set for revolutionary thought. Since then, the conditions most conducive to eudaimonia were well-established. It turned out that civil society is not merely about flourishing, but about justice.

A society characterized by pluralism, secularism, and distributed wealth / power is the only truly civil society. This is characterized by a sense of civic duty, human rights, and democratic governance. By stark contrast: A tribalistic, Reactionary mindset (characterized by hyper-traditionalism, institutionalized dogmatism, and groupthink) is always detrimental—irrespective of the brand. This serves as a precaution: While culture is an engine for social cohesion, when calcified, it can lead to insularity. Generally-speaking, dynamism and diversity are symbiotic with prosperity. (Meanwhile, stasis and homogeneity stifle innovation, thereby precluding societal efflorescence.)

As we've seen, a perk of ethnic diversity is that it enhances memetic cross-pollination between ethnic groups—something that bolsters the prospects for innovation, and thus for progress. What's "progress", though, if it is beneficial to only some? True progress is a boon to the commonweal (or, as the U.S. Constitution's preamble calls it: the general welfare). Synergy, we find, is the lifeblood of novelty. It's what led to samba, sushi tacos, and rock 'n roll. Other than human solidarity, the point of cosmopolitanism is to challenge traditional boundaries, to engage in a shared project in which all of mankind is included. This requires the elevation of cultural awareness, and the promotion of tolerance.

I have argued that cultural exchange plays a crucial role in breaking stereotypes and dispelling misapprehensions. When individuals from different cultures interact, they have the opportunity to learn about each other's customs; and do so via first-hand experience. Direct personal exposure to THE OTHER fosters deeper understanding of—and appreciation for—others' traditions. In this spirit, Shakira blended Latin rhythms with elements of American pop to create a sound that appeals to diverse audiences across the globe—a reminder that music is a universal language (and one of the best ways to bond with those who may not be like us). Under such conditions, Cul-Ap engenders empathy.

I am a White man who has listened to Oscar Peterson while eating soul food and who has watched K-dramas while eating gogi-gui. I have been blessed by the phra at a wat Thai as well as by the pundit at a Hindu temple. Am I a culture-bandit or am I…something else? In such instances, I have done no damage to the source-culture. On the contrary, I cultivated an appreciation for it. Over the course of my travels, I've discovered that participation in exogenous customs is tremendously edifying; and generally welcomed by those in whose culture I am partaking. I've worn traditional Tang attire at the ancient Kai-yuan pagodas in Quan-zhou; and I've worn Gujarati pajamas and a turban at a wedding in Mumbai. In each case, the Cul-Ap was done with respect to the indigenous culture; and was in no way seen as a trespass by my gracious hosts. From Brasil to Burma, from Jamaica to Russia, this was always the case.

We might note that the term, "kosmo-polites" means "world-citizen"—an idea that goes back to the 5th century B.C. When Diogenes was asked where he was from, he replied, "I am a citizen of the world." Thomas Paine—arguably the most important Founding Father of the American Republic—described himself in the same way. To some, this all sounds like a bunch of schmaltzy idealism; but—ambitious as it might be—this should serve as our North Star.

The cultivation of "arete" (moral virtue) is easier said than done. But one thing is for sure: Quibbling over the ownership of cultural elements does nothing to solve the world's most pressing problems. Not only does embroiling ourselves in petty feuds muddy the already-murky waters of public discourse; it only serves to further divide us. Cul-Ap in the midst of power asymmetries, you say? It's the power asymmetries that are the problem. Cul-Ap that is exploitative in nature, you say? It's the exploitation that is the problem. When a surgeon is guilty of malpractice, we don't impugn all of modern medicine; we identify the malfeasance.

When providing a few examples of negative cultural diffusion (from America), I listed soda and Pentecostalism. This is not to say that those two things are on par with one another. Not all maladies are equal; and there are gradations of dysfunction. A carbonated beverage with super-high sugar content is not as bad as The Assemblies Of God (or any other fundamentalist religion, for that matter). But the point stands: It's not good for people. As much as I love guzzling Mountain Dew, the world would probably be a better place without it. It should go without saying that ALL processed sugar is unhealthy; and that ALL cult activity is unhealthy.

As we survey the globe, we find that there are plenty of other regrettable instances of memetic transference. Post-modernism came from France (via Lyotard, Lacan, Derrida, Deleuze, et. al.), which led to a scourge of relativism. Free-market fundamentalism came from Austria (primarily via Hayek and Von Mises), which led to right-wing "libertarianism". ** Neither was a good thing. While these are more philosophical systems than cultural elements, they've had an undeniable impact on the cultures in which they were adopted. Claiming that everything in the universe is a psychical / social construct affects culture in palpable ways. The same goes for the claim that we should conduct ourselves in an "every man for himself, devil take the hindmost" manner. Of course, this doesn't mean that we should discount the salutary cultural contributions from Austria and France. After all, the former gave us Mozart, Schubert, and apple strudel; while the latter gave us Molière, Voltaire, and éclairs.

Unfortunately, since the advent of social media, there has been a profusion of cultural garbage flooding the memetic ecosystem. (We are forced to stand witness to Baby Shark destroying the prefrontal cortexes of toddlers around the world.) Much of this has to do with (what turns out to be) the optimal conditions for virality: shallow thinking, stunted attention spans, and an insatiable craving for instant gratification. As a consequence, rather than edifying content, we covet cheap satisfaction. Pursuant to the law of supply and demand, we wind up with a vast sea of memetic slop—much of it annihilating the critical thinking faculties of almost everyone with an internet connection.

One of the points I make in **Gringos Eating Tacos** is the same one I made in **Robin's Zugzwang**: the litany of frivolous grievances we routinely encounter ends up being an elaborate distraction; diverting our attention away from important matters. Comes the retort: "But we can talk about different problems at once!" No one doubts that there are several different (major) societal problems that are worth addressing. But this is a matter of priorities. We have limited resources (time, energy, attention, political capital, and public funds). The question becomes: Where are these things optimally directed? Yes, we can walk and chew gum at the same time. However…every minute we spend trying to get hoop earrings out of the ears of White women is another minute we're not focusing on trying to get money out of politics. (This is, of course, exactly how corporatist Democrats prefer it.)

So how does all this misdirection work? Political correctness transplants morality with formality. (Put another way: The weaponization of etiquette behooves us to replace probity with propriety—effectively treating the latter as a surrogate for the former.) Meanwhile, identity politics appeals to our baser tribal instincts. Identitarians ask that we engage in one or another form of segregation so as to ameliorate inequities—even if it means requisitioning certain cultural elements.

Instead of seeing the humanity in THE OTHER, we are obliged to assess things in terms of demographic profiles.

In the midst of this, human solidarity soon evaporates.

Such a misguided approach to social justice isn't just a matter of superciliousness, superficiality, and pettiness; it is a matter of shooting an otherwise noble cause in the foot. (Here's a tip: Just as casting a Black actor as James Bond will do absolutely nothing to remedy the structural inequalities that exist along racial lines, prohibiting gringos from opening a tortilla stand will do nothing to empower Mexicans.) Our egregiously-skewed allocation of concern (vis-à-vis those who matter more vs. those who matter less) is testament to the fact that our hierarchy of priorities is way out of wack. Much of this takes the form of virtue-signaling. Potemkin Progressives will hem and haw about non-Filipinos serving Buko (Pandan) here in America, yet be perfectly fine with our government facilitating a genocide in a far-away land.

The anti-Cul-Ap crusade I indict in this book is based on a grave misunderstanding of what culture is and how it works. (Sweat lodges were appropriated from Native Americans, you say? Nope. Nordic, Slavic, and Turkic peoples have been using them for over a thousand years.) As Progressives strive to harness our shared humanity; many seem to think that partitioning mankind according to one or another demographic category is a prudent way to do this. This approach has proven to be a set-back. Strictures on Cul-Ap do not provide remediation to historically marginalized groups; they simply amplify exigent alterity.

The errant thinking within Regressive "Left" circles is akin to the following declaration: "We may not have universal public healthcare (a situation that causes tens of thousands of avoidable deaths each year); but let's talk about whether or not Atlanta's baseball team should be re-named." Refraining from using a tomahawk as a logo is not going to provide Native Americans restitution for the horrible injustices that were visited upon them. All it will do is tie the endeavor to dismantle the for-profit sickness-treatment industry to a bogeyman that has been dreamt up by right-wing polemicists: "cultural Marxism". As if the Progressive cause didn't already have formidable enough obstacles to overcome, this makes things far more difficult.

I have tried to make the (Progressive) case for cultural appropriation; and done so while recognizing how and why some instances of Cul-Ap can be problematic. As we celebrate our shared humanity, it is worth bearing in mind that cosmopolitanism means recognizing that memetic cross-pollination is often a salutary affair; and is—more often than not—a boon to global human solidarity.

* America had long-since embraced music from Germany and Russia. The former had given us Brahms, Beethoven, and Bach; the latter had given us Tchaikovsky, Stravinsky, and Rachmaninoff. We often forget how international contributions to classical music have been. There was Edvard Grieg (Norwegian), Dieterich Buxtehude (Danish), Fryderyk Chopin (Polish), Gustav Mahler (Bohemian), W.A. Mozart and Franz Schubert (Austrian), Franz Liszt (Hungarian), Antonio Vivaldi and Giacomo Puccini (Italian), Constantijn Huygens (Dutch), Claude Debussy and Maurice Ravel (French), and Manuel de Falla (Spanish)…to name some of the most prominent.

** Within the Chicago School, the Austrian school served as a kind of gateway drug—a segue from the Neo-Classical approach of Carl Menger to the anarcho-capitalist lunacy of Murray Rothbard.

About The Author

Originally from the Boston area, Mason Scott lived in New York City from 2000 to 2019. In most of his work, he takes a trans-disciplinary approach to critical inquiry. His undergraduate degrees are in Mechanical Engineering and Analytic Philosophy (Lehigh University). Later, he did graduate work in sociology at Columbia University and New York's Graduate Center. An avid traveler, he loves to explore the world and learn about other cultures. He has spent time in Canada, Mexico, Central America, Brasil, Puerto Rico, Jamaica, Aruba, France, Belgium, Germany, Czechia, Russia, Turkey, India, China, Hong Kong, Taiwan, Burma, Thailand, Lao, Cambodia, Vietnam, Japan, and the Philippines. Mason's influences include Immanuel Kant, Thomas Paine, Arthur Schopenhauer, Eleanor Roosevelt, Isaac Asimov, Douglas Adams, and Noam Chomsky. His peccadillos are narcissism and inauthenticity. He likes chocolate milk, cheesy romantic comedies, Chopin's Nocturnes, and cats.

Made in United States
North Haven, CT
17 April 2025